FORTRESS
BRITAIN

Captain Summers flying prototype K5054 on the very day that the new fighter aircraft was named
'Spitfire'. R.J. Mitchell had designed a machine that would soon come to symbolise British defiance of
would-be invaders.

FORTRESS BRITAIN

ALL THE INVASIONS AND INCURSIONS SINCE 1066

IAN HERNON

The History Press

About the Author

Ian Hernon has been a reporter since 1969, initially on newspapers in the English provinces and the Middle East. He has been a lobby correspondent in the House of Commons for three decades – for 15 years as Parliamentary editor of the news agency Central Press – and correspondent for numerous publications including the Scottish editions of the *Daily Express* and *Sunday Times* and for the *Liverpool Echo* and other Trinity Mirror titles. He was 2010 Avanta regional journalist of the year. He is currently Deputy Editor of *Tribune* magazine.

Ian is the author of the best-selling *Britain's Forgotten Wars* for The History Press (2005), *Assassin! – 200 Years of Political Murder* (2007) published by Pluto, and *The Blair Decade* (2007, Politico's/Methuen). His latest book is *The Sword and the Sketchbook – A Pictorial History of Queen Victoria's Wars* (2012, The History Press).

First published 2013

The History Press
The Mill, Brimscombe Port
Stroud, Gloucestershire, GL5 2QG
www.thehistorypress.co.uk

British Library Cataloguing in Publication Data.
A catalogue record for this book is available from the British Library.

ISBN 978 0 7524 9712 9

Typesetting and origination by The History Press
Printed in Great Britain

CONTENTS

INTRODUCTION

Every schoolchild knows that the last military invasion of Britain occurred in 1066. The arrow that Harold, the last English king, took in the eye (possibly) was certainly a pivotal moment in the history of these isles. But other invasions, two of which achieved their aims, have been erased from popular history and the nation's collective memory. So too have countless raids, attacks, and attempted invasions which in scale were bigger than the Armada and posed an even greater threat than, it can be argued, Adolf Hitler. It is as if the Battle of Hastings was a foretaste of the Battle of Britain in 1940, with not much in between to worry those who stayed safe within these shores.

That is, however, belied by the numerous fortifications around our shores and ports, from round Martello towers to military canals and massive gun emplacements, some preserved in pristine condition, others mouldering brickwork buried in brambles.

This is my attempt to fill the gap in that collective memory. This is not an academic work – for those, see the bibliography – but it does aim to pull together in a straightforward narrative the astonishing events of almost a millennium, which have created the nation of Britain.

My thanks, as always, to my family.

1 AFTER HASTINGS

'... crushed, imprisoned, disinherited, banished'
– the chronicler Odericus Vitalis

Normans preparing to invade England, Bayeux Tapestry.

Before the bloody battle on Senlac Hill and William's conquest, invasions had been an integral part of the patchwork fabric which made Britain: Romans, Angles, Jutes, Saxons, Vikings, Danes and other Scandinavians all planted their standards and all, through assimilation, stayed to varying degrees. As the Roman Empire declined, its hold on Britain loosened. By AD 410, Roman forces had been withdrawn and small, isolated bands of migrating Germans began to invade Britain. There was no single invasion, but the Germanic tribes quickly established control over a mainland not yet a nation. Viking raiders landed near the monastery on Lindisfarne, slew its monks and looted it. Thus began more than two centuries of Viking incursions into England, which was divided into several kingdoms.

❦──❦

In 866, the Viking chief Ragnar Lodbrok was captured by King Aella of Northumbria and thrown into a snake pit. Ragnar's enraged sons, taking advantage of England's political instability, recruited the Great Heathen Army, which landed in Northumbria that year. York fell to the Vikings. Aella was in turn captured by the Vikings and executed. By 1000 the Vikings had overrun most of England and parts of Ireland. In Wessex, King Alfred the Great held off the Vikings during his lifetime, but the Norsemen managed to unite much of England with Norway and Denmark in the eleventh century during the reign of the Danish King Cnut.

When Cnut died he was succeeded by the Anglo-Saxon king Edward the Confessor, who reigned until his death in 1066, when he was succeeded by the powerful Earl of Wessex, Harold Godwinson. The Norwegian king Harald Hardrada invaded the North, only to be defeated with massive losses at Stamford Bridge. But William of Normandy, who also had legitimate claim to the throne, was waiting for good weather to carry his invasion fleet across the Channel.

Harold Godwinson retraced his steps south to take on the threat of the Normans, who landed at Pevensey Bay. He believed that England was now invincible, and that confidence lured him to disaster. The slaughter near Hastings dwarfed even the 901 massacre by Vikings at Maldon, or the defeat of Edmund Ironside by Cnut at Assendon in 1016. So much is common knowledge, along with the debate as to whether Harold died from an arrow in the eye or was hacked apart by Norman knights. Both, probably. But the invasion was not completed in a single battle, famous though it remains.

After the Battle of Hastings, William and his forces marched to Westminster Abbey for his coronation, taking a roundabout route via Romney, Dover, Canterbury, Surrey and Berkshire. From the foundation of the Cinque Ports in 1050, Dover had dominated and it became William's prime target. William of Poitiers wrote:

> Then he marched to Dover, which had been reported impregnable and held by a large force. The English, stricken with fear at his approach, had confidence neither in their ramparts nor in the numbers of their troops ... While the inhabitants were preparing to surrender unconditionally, [the Normans], greedy for money, set the castle on fire and the great part of it was soon enveloped in flames ... [William then paid for the repair and] having taken possession of the castle, the Duke spent eight days adding new fortifications to it.

The Castle was first built entirely out of clay. It collapsed to the ground and the clay was then used as the flooring for many of the ground-floor rooms. William, variously described by chroniclers as cruel, greedy and devoutly pious, replaced the Saxon hierarchy or 'establishment' with his own, amalgamated the Church, imposed new taxation and his own stringent version of the feudal system, and above all wiped out resistance. The chronicler Odericus Vitalis wrote: 'The native inhabitants were crushed, imprisoned, disinherited, banished and scattered beyond the limits of their own country, while his own vassals were exalted to wealth and honours and raised to all its offices.'

After 1066 foreign incursions, real or threatened, continued until William re-forged his realm, bending it to his own will. But it was a drawn-out business. His iron heel quickly assured his rule in London and the South, but rebellions popped up across his new realm, often aided by overseas forces. He brutally subdued the populations of Yorkshire, Nottingham and Warwick, and repeated the exercise in Somerset, Dorset and the West Midlands.

On the Welsh border, Norman earls whose families had settled in the area during the reign of the Confessor snatched lands held by Edric 'the Wild'. There was open warfare. Edric, in alliance with the Welsh princes Bleððyn and Rhiwallon, devastated Herefordshire and eventually sacked Hereford itself. They withdrew back into the hills, knowing full well that William would seek vengeance.

King Harold's mother, Gytha, encouraged the people of Devon to rise up and William only subdued the county after Exeter fell. The other main claimant to the English throne, Edgar Æþeling, grandson of Edmund Ironside, issued a call to arms from his bolthole in Scotland. Later in the year, the men of Dover invited Eustace of Boulogne to help them in their insurrection. This uprising was soon put down with extreme prejudice. But it was in the North that William suffered the greatest defiance. William took his army to crush revolt in Northumberland. The rebels quickly either submitted or fled into Scotland to join the other refugees there in the face of Norman military might.

In the autumn, cousins of Edgar sailed to the Norse-held east coast of Ireland, picked up recruits and raided the West Country, where the Celtic Cornishmen joined them in arms. They plundered and ravaged the countryside so excessively, however, that eventually even the Saxon English joined with local Norman garrisons to expel them.

In 1068, King William appointed Robert de Comines as Earl of Northumberland, instead of the English Earl Morcar. The men of the county promptly killed him and massacred 900 of his men in Durham. Edgar Æþeling travelled to York when he was met by the Northumbrians. William moved up fast from the south and surprised the 'rebels'. Hundreds were slain and the city torched. The conqueror made York his base of operations in the North. He expropriated property and divided half amongst his Norman followers and kept half for himself. William strengthened the defences of the city and built two motte and bailey castles, one on each side of the River Ouse.

The following year Edgar's kinsmen and supporters again rampaged through the West Country, but were defeated by Earl Brian of Penthievre, and fled back to Ireland. Meanwhile Edric the Wild and his Welsh allies broke out from the Marcher hills and took Shrewsbury before moving on to Chester. William, no doubt feeling that he was sailing in a colander, with leaks springing up in all directions, was forced to ignore them while dealing with the Northumbrians led by Morcar and his brother Edwin, supported by the Danish king, Sweyn Estridsson.

Sweyn, the grandson of Harald Bluetooth, was born in England around 1019 and had a solid claim to the English throne as his mother Estrid was the daughter of King Cnut. He grew up as a military leader, courageous in battle but fairly hopeless as a tactician. A long and bitter civil war in Denmark eventually saw him rule supreme, only to be embroiled in another war with Harald Hardrada. Sweyn almost captured Hardrada in a sea battle off the coast of Jutland; if he had succeeded, the events of 1066 may have taken a different course. He was almost killed himself at the naval battle of Nisa in 1062. Harald relinquished his claims to Denmark in 1064, in return for Sweyn's recognition of Harald as king of Norway. After that he sailed off to England to try to enforce his claim on the English crown, with bitter results.

Sweyn was Christian, literate and ruthless, but like many hotheaded rulers of that age, he could be penitent. After one massacre in a church he walked barefoot, dressed in sackcloth, to do penance. While William was away in Normandy, English nobles appealed to Sweyn to claim their throne and revenge his cousin, King Harold. Ever cautious, Sweyn waited almost two years before sending a fleet to the Humber to break William's still-fragile grip on the North. Even then he sent his brother, Asbjorn, to lead the fleet. It was an act that, rather than uniting the English behind one war leader, as they might have behind Sweyn, just complicated what was already confused leadership. and loyalties. The Danes joined the Earls Waltheof and Gospatrick, together with Edgar Æþeling. The Normans in York were slaughtered; Earl Waltheof's exploit of allegedly killing 100 Normans with his long-axe as they tried to escape through a gate provided material for heroic verse.

William was occupied elsewhere. He crossed the Pennine hills to face the threat posed by Edric and the Welsh princes, who now had a formidable army bolstered by the men of Cheshire and Staffordshire. William rode with his men and joined Earl Brian, who had marched up from the West Country after beating Harold's sons. A prudent Edric withdrew to the hills with his Herefordshire and Shropshire men. The Welsh princes marched on and were defeated at the battle of Stafford. William, no surprise here, laid waste to the land. A further revolt in the West Country fizzled out in the face of forces drawn from London and the south east and through internal dissent amongst the insurgents.

William turned back to the North and after a hard march marked by determined resistance, vandalised bridges and swollen rivers, he took and re-entered York without a fight. The Danes had fled and the men of Northumberland took to the hills, pursued by William's force. The Danes withdrew from northern England while William 'harryed' (or harrowed) the North, burning homes and crops, slaughtering livestock and smashing tools and implements in a great scorched earth swathe between the Humber and Durham. The resultant famine wiped out whole villages and the region took generations to recover.

During the extended bloodbath William celebrated Christmas at York, eating off silver plate especially brought up from Winchester. William then inconclusively pursued Teeside insurgents around the Cleveland hills. The devastation, however, forced the rebellion's leaders to pay him fealty, rather than outright submission, to avoid further destruction. William made his way back to York in atrocious conditions, seeking bands of Englishmen as he went, and suffering heavy losses amongst his own men. He re-erected the castles the Anglo-Norse had burned down and re-garrisoned them. He turned to Chester at the northern extremity of the Welsh Marches.

In January 1070, a Norman army including many mercenaries from France's northern provinces set off across the Pennines in bad weather through land that offered them no sustenance as they themselves had previously laid it waste. William's army suffered badly from bad weather and English attacks. Many of the mercenaries mutinied and William simply abandoned them to the enemy and the elements. With only Normans at his back, he reached Chester, which surrendered without a fight. He built castles to hold the North down. He also bought off the Danish leader Jarl Osbjorn.

Meanwhile, the Danes sailed south seeking both loot and assistance from relations in East Anglia who had benefited from Danelaw since before Alfred the Great's reign. They took to the Isle of Ely as a base in the marshy wetlands of the Fens, held by local landowner Hereward the Wake. In June 1070 William made peace with

Sweyn and most Danes left. Sweyn looked away from England and concentrated on consolidating his own kingdom and siring half the royal dynasties of northern Europe through his string of concubines.

The revolt in the Fens had been strengthened by refugees from wasted Northumberland, including Earl Morcar. Hereward paid his remaining Danish allies by allowing them to sack Peterborough and its Cathedral, now controlled by a Norman abbot. William made at least two unsuccessful attempts to take the Isle of Ely. He eventually succeeded after local monks betrayed secret causeways across the marsh. Although Ely fell in 1071, Hereward escaped and, with a band of followers, continued a form of guerrilla warfare for several years.

In 1072 the main threat was from Scotland, where martial numbers were swelled by many English, including Edgar Æþeling. William took an army across the border and confronted King Malcolm at Abernethy. Malcolm made peace.

By 1073 William could feel that his conquest was complete and returned to Normandy to suppress a revolt in Maine. Many in his army were English who worked with a will to devastate the rebel region, just as their home counties had been devastated.

Back in England the 'Revolt of the Earls' erupted in 1075. The two Earls were both half English and half French, and both had supported William in his claim for the throne in 1066. Ralf, Earl of East Anglia, was English on his father's side and had been born in Norfolk, but grew up in Brittany. Roger, Earl of Hereford, English on his mother's side and born in Hereford, was Ralf's brother-in-law. They had both supported William's claim to the throne. Now they plotted to bring him down with Danish support. William crushed both their forces in turn. He then besieged Norwich, held by Ralf's new bride Emma, for three months. Her husband had gone to collect a Danish fleet, but the 200 ships arrived too late to lift the siege. Ralf and Emma made it to France, where they continued their fight against the Normans. Roger was captured and spent the rest of his life in prison. Earl Waltheof, having refused to take part in the revolt, had nonetheless also refused to betray the rebel earls. When that emerged William had him beheaded. The execution appalled the English and many Norman nobles. Waltheof's tomb became a place of pilgrimage.

In 1080 the men of Gateshead killed the Norman Bishop of Durham and 100 soldiers, and six years later Edgar Æþeling was again in revolt. These were suppressed in turn, but another invasion by the Danes remained a real threat throughout William's reign. That was mainly prevented by the lack of co-ordinated resistance by the English and their Danish cousins now settled in England. After Hastings there was no king to give leadership and the English nobles who survived Senlac were driven solely by their own personal interests, co-operating with each other on occasions, only to head off when it suited them. Without decisive leadership, no English army could take the field. And the ordinary folk were cowed by mighty castles, strong garrisons and the enforcement of feudal diktat. Slowly, the English and Normans came together through necessity and marriage.

It was the threat of Danish invasion which prompted the great survey now known as the Domesday Book. William needed to know the precise wealth of his realm in order to levy taxes to pay for an army of defence. Once the massive undertaking was completed with great speed, William summoned all his tenants-in-chief and major land-holders to a court at Salisbury and made them swear an oath of allegiance. His crown was secure. Ironically, that was largely due to fear of invasion.

Between 1066 and William's death in 1087 foreign incursions had been part of a civil war, inter-related dynastic struggles which crossed seas and borders, the inevitable consequence of the Conquest of a still-unformed nation. From then on William's Norman successors concentrated on consolidation of their lands either side of the Channel and extending their empire southwards to Aquitaine and Bordeaux

The immediate consequence of William's death was a war between his sons Robert and William over control of England and Normandy. After the younger William's death in 1100 and the succession of his youngest brother Henry as king, Normandy and England remained contested until Robert's capture by Henry at the Battle of Tinchebray in 1106. Norman rule in England fragmented when two of his grandchildren, Stephen and Matilda, engaged in civil war and created an era of turmoil known as 'The Anarchy.'

Nevertheless, the impact on England of William's conquest was profound and changes in the Church, aristocracy, culture, and language of the country have persisted into modern times. The Conquest brought the kingdom into closer contact with France and forged ties between France and England that lasted throughout the Middle Ages. Another consequence of William's invasion was the sundering of the formerly close ties between England and Scandinavia. William's government blended elements of the English and Norman systems into a new one that laid the foundations of the later medieval English kingdom. Historian Eleanor Searle described William's invasion as 'a plan that no ruler but a Scandinavian would have considered'.

Sir Roy Strong wrote that the Conquest and its aftermath was, for William and the Normans, a remarkable achievement:

> It was to be an enduring one, for unlike the preceding centuries, no other invading force would be successful until 1688 … The new aristocracy saw its first loyalty not to the land they had conquered but to Normandy. England was taxed and exploited in the interests of what was a smaller, poorer and far less cultured country. Henceforth too, for better or worse, English kings were also to be continental rulers and for four centuries the wealth of England was expended in wars aimed at acquiring, defending and sustaining a mainland empire whose final foothold would not be lost until 1558.

King Sweyn died at his farm, Søderup, near the town of Abenra, in either 1074 or 1076. His body was carried to Roskilde Cathedral where he was interred in a pillar of the choir next to the remains of Bishop Vilhelm. He was later named the 'father of kings' because five of his fifteen sons, mostly illegitimate, became kings of Denmark. Sweyn is now regarded as Denmark's last Viking king, and the first medieval one.

In England, Norman rule was cnstantly riven with strife and dominated by events across the Channel.

2 KING LOUIS OF ENGLAND?

'English necks are free from the yoke.'
– Gerald of Wales, 1216

William the Marshal unhorsing Baldwin de Guisnes in jousting, thirteenth century, from Matthew Paris's *Chronica Majora*.

Succession in the Middle Ages was no simple matter. Dynasties fought amongst each other for the crown of England, and inter-marriage, bastardy and Papal decree complicated matters even further. That turmoil, which continued for centuries, produced kings with only tenuous claims, and others with more solid ones. It also produced one king, proclaimed by the most powerful nobles, who has been excised from our collective history.

⊛–⊛

After the chaos of 'The Anarchy' in which England descended into long and bloody civil war, the Anglo-Norman dynasty was ended by an alliance between Geoffrey of Anjou and Robert of Gloucester, with the former's son Henry becoming the first of the Angevin kings of England in 1153. He directly ruled more territory on the Continent than did the French king. His son Richard was vilified, then and since, for spending most of his reign fighting across the sea, either on the Continent or on Crusade, spending only a few months in England itself. Sean McGlynn in *Blood Cries Afar* argues persuasively that Richard's victories abroad meant greater security for England. Unsuccessful campaigns 'were invariably followed by threats of invasion'. After the death of the Lionheart, fears of a French invasion grew. His brother

John inherited a great estate on both sides of the Channel, an Angevin empire which stretched to the Pyrennes splitting modern France in half along the vertical. It provided a great trading zone, combining the wealth of England with the grain and wine of Bordeaux, Aquitaine, Anjou and Pontier, plus all the taxes, tolls and licences involved. Such wealth provided Henry and Richard with influence and political power, buttressed by their willingness to use cold steel. But martial genes appear to have passed John by – his overseas campaigns were ruinous and his realm was wracked by dissent at his despotic rule. His titles included King of England, Duke of Aquitaine, Count of Anjou and Lord of Ireland, but his grip on all those lands was shaky. Philip II of France aimed to exploit John's legal and military weaknesses and by 1204 had succeeded in wresting back control of most of France's ancient territorial possessions.

It was during this age that the concept of chivalry took hold. On the face of it, there is a great dilemma – how do courtly manners and the protection of the weak square with the utmost brutality and the slaughter of the defenceless, both so commonplace that they were barely commented upon? The medieval historian Maurice Keen came closest to an explanation: chivalry was an evolving set of secular values, beginning as a common code of conduct for soldiers and developing into an expression of their social standing. Chivalry limited some of the excesses of warfare – for the nobility if not the common soldiery and civilians – while providing legitimacy for the use of extreme violence.

King John well illustrated the contradictions. He was lustful and lacking in piety, and contemporary chroniclers complained that his mistresses were married noblewomen. He was variously described by his contemporaries as mad, bad and dangerous to friends and minions alike. He was cowardly and vindictive. He was a 'pillage of his own people'. To contemporaries he was known as 'Softsword'. Those chroniclers also catalogued his various anti-religious habits at length, including his failure to take communion, his blasphemous remarks, and his witty but scandalous jokes about church doctrine, including the implausibility of the Resurrection. His attitudes put him at loggerheads with Rome, and he was briefly excommunicated, in common with many other crowned heads. Later, however, he played a canny game with Rome. He agreed that England should be a papal fiefdom of Pope Innocent III owing an annual tribute of 1,000 marks. Nicholas Vincent wrote:

> Regarded by monastic chroniclers at the time as a dangerous invitation to papal imperialism, and derided by later Protestant historians as perhaps the very worst of King John's crimes, the homage was in reality a clever political device, like John's subsequent taking of vows as a crusader, intended to place England under papal protection, and above all to ensure that the Pope was now John's overlord at a time when the French king's claim to overlordship had already led to the confiscation of Normandy and now threatened a French invasion of England.

John focused on trying to retake Normandy but faced several challenges: to secure England against possible French invasion, to keep open the sea-routes to Bordeaux needed following the loss of the land route to Aquitaine and to protect his remaining possessions in Aquitaine following the death of his mother, Eleanor, in April 1204. John planned to use Poitou as a base of operations, advance up the Loire Valley to threaten Paris, pin down the French forces and break Philip's internal lines of communication before landing a maritime force in the Duchy itself. All of this would require a great deal of money and soldiers. At the same time he had to deal with troubles in Wales and Ireland and, most drastically, with Scotland.

Perhaps John's greatest obstacle was the character and ability of Philip II. After becoming monarch aged 14 in 1180 he was overshadowed by the military genius of Richard. Against John, however, he was an experienced leader of men, able to use both military might and courtly skills in a way John could only dream of. Both men were unattractive characters, but Philip's unscrupulous nature bore fruit, unlike John's.

John spent much of 1205 securing England against a potential French invasion. John revived a version of Henry II's Assize of Arms, with each shire organised to mobilise local levies. When the threat of invasion faded, John formed a significant military force in England intended for Poitou, and a large fleet with soldiers intended for Normandy. To achieve this, John reformed the English feudal contribution to his campaigns, creating a more flexible system under which only one knight in ten would actually be mobilised, financially supported by the other nine. John built up a strong team of engineers for siege warfare and a substantial force of professional crossbowmen.

John also built up his Channel navy. Most of these ships were placed along the Cinque Ports, but Portsmouth was also enlarged. By the end of 1204 he had around 50 large galleys available; another 54 vessels were built between 1209 and 1212. William of Wrotham was appointed 'keeper of the galleys', effectively John's chief admiral. Wrotham was responsible for creating a single operational fleet made up of John's galleys, the ships of the Cinque Ports and pressed merchant vessels. John adopted recent improvements in ship design, including new large transport ships called *buisses* and removable forecastles for use in combat.

Baronial unrest in England prevented the departure of the planned 1205 expedition, and only a smaller force under William Longespée deployed to Poitou. In 1206 John set sail himself, but was forced to divert south to counter a threat to Gascony from Alfonso VII of Castille. After a successful campaign against Alfonso, John headed north again, taking the city of Angers. Philip moved south to meet John; the year's campaigning ended in stalemate and a two-year truce. During that truce of 1206-1208, John built up his financial and military resources ready for another attempt to recapture Normandy. John used some of this money to pay for new alliances on Philip's eastern frontiers. The invasion plans for 1212 were postponed because of fresh English baronial unrest about service in Poitou.

Philip seized the initiative in 1213, sending his son, Prince Louis, to invade Flanders, intending to use that as a springboard for an invasion of England. John was forced to postpone his own invasion plans to counter this threat. He launched his new fleet to attack the French at the harbour of Damme. The attack was a success, destroying

Philip's vessels and any chances of an invasion of England that year. John hoped to exploit this advantage by himself invading late in 1213, but baronial discontent again delayed his invasion plans until early 1214.

John began his final campaign to reclaim Normandy. He was optimistic, as he had successfully built up alliances with the Emperor Otto, Renaud of Boulogne and Count Ferdinand of Flanders. In addition, he was again enjoying papal favour, and he had substantial funds to pay for the deployment of his experienced army. Nonetheless, when John left for Poitou in February 1214, many barons refused to provide military service and mercenary knights had to fill the gaps. John's plan was to split Philip's forces by pushing north-east from Poitou towards Paris, whilst Otto, Renaud and Ferdinand marched south-west from Flanders.

Initially, John outmanoeuvred Prince Louis's forces and retook Anjou by the end of June. John besieged the castle of Roche-au-Moine, a key stronghold, forcing Louis to give battle against John's larger army. The local Angevin nobles refused to advance with the king, however, and John retreated back to La Rochelle. Shortly afterwards, Philip won the hard-fought battle of Bouvines in the east against Otto, bringing an end to John's hopes of retaking Normandy. A peace agreement meant to last six years was signed in which John returned Anjou to Philip and paid the French king compensation. John returned to England in October.

Tensions between John and the barons had been growing for several years, as demonstrated by a 1212 plot against the king. Many of the disaffected barons came from the north of England, nobles who had no personal stake in the conflict in France. Many owed large sums to John, thanks to his imposition of *amercements* – a vindictive system of fines for imagined offences against the king's peace – money they did not want to pay. The subsequent revolt has been dubbed 'a rebellion of the king's debtors'. Many of John's military household joined the dissenters, their local links and loyalties outweighing their personal loyalty to John. Tension also grew across North Wales, where opposition to the 1211 treaty between John and Llywelyn (Llywelyn the Great, eventually *de facto* ruler of Wales) was turning into open conflict. The failure of John's French military campaign added to the dissatisfaction as promised plunder failed to materialise. James Holt described the path to civil war as 'direct, short and unavoidable' following the defeat at Bouvines.

Within a few months of John's return, rebel barons in the north and east of England were organising resistance to his rule. John held a council in London in January 1215 to discuss potential reforms and sponsored discussions in Oxford between his agents and the rebels during the spring. John appears to have been playing for time until Pope Innocent III could send letters giving him explicit papal support. This was particularly important as a way of pressuring the barons, but also as a means of controlling Stephen Langton, the Archbishop of Canterbury. In the meantime, John began to recruit fresh mercenary forces from Poitou, although some were later sent back to avoid giving the impression that the king was escalating the conflict. Letters of support from the Pope arrived in April but by then the rebel barons had organised. They congregated at Northampton in May and renounced their feudal ties to John.

The self-proclaimed 'Army of God' marched on London, taking the capital as well as Lincoln and Exeter. Once the rebels held London they attracted a fresh wave of defectors from John's Royalist faction.

John met the rebel leaders at Runnymede near Windsor Castle on 15 June 1215. The agreement John signed was later named Magna Carta, or 'Great Charter'. The charter went beyond simply addressing specific baronial complaints and formed a wider proposal for political reform, albeit one focusing on the rights of free men, not serfs and unfree labour. It promised the protection of church rights, protection from illegal imprisonment, access to swift justice, new taxation only with baronial consent and limitations on feudal payments. A council of 25 supposedly neutral barons would be created to monitor and ensure John's future adherence to the charter, whilst the rebel army would stand down and London would be surrendered to the king.

Neither John nor the rebel barons seriously tried to implement Magna Carta. Despite its lofty reputation, Magna Carta was, as Colin Brown pointed out, 'a shabby deal reached between a gang of landowners who did not wish to see their privileged life destroyed, and a weak king with his back against the wall'. The rebel barons suspected that the proposed baronial council would be unacceptable to John and that he would challenge the legality of the charter; they packed the baronial council with their own hardliners and refused to demobilise their forces or surrender London as agreed. John appealed to Pope Innocent for help, observing that the charter compromised the Pope's rights under the 1203 agreement that had appointed him John's feudal lord. Pope Innocent obligingly declared the charter 'not only shameful and demeaning, but illegal and unjust' and excommunicated the rebel barons. That provided the flashpoint for war. The rebels were led by Robert Fitzwalter and after a few months of half-hearted attempts to negotiate in the summer of 1215, open warfare broke out.

John had already spent £115 on repairs to Rochester Castle, and held it during the year of the negotiations leading up to Magna Carta, but the Charter's terms had forced him to hand it back into the custody of the Archbishop of Canterbury. The rebel barons sent troops under William d'Aubigny to the castle where its constable, Reginald de Cornhill, opened the gates to them. In October while marching from Dover to London, John found Rochester in his way and on 11 October began to lay siege.

The rebels were expecting reinforcements from London but John sent fire ships to burn the city's bridge over the Medway. Robert Fitzwalter rode out to stop the king, fighting his way onto the bridge but was eventually beaten back into the castle. John also sacked the cathedral, took anything of value and stabled his horses in it, all as a slight to Archbishop Langton. Orders were then sent to the men of Canterbury saying 'We order you, just as you love us, and as soon as you see this letter, to make by day and night, all the pickaxes that you can. Every blacksmith in your city should stop all other work in order to make them and you should send them to us at Rochester with all speed'. Ominously, on 25 November John sent a writ to the justicians: 'Send to us with all speed by day and night, forty of the fattest pigs of the sort least good for eating so that we may bring fire beneath the castle.' Five siege engines were then erected and work carried out to undermine the curtain wall. The king's forces entered and held the bailey in early November, and began attempting the same tactics against the keep, including undermining the south-east tower. The mine-roof was supported by wooden props, which were then set alight using the requisitioned pig-fat. The corner of the keep collapsed. The rebels withdrew behind the keep's cross-wall but still managed to hold out. A few were allowed to leave the castle but on John's orders had their hands and feet lopped off as an example.

Winter was now setting in, and the rest of the castle was only taken on 30 November by starvation. John set up a memorial to the pigs and a gallows with the intention of hanging the whole garrison, but one of his captains, Savari de Mauleon, persuaded him that to do so would set a precedent if John ever surrendered. Only one man was actually hanged, a young bowman who had previously been in John's service. The remainder of the rebel barons were taken away and imprisoned. Of the siege – against only 100 rebels, and costing over £1,000 a day – the Barnwell chronicler wrote: 'No one alive can remember a siege so fiercely pressed and so manfully resisted' and that, after it, 'There were few who would put their trust in castles'. Some historians, particularly those who appreciate the strength of medieval castles, argue that the siege showed that John could be a competent and determined general. But Rochester was an exception to the rule of 'Softsword', as was seen as the war progressed.

The war quickly turned into a dynastic struggle for the throne of England through the ambitions of the French Prince Louis. The rebel barons turned to him as both son and heir apparent of Philip, and also a maternal grandson-in-law of the late English King Henry II. The Norman invasion had occurred only 150 years (exactly 150, in fact) before, and the relationship between England and France was an issue of family dispute rather than of patriotic antagonism. The contemporary annals of Waverley recorded, with no sense of irony, that Louis was invited to invade in order to 'prevent the realm being pillaged by aliens'.

Prince Louis, later to be called 'the Lion', was born in 1187. At 12 he had been married to Blanche of Castile, following prolonged negotiations between his father and Blanche's uncle, King John. By 1215 he was judged a suitable claimant and the barons offered him the English throne. At first, in November, Louis simply sent a contingent of knights to protect London. However, even at that stage he also agreed to an open invasion, despite discouragement from his father and from the Pope.

John was well aware of the French threat to his rule and embarked on a ferocious winter campaign to beat the barons and deter Louis. He left London alone, believing it could be retaken later, and divided his army in two. He led one half, stiffened with Flemish knights and Continental mercenaries, northwards, while the other half led by the experienced William Longsword drove the rebels from Exeter in a rampage through the south-west. Both John and Longsword wreaked havoc on the land as his lawless mercenaries pillaged and laid waste. The contemporary ecclesiastic chronicler Roger of Wendover wrote of those mercenaries:

The whole surface of the earth was covered with these limbs of the devil like locusts who assembled … to blot out every thing from the face of the earth, from man down to his castle; for, running about with drawn swords and knives, they ransacked towns, houses, cemeteries, and churches, robbing everyone, and sparing neither women and children; the king's enemies wherever they were found were imprisoned in chains and compelled to pay a heavy ransom. Even the priests, whilst standing at the very altars, were seized, tortured, robbed and ill-treated. They inflicted similar tortures on knights and others of every condition. Some of them were hung up by the middle, some by the feet and legs, some by their hands, and some by the thumbs and arms, and they then threw salt mixed with vinegar in the eyes of the wretched. Others were placed on gridirons over live coals, and then bathing their roasted bodies in cold water, they thus killed them.

Wendover made it clear that the main motivation for such excesses was simple – money. He wrote:

The wretched creatures uttered pitiable cries and dreadful groans, but there was no-one to show them pity, for their torturers were satisfied with nothing but their money. Many who had worldly possessions gave them to their torturers, and were not believed when they had given their all; others, who had nothing, gave many promises, that they might at least for a short time put off the tortures they had experienced once. Their persecution was general throughout England, and fathers were sold to torture by their sons, brothers by their brothers, and citizens by their fellow citizens.

Such venal brutality cowed many but enraged more. The barons could point to John as a tyrant who brought in foreign levies to terrorise his own people, and Louis had his excuse to invade.

Many of France's greatest fighting lords, with their knights, retinues and soldiers gathered in the Channel ports, together with their Flemish allies and mercenaries. Many were veterans of Bouvines and other battles and were enthused by the prospect of booty and a glorious repeat of the conqueror's invasion. Contemporaries, including the anonymous chronicler of Bethune, estimated that there were up to 1,200 knights and their men carried in 800 ships. The fleet was commanded by the infamous Eustace the Monk, of whom more later. Prince Louis boarded Eustace's flagship on Friday 20 May and an oblique course was charted to counter contrary winds. Louis landed unopposed on the Isle of Thanet on 21 May 1216 with just seven ships, as the rest had been dispersed by storms. He insisted on being the first man to step ashore, but slipped and fell into the shallows. A priest emerged from the crowd that had gathered on the shore to welcome him. Louis kissed the priest's crucifix and planted his lance in firm ground. His full fleet arrived the following day and the army marched on the capital.

There was little resistance when the prince entered London and at St Paul's Cathedral, Louis was proclaimed king with great pomp and celebration. Even though he was not crowned, many nobles, as well as King Alexander II of Scotland who controlled estates in England, gathered to give homage.

John fled to the Saxon capital of Winchester. Many of his supporters, sensing a change in the wind, moved to support the barons. Gerald of Wales remarked: 'The madness of slavery is over, the time of liberty has been granted, English necks are free from the yoke.' On 14 June Louis captured Winchester after John had left and soon conquered over half of the English kingdom.

In the meantime, however, King Philip taunted his son for trying to conquer England without first seizing its key: Dover. Matthew Paris, the medieval chronicler, supported this assertion when he referred to Dover as 'Clavis Angliae' (the key of England). The royal castles at Canterbury and Rochester, their towns, and most of Kent had already fallen to Louis but when he did move on to Dover Castle on 25 July, it was well prepared, its constable, Hubert de Burgh, having a well-supplied garrison of men.

Hubert de Burgh, 1st Earl of Kent (born *c.* 1160) was one of the most influential men in England. In his early adulthood Hubert set off for Jerusalem on the Third Crusade. There he received his coat of arms – Richard the Lionheart dipped his finger in the blood of a slain Saracen, put a red cross on the gold shield of de Burgh, and said 'for your bravery this will be your crest.' He rose from being a minor official at Prince John's court in 1197 to Chamberlain the next year, a post he retained when John became king in 1199. He was greatly enriched by royal favour. After John captured his nephew Arthur of Brittany in 1202, de Burgh became his jailor. He may have been complicit in Arthur's murder or, as Shakespeare would have it, refused the king's order to blind the boy. In any case de Burgh retained the king's trust, and in 1203 was given charge of the great castles at Falaise in Normandy and Chinon in Touraine, key to the defence of the Loire valley. After the fall of Falaise, de Burgh held out while the rest of the English possessions fell to the French. Chinon was besieged for a year, and finally fell in June 1205, and Hubert was badly wounded while trying to escape and taken prisoner. After his return to England in 1207, he acquired new and different lands and offices. De Burgh remained loyal to the king during the barons' rebellion but at Runnymede he advised the king to sign the charter, and he was one of the 25 sureties of its execution.

While his army encamped in the town of Dover, Prince Louis spent several days observing the castle and the surrounding area. By mid-July he was prepared to lay siege to the mighty fortress. Leaving half of his army to protect the town, the 29-year-old prince set up an encampment directly in front of the castle. Siege engines, *mangonels* and *perriers*, and a huge stone-thrower called Malvoisin, or 'Evil Neighbour' were erected, along with a wattle siege tower. But, by sending his fleet to sea, he had by now cut off any possible route for supplies or reinforcements from land or sea. The siege began on 19 July, with Louis taking the high ground to the north of the castle. His men successfully undermined the barbican and attempted to topple the castle gate with further undermining. That failed but, through the breach in the wall, the French army stormed the castle. They were held back by de Burgh's men, who managed to close the gap using timbers and enormous cross-beams which had been stripped from the castle's interior.

Meanwhile, William of Cassingham, a Kentish squire, raised a guerrilla force of Wealden archers who opposed the otherwise total occupation by the French of the south-east. A contemporary chronicler, Roger of Wendover, wrote of him:

A certain youth, William by name, a fighter and a loyalist who despised those who were not, gathered a vast number of archers in the forests and waste places, all of them men of the region, and all the time they attacked and disrupted the enemy, and as a result of their intense resistance many thousands of Frenchmen were slain.

The staunch defence of Dover Castle, the failure of his siege artillery to flatten its walls and the activities of Cassingham's guerrilla archers sapped Louis's resolve. After three months, and with a large part of his forces diverted by the siege, Louis called a truce on 14 October – the anniversary of the Battle of Hastings – and soon after returned to London.

The only other castle to hold out against Louis was that at Windsor, where 60 loyalist knights survived a two-month siege, despite severe damage to the structure of its lower ward, possibly due to its having been already besieged by the barons in 1189, less than 30 years earlier. The mighty fortress was commanded by Engelard de Dreux, whom Wendover described as 'a man well tried in war'. Like de Burgh, he favoured surprise sorties, which did much damage to the French in terms of both men and morale. The chronicler of Bethune remarked of the besiegers: 'Long were they there and little did they gain.'

John was heartened by the heroic defence of Dover and Windsor and embarked on his last-ditch campaign. His objectives remain opaque but he aimed to relieve Windsor and to intercept Alexander's army as it marched back to Scotland. The first objective failed – some believe it was merely a feint – and John's armies burnt a swathe through Suffolk and Norfolk, destroying the estates of rebel barons and harvests which would have fed their armies and that of the French invaders. But when it came to a battle near Cambridge, John employed the tactics of a 'cunning traveller' – and ran away. He vented his spleen on the manors and monasteries of Oundle, Peterborough, Boston, Lincoln, Grimsby, Lough and Spalding. It was a whirlwind campaign of terror, fuelled by kingly frustration and desperation. Exhausted, John fell ill at King's Lynn with dysentery, his condition exacerbated by the effects of gluttony. On the morning of October 11, John attempted a well-known short-cut across the fringes of The Wash at low tide. Wendover wrote: 'The land opened up in the middle of the waves and caused whirlpools which sucked in men, as well as horses.' John only narrowly escaped, but his baggage train, including his Crown Jewels, were lost. John, according to Wendover, suffered 'anguish of mind over his possessions swallowed up by the waters.'

A week later, on 18 October 1216, King John died at Newark Castle, Nottinghamshire, and with him the main reason for the fighting. John's body was stripped of all ornaments and clothing by his retainers. His body, minus its heart, was interred in Worcester Cathedral.

John's timely death had, for the barons, changed everything. Historian Sean McGlynn pointed out that there were many aspects of the 1215-17 war, including relations with Rome, the role of castles and foreign mercenaries on all sides, politics, finance and diplomacy. 'But an overarching, dominating theme was personality,' he wrote, 'and now, with John's death, an overarching dominant personality disappeared from the cast. Even the majority who fought for John had little respect for the arbitrary, unstable despot; they were bound to him more by vested interest and fear than by honour and loyalty.' The same could now be said of Louis's allies.

History and literature has certainly been harsh to King John, for many good reasons, but he attracted sufficient men of calibre and self-interest to ensure that his crown passed to his nine-year-old son, Henry, and for them to protect his heir during his turbulent minority. Louis now seemed much more of a threat to baronial interests than the boy Henry. Leading barons, the Papal envoy and the judiciary flocked to support the boy king. His regent, William Marshal, Duke of Pembroke, a tournament fighter described by Stephen Langdon as 'the greatest knight that ever lived', was well respected. Born in 1147 as the son of a minor noble who changed sides during The Anarchy, his start in life had not been auspicious. But he proved a loyal captain to Henry II and a doughty fighter for John in Normandy.

Eleanor of Brittany, the grown daughter of John's late elder brother Geoffrey, imprisoned by John since 1202, was another candidate for the crown as the rightful heiress to England since 1203; but the barons passed her over, leaving her incarcerated. Pierre des Roches, Bishop of Winchester, and a number of barons rushed to have the young Henry crowned as king of England. London was still held by Louis, so, on 28 October 1216, they brought the boy from the castle at Devizes to Gloucester Abbey in front of a small attendance presided over by a Papal Legate and crowned Henry with a band of gold made from a necklace.

On 12 November 1216 Magna Carta was reissued in Henry's name with some key clauses omitted. The revised charter was signed by the young king's regent, William Marshal. A great deal of the country was loyal to Prince Louis but the south-west of England and the Midlands favoured Henry. Marshal was highly respected and he asked the barons not to blame the child Henry for his father's sins. The prevailing sentiment, helped by self-interest, was that depriving a boy of his inheritance was iniquitous. Marshal also promised that he and the other regents would rule by Magna Carta. Furthermore, he managed to get support from the Pope, who had already excommunicated Louis.

William of Cassingham slowly managed to get most barons to switch sides from Louis to Henry and attack Louis. On 6 December 1216 Louis took Gertford Castle but allowed the defending knights to leave with their horses and weapons. He also took the formidable Berkhamstead castle in late December, again allowing the royal garrison to withdraw honourably with their horses and weapons. More success followed with Louis seizing Ely and Lincoln and the castle of Pleshey, Hedingham,

Colchester, Norwich and Orford before a general truce was agreed. By the end of January 1217, three months after John's death, Louis had consolidated his power across most of eastern England, and still seemed unstoppable. William Marshal reported that the boy king's coffers were empty, so troops and mercenaries had to be paid in jewellery and clothing. Pressure was put on the burghers of recalcitrant towns to cough up funds. Nevertheless, at the end of the truce the counter-attack finally began.

Louis and his rampaging troops ran out of supplies and foraging parties were captured or killed. His men went unpaid as they starved in the cold and the rain. Louis decided to return to France for reinforcements, but had to fight his way to the south coast through loyalist resistance in Kent and Sussex, losing part of his force in an ambush at Lewes by William of Cassingham's force. The remainder were chased to Winchelsea.

He was unable to embark because of the offshore presence of English ships. The people in the walled town resisted him, but a French warship commanded by Eustace the Monk sailed from Dover to aid him. Eustace was a notorious pirate who had once belonged to a monastic order before breaking his vows to sail and pillage along with his brothers and friends. The *Romance of Eustace the Monk* portrays him as a foul-mouthed hooligan who blamed his relentless farting on his horse's saddle, but clears him of rumours that he was a sodomite. His successes attracted many lawless men and his pirates became a menace to shipping in the Channel. His English enemies credited him with 'diabolical ingenuity'. He was also a turncoat. From 1205 to 1208, Eustace had worked for King John and with his blessing had seized the Channel Islands and held them for John, while using Winchelsea as his English base. In 1212, Eustace switched his allegiance to France and was chased out of England. He immediately used his ships to transport war engines to the English barons who opposed John.

Eustace captured the English fleet in the harbour and launched a short siege of Winchelsea, with which he was familiar as a former base of operations. He built a large platform on one of the captured ships and on it placed a trebuchet, which hurled large rocks at the town. The people of Winchelsea were in awe of the structure, but that did not stop them mounting a surprise attack on it. They successfully boarded the ship, towed it offshore and chopped up the platform and trebuchet in full view of the French. The success of the sortie had repercussions. The French watchkeepers were blamed for failing to detect the raid in time, and they in turn blamed lack of provisions – they were too hungry to keep a proper watch. Louis displayed true leadership by offering to keep watch himself. The raid, however, did not prevent more trebuchets being landed on shore when more French vessels arrived. They pounded the walls of Winchelsea and Rye across the bay. Finally, the rest of the French fleet arrived and took off Louis and his men, who were close to starvation.

Since the Dover truce, its castle garrison had repeatedly disrupted Louis's communication with France, and so Louis sailed back to Dover to begin a second siege. The French camp set up outside Dover Castle in anticipation of the new siege was attacked and burned by William of Cassingham just as the fleet carrying the reinforcements arrived, and so Louis was forced to land at Sandwich and march to Dover, where he began the second siege in earnest on 12 May 1217. This new siege diverted much of Louis's forces while events in the North were unfolding.

The Regent, William Marshal, had the authority of the king's command. Marshal ordered all nobles with a castle in England to a muster at Newark. Around 400 knights, 250 crossbowmen and a larger auxiliary force of both mounted and foot soldiers were assembled. From there they would march to break a long siege by Prince Louis's army at Lincoln.

Lincoln was an ancient walled city around a Conqueror-built castle straddling a crossroads of two important Roman-built highways, Ermine Street and Fosse Way. Before the relieving force arrived, Louis's army under the Count of Perche took the city but failed to take the stronghold. Its loyal garrison held out bravely. From Stowe, a few miles to the south-west of Lincoln, Marshal's forces made their approach. Though the advance was known to Perche, his knights debated intelligence on the strength of the enemy. Those who believed Marshal's force was relatively small in number favoured going on the attack, hitting the enemy at the base of the hill before Marshal could reach the city gates. Those who believed Marshal had a dangerously large force favoured delaying Marshal at the gates of the city wall, and at the same time pressing the siege, capturing the castle and occupying this much stronger position. The defensive plan was followed, though not without some continuing dissension. The attackers approached in close battle order, and 'struck terror into all those who saw them', according to Wendover. The chronicler reported that Marshal's men 'flew to arms, mounted their horses and struck camp rejoicing … all determined to conquer or die'. Marshal proceeded to the section of the city walls nearest the castle, at the north gate. The entire force of Marshal's crossbowmen led by the nobleman Falkes de Breauté assaulted and won the gate. Perche's forces did not respond, but continued the castle siege.

The north gate was secured by Marshal's main force, while Breauté's crossbowmen took up positions on the rooftops of houses. Volleys of bolts from this high ground caused death, damage and confusion among Perche's forces. Then, in the final blow, Marshal committed his knights and foot soldiers in a charge against Perche's siege. Perche was offered a surrender, but instead fought to the death as the siege collapsed into a scattered rout. Those of Louis' army who were not captured fled Lincoln out through the south city gate, to London. The whole of the battle had taken about six hours. To the south, inhabitants of towns between Lincoln and London ambushed and killed some French soldiers in the flight south. The city of Lincoln – on the pretence of being in league with Louis – was pillaged by the victorious army, in a rapine called the Lincoln Fair. Marshal's unnamed biographer described the pillaging, and worse:

After the battle was thus ended, the king's soldiers found in the city the wagons of the barons and the French, with the packhorses, loaded with baggage, silver vessels, and various kinds of furniture and utensils, all of which fell into their hands without opposition. Having then plundered the whole city to the last farthing, they next pillaged the churches throughout the city and broke open the chests and store-rooms with axes and hammers, seizing on the gold and silver in them, clothes of all colours, ornaments, gold rings, goblets and jewels. Nor did the cathedral church escape this destruction, but underwent the same punishment as the rest, for the legate had given orders to knights to treat all the clergy as excommunicated men. This church lost eleven thousand marks of silver. When they had thus seized on every kind of property, so that nothing remained in any corner of the houses, they each returned to their lords as rich men … Many of the women of the city were drowned in the river, for, to avoid shameful offence [rape], they took to small boats with their children, female servants and household property, and perished on their journey; but there was afterwards found in the river by the searchers, goblets of silver and many other articles of great benefit to the finders.

The Battle of Lincoln was the turning point in the war. Many of Henry's enemies – barons who had supported Louis, and who helped supply, organise and command his military forces – were captured there.

Reinforcements for Louis were then sent across the English Channel under Eustace the Monk. Louis raised his siege of Dover castle and retired to London. Signalling his willingness to negotiate an end to the struggle, he agreed to meet with followers of the boy-king. William Marshal and Louis came close to an agreement. However, in order to pardon the bishops who had gone over to Louis' cause, the new Pope Honorius III's agreement was required. Rome was far away and the negotiations broke down. Louis received the news that reinforcements and supplies would soon arrive from France. Encouraged, he resolved to fight on.

On 24 August, in clear weather, the French fleet set out from Calais. Though the ships were equipped by Eustace the Monk, command of the knights and soldiers was held by Robert of Courtenay. The wife of Prince Louis, Blanche of Castile, was also an important organiser of the relief effort. Opposing the French was Philip d'Aubigney, commander of the south-eastern coast. Marshal had arrived at New Romney on 19 August and summoned the sailors of the Cinque Ports. The English mariners complained bitterly of bad treatment at the hands of King John, but Pembroke convinced them to fight with the promise of great spoils should they defeat the French.

Eustace's own vessel, the Great Ship of Bayonne, led the French squadron. Robert de Courtenay was commander-in-chief while Eustace served as his deputy. Ralph de la Tourniele and William des Barres were third and fourth in command respectively. All told, there were 36 knights on the flagship. The next three troopships were commanded by Mikius de Harnes, William V of Saint-Omer, and the Mayor of Boulogne. Altogether, the first four ships, including the flagship, contained between 100 and 125 knights. Men-at-arms manned the remaining six troopships. There were 70 smaller vessels that carried supplies. All 11 troopships were overloaded, particularly the flagship, which carried a large trebuchet and horses destined for Prince Louis.

The English ships were generally smaller than the French, except for a substantial cog provided by Marshal, who was persuaded to stay ashore. As justicar, Hubert de

Burgh claimed leadership of the fleet, which included between 16 and 18 large ships and 20 smaller vessels. All told, there were no more than 40 English ships. A bastard of King John, Richard Fitz-John, commanded one ship.

The English, who had recovered Sandwich from Louis' forces, let the French armada pass by before attacking. The French fleet, sailing in close order toward the Thames estuary, held the windward position at first. De Burgh's ship, in the lead, lunged at the French in a feint attack, but veered away when threatened. Against the advice of his admiral Eustace, the overconfident Robert of Courtenay ordered the French to attack. As the French shortened sail, the English ships gained the windward. Meanwhile, de Burgh's flagship sailed independently to attack the French from the rear, eventually capturing two French vessels. The English archers, aided by the wind, inflicted considerable losses on the enemy sailors and soldiers before the French bowmen could reply. The English also opened pots of lime, which blew in the faces of the French, blinding them temporarily. Early in the battle, the French flagship engaged Richard Fitz-John's ship. As more English ships came up, they joined the fight against the flagship, while the other French ships maintained their tight formation. Pembroke's cog and Fitz-John's ship grappled Eustace's flagship on each side. After a melee, Robert of Courtenay and the French knights were captured for ransom, while the French sailors and common soldiers were massacred. Marshal's biographer wrote: 'I can tell you that they lost no time at all in killing those on board and throwing them into the sea as food for the fish.' He estimated that during the battle 4,000 were killed in like manner, not counting those who jumped into the sea in panic and sank. Eustace, dragged from his hiding place in the bilge, offered to pay 10,000 marks as ransom. Though his very high price was tempting, Fitz-John and the other English leaders considered Eustace a turncoat because of the pirate's previous employment under King John. Marked for execution by the enraged English, Eustace was tied down and reminded of 'the miseries he had inflicted on land and sea'. A man named Stephen Crabbe struck off his head with one blow. The head was later put on a spear and marched around Canterbury and Dover.

With their flagship taken, the French fleet headed back to Calais. Encouraged, the English attacked, using ramming, grappling, and rigging-cutting to disable the enemy vessels. Nine surviving troopships got away only because the English turned aside to plunder the train of supply vessels. The French sailors were slaughtered or thrown into the Channel, except for two or three men on each captured vessel who were spared. A large part of the loot passed to the English sailors, while some was used to set up the Hospital of Saint Bartholomew at Sandwich.

The English victory – a foretaste of future sea power – was decisive and greatly reduced the French threat to the English crown. After 18 months of war, most of the rebellious barons had defected. Louis's supply routes were severed and his army under pressure. Peace was signed on 12 September at Kingston upon Thames. Prince Louis formally renounced his claims to the English crown in return for being allowed an unmolested departure from England. He also agreed to eject the surviving Eustace brothers from the Channel Islands. A few of Henry's supporters wanted to hold out for unconditional surrender, but Marshal successfully argued for the more moderate terms. In return for Henry III's pardon, the barons who had joined Louis were made to pay the French prince 10,000 marks to expedite his withdrawal. Prince Louis left Dover before the end of the month. His last sight of the citadel he had failed to capture was a reminder of a kingdom he had half conquered but failed to win outright.

The monastic chroniclers clearly saw God's work in his expulsion. The Barnwell annalist wrote: 'It was truly a miracle that the heir to the King of France, having advanced so far into the heart of the country with a great army and having succeeded in occupying so much of it, helped by the barons, and had taken it so quickly, was forced to abandon this kingdom without hope of recovering it. It is because the hand of God was not with him.' Louis himself blamed the lack of support he had received from his father. History suggests that he failed on two fronts, one military, the other political. He failed to capture Dover Castle, his army was routed at Lincoln and his last hope was sunk in a one-sided sea battle. And the changing political allegiances of the day meant that one day he was surrounded by allies, the next by foes. What saved the crown and the country more than anything was the deal John had done with the Pope, resulting in the excommunication of Louis, forcing Philip to be circumspect in his support of his son.

The invasion and expulsion left a gap, many have argued, in the 'correct' chronology of English kingship. Before and after Louis's invasion, other English kings had been more foreign than English. Some, such as Edward V and Edward VIII, were not crowned but only proclaimed. And others gained the crown through more tenuous bloodlines including bastardy. Louis had legitimate blood claims, occupied more than half of England and was recognised as king by the barons as well as by the neighbouring king of Scotland. Therefore, there is a good case for including Louis in the list of English kings.

&—&

The expulsion of Prince Louis and his French army helped in the slow birth of England as a nation independent of foreign blood ties. But such English victories were hollow as the French advanced across English territories on mainland Europe. By 1324 England had lost the whole of Normandy and retained just a few small provinces in Gascony.

Louis VIII succeeded his father on 14 July 1223 and was crowned within three weeks. As King, he continued to seek revenge on the English and seized Poitou and Saintonge. But his reign was most troubled by internal enemies. The Albigensian Crusade had begun in 1209, ostensibly against the Cathar heretics of southern France, though it soon became a contest between lords of northern France and those of the Occitania in the south. The first phase from 1209 to 1215 was quite successful, but this was followed by a series of local rebellions from 1215 to 1225 which undid many of those earlier gains. There followed the seizure of Avignon and Languedoc. A renewed crusade was launched and Louis re-took Avignon after a three-month siege.

While returning to Paris, King Louis VIII became ill with dysentery, and died on 8 November 1226 in the chateau at Montpensier, Auvergne. His son, Louis IX (1226-70), succeeded him. Louis IX concluded the crusade in the south in 1229.

William Marshal's sound statesmanship, marked by compromise and generosity to enemies, helped Henry III consolidate his throne. Both former rebels and the French trusted his word above all others. In March 1219, beset by ill-health, he returned to his estate at Caversham near Reading and called a meeting of the barons, the papal legate, the royal justicar Hubert de Burgh and the Bishop of Winchester, the young king's guardian. He refused to trust the bishop and entrusted the regency to the papal legate. On his deathbed he was invested into the order of the Knights Templar in fulfilment of a vow he had made on crusade. He died on 14 May 1219 and was buried in the Templar Church in London.

More honours and riches were showered on Hubert de Burgh for his pivotal role in expelling the French. He was appointed High Sheriff of Norfolk and Suffolk, and later of Kent. After the death of William Marshal in 1219, de Burgh effectively became regent of England. In this position, de Burgh acquired a number of enemies and rivals. When Henry III came of age in 1227, de Burgh was made lord of Montgomery Castle in the Welsh Marches and remained one of the most influential people at court. In April 1228 he was named Justicar for life. But in 1232 the plots of his enemies finally succeeded and he was removed from office and imprisoned. He escaped from Devizes Castle and joined the rebellion of Richard Marshal, 3rd Earl of Pembroke, in 1233. The following year Edmunch Rich, Archbishop of Canterbury effected a reconciliation. He died in 1243 at the age of 82 or 83 in Banstead, Surrey, and was buried at the church of the Black Friars in Holborn.

At the end of the barons' war, William of Cassingham was granted a pension from the crown and made warden of the Weald and Sergeant of the Peace in reward for his services. Until his death he filled this post, collected his pension and fulfilled minor duties such as fetching logs for the royal household. In Holinshed's Chronicles he was addressed as: 'O Worthy man of English blood!'

3 THE HUNDRED YEARS' WAR

'… slaying, burning, destroying and doing other mischief'
– The Calendar of Rolls 1360

Battle of Sluys, from Jean Froissart's Chronicles, fifteenth century.

Picturesque Winchelsea, which claims to be the smallest town in England, sits on top of a hill overlooking marshes near Rye, East Sussex. It is the epitome of tranquillity, bypassed by the main road and, it seems, by centuries. But on 15 March 1360 it was the scene of unimaginable horrors.

Up to 2,000 French foot soldiers, bowmen, sailors and mercenaries fell upon the townspeople, many of whom took refuge in the stone church. They were butchered. No mercy was shown. The young women were raped before they were killed 'or exposed to even more hideous atrocities'.

It was not the first or last time the little town had suffered so. And the scenes of brutality were repeated along the coastline of England's south-east. They were reciprocated many times by English forces on the other side of the Channel. Most were incursions rather than full-blown invasions, but at stake was the future of both England and France. The bloodletting was relentless in what later became known, inaccurately, as the Hundred Years' War.

Winchelsea was on the 'invasion front'.

The Hundred Years' War, a series of conflicts waged from 1337 to 1453 between England and France, was the result of a dynastic squabble dating back to the Conqueror. As dukes of Normandy, the English kings owed homage to the king of France. That rankled, especially as the royal families of Europe were all inter-linked through bloodlines. Regal pride and a raw patriotism played their part in fomenting disputes, but the biggest factor was wool, by now the chief source of England's wealth. Both sides sought to control the markets and when riches were involved, common humanity and the desire for peace had no chance.

In most of the contests the English had superior firepower – the longbow – and the advantage of enclaves and territories adjoining France. For the English these wars were hugely profitable, enriching mercenaries and the growing landed gentry. Historian Desmond Seward wrote that 'generations of Englishmen went to France to seek their fortunes in rather the same way that their descendants would one day go to India or Africa.' In short, the English were largely the aggressors, the French mainly the victims. But that was no consolation for the peasants, clergy, merchants, artisans and farmers who bore the brunt of French retaliatory action.

When Charles IV of France died in 1328, leaving only daughters, the nearest male in line to the throne was Edward III of England. The French nobility could not stomach that, and an assembly decided that the dead king's cousin, Philip, Count of Valois, should be crowned Philip VI. Despite major friction over Gascony, Edward III of England paid homage to the new French king. But France stepped up pressure on Gascony and a treaty by which France would support Scotland if England invaded northern Britain was renewed. Edward was advised by courtiers and diplomats to start a war to reclaim the kingdom of France.

Edward possessed astonishing energy and determination. He was very tall, handsome, with 'a face like a God' and carried with him an air of dignity. He adored the concept of chivalry, wrote Latin, spoke French and understood German and Flemish. He was also a relentless womaniser with a streak of self-indulgence spelt out in his motto: 'It is as it is.' Seward summed up his contradictions: 'Extravagantly elegant, warm in friendship, mercilessly cruel and hard-hearted in enmity'.

Philip VI had assembled a large naval fleet for a crusade but the plan was abandoned and the fleet, including elements of the Scottish navy, moved off Normandy in 1336, threatening England. To deal with this crisis Edward proposed that the English raise two armies: one to deal with the Scots at a suitable time, the other to proceed at once to Gascony.

At the end of April 1337 Philip was invited to meet a delegation from England, but refused. A call to arms was proclaimed throughout France. In May Philip met with his Great Council in Paris, and it was agreed that Gascony should be taken back on the grounds that Edward III was in breach of his obligations as vassal. Edward responded by challenging Philip's right to the French throne and in 1340 formally assumed the title 'King of France and the French Royal Arms'. The civic authorities of Ghent, Ypres and Bruges proclaimed Edward as king of France, strengthening his alliances with the Low Countries. Channel raids on English merchantmen by

Franco-Spanish ships were stepped up, with English crews massacred as far away as the Bristol Channel.

An early winter forced a pause in the warfare, and by early 1339 English towns had taken the initiative and prepared organised militias to drive off raiders. Responsibility for the militias was given to several leading earls, who faced severe penalties if they failed to defend their stretch of coastline. Although piracy at sea remained a problem, large-scale raids became a relative rarity. An attack on Jersey failed as the island was too strongly defended, and attacks on Harwich, Southampton and Plymouth were driven off with heavy losses, the mercenary elements of the French force unwilling to risk a large-scale battle. The combined Franco-Spanish fleet was reduced to attacking fishing boats and parading the bodies of the crews through the streets of Calais.

An English fleet had also been formed over the winter to take revenge. The fleet's captains realised that attacking and looting the Flemish convoys of Edward's allies was more lucrative than hitting the French, forcing Edward to pay a huge amount of compensation and endure severe diplomatic embarrassment. The fleet, however, proved its worth in July, when 67 French and mercenary vessels attempted to attack the Cinque Ports. The expedition was met by organised militia at Sandwich and turned towards Rye, burning several small villages on the way but failing to land at the town. There the English fleet under Robert Morley caught up with them, forcing the French force to flee back across the Channel. This scare had been too much for the Genoese mercenaries who made up the most experienced part of the French fleet, and they demanded more pay. King Philip VI responded by imprisoning 15 of them, whereupon the others simply returned to Italy, at a stroke costing the French their best sailors and ships.

Morley took advantage of the disarray, taking his fleet to the French coast and burning the towns of Ault and Le Treport and foraging inland, ravaging several villages. He also surprised and destroyed a French fleet in Boulogne harbour. English and Flemish merchants rapidly fitted out raiding ships and soon coastal villages and shipping along the north and west coasts of France came under attack. The Flemish navy was also active, sending their fleet against the important port of Dieppe in September and burning it to the ground. These successes did much to rebuild morale in England and the Low Countries as well as repair England's battered trade.

In March 1338, a French force landed on Jersey but although the island was overrun, the main fortification on the island, Gorey Castle, remained in English hands. The French stayed until September, when they sailed off to conquer Guernsey, Alderney and Sark. In 1339 the French returned, allegedly with 8,000 men in 17 Genoese galleys and 35 French ships. Again they failed to take the castle and, after causing damage, withdrew. The English were able to recapture Guernsey in October 1340 but the French held out in Castle Cornet until 1345.

Despite such successes, French sea power continued to disrupt England's wool trade, the tax on which filled the royal coffers, and the wine trade from Flanders. French and Spanish 'pirates' again raided England's south coast. Edward sailed his fleet from England on 22 June 1340 and arrived the next day off the Zwyn estuary.

The English fleet tricked the French into believing they were withdrawing, but when the wind turned in the late afternoon, they attacked. The French fleet was almost completely destroyed in the Battle of Sluys. The English victory would provide naval superiority in the Channel for decades to come, resulting in the English ability to invade France at several points at once, an advantage that would prove vital in the longer war.

Edward now ran out of funds and the war should have ended. But the Duke of Brittany died, sparking a dispute between the Duke's half-brother and cousin over succession. In the 1341 Breton War of Succession Edward backed John of Montfort and Philip backed Charles of Blois. The next few years saw fortunes change on both sides, as well as further campaigns in Gascony. No-one emerged as clear victor.

In July 1346, Edward mounted a major invasion across the Channel. He captured Caen in just one day, surprising the French who had expected the city to hold out much longer. Philip gathered a large army to oppose Edward, who chose to march northward toward the Low Countries, pillaging as he went. Unable to outmanoeuvre Philip, Edward positioned his forces for battle, and Philip's army attacked. That attack, however, had not been properly prepared and the Battle of Crécy was a complete disaster for the French, cut down by Edward's longbowmen. Philip appealed to his Scottish allies to help with a diversionary attack on England. King David II of Scotland duly invaded northern England but he was captured and his army defeated at the Battle of Neville's Cross. In France, Edward was able to proceed north unopposed and besieged Calais, capturing it in 1347. That enclave allowed the English to keep troops in France safely. Calais would remain under English control until the successful French siege in 1558.

In 1350 Edward learnt that a Castilian fleet was re-equipping in Sluys, Flanders, and would be sailing back home down the English Channel. Castilian ships had fought against England as the allies or mercenaries of France, and both nations had boarded and plundered English trading vessels. On its way to Flanders the Castilian fleet captured a number of English trading ships, and threw the crews overboard, as was common practice at the time. The Castilian merchant fleet was loading cargoes in the Flemish ports to be carried to the Basque coast. The ships were armed and further protected by warships. They were under the command of Don Carlos de la Cerda, a soldier of fortune with Castilian royal blood. On August 10, when the king was at Rotherhithe, he announced he would attack the Castilians on their way home. Later historians have condemned his decision as 'piracy', as the target was mainly a merchant fleet. But Don Carlos was accused of a most heinous crime – the seizure of English wine ships. Wine was an important commodity, vital to the English economy, and any attack on its trade was considered an atrocity. Battle Abbey, whose monks were permitted a pint of wine a day and a gallon on special occasion, relied on imports through Winchelsea.

Edward travelled to Winchelsea by land to rendezvous with his fleet of up to 50 ships. With him were his wife, Philippa of Hainault, and her ladies, his sons, the Black Prince and John of Gaunt, and many nobles. The ladies were placed in the nearby

Greyfriars convent and the king embarked on his flagship, the cog *Thomas*, on August 28. The English fleet remained at anchor, waiting for the appearance of the Castilians.

The naval Battle of *Les Espagnols sur Mer* ('the Spanish on the Sea'), or the Battle of Winchelsea, took place on 29 August 1350. Don Carlos might easily have avoided the English if he had kept well out in the Channel. But he was confident that the size and strength of his 40 large ships, and a large body of mercenary crossbowmen he had recruited in the Flemish ports, would easily see off the English. His mistake was to switch tactics to aggression – in the afternoon he bore down boldly on Edward's ships at anchor. The king was sitting on the deck of his ship, with his knights and nobles, listening to his minstrels who played German airs, and to the singing of Sir John Chandos. When the lookout reported the enemy in sight, the king and his company drank to one another's health, the trumpet was sounded and the whole line stood out.

It proved a classic clash of medieval arms, with bowmen picking off the enemy until ships could be boarded and taken with sword, dagger, spear and mace. But it is also reported to have been the first battle at sea in which primitive guns were also used. The king's own ship, crammed tight with 360 mariners, soldiers and the royal entourage, was rammed by one of the enemy and began to sink. The king's men boarded another Castilian vessel hard alongside and the king had barely reached her deck before the *Thomas* sank. Other Castilian vessels were taken in a ferocious fight. The English slaughtered everyone they could, either by cold steel or by throwing the enemy overboard. Gradually, the English numerical superiority in men overcame the Spanish advantage of larger ships. But it was not a one-sided affair. Don Carlos's crossbowmen slew many, and the Castilian vessels being higher in the water meant the Spanish were able to drop bars of iron or other weights on the lighter English vessels. The English *La Salle du Roi*, which carried the king's household, commanded by the Fleming, Robert of Namur, was grappled by a big Castilian vessel, and was dragged off. The crew called loudly for a rescue, but were either not heard, or could not be helped. As twilight fell a Flemish squire of Robert of Namur, named Hannequin, single-handedly boarded the Castilian and cut the halyards of her mainsail with his sword. The Castilian ship was taken. The remainder fled.

Castilian losses were at least 14 ships captured or sunk – some sources put it as high as 26 – while Edward lost his own flagship and that of the Black Prince. Many of his remaining vessels were damaged, and many of his men were killed. There was no pursuit, and a truce was made with the Basque towns the next year. The battle was certainly a victory for Edward, but a victory which failed to give him dominance in the Channel. That can be seen from the experience a year later of Andrew Offord, a diplomat sent by Edward to attend the Court of Flanders. When he arrived at Dover, no captain was brave or foolhardy enough to ferry him across.

Don Carlos, whose mother was French, was later appointed Constable of France and made Count of Angouleme. That title was claimed by Charles II of Navarre, who hired ruffians to kill Don Carlos in an inn.

In 1356 Edward's son, Edward, the Black Prince, invaded France from Gascony. The French, fearful of the English longbow, shut themselves in castles and fortified towns, avoiding a set-piece battle. The prince adopted a scorched earth policy in a bid to draw them out. His army advanced slowly, killing, pillaging and raping as it went, filling great carts with plunder. Those wagons slowed him down further and his army became weary. The French sent a fresh army on the attack; despite being outnumbered and out of water, the prince won a stunning victory at Poitiers. The Chandos Herald recorded: 'There was many a creature who that day was brought to his end.' John II of France and hundreds of his nobles were captured on the field of battle and taken to England; John's son the Dauphin (later to become Charles V) took over as regent. Chaos reigned, with French nobles and mercenaries rampaging through the countryside. The chronicler Jean de Venette recorded:

...all went ill with the kingdom and the State was undone. Thieves and robbers rose up everywhere in the land. The Nobles despised and hated all others and took no thought for usefulness and profit of lord and men. They subjected and despoiled the peasants and the men of the villages. In no wise did they defend their country from its enemies; rather did they trample it underfoot, robbing and pillaging the peasants' goods.

The anarchy sparked a rebellion against the French nobility. Eager to take advantage, Edward invaded France for the third and last time. The dauphin deliberately avoided a set-piece battle. Edward chose the cathedral city of Reims as the place of his coronation but the citizens reinforced their defences before he arrived. After a failed siege Edward moved on to Paris but retreated after skirmishes in the suburbs. He was forced to negotiate the Treaty of Bretigny in 1360. This gave Edward enlarged sovereignty over Aquitaine and Gascony, and confirmed his possession of Calais, in return for abandoning his claim to the throne of France. It also set John II's ransom at three million crowns. John's son Louis of Anjou stood in as a replacement hostage at English-held Calais, while John returned to France to try and raise funds to pay. When Louis escaped in 1362 John gave himself up and returned to captivity in England. In 1364 he died, still an honourable captive, in London. Charles V succeeded him as king of France.

The Black Prince, now also prince of Aquitaine, taxed his subjects to pay for the war in Castile. Protest was most vociferous in Gascony. The Gascons appealed to Paris for intervention. The reign of Charles V saw the English steadily pushed back. Although the Breton war ended in favour of the English at the Battle of Auray, the dukes of Brittany eventually reconciled with the French throne.

The Black Prince was occupied with war in Spain from 1366 and due to illness was relieved of command in 1371, whilst Edward III was too elderly to fight. England was plagued with internal strife, uprisings in Ireland and Wales, a civil war, the Black Death and a renewed border war with Scotland. That turmoil continued through the reign of subsequent kings until Henry IV took the throne in 1399. It was during this period of relative English weakness that the French made repeated attacks on England's Channel coast.

In July 1373 Bertrand du Guesclin overran Jersey and besieged Gorey Castle. His troops succeeded in breaching the outer defences, forcing the garrison back to the keep. The garrison agreed that they would surrender if not relieved by Michaelmas and du Guesclin sailed back to Brittany, leaving a small force to carry on the siege. Fortunately for the defenders, an English relief fleet arrived in time. The French would not succeed in capturing Jersey during the Hundred Years' War, but did again capture Gorey Castle in the summer of 1461, allegedly as part of a secret deal between Margaret of Anjou and Pierre de Breze to gain French support for the Lancastrian cause. The island was held by the French until 1468, when Yorkist forces and local militia were able to recapture the castle.

The chronicler Jean Froissart is the chief source for the French raids, which some historians have described as mere piracy. The raids were neither isolated nor simply opportunistic, but part of a well-organised naval campaign which had been carefully prepared by the French admiral, Jean de Vienne, during a two-year truce with England. Jean de Vienne was born at Dole and started his military career at 19, being knighted at 21. In 1373 Charles V made him Admiral de France. Working with determination, de Vienne reorganised the navy, started an important programme of construction, created an effective coast guard, navigation police, organised watches along the coasts and distributed licences for the building and selling of ships. He was one of the first to understand that only naval operations could seriously hurt England itself. The Admiral's fleet consisted of 120 ships, including 35 large vessels owned by the Crown, and eight Castilian galleys commanded by Don Fernando Sanchez de Tovar. On board were 4–5,000 troops, plus sailors and oarsmen. In June 1377 the Sussex port of Rye was sacked and burnt. Nearby Winchelsea escaped, as the Abbot of Battle had rapidly garrisoned it.

At some point – the date and sequence of events is contradictory in contemporary accounts – a raid was mounted on Rottingdean, Sussex, where there were rumoured to be rich pickings on the estate of the French-born prior of Lewes. The prior, John de Caroloco, or Cherlieu, had held that post for about 11 years and was a member of the Clunic order, the parent house of which was in France. The prior was defending the coast against his countrymen for two compelling reasons. He responded to orders from King Edward that his bishops 'arm and array' all abbots, priors and other ecclesiastical persons within their respective dioceses. And the lands and peasantry around Rottingdean belonged to his priory – they were valuable assets worth protecting.

Villagers tried to oppose the French landing in the chalk cliff gap south of Rottingdean. That failed and in the early evening the French intruders saw the prior of Lewes and his relief force of 500 men coming towards the village. They set an ambush with 300 horsemen and held their fire until the last moment. The English were surprised and fled with the loss of 100 men. The prior was captured wearing armour covered in red velvet, together with his subordinates, Sir John Falvesley, Sir Thomas Cheyne and the esquire John Brocas. Froissart's account indicates that the battle took place in the village itself. He states that after the French had beaten off local resistance at the landing place, they marched on to meet the prior's forces 'in a convenient square in front of the monastery'. It was no one-sided massacre and the English longbowmen inflicted heavy casualties on the French. Froissart:

> ... a squire born in France being in the service with the said (prior) fought manfully against men of France, in so much that his belly (was) cut, he fought sore, his bowels remaining behind him a great space, and followed his enemies. In which conflict a hundred Englishmen were slain, and many more of the Frenchmen; which took the dead men away with them, other else they burnt their faces with iron that they should not be known, and that Englishmen should not take solace of their death. Where a man of France was taken, confessing afore his death that the realm of England should not have been troubled by the men of France if that the Duke of Lancaster had been made king.

Rottingdean church was burnt, as were many homes in the small town. Nearby hamlets and fine houses were also looted and destroyed. In Sutton by Seafield, the home of Michael de Northburgh, his corn and chattels to the value of £100 succumbed to the raid, according to the following year's Rolls. Despite the claims of Froissart and other French chroniclers (see Appendix 1) there is no evidence that the French reached Lewes itself.

Prisoners were carried back to France where negotiations were undertaken to ensure their release on payment of ransoms. Jean de Vienne held the prior of Lewes prisoner for a year. The prior was eventually released on payment of 7,000 nobles, or approximately twice the annual income of the priory, in 1391. He subsequently returned to Lewes, and remained there until his death in 1396.

The fate of the other hostages was mixed and shines a light on the medieval trade in exalted prisoners. Sir Thomas Cheyne was a retainer of the Prince of Wales and was present with him at the victorious battle of Najera in April 1367, where he captured the famous French commander, Bertrand du Guesclin. Shortly after his return to England in 1371, the Prince promised to pay Sir Thomas £1,483 6s 6d for his captive. In December of the same year, Sir Thomas obtained the manor of Farnborough. Sir Thomas' life retainership ended with the death of the Prince on 8 June 1376. Sir Thomas and Sir John Falvesley were possibly among the 400 knights raised by the Earl of Arundel to defend the Sussex coast, on the understanding that the inhabitants would pay for their upkeep. Both men were stationed in the Earl's castle at Lewes. Sir Thomas was released soon after Easter 1379, for a possible down payment of 300 marks, the first instalment of the debt owed to him by the late Prince of Wales. Sir Thomas died in 1381. He was buried in London, where his brother William was an important officer in the law courts.

Sir John Falvesley, born c. 1335, had at 17 inherited his father's manor in Northamptonshire. It is not clear when Sir John Falvesley was released or how much he was ransomed for. However, he was back in England in 1382. He was a favourite of the Earl of Arundel and later rose high in his service, accompanying him on his naval expeditions to Sluys in March 1387 and France in June 1388. Sir John died in 1392 and was buried in Lewes priory.

After the raid on Rottingdean, the French fleet then moved on to Portsmouth, Dartmouth and Plymouth. In early August, it returned to Harfleur as the men on board had completed their period of paid service. There had also been a serious rift between Jean de Vienne and one of his subordinate commanders, the Sire de Torcy, on whether or not to hold Rye as a counterweight to English Calais. The fleet put to sea again in mid-August to support the Duke of Burgundy's attack on Calais. A gale blew the fleet to the Isle of Wight. The French successfully landed on 21 August, despite opposition from the inhabitants, and plundered the island before being repulsed by the garrison of Carisbrooke Castle under the command of Sir Hugh Tyrill. During the siege, a party of French soldiers on their way to the castle was ambushed and killed. The bodies were buried under a mound still known as 'Noddies Hill'. After extorting 1,000 marks protection money from the island's remaining inhabitants, along with a promise that the locals would not resist if they returned within 12 months, the French left.

The English Crown reacted to the invasion by equipping the castle with cannon and a mill for producing gunpowder. Many more cannon were deployed along the south coast, including at Corfe, Dover, Porchester, Saltwood and Southampton. Further English castles along the Welsh borders and Scotland were similarly equipped, with the Tower of London and Pontefract Castle acting as supply depots for the new weapons.

Meanwhile, the French fleet sailed onto Southampton and Poole, where attempts to land at both places met with fierce resistance. The fleet then sailed eastward to keep its appointment with the Duke of Burgundy at Calais. On the way it attacked Winchelsea with cannon, but without success, the town being well garrisoned again by the abbot of Battle. Hastings was undefended and while the main French force was bombarding Winchelsea, a smaller party, made up mainly of sailors, burnt the town, supposedly in retaliation for a degradation of the Black Prince's army in Northern France. The Church of St Clement's was destroyed in the raid but was rebuilt quickly. The fleet then moved onto Dover and anchored offshore. Finding the defenders alert and well prepared, the fleet returned to Harfleur and was disbanded.

Between 1381 and 1385, de Vienne fought against the Flemish. He still dreamt of threatening the English in their own homes, and in 1385 he used a 180-ship fleet to land an army in Scotland with the intent of invading England, but the force had to withdraw. After Charles VI succeeded his father, the French navy was allowed to decay. Disappointed, de Vienne participated in the siege of Mahdia and joined in the crusade of King Sigismund of Hungary. He was killed during the Battle of Nicopolis in Bulgaria.

❦⸻❦

Although Hastings, Rye, Folkestone, Rottingdean and the Isle of Wight all suffered during this period, the hardest hit was Winchelsea. Before, during and after the 1377 events, it suffered no less than seven attacks.

The original ancient town lies under Rye Bay, having been swamped by storms in the thirteenth century. A high tide that 'flowed twice without ebbing' partially submerged Old Winchelsea in 1250, and another flood in 1287 finished the job. Winchelsea had been an important port, a popular embarkation point for the royal family, and one of the chain of Cinque Ports granted privileges in return for maintaining sea power. The French regarded them as legitimate targets. Edward I was determined that the town must be saved. He planned a new Winchelsea on the hill of Iham at the end of a narrow peninsula; to the north, deep waters formed a natural harbour sheltered from weather and enemy attacks. Edward based the plan of the new town upon the French 'Bastide' design, a gridiron pattern dividing the town into blocks with wide, straight streets. Building began in 1288.

In 1337, the first year of the war, Edward III had ordered a war-galley built at Winchelsea and it was deployed in early skirmishes with the French around Hastings, Rye, Folkestone, Winchelsea itself and Dover. As we have seen, a French force aiming to attack Sandwich was deterred by the strength of the county militia and diverted to Rye and Winchelsea. Considerable damage was done to both towns before an English squadron put them to flight. Nevertheless, for much of this period the French and their Castilian and Genoese allies controlled much of the Channel, while the Black Death ravaged the English southlands, undermining defences.

Despite this, the Cinque Ports could still take effective counter-measures and in 1340 the men of Winchelsea and Rye captured a Boulogne ship and, after killing the crew, interrogated four merchants on board. They revealed that 18 galleys beached at Boulogne were guarded by just six watchmen. The Cinque Ports men entered the enemy harbour unseen, hidden by a heavy mist, sealed off the lower portion of Boulogne and burnt the galleys at their leisure. Before a French relief force drove them off with heavy bloodshed, the English destroyed a further 24 merchant vessels.

After the victory at Poitiers, the 1357 incursions and a short-lived truce, the English defences were further undermined by complacency. The truce over, Edward III again set out for France. The French in turn planned further incursions, aiming to free their King John, imprisoned at Somerton. In the ensuing panic John was hastily moved further inland to Berkhamstead.

A French fleet duly embarked in March 1360 heading for Sandwich, which they wrongly thought was close to Somerton. The fleet was held back for a week by foul weather, but eventually managed to make landfall in Rye Bay. A force of up to 2,000 men, mainly bowmen and foot soldiers, lined up on the beach and on 15 March marched on Winchelsea. Winchelsea was unprepared and its defences were in a sorry state. Two years earlier the town was reported to have been partially 'waste and uninhabited' due to pestilence. Able-bodied men who had survived the Black Death were either with Edward in France as part of the Cinque Ports support fleet, or deployed at the mouth of the Thames following faulty intelligence that London was the main French target.

The French walked up the hill to the town, meeting little resistance. Popular tradition has it that the inhabitants were surprised while at mass. That is unlikely given that warning bells had been rung across southern England. More likely is that the few fit defenders used the thick, crenellated walls of St Giles as a defensive position. Whatever the truth, the defenders were hopelessly outnumbered. In accordance with the custom of medieval warfare when civilians were involved, men, women and children were butchered. Legend has it that whole families perished in the church, which the French torched. The invaders burnt and looted in a leisurely fashion, burning several ships in the harbour. They were in no hurry to leave.

That allowed time for the Abbot of Battle, Hamo of Offingham, to gather around 300 horsemen from the county levies for a counter-attack. He was prompted by reports, later included in the Calendar of Rolls, that

> … enemies landed at Winchelsea on Sunday last a great host of armed men with their horses, took the town, barbarously slew the men therin found, and are riding over the country, slaying, burning, destroying and doing other mischief, and greater damage unless they be speedily and manfully opposed.

That was an exaggeration, and the booty-laden French were in no mood for a real battle. They began to withdraw, increasingly coming under bow-fire, their stragglers surrounded and killed in turn. Some died in the town, but most of the reported 300 casualties fell while trying to board their ships, two of which were beached and unable to refloat.

The revenge taken on the French was poor consolation for Winchelsea. Three years later, despite the efforts of men returned from military service overseas or in the Thames, 409 properties were reported to be still in ruins, their occupants unable to afford the rent. The ships burnt in the harbour were another hammer-blow to a community that relied on maritime trade.

Nationally, too, the raid had a major impact, with the entire country put on a war footing. Many men were ordered away from the fields and from trading enterprise and put on military standby. Food was requisitioned from hard-pressed areas to feed those recruits and seamen. Taxes were collected to both rebuild defences and to raise a fleet for a revenge attack on the French coast.

Around 160 English vessels ferried a large force to Leure on the north bank of the Seine estuary. They took a fort on the beach before moving on to attack Harfleur, three miles inland. The savagery inflicted on that town was a mirror image of that imposed on Winchelsea. But the follow-up was ill thought out and the English were forced to retire. The negotiations which immediately followed led to the Treaty of Bretigny and the release of the French King Henry. It gave Winchelsea a nine-year respite from attack.

It was just as well – Winchelsea remained in a sorry state, its trade further hit by taxes on the export of wool and leather. By 1369-70, however, Winchelsea and Rye were able to contribute to frenzied preparations for the despatch of an invasion fleet to France led by Robert de Knolles. Winchelsea's harbour at the mouth of the River Camber was the rendezvous. A second fleet was sent in 1372 but that was utterly destroyed by the Castilian navy. The English defences were again vulnerable. In May 1376 Rye was told to 'put all able-bodied men at arms to fortify the town that they may be able to resist their enemies.' The decree ordered that no man should leave the town or take away his property. Two years later they did just that, after French raids on ports to the west. The French seized the defenceless town and used it as a base to ravage the surrounding countryside. Hearing that the Abbot of Battle was raising a force against them, the French evacuated Rye. In doing so they killed 64 men and women who resisted looting, stole 42 hogsheads of wine, much rich booty and four of the church bells, which they loaded on their ships along with four ransomable hostages. Before they sailed they torched the town. The removal of the church bells was regarded by the English as a particular insult. Winchelsea escaped this raid, but Hastings was again set ablaze.

The men of Rye and Winchelsea combined the following year and sailed for Normandy, hell-bent on revenge. They arrived by night at the small town of Portus Petri and 'slew all who resisted' before taking hostages and burning as many buildings as they could. They repeated their deprecations at the Hamlet of Wylet and returned home laden with booty. This included, thanks to good intelligence, the stolen church bells of Rye.

The Castilians, meanwhile, were still keen to avenge their losses in the sea battle off Winchelsea. In 1380 seventeen galleys from Seville and two from Santander, along with a solitary French vessel, sailed from Harfleur to Winchelsea. They landed a force which, according to tradition, was treacherously admitted to the hill-top town through the New Gate. It is a fair assumption that the previous butchery was repeated, but there is scant evidence of exactly what happened. The stone Pipewell Gate and part of St Thomas's Church were ruined and most if not all of the wooden buildings burnt; but details of the destruction remain sketchy and are based mainly on archaeological evidence rather than records. Thomas Walsingham merely noted in a wider history of the wars: 'Amongst the dreadful damage which befell our country was that they took the town of Winchelsea and put to flight the Abbot of Battle and all his followers when they tried to assist the town.' Winchelsea was all but wiped out, and the town briefly abandoned.

The people of Winchelsea began to rebuild, but the country was hit the following year by the Peasants' Revolt following John of Gaunt's unjust imposition of a poll tax. The war with the French continued, but Winchelsea's ability and will to fight on the front line was sapped. Nearby Rye responded better to further invasion threats, using a 3d levy on each boatload of fish landed to maintain a constant watch from what is now known as Ypres To and preparing supplies of molten lead and boiling oil to pour on the heads of attackers.

In 1386 the French constructed an enormous palisade 20ft wide and 3,000 paces long, in sections which could be transported across the Channel and erected to protect the beachhead of an invading army. Luckily for the English, ships carrying the sections were captured by Sir William Beauchamp, Constable of English-held Calais. The sections were taken to Sussex and erected around the approaches to Winchelsea.

Despite that extra defence, Winchelsea never again regained its confidence, its once-booming trade or its importance to national defence. Its river silted up and the sea receded, stranding it inland. The war, like subsequent history, passed it by, although there is some flimsy evidence of a last French raid in 1418.

&–&

In the early 1380s England's economy was in meltdown. The wool trade was throttled by taxes to pay for war, and the need for armed merchant convoys to bring in wine had doubled its price. Between 1381 and 1383 Parliament three times refused to grant taxes for war, and soldiers' pay was cut, in some cases, by 80 per cent. Military setbacks in the Low Countries threatened a blockade of all England's trade. And in July 1386, England was facing the greatest invasion threat since the Conquest.

A French army of 30,000 gathered at Sluys to, according to chroniclers, 'invade these miserable English folk who have caused such mischief and destruction in France, and avenge ourselves for our fathers and mothers and friends whom they have killed.' Huge quantities of supplies were collected at special depots, while an armada of 1,200 cogs, galleys and barges assembled in the harbour to transport them.

When intelligence of the build-up reached England there was panic. Londoners, 'maddened by wine', demolished their suburbs to make their walled city more defensible. Many of the rich went on a wild spending spree, convinced that the end was nigh. Troops, fed up with waiting for their pay, rampaged through the countryside looting and scavenging whatever they could; their behaviour was so excessive that they were forbidden to go within 50 miles of the capital. Other units were disbanded despite the French threat, such was the fear of out-of-control soldiery. The English defence plan was to keep the fleet in the Thames until enemy troops were well inland and then attack the French fleet in the Channel, cutting off the line of retreat. Trusted English units retreating before the French troops would unite around London and together slaughter the isolated enemy army.

It was a sensible plan, but one that proved unnecessary. The invasion was delayed until the autumn because Philip of Burgundy, the invasion architect, was taken ill. When the new invasion deadline arrived the weather had, quite naturally, changed. French sailing masters told the High Command:

Most dread and powerful lords: of a truth, the sea is foul and the nights be too long, too cold, too dark, too wet and too windy. We are short of victuals, while we must have a full moon and a favourable wind with us. Moreover the English coast and English havens are dangerous. Too many of our ships are old and too many are small and might be swamped by those that are large. And the sea is at its worse between 29 September and 25 November.

The invasion was called off.

Although Henry IV planned campaigns in France, he was unable to put them into effect during his short reign. In the meantime, though, the French King Charles VI descended into madness – he killed four of his entourage while hunting in a forest, ran through his palaces howling like a wolf, and believed that his body was made of glass – and an open conflict for power began between his cousin, John the Fearless, and his brother, Louis of Orleans. After Louis's assassination, the Armagnac family took political power in opposition to John. By 1410, both sides were bidding for the help of English forces in a civil war.

The rebellion of Owain Glyndwr in Wales, the 1402 Scottish invasion, and a dispute between Henry and the Earl of Northumberland which wiped out the power of the Percy family in 1408, effectively delayed any formal renewal of hostilities with the French until 1415, although there were raids by French privateers on the Isle of Wight and Dartmouth. Then there were two decades of savagery.

Amongst the first actions was yet another invasion of the Isle of Wight. The French were repulsed by the inhabitants who re-took the French plunder and captured many prisoners. Shortly after, another French fleet arrived and demanded money. The Islanders refused, but invited the French to land without hindrance, refresh themselves for six hours and then meet them in the field. The French, who included veterans of the previous debacle, declined the invitation and left.

The new English king, Henry V, turned down an Armagnac offer to restore the Brétigny frontiers in return for his support. Instead, he demanded a return to the territorial status during the reign of Henry II. In August 1415, he landed with an army at Harfleur and took it, although the city resisted for longer than expected. By then most of the campaigning season was over. Henry decided to raid through northern France and reach English-occupied Calais. His army grew low on supplies and he found himself outmanoeuvred, forced to make a stand against a much larger French army at Agincourt, north of the Somme. The French nobility and men-at-arms were slaughtered by English and Welsh bowmen, and more died when Henry ordered the prisoners killed.

Henry took much of Normandy, including Caen in 1417 and Rouen in January 1419, making it English for the first time in two centuries. He made a formal alliance with the Duchy of Burgundy, who had taken Paris, after the assassination of Duke John the Fearless in 1419. In 1420, Henry met with the mad king Charles VI, who signed the Treaty of Troyes under which Henry would marry Charles' daughter Catherine and their heirs would inherit the throne of France. The Dauphin was declared illegitimate. Henry formally entered Paris later that year.

Henry's relentless progress was stopped by the arrival in France of a Scottish army of around 6,000 men. In 1421, a combined Franco-Scottish force led by John Stewart, Earl of Buchan, crushed a larger English army at the Battle of Bauge, killing the English commander, Thomas, 1st Duke of Clarence, and killing or capturing most of the English leaders. The French were so grateful that Buchan was immediately promoted to High Constable of France. Soon after, Henry V died at Meaux in 1422. Henry's infant son, Henry VI, was immediately crowned king of England and France, but the Armagnacs remained loyal to Charles' son and the war continued in central France.

The English continued to attack France and in 1429 were besieging the important French city of Orléans. An attack on an English supply convoy led to the skirmish that is now known as the Battle of the Herrings, when John Fastolf circled his supply wagons, largely filled with fish, around his archers and repelled a few hundred attackers. The English laid siege to Orléans. Their force was insufficient to fully invest the city, but larger French forces remained passive. In 1429 a young peasant girl, later to be known as Joan of Arc, convinced the Dauphin to send her to the siege, saying she had received visions from God telling her to drive out the English. She raised the morale of the local troops and they attacked the English redoubts, forcing the English back. Inspired by Joan, the French took several English strong points on the Loire. Shortly afterwards, a French army, some 8,000 strong, broke through English archers at Patay with 1,500 heavy cavalry, defeating a 3,000-strong army commanded by Fastolf and the earl of Shrewsbury. This victory allowed the Dauphin to march to Reims for his coronation as Charles VII. Joan was captured by the Burgundians in 1430 and later sold to the English, tried by an ecclesiastic court and executed. The French advance stalled in negotiations. In 1435, the Burgundians under Philip III switched sides, signing the Treaty of Arras and returning Paris to the king of France. A long truce gave Charles time to reorganise his army and government, replacing his feudal levies with a more modern professional army that could put its superior numbers to good use. The French recovered town after town.

By 1449, the French had retaken Rouen, and in 1450 the Count of Clermont and Arthur de Richemont, Earl of Richmond, caught the English army attempting to relieve Caen at the Battle of Formigny and defeated it. The French captured Caen and then Bordeaux and Bayonne in 1451. An attempt to recapture Gascony, although initially welcomed by the locals, was crushed by Jean Bureau, who brilliantly deployed cannon at the Battle of Castillon in 1453. This is considered the last battle of the Hundred Years' War.

During those many decades of strife, weapons, tactics, army structure, military technology and the nature of war evolved. When they began, heavy cavalry was the most powerful unit in an army; when they ended the heavy horse was made almost redundant by the longbow and later by firearms, together with the effective use of fixed defensive positions by men-at-arms. The English began using lightly armoured mounted troops – later called dragoons – who would dismount in order to fight battles. By the end of the Hundred Years' War, the days of the heavily armoured knight as a military force and the nobility as a political one were all but over. Cannon and firearms changed the face of battle and stone castles fell to their thunder, changing both defensive and offensive tactics forever. As General George S. Patton would later observe, 'Fixed fortifications are monuments to man's stupidity.'

The Hundred Years' War devastated France as a land, but it also awakened French nationalism. The conflict accelerated the process of transforming France from a feudal monarchy to a centralised state. It became a struggle not just between English and French kings but one between two peoples. The English came to regard the French as both enemy and prey, developing both hatred and contempt. The contemporary poet Eustache Deschamps credited an English soldier with the words: 'Dog of a Frenchman, you do nought but drink wine.' On the other hand, there were constant rumours in England that the French meant to invade and destroy the English language. National feeling that emerged out of such rumours, ignorance and bigotry unified both France and England further and set each against the other.

The lasting English patriotism stirred up by the three great victories at Poitiers, Crécy and Agincourt disguised the fact that it was the French who won the war. Nicholas Vincent wrote:

> In this stark paradox lies a fundamental truth. No matter how many times the French were defeated in battle, the war itself was not to be decided by a few brief hours of slaughter. At Agincourt, Henry V proved that his cause was just and that God was on his side. His victory was greeted with general celebration in England. By Parliament he was accorded the unprecedented honour of a lifetime grant of the custom on wool. Bishop Henry Beaufort, his cousin, proclaimed the invincibility of the English nation, comparing Henry to David and the great heroes of the Biblical Old Testament. In reality, in France, little had changed.

Opposition to the war helped to shape England's early modern political culture. Although anti-war and pro-peace spokesmen generally failed to influence outcomes at the time, they had a long-term impact. England showed decreasing enthusiasm for a conflict deemed not in the national interest, yielding only losses in return for the economic burdens it imposed. Conversely, the French understood that warfare was necessary to expel the foreigners occupying their homeland.

Bubonic plague and warfare depleted the overall population of Europe in the fourteenth and fifteenth centuries. France's population, about 17 million in the 1330s, was roughly halved. Normandy lost three-quarters of its population during the war. In the Paris region, the population between 1328 and 1470 was reduced by at least two-thirds.

The Hundred Years' War bankrupted the English government and fatally discredited the Lancastrian dynasty. In August 1453 Henry VI went into a catatonic state of lethargy and the Duke of York became Protector of England. When Henry recovered and tried to reinstate his regime, the drawn-out bloodbath known as the War of the Roses broke out. As Seward put it: 'Veterans used the combat skills they had learnt in France on each other.' And that civil war saw more invasions.

4 THE PRETENDERS

'… merely a commonplace tool to be used for important ends.'
– James A. Williamson on Simnel, *The Tudor Age*

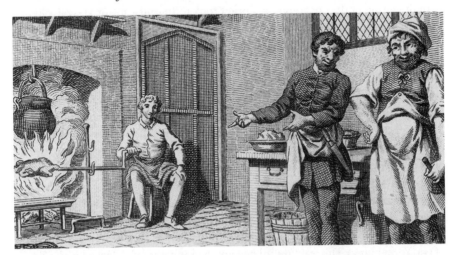

Figurehead of the Yorkist conspirators, Lambert Simnel provided the first challenge to Henry VII's newly
established reign in 1487, two years after the Battle of Bosworth, claiming to be the Earl of Warwick.
Following the defeat of the invading army of mostly Flemish and Irish troops at the Battle of Stoke Field,
Henry forgave young Simnel and gave him a job in the royal kitchens as a spit turner.

The Wars of the Roses were fought sporadically between 1455 and 1486 between
the two rival Plantagenet houses of Lancaster and York. Virtually all the leading participants were related and they are also known as the 'cousins' wars' in which, over
less than 25 years, the crown of England changed hands no less than five times. As
in all civil wars, no quarter was given or expected, and the battle of Towtown on
Palm Sunday in March 1461 has claim to be the bloodiest on English soil. Fought in
a raging snowstorm it, and many other ferocious battles, wiped out entire dynasties.
Unusually for the medieval era, the viciousness displayed swept away aristocrats as
well as the common soldiery. After the battle of Mortimer's Cross, Henry VI's stepfa-
ther, Owen Tudor, was beheaded in Hereford and a mad woman combed his hair and
placed his severed head at the market cross, surrounded by 100 candles. The final victory went to a relatively remote Lancastrian claimant, Henry Tudor, who defeated the
last Yorkist king, Richard III, at the Battle of Bosworth in 1485. He married Edward
IV's daughter Elizabeth of York to unite the two houses.

Henry's claim was to the throne was shaky: he was half Welsh and half French and was most closely related to the French royal family as great-grandson of Charles VI. In England he was merely the great-great-great grandson of Edward III. But he was backed by French and Breton silver, his army boosted by mercenaries – and most importantly – he had won a clear victory at Bosworth.

That bloodbath had ended the Wars of the Roses and put Henry VII on the throne, but his troubles were far from over. He was beset by enemies at home and at the court of Burgundy, and in the spring of 1487 a serious insurrection was launched from Ireland.

In the spring of the previous year a priest took to Ireland a 10- or 11-year-old boy, Lambert Simnel. The lad had been born around 1477 and his real name is not known – contemporary records call him John. According to subsequent legends he was the son of a baker, or an organ builder, or a tradesman. He was certainly of humble origin. He was taken as a pupil by an Oxford-trained priest, Richard Simon (or Symonds or Simons or Symonds) with ambitions to be a king-maker in such turbulent but opportunistic times. He tutored the handsome boy in courtly manners and gave him an excellent education. Simon noticed a striking resemblance between Lambert and the supposedly murdered sons of Edward IV, so he initially intended to present Simnel as Richard, Duke of York, son of Edward IV, the younger of the vanished princes in the Tower. However, when he heard rumours that the Earl of Warwick, a boy of the same age and of similar appearance to his pupil, had died during imprisonment, he changed his mind and put forward Simnel as the Earl. Warwick was the son of the Duke of Clarence, King Edward IV's brother, and as such had been the nephew of two Yorkist kings. The real Edward had not died and was safely locked in the Tower, but Yorkist propaganda now claimed that the prisoner was an imposter. That claim was widely promoted by Margaret, Dowager Duchess of Burgundy, who was sister of both Edward IV and Richard III. She was supported by several nobles, including John De la Pole, Earl of Lincoln, who was himself the son of Elizabeth, another of the sisters of the two Yorkist kings. However, Lincoln's claim was too tenuous and an attempt to raise a rebellion in north and west England in 1486 came to nothing. Lincoln had fled the English court in March and although he doubted Simnel's claim, he saw in him an opportunity for revenge and personal advancement. Lincoln was joined by a number of rebel English Lords at Mechelen, including Richard III's loyal supporter, Francis Lord Lovell, Sir Richard Harleston, the former governor of Jersey and Thomas David, a captain of the English garrison at Calais.

The indomitable Margaret provided between 1,500 and 2,000 German, Swiss and Flemish mercenaries under Captain Martin Swartz. They were mostly foot soldiers carrying bill and pike, with some crossbowmen and a few who carried the relatively new firearm, the *arquibusier*. The rebel army was put together in Ireland, where opposition to Henry Tudor was strong. Simon took the boy to Ireland, now claiming that Warwick had escaped the Tower and taken refuge under his care. He presented him to the Irish governmental head, the Earl of Kildare, who was willing to swallow the story as it gave him a pretext to invade England and overthrow Henry. The frightened and bemused Simnel was crowned King Edward VI of England in Dublin 24 May 1487.

By then the Yorkist fleet had arrived in Dublin. Kildare and his brother Thomas Fitzgerald of Laccagh, the Lord Chancellor of Ireland, recruited 4,500 Irish mercenaries, lightly armoured infantry, for the cause.

On 5 June, accompanied by Lincoln and Lovell, Simnel was landed on Piel Island near Furness, Lancashire, and were joined by some English supporters. Most local nobles, apart from Sir Thomas Broughton, stayed away. The pretender's army advanced through Yorkshire, picking up recruits as they went, and swelled to between 7,000 and 8,000, including some English knights and their retinues. By forced marches they covered over 200 miles in five days. On the night of 10 June, at Bramham Moor outside Tadcaster, Lovell led 2,000 men on a night attack against 400 Lancastrians under Lord Clifford, and easily overwhelmed them. Lincoln then outmanoeuvred Henry's northern army, under the Earl of Northumberland, by ordering a force under John, Lord Scrope, to mount a diversionary attack on Bootham Bar, York, on 12 June. Scrope then withdrew northwards, drawing Northumberland's army after him.

From Doncaster a Royalist force of some 6,000 men under Sir Edward Woodville challenged the main rebel force but retreated when they saw they were outnumbered. For three days the rebels advanced through Sherwood, skirmishing all the way. Nottingham was evacuated as they approached. But the fighting had delayed the Yorkists, allowing time for reinforcements under Lord Strange to bolster the city's defences and deter the rebel advance. Near Farnsfield the rebels turned off the Nottingham road and headed towards Newark into the security of the Earl of Lincoln's lands.

Henry was at Kenilworth but swiftly set off for Nottingham. He arrived there on 14 June and found that the rebels were at Southwell, 12 miles to the north-east. Henry moved to Radcliffe, between Nottingham and Bingham, the following day, while the rebel army crossed the Trent by the ford below Fiskerton and took up a position on an open escarpment some 1,500yds south of East Stoke. Here the king met them on the morning of the 16th as he was marching towards Newark. The rebels had an advantage in numbers, perhaps 9,000 to 6,000, but apart from the German mercenaries their soldiers were not well armed or trained. The English army was split into three parts of fairly equal size. The van, with heavy cavalry, was under the Earl of Oxford. Their two great advantages were their better armour and their large number of longbowmen.

Lincoln and the rebels had camped overnight on the high ground south and west of the village of East Stoke above the Fosse Way. The two sides were facing each other by 9 a.m. and rather than wait for the rest of the royal army, Oxford began a withering bow fire upon the rebels on the higher ground in front of him. The unarmoured Irish suffered gravely under the hail of arrows and Lincoln was forced to charge down the hill rather than stand his ground.

For three hours the battle was fiercely contested. The rebels were well served by the German mercenaries and the English shuddered under the shock of the initial charge. But after a while their poor equipment and armour, and the lack of training amongst the Irish levies, saw the fight swing to the English. A counter-attack by Oxford was enough to break the resistance of much of the rebel army. Unable to retreat, the German and Swiss mercenaries fought on, mainly to the death. Their commander, Martin Swartz, and Lincoln were killed, as were Broughton and Fitzgerald. Of the Yorkist commanders, only Lord Lovell escaped, by swimming the Trent and, according to legend, died hidden in a secret room at his house. He was never seen publicly again. The terrified Simnel was captured.

The rebels were slaughtered in a gully at the foot of the ridge and in the marshy fields. Between 4,000 and 5,000 died either in the battle or in the aftermath as the fugitives were hunted down. All captured Irish or English rebel soldiers were immediately hanged. The Irish nobles who had supported Simnel were spared, as Henry needed their support to govern Ireland effectively. The German mercenaries who survived the grim slaughter were allowed to go free but without their pay. Most of those who died on the field were buried in mass graves on the same day.

Simon avoided execution due to his priestly status, but was imprisoned for life. Henry pardoned young Simnel, acknowledging that he had been a mere puppet in the hands of adults, and gave him a job in the royal kitchen as a spit-turner. When he grew older, he became a falconer. He died around 1525.

The rebels had inflicted heavy casualties on Henry's army, possibly as many as 2,000 men. But his victory at Stoke secured the safety of the Tudor dynasty. The threat was not over, however. Another pretender emerged.

❦—❦

Perkin Warbeck was born around 1474 and his youth is clouded in mystery. According to his later confession, procured under duress, his father was John Osbeck, the Flemish comptroller to the city of Tournai. At 10 he was taken by his mother to Antwerp to learn Dutch. He served several masters before being employed by a local English master, John Strewe, for some months before being hired by a Breton merchant, who took him to Cork when he was about 17. There he learnt to speak English. Dressed in silk clothes, he was approached by Yorkists who saw a resemblance to the younger son of Edward IV, Richard, who had died in the Tower.

He returned to the Continent and first claimed the English throne at the court of Burgundy in 1490. He went back to Ireland in that guise hoping to raise support as Lambert Simnel had done four years earlier. He impressed few and was forced home. He was received by Charles VIII of France in 1492, but expelled by the French king under the terms of a treaty in which he agreed not to shelter English rebels. It was back at the Burgundian court, a hotbed of Yorkists, that his fortunes changed. He was officially recognised as Richard of Shrewsbury by Margaret of York, now the widow of Charles the Bold, who cynically tutored him in the ways of the Yorkist court. Simnel's mentor, Margaret of Burgundy, also opportunistically hailed the young man. Warbeck's claims echoed around the European courts and Henry imposed a trade embargo on Burgundy. At the invitation of Duke Philip's father, King Maximilian I, he attended the funeral of Emperor Frederick III in 1493 and was recognised as

King Richard IV of England. Warbeck in turn promised that if he died before becoming king, his claim would fall to Maximilian. The determined and vengeful Margaret of Burgundy funded another invasion attempt.

In July 1495 Warbeck landed at Deal in Kent, hoping to spark an uprising behind his bogus banner. Instead, his small army was routed and 150 of his troops killed before Warbeck even managed to step ashore. He retreated immediately to Ireland where he was supported by the Earl of Desmond. He laid siege to Waterford but strong resistance forced him to flee again, this time to Scotland.

Warbeck was well received by James IV of Scotland, who knew the political leverage to be had from having an English pretender at his court. Ferdinand and Isabella of Spain in particular were inclined to help him in his struggles with England, in order to prevent the situation escalating into war with France. Warbeck was permitted to marry James's distant cousin, Lady Catherine Gordon, a daughter of the Earl of Huntly. The marriage was celebrated in Edinburgh with a tournament. James gave Warbeck clothes for the wedding and armour covered with purple silk. So clothed, he may have fought in a team with the king and four knights.

In September 1496 James IV prepared to invade England with Warbeck. A red, gold and silver banner was made for Warbeck as the Duke of York; Roderic de Lalanne, a Flemish knight arrived with two little ships and 60 German soldiers. Two great French guns, 10 smaller cannon and 30 iron breech loading 'cart guns' were rolled out with 16 wagons for the munitions. An English spy in Edinburgh estimated that the invading army would last just five days in England before it ran out of provisions. His assessment was to be proved correct.

The Scottish army assembled near Edinburgh and James IV and Warbeck offered prayers at Holyrood Abbey on 14 September. Seven days later the army crossed the River Tweed at Coldstream. Miners set to work to demolish the tower of Castle Heaton on 24 September, but the army quickly retreated when resources were used up, and hoped-for support for Perkin Warbeck in Northumberland failed to materialise. In all, the invading army marched just four miles into England, destroyed four small defensive towers and burnt a few of Henry's royal banners. They retreated to Scotland on 25 September when an English army commanded by Lord Neville approached from Newcastle. James's allies, including Spain, pressed him to make peace with England.

Warbeck was now an embarrassment rather than an asset and James provided a ship, the *Cuckoo*, and a hired crew under a Breton captain, which returned him to Waterford in shame in July 1497. James IV did indeed make peace with England. Once again, Warbeck laid siege to Waterford, but this time his effort lasted only eleven days before he was forced to flee Ireland, chased by four English ships. He was left with only 120 men on two ships.

In September 1497, Warbeck landed at Whitesand Bay in Cornwall hoping to take advantage of Cornish resentment at the defeat of their own rising three months earlier. Warbeck proclaimed that he would put a stop to extortionate taxes levied to help fight a war against Scotland and was warmly welcomed. The Cornish fell for his rhetoric because they wanted to believe it. He was declared Richard IV on Bodmin Moor and his Cornish army of around 6,000 entered Exeter before advancing on Taunton. Henry sent his top general, Giles, Lord Daubeney, to attack the Cornish and when Warbeck heard that the king's scouts were at Glastonbury, he panicked and deserted his army. Warbeck surrendered himself at Beaulieu Abbey in Hampshire.

Henry reached Taunton on 4 October 1497, where he received the surrender of the remaining Cornish army. The ringleaders were executed and others fined. Warbeck was imprisoned, first at Taunton, then at the Tower of London, where he was, according to an eyewitness, 'paraded through the streets on horseback amid much hooting and derision of the citizens'.

Warbeck was held in the Tower alongside Edward, Earl of Warwick. Both tried to escape but were quickly re-captured. Unlike the boy Simnel, the 25-year-old Warbeck could not claim that he had been the pawn of unscrupulous adults. It is estimated that Henry spent £13,000 on countering Warbeck's adventures, putting a strain on the royal finances and making him disinclined to mercy. On 23 November 1499, Warbeck was drawn on a hurdle from the Tower to Tyburn. On the scaffold he read out his confession before being hanged.

Many historians credit Henry's victory at Bosworth as marking the beginning of the modern nation. Others qualify that judgement. Nicholas Vincent wrote:

> … by the time that Henry Tudor placed a crown upon his head, England had acquired both a history and a national identity. Wealth and the bounty of nature were England's birthrights, a consequence of geography, of the constant presence of the sea, and of the toil of those who first cleared the land, dug the mines and tilled the soil. From at least the age of Bede, as far back as the eighth century, came an idea of Englishness and of united destiny united under Christian kingship. For all the shattering uncertainties and usurpations of the fifteenth century, the kingdom of England, unlike the kingdom of France or the empire of Germany, remained a united and indivisible whole.

Attempted invasions, hopeless though they were, helped to cement that birthright, that national identity.

5 HENRY'S CASTLES AND THE INVASION OF THE ISLE OF WIGHT

'The bravery of his enemies who come so near his nose'
– Sir Peter Carew, 1545

Depiction of Henry embarking at Dover, c.1520, unknown artist, 1775, from the Royal Collection.

Henry VIII, a martially minded king and keen jouster, was left politically isolated after his divorce from Catherine of Aragon. At the Peace of Nice, Europe's Catholic overlords, France and Spain, rattled their swords and threatened an invasion blessed by the Pope. Henry responded by building the strongest set of coastal defences ever seen, surpassing the Roman fortifications of the Saxon Shore. The great stone castles built by the Normans and Plantagenets, most notably the chain built around Wales by Edward I, had been intended more for suppressing local populations and potential rebels than as a bulwark against foreign invasion. True, the growing ports and river-crossings were heavily fortified throughout the Middle Ages, but the coming of cannon made many of the works next to useless against an overseas army with the latest martial technologies. Stone was replaced with brick, masonry and earthen banks. Henry, as befitting a Renaissance prince, was interested in every new advance and employed the best architects and engineers. His defences proved to be a solid legacy, but one dwarfed in effect by his marital complexities, which saw the creation of the Church of England and ensured centuries of bloodshed.

Henry came to the throne, aged 18, in 1509. He was a giant, single-minded, fit and interested in everything the age could provide – the opposite of later caricatures after his body and soul went to seed. His realm was small – barely four million people – and what wealth there was depended on wool. And that meant trade. He could not afford expensive campaigns of conquest, but he understood early the necessity of keeping the Channel ports open. He still had Calais, the last bit of mainland Europe left after the Hundred Years' War. But trade routes were threatened by the powers of France and Spain. Henry took the diplomatic route to survival and prosperity in those turbulent times. He played with the dynasties which ruled and brokered power. He forged family links with both super-powers. First, he married Catherine of Aragon, the aunt of the Spanish Emperor Charles V. Then he married his favourite sister, Mary, to the elderly King Louis XII of France.

The dynastic job done, he then focused on defence. He improved existing coastal forts and constructed new ones. He encouraged an astonishing surge in the art of gun-making, emulating his brother-in-law James IV of Scotland, who created a small but efficient navy backed by the most modern weapons the foundries could produce. Henry appointed his father's gunner, Humphrey Walker, as gunfounder and bought enough tin to be used in the smelting of 100 large cannon. Henry ordered another 48 from the master gun-maker of Belgium in 1512 and within two years his arsenal was the envy of many Continental rulers.

Henry had inherited a weak and obsolete navy from his father, and set about transforming it. It had been customary that such ships were merchantmen in peacetime and only reverted to warships at times of crisis, and that the main function of such part-time warships was either to transport troops or to engage at close quarters with a potential invader. Henry, using the very best craftsmen and innovators, changed all that. His warships were to be genuine ships of war: mighty, threatening, fit for all purposes. Henry bought eight acres of land at the entrance to Portsmouth harbour and built the world's first dry dock. His claim to be the founder of the British navy is a strong one.

This was a time of great technological change, and matching changes in the strategies of warfare. Before Henry, the firepower of ships was limited by the weight of guns each could carry. And the effectiveness of such guns was ruled by how close to the water-line they could be positioned. The key issue was how to cut gun-ports low down while ensuring they were watertight when exposed to conditions at sea. That was impossible as long as the hulls were clinker-built with overlapping planks. The turn of the century saw the development of hulls built with smooth planks set edge-to-edge. It proved a major breakthrough, but no fail-safe, as events were to prove.

Henry embraced the new technology, but so did potential enemies, with the new hulls appearing simultaneously in Spain and Portugal, and the French credited with inventing effective gunport lids. By the time of the Field of the Cloth of Gold in 1520, contemporary illustrations clearly show heavy guns protruding from lower decks. Such improvements were developed and refined during the 1520s and 1530s. Henry's flagship *Mary Rose* spanned both ages. Her keel was laid in Portsmouth in 1509 and her hull was built in the old clinker style. But she was extensively rebuilt twice.

In 1512 Henry and his parliament joined an alliance of the Pope and the king of Aragon against Louis XII. English merchantmen were called back into service and crews were lured with promises of 6d a day conduct money, plus food and uniforms. Admiral Sir Edward Howard was tasked with keeping the Channel clear while a flotilla packed with soldiers crossed to capture Boulogne. This he did successfully and in August the *Mary Rose* led 25 ships in an attack on the 222-strong French fleet anchored off Brest. Fire arrows burnt several French warships to the waterline, a further 32 vessels were either partially burnt or captured, and 800 soldiers were taken prisoner. The *Mary Rose* was at the fore of many such actions until she was refitted and partially rebuilt in the Medway. Modifications were made to allow great cannon to be more efficiently situated on her gundecks.

The threat of a combined Franco-Spanish attack in 1538, following his divorce from Catherine of Aragon, put Henry's realm in the greatest danger. He knew by then that the combined might of Catholic Europe was ranged against him, its rulers and populace outraged by his sacrilege. His 1533 excommunication and the annulment of his marriage to Charles V's aunt had made war inevitable. The Pope reconciled the French and Spanish and preached holy war against Henry, whom he compared to 'the Turk'. In the Vatican, and in Catholic royal courts, it was believed that Henry's subjects would welcome an invasion force as their deliverance. Furthermore, Henry's best advisor, Cardinal Wolsley, was disgraced and dead. Wolsley had always advocated an alliance with Emperor Charles, whose Spanish possessions included the Netherlands and its Channel ports, through which much of England's wool trade passed. Such restraint was no more and Henry was truly on his own. He turned his mind to more fortifications.

This first phase was known as the 1539 device programme. Henry's coastal defences ranged from earthen bulwarks to small blockhouses and artillery towers to state-of-the-art Italianate style fortifications. Henry took a personal interest in the military engineering techniques of the time, and approved and amended the designs himself.

Henry started with the North, to secure those borders, concentrating mainly on modernising existing castles at Berwick and Carlisle. But it was along the south coast, which faced the greatest threat, that he got into his stride, building 30 castles and forts. They were placed at points overlooking key invasion routes or anchorages, and spaced to allow interlocking fire between them. The result was an impressive defensive line, paid for in part at least by the revenue raised by the dissolution of the monasteries.

Military historian D.J. Cathcart King contrasted Henry's device forts with medieval fortifications, noting that 'by medieval standards their profile is squat; their battlements, unpierced by loops, have rounded *merlons* and widely splayed embrasures with sloping sills, to reduce damage by gunfire; and they are robustly built.' The early artillery forts were generally a central round tower surrounded by a variety of concentric elements. They were short and squat, with three tiers of long-distance offensive armament and two tiers of defensive armament. The bays had wide splays for easy traverse of the guns, walls were thick and curved to deflect shot, but the medieval portcullis, murder hole and drawbridge were retained as protection against infantry attacks from the landward. They were linked by earthworks and bulwarks to provide further defences.

The Elizabethan writer Lambarde wrote that Henry, 'having shaken off the intolerable yoke of the Papish tyrannie ... with all speede, and without sparing any cost, builded Castles, platfourmes, and blockhouses, in all needful places of the Realme.' For almost the first time, the State was involved in the construction, rather than fortifications being left to individual nobles.

The key section became known as the Castles of the Downs at Walmer, Deal and Sandown covering the stretch of water between the Kent coast and the Goodwin Sands. That waterway was a favoured anchorage for both merchant and military vessels, a place for victualing and an embarkation point. And an incoming invasion fleet would be channelled along it, running the gauntlet of the land forts. Emperor Charles V knew it personally, having departed from there after his 1520 meeting with Henry at Canterbury. By May 1539 at least 1,400 men were working on the chain of forts and associated defences. All three were built to a similar design, but with different modifications. The work was carried out speedily and efficiently, benefiting from the (sometimes) concomitant organisation of a state project.

Deal was the most impressive of the device forts and was built by the famed Bohemian engineer Stefan von Haschenperg. The design, although considered revolutionary in England, was in line with continental trends, notably the pointed, angled bastions favoured in Italy. It was a pure fortress, with none of the comforts of noble edifices. Many of the walls were made from recycled monastic Caen stone, smoother and paler than the Kentish ragstone. It had a permanent garrison of 35, captained by Thomas Wynkfelde of Sandwich. By December 1539 the castle was sufficiently complete to host a state banquet to welcome Anne of Cleves on her journey to London and a brief marriage to Henry.

Walmer was a circular keep, surrounded by an open courtyard and protected by a concentric wall, from which four squat, semi-circular bastions projected. The northern bastion formed the gatehouse with a gun on its roof; the others had guns mounted inside them and on the roof. The central keep would also have had guns mounted on its roof giving the castle the capacity to mount 39 guns. A gallery running around the castle at basement level had 32 loops for hand-guns covering the moat. Sandown, which completed the trio, was similar to Walmer, and protected by a stone-lined dry moat, with a drawbridge on the landward side. The three forts were initially linked by a two-mile-long earthen 'fosse', or rampart, strengthened by three small earth bulwarks. The whole scheme for the defence of the Downs was completed, and the castles garrisoned, by the autumn of 1540 and placed under the control of the Lord Warden of the Cinque Ports.

Henry's scheme continued along the south coast. Hurst Castle was built at the end of a long shingle spit at the west end of the Solent to guard the approaches to Southampton. The site was well chosen at the narrow entrance to the Solent, where the ebb and flow of the tides creates strong currents, putting would-be invaders at its mercy. By 1540 some kind of fortification existed but details are scant. The work on the castle proper took several years and was finished by the end of 1544.

St Mawes Castle, Cornwall, and its larger sister castle, Pendennis, were built on the shores of the River Fal estuary to provide protection to the large inland expanse of water known as the Carrick Roads near Falmouth, one of the largest natural harbours in the country. The building of both was supervised by Thomas Treffrey to a clover-leaf plan with massive bastions designed to mount 'ship-sinking' guns, which covered every angle of approach.

Such defences were certainly impressive, but they were not continuous. Faced with a renewed threat from the French, Henry built a second phase, concentrating on the vulnerable area around the Solent estuary and the ports of Southampton and Portsmouth. This later programme of coastal defences reflected new developments in fortifications, especially in the introduction of Italianate designs using angular features. The earlier curvilinear designs of castles were replaced by square keeps surrounded by angular or arrowhead-shaped bastions. Southsea Castle was built in 1544 on the waterfront at the southern end of Portsea Island. Shortly afterwards, Yarmouth Castle was erected, a small square blockhouse guarding Yarmouth harbour on the Isle of Wight.

The device forts were certainly needed. By the spring of 1545 a new force was gathering, intent on invading across the Channel. Francis I's plan was to send his fleet to attack Portsmouth and cut off essential supply lines with Boulogne, still in English hands. The French fleet was assembled in the Seine estuary between Le Havre and Honfleur. In June Henry sent two task forces in a failed bid to scatter and destroy it. By July, the French were ready. The fleet was fully equipped and loaded with 30,000 men to attack Portsmouth and destroy Henry's fleet in anchorage. At the same time an army under Marshal de Briez was ordered to march on Boulogne. It was to be a classic attack by land and sea on two fronts.

Francis dined on board the flagship, the 800-ton *Carraquon*, before going ashore to wave them off. His dinner party was later blamed for the fire that spread through the flagship from its galley. The French Admiral Claude d'Annebault, Baron de Retz, Governor of Normandy, abandoned ship just before the guns and ammunition exploded. He switched to the carrick *La Maitresse*, but that ran aground near Honfleur. Such mishaps delayed the invasion, but by Saturday 18 July the fleet, after a fair passage, dropped anchor in St Helen's Roads on the north-east corner of the Isle of Wight.

Henry was ready for them. He had received good intelligence from spies and other informants and had been in Portsmouth for three days to prepare the defence and set up his HQ and a tented army encampment around Southsea Castle. His brother-in-law, Charles Brandon, prepared the soldiers to repel any landings if the French broke through the sea defences. But in Portsmouth harbour Henry could gaze on just 60 ships – carricks, *gallaises* and galleys – under the command of John Dudley, the Viscount Lisle. Against them, the French fleet numbered 225 vessels, much larger than the Spanish Armada that Henry's daughter would confront 43 years later. And Henry's 12,000 soldiers were up against Francis's 30,000. A contemporary source said that the king 'fretted and his teeth stood on edge to see the bravery of his enemies who come so near his nose and he not able to encounter with them'.

The topography of the area, however, was very much in Henry's favour. The serpentine channel into Portsmouth harbour is bounded by the shallow waters around Spit Bank, Horse Sands and No Man's Land Sands. In front of the harbour entrance is the Hamilton bank, then called The Spyte, which appeared heaven-sent to trap the unwary or ignorant navigator. Those waters were made all the more dangerous by the guns on Southsea Castle and two more towers, the Round and the Square, commanding the deep water channel. Henry's tactics were simple: sit tight and draw the enemy into the killing zone.

Henry was reinforced as he waited by ships from the Thames and the West Country, but with around 100 vessels he was still heavily outnumbered. The King dined aboard the flagship *Henry Grace à Dieu* and issued his orders to Admiral Lisle and Vice-Admiral Sir George Carew. A look-out reported a large number of men-o'-war approaching and Henry left for his vantage point on the shore. The English fleet set out from their anchorage to pass the harbour mouth and fan out south, sailing between Spit Sands and Horse Sands. The quayside was thronged with families and friends of the officers and crews. Local knowledge of the sandbanks and channels was invaluable. But the first day's action was hardly a grand battle.

Sir John Oglander, the deputy governor of Portsmouth, writing many decades later, described it as 'a little skirmish between our ships being in number 60 but it is true that we were too weak and withdrew to the Horse.' In the invasion fleet, cavalry officer Martin du Bellay recalled:

> After a long fight with gunshot the enemy began to slip to the left to the shelter of the land. This was the place where the ships were defended by a few forts which stood on the cliff behind them and on the other side by hidden shoals and rocks, with only a narrow and oblique entrance for a few ships at a time. This withdrawal and the approaching night put an end to the first day's fighting without our suffering notable loss from their cannon shot.

La Maitresse was on the point of sinking due to the damage she had sustained earlier but although d'Annebault had to change his flagship again, she was saved from foundering.

The following day, 19 July, the English fleet were becalmed, with barely a breath of wind. They were at the mercy of the French galleys, which Admiral Annebault ordered forward. Annebault later reported: 'This order was executed with a great deal of intrepidity and the weather favoured our attempt beyond our wishes for in the morning it was proven a perfect calm. Our galleys had all the advantages of working which we could desire to the great damage of the English who for want of wind not being able to stir laid exposed to our cannon and being so much higher and bulkier than our galleys, hardly a shot missed them while they, with the help of their oars, shifted at pleasure, and thereby avoided the danger of the enemy's artillery.' As the morning progressed an offshore breeze began to blow and the battered English carracks hoisted sail. The outcome was a disaster for the pride of Henry's fleet. Sir Peter Carew, in his contemporary memoirs, described the events:

Sir George Carew being entered into his ship commanded every man to take his place and the sails to be hoist but as the same no sooner done than that the *Mary Rose* began to heel to one side. Sir George Carew being in his own ship and seeing the same called for the master of the ship and told him thereof and asked him what it meant, who answered that if she does heel she is likely to be cast away. Then the said Sir Gawain passing by the *Mary Rose* called out to Sir George Carew asking him how he did, who answered that he had the sort of knaves whom he could not rule and it was not long after that the said *Mary Rose* thus heeling more and more was drowned with 700 men which were in her with very few escaped.

Sir George Carew went down with his ship. Historians and marine archaeologists have long argued about the exact cause of the loss. The likeliest explanation is that the *Mary Rose*, hoisting sail to go to the aid of the *Henry Grace à Dieu* under attack from French galleys, swung too steeply and heeled over. The gunports were open for action – the gunners were later blamed for not closing them after firing once – and the sea-water poured in. The heeling was exacerbated when heavy cannon broke loose and ammunition lockers burst open, with the munitions rolling to starboard and causing her to capsize. A French witness claimed that she was sunk by fire from a galley, but his account was not supported by other contemporary accounts or from the physical evidence when the ship was lifted in 1982. The high casualty rate – less than 40 men survived – may have been because anti-boarding netting had been strung up, trapping the crew, marines and around 100 soldiers. Henry and thousands of others looked on horrified from the shore.

Despite that huge and shocking loss, the battle proved inconclusive. The French withdrew to the Isle of Wight. French strategy was to land at Whitecliff Bay and cross Bembridge Down to attack Sandown, with another landing at Bonchurch, which would link up at Sandown. Contemporary accounts suggest that the French (or their mercenaries) sacked the area in order to draw out the English fleet.

The French landed 2,000 men at three undefended points and then attacked defences from inland. At Whitecliff Bay and at Bonchurch they moved swiftly to seize the high ground. However, the attacks were expected and in both cases local forces reached the high ground to oppose them. The Island's militia fought back ferociously. Martin Du Bellay wrote:

To keep the enemy's forces separated, a simultaneous descent was made in three different places. On one side Seigneur Pierre Strosse was bidden to land below a little fort where the enemy had mounted some guns with which they assailed our galleys in flank, and within which a number of Island infantry had retired. These, seeing the boldness of our men, abandoned the fort and fled southwards to the shelter of a copse. Our men pursued and killed some of them and burned the surrounding habitations …

A later account from Sir John Oglander: 'They landed at three several places at one time, purposely to divide our forces. Pierre Strosse landed at St Helens where there was a little fort, and beat our men, being divided from the fort, into the woods. Le Seigneur de Tais, General of the Foot, landed at Bonchurch, where there was a hot skirmish between them and us, and on either party many slain.'

The area around Bonchurch was important in its own right because nearby Dunnose Point offered a safe anchorage for French ships. There were also sources of fresh water nearby that could be used by the soldiers and sailors of the fleet. The French landed 500 men at Monk's Bay, but were then faced with the difficulty of breaking out from the Undercliff. They ascended the steep and thickly wooded slopes of St Boniface and Bonchurch Downs, which are over 700ft high. They were met by 300 local militia under Captain Robert Fyssher. Accounts of the fighting are confused, but it appears to have started at dawn and continued to noon. Some reports inflated the numbers involved to 2,800 on both sides, but they are unsubstantiated. More believable records suggest that local women archers participated. The first French attack was repelled but de Tais rallied his troops. A second French attack was launched, with the French forces arranged into the 'array' fighting formation. A French account concluded that after heavy casualties were sustained by both sides, the English line broke and the militia were routed as a result of the second attack. It also stated that Captain Fyssher offered £100 for a horse as he was too fat to run. Oglander reportedly confirmed this, adding: 'but none could be had even for a kingdom'. The Captain was never heard from again. He was probably either killed, or captured and eventually buried at sea.

The casualties for both sides were heavy. The French, whether or not they claimed victory, were thinly stretched and re-embarked. Another skirmish took place at Bonchurch several days after the battle, when English forces engaged with Frenchmen who had disembarked from French ships retreating from Portsmouth looking for water. A senior French commander, Chevalier D'Aux, was killed in the engagement.

There is still argument about whether the French invasion of the Isle of Wight was just a feint to draw out the English fleet, or a serious strategic endeavour. If the French had captured the island in serious numbers, and held it, the course of the war could have been very different. The island would have been used as a staging post for a full-scale invasion of England. The French Admiral d'Annebault wrote that 'having it [the Isle of Wight] under our control, we could then dominate Portsmouth ... and so put the enemy to extraordinary expense in maintaining a standing army and navy to contain us.'

The French fleet withdrew without a large-scale landing and attacked Seaford, inflicting some casualties, before sailing back across the Channel. Margaret Rule summed things up: 'The potentially great and bloody invasion had been reduced to a skirmish at sea, with a few raids of nuisance and attrition.'

The fiasco brought France to the negotiating table. In the Treaty of Camp, Henry secured Boulogne for eight years, after which the French would get it back if 2 million crowns were paid, or £750,000. Henry's motivation was now financial; his 1544 campaign had cost £650,000 and England was once again bankrupt.

Henry's later years of remarriage and decline belong in another book. He embarked on a wave of judicial executions in an increasingly psychotic bid to secure his succession. He grew into his obese incarnation and had to be moved about with the help of mechanical hoists. He was covered with painful, pus-filled boils and possibly suffered from gout. His obesity and other medical problems can be traced from a jousting accident in 1536. The fall re-opened and aggravated a previous leg wound, which festered for the remainder of his life and became ulcerated. It was a factor in Henry's violent mood swings. Henry's obesity hastened his death at the age of 55 on 28 January 1547 in the Palace of Whitehall, after allegedly uttering these last words: 'Monks! Monks! Monks!' Guilty conscience? Or terror at what he believed was in store for him after death?

❦–❦

Most of Henry's fortifications never saw action during his reign, but their value had been demonstrated in the Solent. Subsequent monarchs built on them, particularly his daughter Elizabeth.

The importance of the Medway became clear with the growth of the Chatham dockyards building and servicing Her Majesty's fleet. Storehouses were built, and the dockyard served as a nursery for Elizabethan seamen, including Sir Francis Drake. The massive medieval castle at Rochester loomed over the bridge, but the defences downriver were scanty. In 1559, the year after Elizabeth was crowned, she ordered a bulwark built at Upnor. Initially, it was a an angular bastion jutting into the river, but over the following decades it was improved and expanded in line with the development of heavy ordnance. Its aim was to deter enemy ships sailing up to attack the fleet when it was most vulnerable, in the dockyards.

As the dockyard grew it became clear that more defences were needed to protect the valuable naval stores at Chatham. A 'Cold War' existed with Spain, and the Medway was wide open to raids from the Spanish-controlled ports of the Netherlands. The Surveyor of the Navy, Sir William Winter, rejected Sheerness and the Isle of Grain in favour of another fort at Swaleness, opposite Queenborough, to prevent an enemy raiding up the Swale and into the Medway. That fort was erected in 1575. But master gunner William Bourne warned that shore batteries alone would not stop enemy incursion; they might batter the super-structures or heavy ships and bring down rigging, but the guns were not powerful enough over distance actually to sink them. He recommended that a heavy chain be placed across the Medway, capable of being lowered to let through friendly vessels and raised to block enemy ones. In 1588 maintenance of the chain cost £80.

That same year, it would do nothing to deter the most serious invasion attempt since 1216.

6 THE SPANISH ARMADA

'Distorted by a golden mist'
– Garrett Mattingley, 1959

Elizabeth I – The Armada Portrait, oil on panel by George Gower (1540-1596), Woburn Abbey.

Of all the great, epochal events in British history, the story of the Spanish Armada is probably the most riddled with myths and half-truths. Generations have been taught that the Spanish king launched his 'invincible' Armada to avenge the execution of Mary, Queen of Scots and re-impose Catholicism; and that the doughty little British fleet took on a leviathan and won by sheer pluck and superior seamanship. I was taught, for example, that our ships were so small that the Spanish shot sailed over them, allowing Drake's lads to engage in close combat; that the Spanish turned into an undisciplined rabble who took the wrong way home and were annihilated on the rocky coastlines of Scotland and Ireland. Spanish seapower was forever smashed, leaving the seas clear for British imperial expansion. None of the above is true to any appreciable extent. The expedition was doomed from the start and was the product of kingly over-ambition combined with the scepticism of military commanders. For Britain, it was a lucky escape which, until the Tudor spin doctors wove their spells, underlined the vulnerability of these shores, rather than their strength.

Philip II of Spain may have been a robust Catholic, but his driving interests were, like all contemporary monarchs, wealth, security and power. To maintain all, he looked west. The Americas were by then Spain's main source of all three. And it was this, rather than opposing religious dogma, which made Queen Elizabeth his enemy. Sir Francis Drake and her other sea dogs seriously interrupted the flow of bullion and other precious goods from South America. That was the principal cause of Philip's decision to invade England. But there were other factors. England had for almost 20 years aided the Dutch in their rebellion against Spanish rule of the Netherlands. English reinforcements had in 1586 seriously impeded the great Spanish General the Duke of Parma in his re-conquest of Flanders. Conversely, Parma's success in occupying 10 of the 17 provinces in what is now Belgium offered the potential to control deep-water ports in the Channel, the ideal springboard for an invasion. Parma had many doubts about an invasion of England, particularly due to well-founded fears that if his men were engaged in England, the French might invade the undefended southern provinces of the Netherlands. Parma eventually favoured an invasion because knocking the English out of the game would help him complete the total suppression of the Dutch.

All the pieces for the game were in place, and Mary, Queen of Scots provided the opener. There had been previous plans for a lightning Spanish strike across the Channel to rescue the imprisoned Catholic heroine. One such plot, hatched by the hero of Lepanto, Don Juan of Austria, was only scotched when he died of typhoid. While Mary lived, she would inherit the English crown on Elizabeth's death, sparking a counter-Reformation and upholding the honour of Catholic Christendom. But Philip knew that any rescue was fraught with danger – Mary could be executed as soon as one foreign foot landed on English soil. Mary's execution removed that reason for restraint. And it allowed Philip to declare a holy cause.

During this violent era Elizabeth was regarded by many Catholics as a harlot of Satan, worthy of an assassin's bullet to send her straight to Hell. Pius V's Papal bull *Regnans in Excelsis* in 1570 not only excommunicated her but also absolved all her subjects of oaths of obedience to her. Elizabeth responded with draconian legislation which made even the uttering of a word of criticism against her a capital offence. Elizabeth's judges and law enforcers responded with enthusiasm and she vies with her father as the monarch who authorised the greatest number of judicial executions during her reign. Her spymaster Walsingham built a formidable network of informers and, by torture and trickery, foiled at least three serious plots to kill Elizabeth and replace her with Mary – plus a few bogus ones used as a pretext to pursue personal vendettas. The threat of invasion from Catholic Europe was all too real, but it was also a useful tool in domestic control. Walsingham summed up invasion paranoia with the words: 'There is less danger in fearing too much than too little.' And the imagined consequences of a successful assassination of Elizabeth are all too plausible: the isolation of the royal council in the Tower of London, a swift Spanish invasion, the execution of Elizabeth's loyal ministers and the coronation of Philip, Mary Tudor's widower, as the first Hapsburg king of England.

Philip, who certainly regarded Elizabeth as a heretic and an illegitimate ruler of England, had indeed previously supported plots to have her overthrown in favour of her Catholic cousin. Yet Elizabeth had been on the throne for 30 years and it was 18 years since she had been excommunicated. Such tardiness suggests that political and military considerations were uppermost, rather than religious zeal. Nevertheless, Pope Sixtus V supported the invasion, declaring it a crusade and promising a subsidy if the Armada landed. The Pope allowed Philip to levy crusade taxes and granted his men indulgences.

By early 1587 Philip had made his decision. The 'invincible' armada would sail from Spain and pick up the main invasion army on the Dutch coast. But the invasion plan was undermined from the start by a confusion of intentions. His greatest general, Parma, saw the subjugation of the Netherlands as the greatest prize and the invasion of England purely as a means to that end. For Philip, the reverse was true. Was it feasible to mount an invasion from Spain alone, or from captured Channel ports, or combine the two? The invasion, many have subsequently argued, was sunk before it started.

Historian Frank McLynn summed it up succinctly:

> It was difficult enough even on paper to assemble a fleet at an Atlantic port while the army was made ready on the shores of the North Sea more than a thousand miles away. Even if Spain had total control of the Netherlands ports, co-ordinating the two strands of the expedition would have been a tall order, especially given the slowness of communications between Philip and Parma. The Armada would still have to beat up the length of the Channel, in the teeth of the English fleet and possibly in adverse weather, to embark Parma's formidable veterans. But the incredible fact about 1588 was that the central problem of the invasion was never addressed. No-one in Spain seemed to have realised that without control of the seas around the Netherlands – and it was surely well enough known that the Dutch admiral Justin of Nassau had these in a tight grip – the enterprise of England could never succeed, even if the Spanish had scored a victory as great as Lepanto over the English fleet in the Channel.

But Philip was by now determined to invade whatever the logic of the situation. Don Alvaro de Bazan, the Marquis of Santa Cruz and proposed admiral of the Armada, put forward a plan involving 64,000 soldiers and 30,000 sailors, which was logistically realistic given the task but prohibitively expensive. Parma, however, argued that he could ferry 30,000 infantry and 4,000 cavalry across the Channel in a single night using barges and the element of surprise. That was a fantasy, given the strength of the English and Dutch navies and the impossibility of keeping the army's build-up a secret. Philip decided on a compromise that was worse than both propositions. The armada would sail from Spain, Parma would load 34,000 men into barges and they would meet up somewhere in the Straits of Dover.

Throughout the rest of 1587 preparations were made, delayed but not destroyed by Sir Francis Drake's famous fireship raid on Cadiz. Parma tightened his grip on the Netherlands, and Spain attempted to close German ports to British cloth, a declaration of economic war.

The Armada preparations were known about the length and breadth of Europe, but Queen Elizabeth enraged some of her critics by keeping the English fleet in port through the winter and vetoing further raids on Spain. Drake, eager to go on the attack, was kept in Plymouth. Sir John Hawkins, eager to blockade the Spanish coast, was also kept at home straining at the leash. Elizabeth, reluctant to have an open war with Spain, kept all her tall ships tied up and unrigged in their docks, while their guns were kept in the Tower of London. Only skeleton crews manned the vessels. If Santa Cruz, a bold and experienced campaigner, had been able to launch his attack in the autumn, the sea and river lanes to London would have been wide open to him.

In December, Walsingham reported intelligence that Santa Cruz could arrive before Christmas. Within a fortnight the whole fleet was mobilised, armed ready for action, crewed and at least partially provisioned. But when Walsingham's report proved premature, Elizabeth again angered and perplexed her captains by reducing the fleet again. Four galleons and other ships were sent to help the Dutch patrol their coastline, and the rest of her fleet were told to tie up in the Medway or Plymouth harbour with only half their complements. Reduced crews meant that the Queen could save £2,433, 18s and 4d a month in wages and food. Elizabeth had legitimate money troubles. The Low Country war had cost a fortune without noticeable benefit, and an open war with Spain would cause trouble in Ireland. She believed that while her parliament was against popery, they would not want to pay for a war on three fronts – in Flanders, in Ireland and on the open seas. She may have had good reasons, but Elizabeth's parsimony and her naïve belief that the Spanish did not really mean business was a regal gift to Philip.

But in the New Year Philip was hit on two fronts. Santa Cruz, a highly capable and realistic commander, died; and the Spanish army in the Netherlands was devastated by plague, leaving only 17,000 of the planned 30,000 infantry alive or operationally fit. Philip, however, was a determined man and brushed aside both disasters. He appointed the Duke of Medina Sidonia as commander. The seventh Duke was a highborn courtier with no experience at sea, but when he inspected the fleet he was appalled. Only 13 of the intended 50 galleons were ready and just 70 smaller vessels instead of the 400 Santa Cruz had ordered. Weeks of feverishly intense activity by Sidonia filled many, but not all, of the gaps.

By May 1588 the Duke could look out on his Armada: in the front line 20 galleons, four *galleasses* (galleons fitted with oars), and four large merchant galleys fitted with guns. In the second line were 40 armed merchantmen and numerous smaller vessels. The total came to 151 ships with 1,500 brass guns and 1,000 iron guns, 8,000 sailors and 18,000 soldiers. The remainder of the heavy vessels were mostly armed carracks and hulks; there were also 34 light ships. Their total tonnage pretty much matched that of the English navy, but the Armada was significantly inferior in long-range firepower.

The Armada's banner was blessed in a formal ceremony and it set sail from Lisbon harbour on 28 May. It took two days to clear the harbour and then crawled up the Iberian coastline in the teeth of ferocious winds. The fleet kept together but that meant, as Sidonia reported, 'governing our progress by the speed of the most miserable tub amongst us'. The wind could blow in all four directions during a single day and sometimes there was no wind at all, leaving the fleet rolling at the mercy of the long Atlantic swell. Progress was painfully slow. Shortages of water and provisions – much of the victuals loaded at Lisbon proved to be spoilt, while most of the water barrels had been dishonestly made of green wood – forced Sidonia to stop at Corunna to re-stock, but sudden squalls scattered the ships. It was not until 20 July that the ships regrouped and he was able to leave the safety of the harbour. Five days later he was hit by a full gale, which again scattered the fleet. Four galleys and a galleon took refuge in French ports and did not re-emerge.

Sidonia, angered by the crookedness of the provisioning and frustrated at the vagaries of the weather, saw his Armada being degraded daily. He became both depressed and disillusioned with his mission. Showing a greal deal of moral courage for a courtier, he wrote to Philip asking to be relieved of command and urging that peace should be reached with the English. He pointed out that his fleet was being scattered and buffeted even in June, the best sailing month of the year; his provisions were woefully inadequate; illness was cutting swathes through his men and those of Parma. Philip's response was succinct, repeating his embarkation order: 'Forward, in God's name.' Sidonia's qualms would prove to be prophetic.

The Armada finally reached the approaches to the Channel on 30 July and held a council of war within sight of the Lizard. The admiral and his commanders agreed that it was too risky to progress past the Isle of Wight until the rendezvous with Parma, its timing and precise location, was established. Shortly afterwards the English fleet was sighted.

On the day the Armada set sail, Elizabeth's ambassador in the Netherlands met Parma's representatives in peace negotiations. On 16 July those negotiations were abandoned, and the English fleet stood prepared, if ill-supplied, at Plymouth, awaiting news of Spanish movements. The English fleet, with almost 200 ships, outnumbered the Spanish. On paper, the Spanish fleet outgunned the English – its available firepower was 50 per cent more than that of the English – but there were generally short-range, outdated guns. The English fleet consisted of the 34 ships of the royal fleet and 163 other ships, a dozen of which were privateers owned by Lord Howard of Effingham, Sir John Hawkins and Sir Francis Drake. Effingham, as The Admiral of the Fleet, had under his direct command no less than 18 full galleons. The English full-rigged ship was one of the greatest technological advances of the century and permanently transformed naval warfare. In 1573 English shipwright had introduced designs, first demonstrated in the 'Dreadnaught', that allowed the ships to sail faster and manoeuvre better and permitted heavier guns. Effingham's craft were faster than the Spanish, more manoeuvrable, better armed with longer ranges, and he was fighting close to his home base where the winds favoured him. Effingham, well past 50 and only three years in the job, owed his position mainly to social rank, his ardent Protestantism and his unquestioned loyalty rather than ability. But he had proved to be a quick learner and had tirelessly inspected every ship under his command, bringing each up to scratch. He also shared the aggressive, go-at-'em instincts of Drake and Hawkins.

The first sight of the Armada had been conveyed to London by a system of beacons along the south coast. According to myth, Drake was playing bowls on Plymouth hoe when he heard of the impending battle and refused to halt the game, saying there was plenty of time to finish and still beat the Spanish. There is no known eyewitness account of this incident and the earliest retelling of it was printed 37 years later. Adverse winds and currents caused some delay in the launching of the English fleet as the Spanish drew nearer, perhaps prompting the popular myth of Drake's cavalier attitude to the Spanish threat. On that evening the English fleet was trapped in Plymouth Harbour by the incoming tide. As the tide turned, 55 English ships set out to confront the Armada under the overall command of Effingham, with Drake as Vice-Admiral and Hawkins as Rear Admiral.

A confused running battle began along the Channel on 1 July and continued to 9 August. Spanish seamanship proved to be remarkable and the Spanish commanders used their considerable skills to avoid annihilation. Sidonia's tactics were to try to force close engagements and hand-to-hand combat, at which the outgunned Spanish excelled. Employing the extraordinary seamanship of his Portuguese and Spanish seafarers, he formed his ships into crescents, with the biggest galleons on the wings to try to draw the English into the weaker centre, where they would lose the wind advantage and be enveloped. But the English tactics were to stand back and batter the Spanish with their long-range guns.

Off Eddystone Rocks the English tacked upwind of the Armada overnight and at daybreak engaged the enemy. The Armada was in its crescent-shaped defensive formation, convex towards the east. Opposing them the English were in two sections, Drake to the north in *Revenge* with 11 ships, and Howard to the south in *Ark Royal* with the bulk of the fleet. Given the Spanish advantage in close-quarter fighting, the English ships used their superior speed and manoeuvrability to keep beyond grappling range and bombarded the Spanish ships from a distance with cannon fire. However, the distance was too great for this to be effective and at the end of the first day's fighting neither fleet had lost a ship in action, although the Spanish carrack *Rosario* and galleon *San Salvador*, flagship of Don Pedro de Valdes, were crippled after they collided. Another ship blew up mysteriously – rumoured to be as a result of a pressed Dutchman, or possibly Englishman, laying a fuse to a powder keg. When night fell, Drake turned his ship back to loot the crippled Spanish flagship, capturing supplies of much-needed gunpowder, as well as gold. That material opportunism cost the English fleet dear. Drake had been guiding the fleet with a lantern that was snuffed out when he slipped away. The rest of his fleet became scattered and was in complete disarray by dawn. It took an entire day for the English to regroup and the Armada gained a day's grace.

No-one seemed to blame Drake, particularly when he presented Don Pedro, now his captive and guest, to the Lord Admiral. His excuse was risible, claiming that he had peeled off to investigate a mysterious flotilla, which turned out to be harmless German merchantmen, and had come across the flagship by accident. Drake's buccaneering was legendary and, even during a battle for the survival of England, no-one appeared ready to blame him for capturing a prize they all envied.

In general the English had little reason to be proud of their performance at this stage: they had dissuaded an attack on Plymouth and engaged the enemy, but the Armada was still making stately and deliberate progress towards its rendezvous with Parma's forces. Drake and co used their superior speed to catch up with the Spanish fleet after a day of sailing. But Effingham, previously bullish, became ultra-cautious and for a while the fleet did little more than snap at the Spaniards' heels. The first battle had been a low-score draw. The Spanish could not draw in the English, while the English guns could not destroy the Spanish. On 2 August, two more Spanish vessels were separated from the rest.

The two fleets engaged once more, off Portland. This time a change of wind gave the Spanish the weather-gauge, and they sought to close with the English, but were foiled by the smaller ships' greater manoeuvrability. Howard formed his ships into a line of battle, to attack at close range bringing all his guns to bear, but this was not followed through. Captains on both sides spoke of the ferocity of the action, with the sound of cannon rolling continuously like thunder and vast clouds of smoke turning friend and foe into ghostly apparitions lit up by balls of fire. The Spanish San Juan was cut off from the main fleet and surrounded by the English, but she blazed away, keeping the English at a distance. That heroic action, however, could not mitigate the frustration of the Spanish commanders at their inability to bring the English within range of their grappling hooks.

If the Armada could create a temporary base in the protected waters of the Solent they could wait there for word from Parma's army. However, in a full-scale attack, the English fleet broke into four groups, Drake coming in with a large force from the south. At the critical moment, Sidonia sent reinforcements south and ordered the Armada back to open sea to avoid sandbanks. As there were no other secure harbours farther east along England's south coast, the Armada was compelled to make for Calais, without being able to wait for word of Parma's army. On 4 August the Spanish came close to running onto rocks but escaped disaster. By 6 August the Armada was at the Calais Roads, ready to join up with Parma's army. It was battered, but its ability to carry out its purpose was barely dented.

But at Calais the in-built flaws in the dual invasion plan became all too clear. Sidonia was expecting 50 fly-boats to help in the operation, but Parma did not have them. Even worse, Parma's barges could not come out of harbour because of the Dutch blockade. Historians have found Parma's lack of preparedness rather strange. He had had months to build the fly-boats but the boat-builders had downed tools when their pay became heavily in arrears. But Parma had faced such difficulties before and, a logistical genius, had always overcome them. Discipline and inspections had grown lax, again uncharacteristically so given Parma's record. A contemporary, Cabrera de Cordoba, said: 'He acted as if he did not believe that the news of the Armada's coming could be true.' Some believed that he had lost belief in a project for which he had only had lukewarm support from the start. Others believed that his earlier support had simply been a ruse, allowing him to build up a reserve which would never go to sea. Or it could simply be that as his army was diminished by plague, desertions and poor provisions, so his generalship was also diminished.

The Armada galleons drew up to 30ft of water and had to stay well out of the shallows. Sidonia, having fought storms and the English, ran into the undeniable truth, brushed aside by his king, that the landing of soldiers would only be possible with control of the seas off the Netherlands – a control he did not possess. His Armada was packed in a tight defensive formation.

Effingham spotted his enemy's predicament and saw that wind and currents made the Armada particularly vulnerable to fireships. Eight filled with pitch, tar, brimstone and gunpowder were launched at night on 7 August and were spectacularly successful. The Spanish feared that these uncommonly large fireships were 'hell-burners', filled with large gunpowder charges, which had been used to deadly effect at the Siege of Antwerp. Two were intercepted and towed away by small pinnaces, but the remainder bore down on the fleet. Medina Sidonia's flagship and the principal warships initially held their positions, but the rest of the fleet cut their anchor cables in panic and scattered in confusion.

In that confusion the galleass *San Lorenzo* ran aground at Calais. Effingham led his own squadron to take the crippled monster. He was hampered by the bigger draught of his galleons compared to the shallower one of the galleass, which meant his ships could not get within range for effective cannon fire. On the other hand, the *San Lorenzo* was canted at such an angle that her big guns were useless. The answer was a tactic which the Spanish had been trying to engage in for the entire enterprise – close contact and boarding. Initial boarding attempts by the English in a flotilla of ships' boats were beaten back. The listing sides of the ship were hard to scale, there were too many shoals to get around to the more vulnerable landward side and the small arms fire from the French defenders was intense. But then the San Lorenzo's commander, Don Hugo de Moncada, was shot clean through his head. The crew saw no purpose in continuing and jumped over the landward rail to scramble for shore. The English clambered up the other side and took away everything of value they could carry, in accordance with the contemporary rules of warfare. The Mayor of Calais, however, claimed the vessel itself, its guns and rigging, as his. When it looked like the English would ignore that claim, he opened fire from Calais Castle at the boats below. The English retired, laden with booty.

Sidonia had at first returned to his original position, apparently prepared to rally his fleet for a do-or-die stand. But the crescent formation had been broken, and the fleet now found itself too far to leeward of Calais in the rising south-westerly wind to recover its position. Sidonia rejoined his fleet, which had settled down after the first panic. The English followed and caught up with Sidonia at Gravelines the following afternoon.

Off the small port Sidonia tried to re-form his fleet and was reluctant to sail farther east, knowing the danger of the shoals off Flanders, from which his Dutch enemies had removed the seamarks. The English commanders had learnt a lot about their enemy's strengths and weaknesses during the fights up the Channel. They had learnt that the Spanish heavy guns could not easily be run in for reloading because of their close spacing and the quantities of supplies stowed between decks. Instead the gunners fired once and then jumped to the rigging, ready to board enemy ships. Evidence from Armada wrecks in Ireland shows that much of the fleet's ammunition was never spent.

Drake in the *Revenge* was given the first English charge and, understanding that no Spanish ship had been yet sunk by direct gunfire, he held fire until a 'half-musket shot' so that his cannon could have maximum effect on the Spanish hull. The *Revenge*'s broadside was answered by the *San Martin*, Sidonia's flagship, and Drake's ship was 'pierced through by cannon balls of all sizes'. Drake veered off. Sir Martin Frobisher, who the following day condemned Drake as either a 'cowardly knave or traitor', followed and engaged the *San Martin* in earnest. His *Triumph* was larger and her castles taller than the Spanish flagship and he lay close while the rest of his squadron swarmed around, riddling the Spanish. The flagship was only saved by the timely arrival of other Spanish warships.

With its superior manoeuvrability, the English fleet provoked Spanish fire while staying out of range. The English then closed, firing repeated and damaging broadsides into the enemy ships. This also enabled them to maintain a position to windward so that the heeling Armada hulls were exposed to damage below the water line. Many of the gunners were killed or wounded, and the task of manning the cannon often fell to the regular foot soldiers on board, who did not know how to operate the guns. The ships were close enough for sailors on the upper decks of the English and Spanish ships to exchange musket fire. It was a keenly fought and close-run battle for, both sides believed, God, country and monarch.

For the first time English cannon were inflicting real damage on the Armada's fabric, bringing down masts, gouging into the hulls and smashing through the wooden castles. Among the crews there was carnage. The *San Felipe* lost 60 men dead and 200 wounded. And hers were not the highest casualty rates. An unnamed ship, probably the *San Mateo*, was seen to have blood pouring obscenely from her gunwales. But the Spanish crews fought on bravely, taunting the English as 'Lutheran hens' even as they were cut down. An English ensign called on one battered ship to yield with honour and was killed by a musket ball, one of the few English fatalities. The under-gunned *Maria Juan* was cut off, surrounded and shot to pieces by the *Hope*. Those crew members who survived the pounding did attempt to surrender, but as terms were being shouted across the choppy waters, the *Maria Juan* broke it two and sank. Only a few of the 272-strong crew survived the pounding of both cannon and sea. That vessel was the only one in the entire Armada to be destroyed solely by English firepower.

The key decider came down to simple logistics. As Mattingley wrote in his superb *Armada* chronicle:

> With high courage and bold leadership on both sides, the victory goes to the best ships and the best guns. The superiority of the English ships had been demonstrated already, time and again. They could outflank and worry the enemy at will, keep the weather-gauge, choose their own range, and always be sure of disengaging when they liked. The superiority of English guns and gunnery the Spanish were inclined to concede, but the chief superiority of the English off Gravelines lay in the fact that they still had ammunition. When they decided to close the range, as must have been agreed Sunday morning, they cannot have known how short the Spanish were; but in the second phase of Monday's battle, when all five English squadrons were harrying and jostling the Spanish crescent and trying to worry it into bits, they found that they could close to easy hailing distance and not suffer too much punishment.

After eight hours, the English ships began to run out of ammunition, and some gunners began loading objects such as chains into cannons. Around 4:00 p.m., the English fired their last shots and were forced to pull back.

Meanwhile, the galleons *San Mateo* and *San Felipe* drifted away in a sinking condition, ran aground on the island of Wallcheren the next day and were taken by the Dutch. One carrack ran aground near Blankenberge; another foundered. Many other Spanish ships were severely damaged, especially the Spanish and Atlantic-class galleons which had to bear the brunt of the fighting during the early hours of the battle in desperate individual actions against groups of English ships.

The Spanish plan to join with Parma's army had been defeated and the English had gained some breathing space, but the Armada's presence in northern waters still posed a great threat to England. The threat of invasion from the Netherlands had not yet been discounted by the English, and the earl of Leicester maintained a force of 4,000 soldiers in Essex, to defend the Thames Estuary against any incursion up-river towards London.

On 18 August Queen Elizabeth went to Tilbury to encourage her forces, and the next day gave to them what is probably her most famous speech:

> My loving people, we have been persuaded by some that are careful of our safety, to take heed how we commit ourselves to armed multitudes for fear of treachery; but, I do assure you, I do not desire to live to distrust my faithful and loving people. Let tyrants fear, I have always so behaved myself, that under God I have placed my chiefest strength and safeguard in the loyal hearts and goodwill of my subjects; and, therefore, I am come amongst you as you see at this time, not for my recreation and disport, but being resolved, in the midst and heat of battle, to live or die amongst you all – to lay down for my God, and for my kingdoms, and for my people, my honour and my blood even in the dust.

I know I have the body of a weak and feeble woman; but I have the heart and stomach of a king – and of a king of England too, and think foul scorn that Parma or Spain, or any prince of Europe, should dare to invade the borders of my realm; to which, rather than any dishonour should grow by me, I myself will take up arms – I myself will be your general, judge, and rewarder of every one of your virtues in the field. I know already, for your forwardness, you have deserved rewards and crowns, and, we do assure you, on the word of a prince, they shall be duly paid you. In the meantime, my lieutenant general shall be in my stead, than whom never prince commanded a more noble or worthy subject; not doubting but by your obedience to my general, by your concord in the camp, and your valour in the field, we shall shortly have a famous victory over those enemies of my God, of my kingdom, and of my people.

The Armada had already been effectively defeated and there is strong evidence that Elizabeth was well aware of that. Colin Brown wrote: 'Elizabeth's speech at Tilbury, and her review of her troops, appears to have been all part of an elaborate pageant to create a gigantic heroic myth that has lasted to this day.'

By then the Spanish were suffering from thirst and exhaustion, and the only option left to Sidonia was to chart a course home to Spain to save what he could of his 'invincible' armada. That was by a very hazardous route, northwards around the top of Scotland and then south-west along Ireland. For four days the English pursued in the North Sea before turning into the Firth of Forth.

The Armada was by now in a sorry state. A long outward voyage through storms, and the stress of battle, had left some galleons barely floating. The *San Marcos* was so weak that its hull was bundled up with cables. The flagship *San Martin* was shot through like a colander, with one large hole only just above the waterline. The *San Juan's* mainmast was too weak to carry sail. Others wallowed deeper every hour. Supplies of food and water ran short, and the cavalry horses were thrown overboard.

Sidonia's intention was to keep well to the west of the coast of Scotland and Ireland, in the relative safety of the open sea. However, the Spanish were unaware of the Gulf Stream and committed a devastating navigational error by turning south too far to the east. Off the coasts of Scotland and Ireland the fleet ran into a series of powerful westerly gales, which drove many of the damaged ships further towards the lee. Because so many anchors had been abandoned during the escape from the English fireships, many were unable to take shelter as they reached the coast of Ireland and were driven onto the rocks. Many more ships and sailors were lost to cold and stormy weather than in combat.

Some shipwrecked survivors were concealed by ordinary Irish people, fellow Catholics, but they were the few lucky ones. Most were slaughtered on the direct orders of the English authorities. In all, up to 5,000 men died by drowning, starvation or butchery after they saw Ireland.

In the end, 67 warships and around 10,000 men survived. Many of the men were near death from disease and starvation and many later died in Spain, or on hospital ships in Spanish harbours. It was reported that when Philip II learned of the result of the expedition, he declared, 'I sent the Armada against men, not God's winds and waves.' Nevertheless, Sidonia took home two-thirds of his fleet, including 20 galleons, although around half the survivors were unfit for further service. And Parma's army was intact.

Sidonia's achievement in getting home the bulk of his battered fleet has rarely been acknowledged. Every vessel whose commander followed his set course survived, although often in a dreadful state. For much of the return trip Sidonia stayed in his cabin, wracked by fever. He was helped by the best navigators then available on the last leg – there were four pilots aboard the *San Martin*, one of them an Englishman. But three died on the voyage and the survival of so many of the Armada's men despite such horrific circumstances must be down in part at least to the determination and leadership of its commander.

Sidonia, no doubt hit by aristocratic torments over the failure of the enterprise, never used the remarkable voyage home to in any way excuse the Armada's failure. When his flagship finally reached Santander he was too weak to sit upright, but signed letters to the king pitifully asking for help. From his sick-bed he tried to cope with his fleet's ongoing troubles – half-clothed, starving and unpaid crews who continued to sicken and die in the squalor of their stinking hulks because there was no money either to house them ashore or pay them off. Sidonia survived, unlike so many under him, but a friend who ran into him 15 years later remarked that he was a 'haunted man'.

There is no doubt that the defeat of the Spanish Armada was a pivotal moment in British history, and one that helped define a nation. But England had been exhausted by the effort of repelling the invaders. She may only have lost 50-100 dead and 400 wounded, and none of her ships had been sunk, but after the victory, typhus, dysentery and hunger killed many sailors and troops (estimated at 6,000-8,000) after being discharged without pay. So much for Elizabeth's fine words at Tilbury.

However, the English victory revolutionised naval battle tactics with the promotion of gunnery, which until then had played a supporting role to the tasks of ramming and boarding. The Battle of Gravelines started a lasting shift in the balance of naval power in favour of the English. Geoffrey Parker wrote that 'the capital ships of the Elizabethan navy constituted the most powerful battle fleet afloat anywhere in the world.' The English navy yards were leaders in technical innovation, and the captains devised new tactics.

Superior English ships and seamanship had foiled the invasion. The Armada failed because Spain's over-complex strategy required coordination between the invasion fleet and the Spanish army on shore. But the poor design of the Spanish cannon meant they were much slower in reloading in a close-range battle, allowing the English to take control. Spain still had numerically larger fleets, but England was catching up.

Elizabeth became known as 'Gloriana'. The 'Protestant wind' had worked in England's favour. On these shores at least, Protestantism ruled and the Catholic bogeymen were seemingly banished. Clerics preached that God and Protestant England were as one and Papists were promised hell in the Channel and in the afterlife. In the words of the bishop of Salisbury, John Piers, God had executed 'justice upon our cruel enemies; turning the destruction that they had intended on us upon their own heads'.

Sir Roy Strong:

> To England and Protestant Europe this was seen as God's judgement and his handmaiden went in triumph through the streets of London to St Paul's to give thanks amidst the acclamation of her people. In a sense she became England. The defeat of the Spanish Armada made a reality of what her government had striven to achieve, a united people held together by the crown, Protestant, patriotic, fearless in defence of Queen and country. Although in political terms the victory may have changed little and the country was to remain involved in a costly war for the rest of the reign, in moral ones it gave confidence and creative energy to what was in essence a new civilisation and society …

The boost to national pride lasted for years, and Elizabeth's legend persisted and grew long after her death.

❦

The Spanish appear to have shrugged off their defeat as nothing more than an unfortunate setback. The Spanish navy underwent a major organisational reform that helped it to maintain control over its trans-Atlantic routes. High-seas buccaneering and the supply of troops to Philip II's enemies in the Netherlands and France continued, but brought few tangible rewards for England.

Within a few years Spain, opposed to Henry of Navarre's claim to the French throne, invaded Normandy and Brittany, captured Amiens and Calais and threatened the key Channel port of Brest. The English sent 4,000 men to Brittany and, with their French allies, saw off that threat. But a Spanish raid from Blanet in galleys not at the mercy of English winds exposed again the vulnerability of Elizabeth's realm and her navy was recalled from overseas duties. The danger was very real as Philip was planning a second invasion Armada. It set off in winter 1596 but was thwarted not by English galleons, but by the weather.

The following year Elizabeth sought to retaliate by planning her own armada against Spain. A hundred ships and 6,000 men were to be sent to burn the port of Ferrol, where the Spanish were preparing yet another invasion fleet, but the task proved to be beyond England's cash-strapped capacity. Drake also set sail with a fleet of privateers to establish a base in the Azores, attack Spain and raise revolt in Portugal. The expedition raided Corunna, but withdrew from Lisbon after failing to co-ordinate its strategy effectively with the Portuguese. Elizabeth fell back on the strategy of building up her country's defences.

In October 1597 the third Armada set off. The Spanish plan was to sail 9,000 troops, protected by galleons, from Ferrol, while another 1,000 sailed in barges from Brittany with the apparent purpose of a swift raid. In reality, they were to meet at Falmouth, land and join up with a supposed rebellion by English Catholics. Again, the weather came to the rescue and the invaders were scattered by a storm off the Lizard.

Still the Spanish refused to give up. By then Henry IV was firmly in control of France and by the 1598 Peace of Venins he abandoned his support for England in return for the Breton and Normandy ports captured by the Spanish. Philip of Spain's successor, Philip III, then tried to negotiate a leaseback of those ports for use as a springboard to England. Luckily for England, Henry rejected that plan.

In 1601 Spanish attention turned to Ireland, then in a turmoil of revolt led by Hugh O'Neill, Earl of Tyrone. The rebels defeated Elizabeth's favourite, the Earl of Essex, and the Spanish saw their chance. Forty ships and 5,000 troops sailed for the Irish coast. The fleet was battered by storms and half turned back, but the remainder made landfall, landing at Kinsale in September. By then, however, the rebels had been defeated. The Spanish became bogged down in the beachhead, and when news came through that the remnants of the rebel armies coming to join them had been crushed, they surrendered on honourable terms.

On Elizabeth's death in 1603, James VI of Scotland became king of England offered Philip III a negotiated peace. Both sides were exhausted by 20 years of war and the August 1604 Treaty of London offered an honourable settlement. Spain effectively recognised that they could not reverse the Reformation in England; the English agreed to halt efforts to destroy Spain's trading monopoly in much of the Americas.

Mutual suspicion and tension, however, continued for decades until the French once again became England's main threat.

The myths of the Armada became reality for most Britons up to the Second World War and beyond. They helped define a sense of Englishness driven by both fear and certainty. Its fury, brief though it was, and bungled as much of the enterprise was, gave the nation a moment of invigoration and renewal. As Garrett Mattingly wrote in 1959: 'Its story, magnified and distorted by a golden mist, became a heroic apologue of the defence of freedom against tyranny, an eternal myth of the victory of the weak over the strong, of the triumph of David over Goliath. It raised men's hearts in dark hours, and led them to say to one another: "What we have done once, we can do again."'

The Armada myths continue to inspire.

Note that dates used are from the then-new Gregorian calendar, which added 10 days to the English calendar of the time.

7 MOUSEHOLE

'... burn'd and spoil'd by the Spaniards'

The picturesque town of Mousehole in Cornwall today.

The official report sent to the king of Spain by the commander of the raid stated:

> In this town we burned more than four hundred houses, some outlying hamlets and three ships which were laden with wine and other goods. The mosque where they gather for their conventicles was not burned because Captain Richard Burley, an English gentleman entertained in your Majesty's Royal Navy, said that this mosque had first been English and that Mass had been celebrated in it previously. Friar Domingo Martinez, principal chaplain of the galleys, wrote two verses in English in which he declared the reason for not burning it and his trust in God that Mass would be celebrated in it again within two years. This done our men withdrew to another town called Newlyn, burning it and all the outlying houses.

It was seven years after the Armada, and the Spanish had finally landed on English soil in a daring hit-and-run raid. That 1595 attack was a tiny part of the fierce and fanatical contest between Catholicism and Protestantism which tore Europe apart for three centuries, hence the reference to an ungodly Protestant 'mosque'.

❦ ❦

During the 24-year war with Spain, of which the defeat of the Armada was the highlight, Cornwall was in the front line as the nearest British landfall from Iberia. Spain controlled coastal areas of France and the threat of possible invasion by a Spanish force was a continuing fear shared by all Cornishmen, particularly those of the vulnerable fishing villages of Mounts Bay.

The Spanish force was part of a Spanish fleet based in the Blavet estuary (now Port Louis and Lorient) in Southern Brittany to support the Breton Catholic faction, led by the Governor of Brittany, the Duke of Mercoeur, in the religious civil war which divided France. The opposing Huguenots and Royalists factions had appealed to England and had initially received 2,500 English troops, plus naval support.

Cornwall had some warning. In January 1595 the English troops in Brittany, having prevented the Spaniards from capturing Brest, were withdrawn. That set the galleys at Blavet free to prowl round the Cornish coast. At Plymouth Drake and John Hawkins were fitting out their last voyage to the West Indies, where they would both die, and the Spaniards were very anxious to learn its destination. In May a fast boat from Blavet, manned by 16 sailors and 24 soldiers, appeared in Falmouth Bay and captured a fishing boat out of St Keverne, carrying the men over to Brittany. There they were examined, but could tell the Spanish general nothing of the objectives of the expedition. A captured English gunner from Bristol told the fishermen to report to the first justice of the peace they met on their release that there were four galleys and 10 ships of war at Blavet, and that they were expecting seven more galleys and ten ships with which to surprise shipping at Scilly. The fishermen duly told their story on their return. On 10 July 1595 Sir Francis Godolphin, deputy Lord Lieutenant of Cornwall, wrote to Lord Essex that more men would be needed for the defence of Scilly: 'I rest still of the same mind that it needeth a stronger garrison, for the gathering of those Spaniards seemeth as a cloud that is like to fall shortly in some part of her Majesty's dominions.'

Over the next 10 days galleys were seen at several places off the Cornish coast: at St Eval, and Padstow where Grenville's son hastily mustered some sort of miliatia, the sight of which discouraged the Spaniards from landing; at St Keverne a number of foreign ships were seen cruising around the Manacles reef; and at dawn on 23 July the four Spanish galleys were seen close-in to the shore, immediately off the small fishing town of Mousehole.

Carlos de Amesquita commanded three companies of *arquebusiers* consisting of about 400 men, and four galley (*Capitana*, *Patrona*, *Peregrina* and *Bazana*) from the fleet under Pedro de Zubiaur. He sailed from Port Louis in Brittany on July 16.

After calling at Penmarch, they sank a French barque manned by an English crew and with a cargo bound for England. Amésquita's forces eventually landed at Mount's Bay, in search of water, supplies and booty. He was guided by English turncoat Captain Richard Burley of Weymouth.

The English militia, which formed the cornerstone of their anti-invasion measures, fled in panic. The unarmed civilians ran pell-mell towards the villages of Paul and Newlyn. Squire Jenkin Keigwin was killed making a stand to protect his granite mansion. Most of the buildings on the Spanish route were thatched and were set ablaze by firing parties which then, unopposed, continued towards Paul where they burned not only the houses but also the church.

The panic-stricken civilians reached Penzance where by chance Godolphin was visiting. A contemporary account recorded: 'Godolphin met them upon the green to the west of the town and tried to put them in order to resist [but] they were virtually unarmed.' Godolphin sent a messenger to Drake and Hawkins at Plymouth 'to consider what is to be done for your own safety and our defence'. He clearly thought that the raid was the prelude to invasion. He gathered around 100 men and headed towards the landing site via Penzance.

But the Spaniards upset his plan by leaving Mousehole, returning to their galleys and landing their whole force at Newlyn. They sent two ranks of soldiers to the top of the hill to spy out the country, and when they saw the smallness of Godolphin's forces, they made for Penzance. The galleys kept up a fire upon the Cornishmen. Godolphin hoped to make a stand at the market place; but nothing could induce his men to stay, not even threats with his drawn rapier. Only a dozen or so of his own servants stood with him at the rear of the retreating mob. The Spaniards were in possession of three parts of the town. There was nothing for Godolphin to do but withdraw to protect the Mount and the main route inland. The enemy then set fire to Penzance as they had fired Newlyn and Mousehole. They held a mass on the western hill, where they vowed to build a friary upon the conquest of England. They then returned once more to their galleys.

By evening an encouraging number of volunteers and local militiamen had turned up to help Godolphin, and they encamped upon the green outside Marazion, further along the bay, for the defence of that place and the Mount. Hannibal Vyvyan sent word to Drake, asking him to send down some of his leaders who had commanded in war and to put ships in readiness. The success of the Spaniards might encourage them to land elsewhere further to the east, as well as on the north coast.

Meanwhile, the Spanish took all they needed and, learning of the nearness of English reinforcements, took advantage of a favourable wind and made off for Brittany. They left all prisoners on the shore. It was the first time that Spanish soldiers had landed on English soil, and the weakness of the opposition led to increased fortification of the Cornish coast.

In two days devastation had struck the area around Mousehole, an important trading centre and market town before 1595, which was never to recover that status. The raid was recorded by Richard Carew in his 'Survey of Cornwall' (1602) following conversations with Godolphin. In writing of the destruction of Paul Church he claimed that even 'the great stonie pillers thereof' were ruined. The fire destroyed church records and its 1595 register starts with a reference to the raid:

> *Jesu spes et salus mea* [Jesu my hope and my salvation]. A register of the names of all those that were baptised, married, and buried in the Parish Church of St Pawle, in the Countie of Cornwall, from the 23rd Daie Julie, the year of our Lord God 1595, on which Daie the Church, towre, bells, and all other things pertaining to the same, together with the houses and goods, was burn'd and spoil'd by the Spaniards in the said parish, being Wensdaie, the Daie aforesaid, in the 37th yeare of the Reign of our Sovereigne Ladie Elizabeth, by the Grace of God, of England, Fraunce and Ireland, defender of the Faith. *Per me Johannem Tremearne, Vicarium Ejus.* The first names recorded are of those who perished in defence of their town: Jenkin Keigwin of Moussell being kild by the Spaniards was buried the 24th of July. John Pearce Peiton was buried the 24th daie of July. Jacobus de Newlyn *occisus fuit per inimicos* [slain by enemies] *et sepultus est 26th die Julii.*

The day after, Sir Nicholas Clifford and other captains arrived from Plymouth, while Drake sent down some of his ships to the Lizard. The plan was to cut off the retreat of the Spaniards if they should land again in search of water. The wind was strong at south-east, which prevented them getting away. But within an hour of the captains' arrival from Plymouth, it suddenly shifted north-west, and the galleys seized the opportunity to get clear away.

The freed English prisoners, mainly fishermen and merchant crews, were examined. They told Godolphin that the galleys would have stayed longer and done more spoil along the coast, had they not stood in fear of Drake's fleet. The Spanish had intended to go to St Ives and Padstow, and thence into the Bristol Channel, but they were short of fresh water. The Spaniards also intended to take Scilly, where they would keep their galleys under the protection of the fort.

Sir Nicholas Clifford reported on Godolphin's conduct:

> For the town of Penzance, had the people stood with Sir Francis Godolphin, who engaged himself very worthily, it had been saved; but the common sort utterly forsook him, saving four or five gentlemen. Those same common people took refuge in an ancient prophecy, in their own language… that hath long run amongst them, how there should land upon the rock of Merlin, those that would burn Paul church, Penzance and Newlyn. And indeed so is the rock called where the enemy first stepped on shore.

Amezquita evaded a fleet sent against them under Drake and Hawkins. He met a Dutch squadron of 46 ships, sinking two of the Dutch ships and causing much damage to the others but also suffering at least 20 men killed before the rest of the Dutch ships escaped. Thomas Treffry recorded the Spanish losses as 140 men with 'one of their galleys so torn as they could not carry her to Blavet.' Amezquita stopped at Penmarch for repairs and finally arrived back at Port Louis on the 4 August.

The affair, small-scale in terms of casualties, delivered a disproportionate shock to the English government. The entire defence position of the country was carefully surveyed by Burghley. Sir Walter Raleigh was sent to view the Cornish levies and improve discipline and training, while the deputy-lieutenants barricaded the port towns at their own cost. Raleigh told his friend Cobham of his 'miserable journey into Cornwall' away from the pleasant pursuits of Sherborne. To the government he wrote critically of Cornwall's state of unreadiness at the end of November. He described the defensive preparations as woefully inadequate when compared with neighbouring Devon. He detailed the difficult geography of Cornwall, 80 miles in length and divided into three parts by deep river estuaries, making it near-impossible to transport relief forces around the Tamar to aid Plymouth. He concluded that

> ... there is no part of England so dangerously seated, so thinly manned, so little defenced and so easily invaded, having the sea on both sides, which no other county of England hath, and is so narrow that if an enemy possess any of the two or three straits, neither can those of the west repair eastward nor those of the east westward.

He drew attention to the Falmouth estuary,

> ... which is as much of Cornwall as the enemy should need, for within so much as lieth to the west ... are the best ports, and are very sufficient to receive the greatest fleet that ever swam, and containeth 27 miles of length very guardable, which in my simple judgment is every way more to be sought for by the enemy than Plymouth, at least if the same were so well understood by them, which is not unlikely.

His report proved prophetic, as the objective of the Adelantado's 1597 Armada was Falmouth.

Between 1595 and 1597 large-scale operations were resumed; Drake was called out from his retirement and placed, with Hawkins, in command of another expedition. Raleigh and Lord Essex brilliantly attacked Cadiz, capturing the city and temporarily bankrupting King Philip of Spain. But the delayed West Indies expedition accomplished little; both Drake and Hawkins died and were buried at sea, disease ravaged the fleet and in April 1596 several of their ships reached Falmouth in great want and distress.

Soon Philip was preparing another great armada and Elizabeth called up an army to defend her regal frame, to which Cornwall and Devon were to contribute 2,000 men. They were not necessary as the fabled 'Protestant wind' came to the rescue – the armada was struck by fierce gales off Finisterre (see previous chapter).

At Plymouth, the military Governor raised his garrison to 100, and while under his supervision many more hundreds of pounds were spent upon the fortifications of

Plymouth Citadel. The strain was being felt: notification was given that there would not be sufficient funds out of the revenue of Devon and Cornwall to meet his half-yearly charges, now amounting to £900.

Ralegh and Essex were fitting out another joint expedition at Plymouth, this time for the Azores, to intercept the Plate fleet. Meanwhile, information was coming into the west country of the renewed preparations in Spanish harbours: an armada of 100 sail. It was thought that, as in 1588, they would be heading for Calais. In the Azores, the English fleet of Raleigh and Essex just missed the Plate treasure fleet bound for Spain: the narrowest escape King Philip had had. Essex and Ralegh quarrelled bitterly and, their fleet battered by the gales of that summer and in no condition to fight, made for home.

Two days before they left, the Adelantado weighed anchor from Ferrol (Spain) and with all his armada kept company 'with great joy' until within twenty-five leagues from the Scilly Isles off Cornwall. Then it transpired what his objective was not Calais at all, but Falmouth. His instructions were a new and elaborated version of the great Menendez's plan of the 1570s: to seize, fortify and garrison Pendennis Castle at Falmouth, then take his fighting ships to the Scilly Isles, wait there and destroy the English ships returning from the Azores. If successful in this, he was, with the other half of his forces, some 10,000 men, to march eastward and capture Plymouth. It was an ambitious plan, and some part of it might have achieved success. But again, the Channel winds prevented it being put to the test. It was October when the armada put out. It was within two days' sail of Land's End when the autumn gales struck it and forced it to turn back.

The immediate consequence of the failed invasion was that the fortification of Pendennis Castle was undertaken in real earnest. Lord Essex gave his opinion that it was not defensible as it was against an army landed, and that an engineer should be employed to make the ground better to resist fire. It was reported that the Adelantado had meant to establish himself on the headland and turn it into an island by cutting the narrow neck of the peninsula.

At the moment of danger, Raleigh had drawn 500 levies into Pendennis, a crippling burden for a poor county. When it had passed, Godolphin wrote to him: 'Our country poor people do and will much repine at the burden of maintaining these small forces, of 400 or 500 at Penryn for guard thereof, which guard to the intended force is of ineffectual moment.' He suggested a further garrison to lie in readiness about Truro. 'But what speak I of beggarly country aid against princes' royal armies, which cannot but by our prince's purse and munition be resisted?' The strain of defence, the constant responding to calls on levies, maintaining them in service, was becoming too expensive for Cornwall's meagre resources.

Relief came with the accession of King James, an end to war and the end of the fighting Elizabethan age.

8 THE BARBARY PIRATES

'… all their bodies pearled with a bloody sweat'

Bombardment of Algiers, 1682, by unknown artist.

Two Algerian galleys crewed by Dutch, Algerians and Ottoman Turks landed in the dead of night in West Cork, Ireland, on 20 June 1631. The force was captained by a Dutchman, Jan Janszoon van Haarlam, also known as Murad Reis the Younger, a Flanders mariner turned corsair. A Dungarven man called Hackett, captain of a fishing boat Janszoon had captured earlier, led the ships through intricate channels to the remote village and port of Baltimore in return for his freedom.

The motley crew sacked the village and captured 108 English settlers who worked in the pilchard industry, and some local Irish people, pretty much the entire population of Baltimore. Of the settlers, two dozen men, 34 women and 50 children, 'even those in the cradle', were abducted, principally the descendants of dissenting Protestant settlers from Cornwall, Somerset and Devon. They were put in irons and taken to a life of slavery in North Africa. A French missionary priest working in Algiers saw several of the Irish captives put up for auction. After that, very little more was heard of them. Some prisoners died as galley slaves, others worked as labourers within the sultan's palace, while some of the women lived out their days in the seclusion of the Sultan's harem. At most, only three of them ever saw Ireland or England again.

Conspiracy theories abound relating to the raid. It was suggested that Sir Walter Coppinger orchestrated the raid to gain control of the village from the local Gaelic chieftain, Fineen O'Driscoll. It was O'Driscoll who had licensed the lucrative pilchard industry in Baltimore to the English settlers. In the aftermath of the raid, the remaining settlers moved to Skibereen, after hanging Hackett from the clifftop.

A decade later, in April 1641, the Reverend Devereux Spratt was one of those captured when trying to cross the Irish Sea from County Cork to England. After several years' captivity he wrote: 'When we had arrived [in Cork], I made a request to Lord Inchaquoin to give me a passport for England. I took boat to Youghal and then embarked on the vessel *John Filmer*, which set sail with 120 passengers. But before we had lost sight of land, we were captured by Algerine pirates, who put all the men in irons.'

The diarist Samuel Pepys gave a vivid account of an encounter with two men who had been taken into slavery in his diary of 8 February 1661:

> ... to the Fleece tavern to drink and there we spent till 4 a-clock telling stories of Algier and the manner of the life of Slaves there; and truly, Captain Mootham and Mr Dawes (who have been both slaves there) did make me full acquainted with their condition there. As, how they eat nothing but bread and water ... How they are beat upon the soles of the feet and bellies at the Liberty of their Padron. How they are all night called into their master's Bagnard [prison], and there they lie.

The casualness of the account makes it clear just how commonplace unfortunates like Moontham and Dawes were in seventeenth-century Britain. Britons in later years have boasted that they 'never will be slaves' but during these years they were enslaved all too often.

According to observers of the late 1500s and early 1600s, there were around 35,000 European Christian slaves held throughout this time on the Barbary Coast – many in Tripoli, Tunis and various Moroccan towns, but most of all in Algiers. Most were mariners, taken with their ships, but a good many were fishermen and coastal villagers. The British were a minority in slavery; the majority were from lands closer to Africa, especially Spain and Italy. They were taken by the thousands, by slavers who raided the coasts of Valencia, Andalusia, Calabria and Sicily so often that eventually it was said that 'there was no one left to capture any longer'.

There are no records of how many men, women and children were enslaved, but it is thought that around 8,500 new slaves were needed annually to replenish numbers – about 850,000 captives over the century from 1580 to 1680. For the 250 years between 1530 and 1780, the figure could easily have been as high as 1,250,000 – little more than a tenth of the Africans taken as slaves to the Americas from 1500 to 1800, but still a considerable figure, a tally of utter misery.

In the first half of the 1600s, Barbary corsairs ranged all around Britain's shores. Admiralty records show that during this time the corsairs plundered British shipping pretty much at will, taking no fewer than 466 vessels between 1609 and 1616, and 27 more vessels from near Plymouth in 1625. As eighteenth-century historian Joseph Morgan put it, 'this I take to be the Time when those Corsairs were in their Zenith'. Unfortunately, it was hardly the end of them, even then. Morgan also noted that he had a 'List, printed in London in 1682' of 160 British ships captured by Algerians between 1677 and 1680. Considering what the number of sailors who were taken with each ship was likely to have been, these examples translate into a probable 7,000 to 9,000 able-bodied British men and women taken into slavery in those years.

None of the raids can be categorised as invasions, but the casualty rate and pressure on the Exchequer was greater than many wars of the age. And the raids of the Barbary pirates were politically entwined with the European turmoil that kept Britain continuously on invasion alert.

❧—☙

The Barbary pirates, sometimes called Barbary corsairs or Ottoman corsairs, were based primarily in the ports of Tunis, Tripoli and Algiers, known by Europeans as the Barbary Coast, a term derived from its Berber inhabitants.

The slave trade had existed in North Africa since ancient times, with a supply of African slaves arriving through trans-Saharan trade routes. The towns on the North African coast were recorded by the Romans for their slave markets, and this trend continued into the medieval age Their hunting grounds extended throughout the Mediterranean, south along West Africa's seaboard and even South America and as far north as Iceland. In addition to seizing ships, they engaged in raids on European coastal towns and villages, mainly in Italy, France, Spain, and Portugal, but also in England, Scotland, Wales, Ireland and the Netherlands. Their chief aim was to capture Christian slaves for the Islamic markets in North Africa and the Middle East.

While such raids had occurred since soon after the Muslim conquest of the region, the term 'Barbary pirate' is normally applied to the raiders active from the sixteenth century onwards, when the frequency and range of the slavers' attacks increased and Algiers, Tunis and Tripoli came under the sovereignty of the Ottoman Empire, either as directly administered provinces or as autonomous dependencies known as the Barbary States. Unlike the pirates of Robert Louis Stevenson and popular legend, the Barbary corsairs were an integral part of their society and the economy of their countries. As Linda Colley wrote:

> Need, greed and aggression linked all of these seafarers, but most North African 'pirates' were not independent agents operating outside of their home communities' laws, so much as a vital and officially recognised part of their revenue-raising machinery.

Pirates had been known in Mediterranean since at least the ninth century and the short-lived Emirate of Crete. Despite the animosity generated by the Crusades, the level of Muslim pirate activity was relatively low and in the thirteenth and fourteenth centuries it was rather Christian pirates out of Catalonia that posed the greatest threat to merchants. It was not until the late fourteenth century that Tunisian corsairs became enough of a threat to provoke a Franco-Genoese attack on Mahdia in 1390, also known as the 'Barbary Crusade'. Moorish exiles of the Reconquista and Maghreb pirates added to the numbers, but it was not until the expansion of the Ottoman Empire and the arrival of the privateer Kemal Reis in 1487 that the Barbary corsairs became a true menace to Christian shipping. The Barbary ships were armed with a cannon mounted in the bow with which, using chain shot, they could bring down the rigging of the slower English ships and then board them and capture them intact with their crew.

Spanish Moors and Muslim adventurers from the Levant increased the number of raids around the turn of the fifteenth century. In response, Spain began to conquer the coast towns of Oran, Algiers and Tunis. The most famous of the corsairs were Oruç and Hızır Hayreddin, named the Barbarossa brothers because of their red beards. The eldest, Oruç, captured the island of Djerba for the Ottoman Empire in 1502 or 1503. He often attacked Spanish territories on the coast of North Africa; during one failed attempt in 1512 he lost his left arm to a cannon ball. The elder Barbarossa also went on a rampage through Algiers in 1516 and captured the town with the help of the Ottoman Empire. He executed the ruler of Algiers and everybody he suspected would oppose him. He was finally captured and killed by the Spanish in 1518 and his body put on display.

After that, his brother Hızır appealed to Selim I, the Ottoman sultan, who sent him troops. Hızır (later called Hayreddin or Kheir ed-Din) was a more traditional corsair. He was a capable engineer and spoke at least six languages. He dyed the hair of his head and beard with henna to redden it like Oruç's. After capturing many crucial coastal areas, Hayreddin was appointed admiral-in-chief of the Ottoman sultan's fleet. Under his command the Ottoman empire was able to gain and keep control of the eastern Mediterranean for over thirty years. In 1544, Hayreddin captured the island of Ischia, taking 4,000 prisoners, and enslaved some 9,000 inhabitants of Lipari, almost the entire population. Barbaros Hızır Hayreddin Pasha died in 1546 of a fever, possibly the plague.

From about 1518 till the death of Uluch Ali in 1587, Algiers was the main seat of government of the beys of northern Africa, who ruled over Tripoli, Tunisia and Algeria. From 1587 to 1659, they were ruled by Ottoman pashas, sent from Constantinople to govern for three years; but in the latter year a military revolt in Algiers reduced the pashas to nonentities. From 1659, these African cities, although nominally part of the Ottoman Empire, were in reality military republics that chose their own rulers and lived by war booty captured from the Spanish and Portuguese. There are several cases of Sephardic Jews, including Sinan Reis and Samuel Pallache, joining the corsairs after fleeing Spain and attacking the Spanish Empire's shipping under the Ottoman flag, a profitable strategy of revenge for the Inquisition's religious persecution.

From 1518 to 1587, the beys were admirals of the sultan, commanding great fleets and conducting war operations for political ends. They were slave-hunters and their methods were ferocious. After 1587, the sole object of their successors became plunder, on land and sea. The maritime operations were conducted by the captains, or *reises*. Cruisers were fitted out by investors to go raiding. Ten per cent of the value of the prizes was paid to the pasha or his successors.

At various times the corsairs used Lundy Island in the Bristol Channel as a short-term operations base to intercept trading vessels between Bristol, Ireland and the Americas. Prisoners taken included the brother of the mayor of Bristol. Around 1645 the Dutch corsair Jan Janszoon used Lundy as a staging post, having taken 310 prisoners off the surrounding coastline for sale in Salee Castle, Algiers.

In 1520 King James I sent a battle squadron to blockade the Barbary ports to demand the release of the captives, but it was Oliver Cromwell, over a century later, who took more effective punitive action. Aware that the corsairs were crippling his south-west ports and drastically raising insurance costs for the entire merchant fleet, he decreed that any Arab taken in those waters should be taken to Bristol and slowly drowned. He commissioned Robert Blake and William Penn, both of solid West Country stock, to clear the corsairs off Lundy. They bombarded the makeshift enemy stronghold and those not killed or captured fled back to Barbary. Penn had been paid privately by Bristol merchants, including the mayor, to clear the Severn. He could speak Arabic as his father Giles senior had been ambassador in Africa on behalf of King Charles. Ironically, Penn had previously turned to piracy himself when he and his brother were refused trade permits by the Bristol cartel, and had done much business with the corsairs. Despite the Lundy setback, the corsairs continued to mount raids on the coastal towns and villages in Cornwall, Devon, Dorset and the west coast of Ireland. Fishing vessels were particularly vulnerable.

The worst culprits were not Muslim, or Arab, or North African, but English privateers and Dutch captains who exploited the changing loyalties of an era in which friends could become enemies and enemies friends with the stroke of a pen. They included Zyman Danseka, Henry Mainwaring and Jack, or John, Ward, who was called 'beyond doubt the greatest scoundrel that ever sailed from England' by the English ambassador to Venice. Ward was a privateer for Queen Elizabeth during her war with Spain. He captured a ship in about 1603 and sailed it to Tunis, where he and his crew converted to Islam as a prerequisite for success and wealth. He introduced heavily armed square-rigged ships, used instead of galleys, to the North African area, a major reason for the Barbary's dominance of the Mediterranean and far beyond. He died of plague in 1622. Danseker and other fellow countrymen used the Barbary ports as bases for attacking Spanish shipping during the Dutch Revolt. They cooperated with local raiders and introduced them to the latest Dutch sailing rigs, enabling them to brave Atlantic waters. Some of these Dutch corsairs converted to Islam and settled permanently in North Africa. Two examples are Süleyman Reis (De Veenboer), who became admiral of the Algerian corsair fleet in 1617, and his quartermaster Jan Janszoon. Both worked for Danseker.

In 1624 it was reported that over 1,500 Britons were held captive. Many families had difficulty in raising the ransoms and made pleas for help in paying them. Typical of such pleas are two made in 1621 and 1623 of men taken in the Straits of Gibraltar: 'Henry Hammon, mariner late of Gravesend, was on the *Long Robert* of London on a voyage to the Straits about 5 years ago when the ship was taken by Turkish pirates. He and others were carried to Tunis in Barbary where he is credibly reported to have been held ever since, in great misery. His ransom is set at £80, which the poor young man and his friends cannot raise.' And: 'He was carried to Algiers and will remain there in miserable captivity unless charitable provision is made for his ransom, which is great and which he cannot pay because his adventure was lost. His wife and children are likely to starve in his absence.'

The corsairs began to attack the merchant ships sailing to the new settlements in Virginia and Newfoundland. In 1625 the Mayor of Poole wrote to the Privy Council demanding that protection be supplied for the ships returning from Newfoundland or they would be lost to the pirates. He reported that 'Twenty-seven ships and 200 persons had been taken by Turkish pirates in ten days.'

The North Wales coast was also a hunting ground for slavers, particularly around Conwy, and as the value of slaves increased, they ventured further inland. Landowners and merchants in Chester petitioned the king and Admiral Sir Thomas Button, a famous navigator and explorer appointed 'Admiral of the King's Ships on the coast of Ireland' by James, was sent with one warship to patrol the seas around Anglesey. The corsairs chased him back to harbour.

A small fleet, under Sir John Pennington, and comprising a number of ships called the Lion's Whelps, cruised the Channel for several years to suppress the Barbary pirates, who are described as 'the scourges of all Christian navigations'. St Keverne suffered severely at their hands in June 1636, The Calendar of state papers recorded that seven boats fishing off the Manacles were taken by the 'Turks' and their crews, totalling around 50, carried away as captives. The same pirates also took five boats of Looe, which were engaged in deep sea fishing between England and Ireland. Empty vessels were seen drifting without crews or sails. Women wept in the knowledge that they would not see their men again. One witness, the captain of a barque of Plymouth, reported that he sailed from Plymouth for St Keverne and

> ... arrived there on Thursday morning last, where he heard it credibly reported, with sorrowful complaint and lamentable tears of women and children, that on the 15th instant three fisherboats belonging to St Keverne, three others of Helford, and one more of Mollan [Mullion] and about 50 men in them, being on the coast fishing near Black Head, between Falmouth and the Lizard, not three leagues off the shore, were taken by the Turks who carried both men and boats away. During the time of his abode at St Keverne, which was from Thursday till Sabbath-day then following, there was no news heard of either men or boats, so that it goes for an absolute truth thereabouts that they were all surprised by the Turks and carried away.

Another account given by the Justices of the Peace sitting in quarter sessions at
Bodmin told how the men of Looe, 'through terror of that misery whereunto these
persons are carried by these cruel infidels' would rather 'give over their trade than
put their estates and persons into so great peril, there being now 60 vessels and about
200 seamen without employment'. The Justices added: 'These Turks daily show themselves at St Keverne, Mount's Bay, and other places, that the poor fishermen are fearful
not only to go to the seas, but likewise lest these Turks should come on shore and
take them out of their houses.' The Earl of Northumberland, in command of the fleet
at Plymouth, sent two vessels in pursuit of these pirates, who were suspected to have
gone into the Severn estuary, but they were not caught.

Other corsairs in 1640 took three barks 'in the open view of Penzance' and stole
three other ships the same night at Mousehole and Land's End, while three other vessels were pursued and escaped, one after eight hours' fighting. In one official account
there were reported to be 60 'Turkish men-of-war' on the coast. In another, 60 men,
women and children were taken from about Penzance. Villagers along the south coast
of England petitioned the king to protect them from abduction by Barbary pirates.
Item 20 of The Grand Remonstrance, a list of grievances against Charles I and presented to him in 1641, contained the complaint:

> … And although all this was taken upon pretense of guarding the seas, yet a
> new unheard-of tax of ship-money was devised, and upon the same pretense, by
> both which there was charged upon the subject near £700,000 some years, and
> yet the merchants have been left so naked to the violence of the Turkish pirates,
> that many great ships of value and thousands of His Majesty's subjects have been
> taken by them, and do still remain in miserable slavery.

The Domestic State Papers of 1649 include almost daily accounts of piracy and
related petitions. The Council of State drew the attention of the Generals at sea to
the 'growing strength of pirates at sea' and 'The great danger the fishermen are in to
be deprived of the fruit of their labour', and dictated a general policy of suppression.

The European states constructed new-style frigates, light, fast and manoeuvrable
galleys, designed to run down Barbary corsairs trying to get away with their loot and
slaves. Other measures included coastal lookouts to give warning for people to withdraw into fortified places and rally local forces to fight the corsairs. Too often such
tactics were fruitless as the corsairs engaged in well-planned banditry along isolated
coastlines, often with the advantage of local knowledge through turncoats or, as in the
case of Baltimore, captive locals. In desperation some villages were abandoned and
rebuilt farther inland, with the church tower used as a lookout.

Being captured was just the first part of a slave's nightmare journey. Many died on
the ships during the long voyage back to North Africa of disease or lack of food and
water. On arrival those who survived the journey were walked in chains through
town on their way to the slave auction, where they would stand to be viewed for
up to six hours. For many Christians that was the greatest humiliation. During the

auctions the slaves would be forced to run and jump around to show their strength and stamina. After purchase, these slaves would either become slaves for ransom, or they would be put to work.

Christian slaves were used for a wide variety of jobs, from hard manual labour to housework for most of the women. Nights were spent in hot and overcrowded prisons called *bagnios*. However, by the eighteenth century some *bagnios* had chapels, hospitals, shops, and bars run by slaves. Those were uncommon, and conditions were generally grim. A petition of English captives in Algiers to King Charles in 1640 gives some insight:

> Here are about 5,000 of your subjects, in miserable captivity, undergoing most unsuffrable labours, as rowing in galleys, drawing in carp, grinding in mills; with divers such unChristian like works, most lamentable to express and most burdensome to undergo, withal suffering much hunger and many blows on their bare bodies, by which cruelty many not being able to undergo it, have been forced to turn Mohamedans, so that these burdensome labours will cause many good seamen and others your subjects to perish unless some course be by you taken for our release, which we of ourselves cannot procure by reason of our great losses, and the extraordinary ransoms imposed on us.

To this petition dated 3 October 1640, was appended a list of 957 prisoners taken since 18 May 1639.

Although the conditions in *bagnios* were harsh, they were paradise compared to the galleys. Most Barbary galleys were at sea for around eighty to a hundred days a year, so the slaves were not on them constantly, but when they were not rowing the galleys they were forced to do hard manual labour on land. There were exceptions: galley slaves of the Ottoman Sultan in Istanbul would be permanently confined to their galleys, and often served extremely long terms, averaging around 19 years. Rowers were shackled and chained where they sat, and never allowed to leave. Sleeping, eating, defecation and urination took place at the seat to which they were shackled. Overseers would crack the whip over the bare backs of any slaves considered not to be working hard enough. Any moderately healthy man-captive could expect to go to the galleys. Before 1650 the Algerian galley-fleet alone comprised of 70 vessels, with up to 25 banks of oars and three to five men at each oar. The Englishman Francis Knight recalled his enforced service, shackled to the oars for up to 20 hours a day:

> Not having so much room as to stretch legs. The stroke regular and punctual, their heads shaved unto the skull, their faces disfigured by disbarbing, their bodies all naked, only a short linen pair of breeches to cover their privities … all their bodies pearled with a bloody sweat.

Barbary slaves could hope to be freed through payment of a ransom. Despite the efforts of middlemen and charities to raise money to provide ransoms, they were still very difficult to come by. As charity funding for ransoming slaves increased, North African states increased the ransom required. No real system of raising relief funds emerged until around 1640. Then the attempts became more systematic and were sometimes state-subsidised, as in Spain and France. Almost all the actual work, however – from collecting the funds, to voyaging to Barbary, to negotiating with the slave owners there – was carried out by clergy.

Parish churches across Spain and Italy kept locked collection boxes marked 'for the poor slaves', with clerics constantly reminding their wealthier parishioners to include ransoming societies in their wills, Ransoming slaves was promoted as being one of the best of the charitable works. By the 1700s, the ransoming orders had significantly reduced slave populations in Barbary, eventually even inflating slave prices, as more cash chased fewer captives.

Compared to Catholic Europe, however, Protestant states could be lax and disorganised in freeing their subjects. Thousands of British, Dutch and German slaves 'languished for years in the chains of Barbary' without the aid of organised clergy or state funds for their release. Large-scale ransomings – like that headed by Edmund Casson that freed 244 men, women, and children in 1646 – were rare, with the result that Protestant Britons were often more demoralised and likely to die in captivity than European Catholics. As one ex-slave noted:

> All of the nations made some shift to live, save only the English, who it seems are not so shiftful as others, and … have no great kindness one for another. The winter I was in [captivity], I observ'd there died above twenty of them out of pure want.

After payment of a ransom slaves often went through a port to wait for the ransom to be finalised; in some cases in the seventeenth and eighteenth centuries, slaves were kept at these ports under quarantine for fear of the plague.

Not many Barbary slaves could depend on being ransomed. Escaping was another possibility, but rarely successful; Cervantes, author of *Don Quixote*, who had been captured and enslaved, made four unsuccessful attempts to escape and was eventually ransomed by his family. The most famous of runaway slaves was Thomas Pellow, who had the story of his journey published in 1740. After several failed attempts, in which he was nearly killed, Pellow was finally able to escape to Gibraltar in July 1738.

But return to Britain, whether by ransom or escape, could be uncomfortable, particularly for those who admitted they had professed the Muslim faith to survive. John Kay, for example, was first an indentured apprentice, then a pressed soldier and while serving a Venetian merchant was captured by corsairs and spent three and a half years as a slave. When he made it back, destitute, to the north of England, he was promptly arrested for begging. His entire life, it can be said, was one of captivity.

As they aged or their owner's fortunes changed, slaves were resold, often repeatedly. The most unlucky ended up stuck and forgotten out in the desert, in some sleepy town such as Suez, or in the Turkish sultan's galleys, where some slaves rowed for decades without ever setting foot on shore.

Many slaves converted to Islam, though, as Morgan put it, this only meant they were 'freed from the Oar, tho' not from [their] Patron's Service'. Christian women who had been taken into the pasha's harem often 'turned Turk' to stay with their children, who were raised as Muslims. Men sought easier labours, usually as overseers for other slaves, and some gained real power and occasionally their freedom. Between 1580 and 1680, there were typically around 15,000 of these 'renegades' in Barbary.

Barbary was a term that conjured up sheer horror in the minds of Britons. The clergyman and traveller Samuel Purchas wrote of Algiers: '... the cage of unclean birds of prey, the habitation of sea-devils ... the whip of the Christian world, the wall of the barbarian; terror of Europe ... scourge of the islands, den of pirates.'

In 1607, the Order of Malta, with the help of the Knights of St Stephen, went on the offensive, capturing and pillaging the city of Bona in Algeria. But corsair attacks continued along the coasts of the Iberian peninsula, the Canaries, Corsica. Elba, Italy, Sicily and Malta. Occasionally, coastal raids reached farther afield. Iceland was a target in 1627. Jan Janszoon took 400 prisoners and 242 of them were sold into slavery. The corsairs took only young people and those in good physical condition. All those offering resistance were killed and the old people were gathered into a church which was set on fire.

More than 20,000 captives were said to be imprisoned in Algiers alone. The rich were often able to secure release through ransom, but the poor were condemned to slavery. Their masters would on occasion allow them to secure freedom by professing Islam. While the chief victims were the inhabitants of the coasts of Sicily, Naples and Spain, all traders of nations which did not pay tribute for immunity were liable to be taken at sea. Religious orders worked for the redemption of captives and large legacies were left for that purpose in many countries.

The continuation of piracy was assisted by competition among European powers. France encouraged the corsairs against Spain, and later Britain and Holland supported them against France. By the second half of the seventeenth century, the greater European naval powers were able to strike back effectively enough to intimidate the Barbary States into making peace with them. However, those countries' commercial interests then benefited from the impact of continuing attacks on their competitors and as a result there was little interest in imposing a more general cessation of corsair activity.

The most successful of the Christian states in dealing with the corsair threat was England. From the 1630s onwards she had signed peace treaties with the Barbary States on various occasions, but invariably breaches of these agreements led to renewed wars. A particular bone of contention was the tendency of foreign ships to pose as English to avoid attack. However, growing English naval power and increasingly persistent operations against the corsairs proved increasingly costly for the Barbary States. During the reign of Charles II a series of English expeditions won victories over raiding squadrons and mounted attacks on their home ports, which permanently ended the Barbary threat to English shipping. In 1675 a Royal Navy squadron led by Sir John Narborough negotiated a lasting peace with Tunis and, after bombarding the city to induce compliance, with Tripoli. Peace with Sale followed in 1676. Algiers, the most powerful of the Barbary States, returned to war the following year, breaking a treaty made in 1671, but further defeats at the hands of an English squadron under Arthur Herbert forced Algiers to make peace again in 1682. The treaty would last until 1816. France, which had recently emerged as a leading naval power, achieved comparable success soon afterwards, with bombardments of Algiers in 1682, 1683 and 1688 securing a lasting peace, while Tripoli was similarly coerced in 1686.

In 1783 and 1784 it was the turn of Spaniards to bombard Algiers. The second bombardment under Admiral Barcelo damaged the city so severely that the Algerian Dey negotiated a peace treaty and Spanish vessels and coasts were safe for several years.

Until the American Declaration of Independence in 1776, British treaties with the North African states protected American ships from the Barbary corsairs. Morocco, which in 1777 was the first independent nation to recognise the United States, became in 1784 the first Barbary power to seize an American vessel. The Barbary threat led directly to the creation of the US Navy in March 1794. Payments in ransom and tribute to the Barbary States amounted to 20 per cent of United States government annual expenditures in 1800. Two short, sharp wars in 1801 and 1815 led to more favourable peace terms ending the payment of tribute.

The end of the Napoleonic Wars meant the Royal Navy no longer needed the Barbary states as a source of supplies for Gibraltar and the Mediterranean. It also increased consensus on the need to achieve a general halt to Barbary raiding. The sacking of Palma, Sardinia, by a Tunisian squadron, which carried off 158 inhabitants, roused widespread indignation. Britain had by this time banned the slave trade and was seeking to induce other countries to do likewise. This led to complaints from states which were still vulnerable to the corsairs that Britain's enthusiasm for ending the trade in African slaves did not extend to stopping the enslavement of Europeans and Americans by the Barbary States.

In early 1816, Edward Pellew, Lord Exmouth, undertook a diplomatic mission, backed by a small squadron, to Tunis, Tripoli and Algiers to convince the Deys to stop the practice and free the Christian slaves. The Deys of Tunis and Tripoli agreed without any resistance, but the Dey of Algiers was more recalcitrant and the negotiations were stormy. Exmouth believed that he had negotiated a treaty to stop the slavery of Christians and returned to England. However, due to confused orders, Algerian troops massacred 200 Corsican, Sicilian and Sardinian fishermen who were under British protection just after the treaty was signed. This caused outrage in Britain and Europe and Exmouth's negotiations were seen as a failure.

Pellew was ordered back to punish the Algerians. He gathered a squadron of one 50-gun ship and four frigates. The 100-gun HMS *Queen Charlotte* was his flagship and Admiral David Milne was his second in command aboard HMS *Impregnable* with 98 guns. This squadron was considered by many to be an insufficient force, but Exmouth had already surveyed the defences of Algiers unobtrusively, spotting a weakness in the field of fire of the defensive batteries. On arrival in Gibraltar, a squadron of five Dutch frigates and a corvette led by Vice-Admiral Theodorus Frederick van Capellen offered to join the expedition. Exmouth decided to assign them to cover the main force from Algerian flanking batteries, as there was insufficient space in the mole for the Dutch frigates. The day before the attack, the frigate *Prometheus* arrived and its captain, Dashwood, attempted to secretly rescue the British Consul and his wife and infant but some of the rescue party were discovered and arrested.

The plan of attack was for the larger ships to approach in a column. They were to sail into the zone where the majority of the Algerian guns could not be brought to bear. Then, they were to come to anchor and bombard the batteries and fortifications on the mole to destroy the defences. Simultaneously, the 50-gun *Leander* was to anchor off the mouth of the harbour and bombard the shipping inside the mole. To protect Leander from the shore battery, two frigates – *Severn* and *Glasgow* – were to sail inshore and bombard the battery.

Pellew in *Queen Charlotte* anchored 80yds off the mole facing the Algerian guns. However, most of the other ships, notably Admiral Milne aboard HMS *Impregnable,* anchored out of position, both reducing their effectiveness and exposing them to fiercer Algerian fire. In their earlier negotiations, both Pellew and the Dey of Algiers had stated that they would not fire the first shot. The Dey's plan was to allow the fleet to anchor and then to sortie from the harbour and board them with large numbers of men in small boats. However, Algerian discipline did not hold and one Algerian gun fired at 15:15. Pellew immediately began the bombardment. The Algerian flotilla made an attempt to board but 33 of their little boats were sunk. After an hour, the cannon on the mole were silenced and Exmouth turned his attention to the shipping in the harbour. Although the fleet also bombarded the city, there was comparatively little damage as the cannon balls passed through the flimsey walls. At 20:00, Milne asked that the bomb vessel *Vesuvius* be used against the battery that was mauling his ship. The commander of the bomb vessel made an error of navigation and she exploded ineffectively beside the wrong battery. Despite this, the Algerian batteries were no longer able to maintain fire and by 22:15, Exmouth gave the order for the fleet to weigh anchor and sail out of range, leaving HMS *Minden* to keep firing to suppress any further resistance. By 01:30 the next morning, the fleet was anchored out of range, the wounded were being treated and the crew were clearing the damage caused by the Algerian guns.

At noon, Exmouth sent a letter to the Dey: 'Sir, for your atrocities at Bona on defenceless Christians, and your unbecoming disregard of the demands I made yesterday in the name of the Prince Regent of England, the fleet under my orders has given you a signal chastisement, by the total destruction of your navy, storehouse, and arsenal, with half your batteries. As England does not wage war for the destruction of cities, I am unwilling to visit your personal cruelties upon the unoffending inhabitants of the country, and I therefore offer you the same terms of peace which I conveyed to you yesterday in my Sovereign's name. Without the acceptance of these terms, you can have no peace with England.' He warned that if they were not accepted, then he would continue the action. The Dey accepted the terms. It was a complete bluff on Pellew's part as the fleet had already fired off all of its ammunition. A treaty was signed on 24 September 1816, 1,083 Christian slaves and the British Consul were freed and the ransom money repaid. Over 3,000 slaves in total were later freed.

However, securing a uniform ban on slave-raiding, which was traditionally of central importance to the North African economy, proved impossible. Algiers subsequently renewed its slave-raiding, though on a smaller scale. In 1824 another British fleet under Admiral Sir Harry Neal again bombarded Algiers. Corsair activity based in Algiers did not entirely cease until its conquest by France in 1830.

For many Britons, over 300 years in which their own nation was consolidated, fear of the Barbary pirates was very real. Linda Colley:

> So visceral were these terrors, indeed, that they long outlasted the corsairs' capacity to do serious harm. This infected the British vision of slavery in ways that have been scarcely been acknowledged. It is often suggested that, after 1600, slavery became 'geographically and racially marginalised', a fate that whites in Europe were able to inflict on people of a different skin colour in regions of the world safely distant from their own.

The transatlantic slave trade carried on by whites in black flesh sold by Arabs was given legitimacy in many minds. Conversely, slaves in Barbary could be black, brown or white, Catholic, Protestant, Orthodox, Jewish or Muslim. That undermined contemporary claims that slavery was a natural order of race or religion. Some preachers on both sides of the Atlantic could not see any difference between the fates of whites in corsair galleys and blacks on American plantations. Early abolitionists used Barbary slavery as a way to attack the universal degradation of slavery in all its forms.

9 THE BATTLE OF THE MEDWAY

'I think the Devil shits Dutchmen.'
– Samuel Pepys, 1667

Admiral de Ruyter, de Witt and other senior officers go
on board the Dutch flagship, by E. Koster, 1857.

On 13 June 1667 Samuel Pepys wrote in his diary: 'I do fear so much that the whole kingdom is undone, that I do this night resolve to study with my father and wife what to do with the little that I have in money.'

He, like many Londoners, was thrown into a panic by an extraordinary raid on the Royal Dockyards of Chatham, which contained in oak the defensive strength of England. Only a rusty chain and a tiny river-fort provided the last defence against invasion. That panic was shared by the government. A coastal town was captured and three capital ships and 10 lesser vessels were burnt, while around 30 vessels were scuttled and two others – including the pride and flagship of the navy, were towed away. The one-sided attack proved to be, it can be argued, the worst defeat in the Royal Navy's history. And it vies with Majuba Hill (1881) and the fall of Singapore (1941) as the most humiliating defeat of British arms.

The Stuarts, by making friends of the Spanish and French, ensured that the threat from those two rival powers would be diminished for the best part of a century. That peace was interrupted when it became clear that the Parliamentarians were winning the Civil War against Charles I. A French squadron with transports evaded the navy in the North Sea and reached Bridlington, but was then destroyed in the harbour. Cromwell's Commonwealth was not threatened from overseas, partly because in a Europe hit by financial crisis, no power was strong enough to mount a serious challenge. That did not change much when the Stuarts were restored. But the Dutch, sometimes allies, sometimes enemies, were a different matter.

During the Commonwealth, Cromwell had successfully seen off the Dutch in a war sparked by trade disputes and fought entirely at sea. The English were victorious at the Battle of Scheveningen and the Dutch were forced to accept an English monopoly on trade with England and English colonies. Cromwell sought to avoid further conflict with the Dutch Republic.

The restoration of Charles II saw widespread demands at home to reverse the Dutch dominance in world trade. Charles, however, was personally greatly in debt to the House of Orange, which had lent enormous sums to his father during the Civil War. But a conflict soon developed over the education and future prospects of his nephew, William III of Orange. That dispute, which had wide implications for the royal houses of Europe, was temporarily solved, thanks largely to the diplomacy of Lord Clarendon, a favourite of the king. In 1664, the situation quickly changed when Clarendon's enemy, Lord Arlington, superseded him as the king's favourite. Arlington and the king's brother James, Duke of York, the Lord High Admiral, saw the opportunity for great personal gain in a war with the Dutch. James headed the Royal African Company and hoped to seize the possessions of the Dutch West India Company. The two were supported by the English ambassador in The Hague, George Downing, who despised the Dutch. He, either falsely or over-optimistically, reported that the Republic was politically divided between Orangists, who would gladly collaborate with an English enemy in case of war, and a faction of wealthy merchants that would give in to any English demand in order to protect their trade interests. Arlington planned to subdue the Dutch completely by permanent occupation of key Dutch cities. Charles was easily influenced and became convinced that a popular and lucrative foreign war at sea would bolster his authority as king. Naval officers were hungry for promotion and fortune in a conflict which they thought would be a walk-over.

Enthusiasm for war became infectious. English privateers attacked Dutch ships, capturing about 200. Dutch ships were obligated by treaty to salute the English flag first. In 1664 English commanders provoked the Dutch by not saluting in return. Many Dutch commanders could not bear the insult. English propagandists got to work, invoking the Amboyna Massacre of 1623 when ten English residents in the Dutch fortress of Victoria were executed by beheading for alleged treason, after first being tortured by a seventeenth-century version of water-boarding. Scurrilous broadsheets demonised the Dutch as drunken and profane. Pamphlets documented, without any real evidence, Dutch atrocities in the colonies. Under such a mountain of print, most Englishmen believed, in the poet Andrew Marvell's words, that the Dutch were the 'undigested vomit of the Sea'. Such vilification was at least partially an expression of unease with the presence of notable Cromwellians in exile in Holland. Charles had some reason to be nervous about at least the possibility of a Dutch invasion coordinated with an uprising within England.

Behind such fear-fuelled bigotry was of course the time-honoured motive for war – mercantile competition. The English sought to take over the Dutch trade routes and colonies while excluding the Dutch from their own colonial possessions. Contraband shipping had gone on from English colonies in America and Surinam for a decade, and the English were in no mood to give up such revenues. The Dutch, for their part, considered it their right to trade with anyone, anywhere. They too suffered from myopic double standards as they themselves enforced a monopoly in the Dutch Indies and threatened to extend it to India, after having expelled the Portuguese from that region.

Relations were decidedly tense on all fronts. James sent the Royal African Company's Robert Holmes to capture Dutch trading posts and colonies in West Africa. With royal authority, the English invaded the Dutch colony of New Netherlands in North America on 24 June 1664, and controlled it by October. The Dutch responded by sending a fleet under Michiel de Ruyter, which recaptured their African trade posts, seized most English trade stations there and then crossed the Atlantic for a punitive expedition against the English in America. In December 1664, the English suddenly attacked the Dutch Smyrna fleet. Although the attack failed, the Dutch in January 1665 decreed that their ships could open fire on English warships in the colonies whenever threatened. Charles used this as a pretext to declare war on the Netherlands on 4 March 1665.

Since their defeat in the First Anglo–Dutch War, the Dutch had become much better prepared. Beginning in 1653, a 'New Navy' was constructed, a core of 60 new, heavier ships with professional captains. However, these ships were still much lighter than the 10 biggest ships in the English navy. With the threat of war growing, in 1664 the Dutch decided to replace their fleet core completely with still heavier ships. Upon the outbreak of war the following year, the new ships were quickly completed, with another 20 ordered. In the run-up to hostilities, cash-strapped England could only build a dozen ships. During the course of the war the Dutch shipyards built seven vessels to England's one.

Still, on paper England appeared, fallaciously as it turned out, to be a giant facing the little Dutch boy. Her population was four times as big and its confidence was still on a par with its post-Armada period. But money was tight, with few cities able to dig deep into their coffers. The Dutch burghers were able to spend the equivalent of £11 million on the war, the English barely half that. And God seemed to have deserted England. The outbreak of war was swiftly followed by both the Great Plague and the Great Fire of London, bringing England virtually to her knees. Furthermore, the English fleet had already suffered severe cash shortages, despite having been voted a record budget of £2,500,000 by Parliament. The navy could only pay its sailors with 'tickets', or debt certificates, as Charles lacked an effective means of enforcing taxation. The only way to finance the war was to capture Dutch trade fleets.

The first encounters were, unsurprisingly, at sea and British naval power at first seemed supreme. At the Battle of Lowestoft on 13 June the English gained a great victory. It was the worst defeat of the Dutch Republic's navy in history. However, the English proved unable to capitalise on the victory. The leading Dutch politician, Johan de Witt, quickly restored confidence by joining the fleet personally. He sacked ineffective captains and introduced modern tactics.

In August, de Ruyter returned from America to a hero's welcome and was given supreme command of the confederate fleet. The 60-year-old de Ruyter was highly respected, even loved, by his sailors and soldiers, who used the term of endearment Bestevaêr ('Grandad') for him. A pious, lowly born man, cautious in his personal nature, he always led from the front and refused to back away from danger. He also, unusually for one of his standing, had an utter disregard for rank. Meanwhile, the Spice Fleet from the Dutch East Indies managed to return home safely after the Battle of Vagen. That hit English pockets hard.

Charles and his ministers sought foreign help. In the summer of 1665 the bishop of Münster, an old enemy of the Dutch, had been induced by promises of English subsidies to invade the Republic. At the same time, the English made overtures to Spain. Both strategies backfired. Louis XV was greatly alarmed by the attack by Münster and the prospect of an English–Spanish coalition. He feared that a collapse of the Republic could create a powerful Habsburg entity on his northern border, as the Habsburgs were the traditional allies of the German bishops. He immediately promised to send a French army corps and French envoys. There was consternation at the English court. It now seemed that the Republic would end up as either a Habsburg possession or a French protectorate. Either outcome would be a disaster for England. Clarendon, always having warned about 'this foolish war', was ordered to quickly make peace with the Dutch without French mediation. Instead, he encouraged the Orangists to seize power, but that was foiled by the return of de Witt from his fleet.

The Dutch created a strong anti-English alliance. On 26 January 1666, Louis declared war and days later Frederick III of Denmark was bribed into doing the same. Charles made a new peace offer, which vaguely promised to moderate his demands if the Dutch would only appoint William to some responsible function and pay £200,000 in 'indemnities'. De Witt considered it a mere feint to divide the Dutch and their French allies. He was having none of it and decided to strike hard with a fleet of 85 ships.

Eighty English ships, under General-at-Sea George Monck, the Duke of Albemarle, set sail at the end of May to confront the threat. But 20 of them under Prince Rupert peeled off to intercept a phantom French squadron believed to be joining up with the Dutch – in fact, most French vessels were in the Mediterranean. Albemarle came upon de Ruyter's fleet at anchor on 1 June and immediately attacked the nearest Dutch ship before the rest of the fleet could come to her aid. The Dutch rearguard under Lieutenant-Admiral Cornelius Tromp set upon a starboard tack, taking the battle toward the Flemish shoals and compelling Albemarle to turn about. A ferocious battle raged until nightfall. Albemarle's strength was reduced to 44 ships, but with these he renewed the battle, tacking past the enemy four times in close action. With his fleet in too poor a condition to continue to challenge, he retired towards the coast with the Dutch in pursuit.

The following day Prince Rupert returned with his 20 ships, joined Albemarle. During this stage of the battle, Vice-Admiral George Ayscue, on the grounded *Prince Royal*, surrendered, the last time an English admiral did so in battle. On the fourth day the Dutch broke the English lines several times. The English again retreated, but de Ruyter was reluctant to follow because gunpowder was running low. The battle ended with both sides claiming victory, even though the English had lost 10 ships against the Dutch four.

One more major action was fought – the St James's Day Battle on 4 and 5 August ended in English victory because they lost one ship to the Dutch two. It failed to decide the war as the Dutch fleet escaped annihilation and at this stage simply surviving was enough for the Dutch. Five days later, Charles made another peace offer to de Witt using the notorious Henri Buat, a Dutch cavalry officer with a track record of conspiracy, as an intermediary. Among the letters he took to The Hague, presumably by mistake, was one containing the secret English instructions to their contacts in the Orange party, outlining plans for an overthrow of the state's regime. Buat was arrested, condemned for treason and beheaded. His accomplices in the conspiracy fled the country to England. De Witt now had proof of treachery within the Orange movement.

The mood in the Republic now turned grimly belligerent. To raise tempera-tures even higher, in August English Vice-Admiral Robert Holmes, during his raid on the Vlie estuary in August 1666, destroyed merchantmen and sacked the island of Terschelling, setting the main town aflame. In this he was assisted by a Dutch cap-tain, Laurens Heemskerck, who had fled to England after having been condemned to death for cowardice shown during the Battle of Lowestoft.

After the Great Fire of London in September, Charles again reduced his demands in an attempt to withdraw from the war without losing face. He was rebuffed.

By the beginning of 1667 Charles's active fleet was in a poor state owing to spend-ing cuts and the remaining big ships were laid up. Johan de Witt saw his chance. Negotiations had been in progress at Breda since March, but Charles had been procrastinating over the signing of peace, hoping to improve his position through secret French assistance. De Witt vowed to end the war quickly with a clear victory, thereby ensuring a more advantageous settlement for the Dutch Republic. He sent his brother Cornelis to supervise the fleet's preparations. The Dutch commanders, fearing the treacherous shoals in the Thames estuary, hired two English pilots, one a dissenter named Robert Holland, the other a smuggler who had fled English justice.

Admiral de Ruyter gathered together his various squadrons and set sail for the Thames on 4 June with 62 frigates or ships-of-the-line, about 15 lighter ships and

12 fireships. The fleet was in three squadrons: the first was commanded by de Ruyter himself, the second by Lieutenant-Admiral Aert Jansse van Nes, and the third by Lieutenant-Admiral Baron Willem Joseph van Ghent. The latter, on the frigate *Agatha*, was the real commander of the expedition; he had done all the operational planning as he had been the former commander of the Dutch Marine Corps, the first in history created for specialised amphibious operations. That was now headed by the English Cromwellian Colonel Thomas Dolman.

On 6 June a break in the fog bank revealed the Dutch task force sailing into the mouth of the Thames. The attack caught the English unawares. Despite ample warning from spies, no serious preparations had been made. Most frigates were at Harwich and in Scotland. Sir William Coventry had earlier dismissed the likelihood of the Dutch landing anywhere near London, believing that purely as a morale-booster they would launch a token attack on Harwich. That port was strongly fortified, leaving London protected by only a small number of active ships, most of them prizes taken earlier in the war from the Dutch. In March the Duke of York had ordered the discharge of most of the crews of the prize vessels, leaving only three guard ships at the Medway. The number of fireships was hastily increased from one to three, and 30 large sloops were prepared to row ships to safety in an emergency. But such measures merely underlined the lack of a clear line of command, with most responsible authorities giving hasty orders without bothering to coordinate them first. The result was utter confusion. King Charles stood aloof and English morale plummeted. English soldiers, not having been paid for months or even years, were not over-eager to risk their lives. England dithered while the main Dutch fleet took five days to manoeuvre around the shoals and reach the approaches to Chatham.

At the Royal Dockyard, Commissioner Peter Pett, despite having raised the alarm, sat on his hands until 9 June when, late in the afternoon, about 30 Dutch ships, Van Ghent's squadron of frigates, were sighted off Sheerness. Pett sent a gloomy message to the Navy Board, lamenting the absence of Navy senior officials whose help and advice he believed he needed. When decisive action was required, Pett was more interested in avoiding future blame.

Van Ghent's frigates carried marines who were landed on Canvey Island in Essex. They had strict orders not to plunder, as the Dutch wanted to shame the English whose troops had sacked Terschelling. Nevertheless, tCaptain Jan van Brakel's crew couldn't control themselves and commenced looting rather than soldiering. They were driven off by English militia and upon returning to the Dutch fleet found themselves under threat of severe punishment. Van Brakel offered to lead the attack the next day to avoid the penalty.

King Charles was finally spurred into action and ordered the Earl of Oxford to mobilise the militia of all counties around London. All available barges were gathered to lay a ship bridge across the Lower Thames, so that the English cavalry could quickly switch positions from one bank to the other. Musketeers from the Sheerness garrison were sent to investigate reports of Dutch raiding parties on the Isle of Grain. It was only in the afternoon of 10 June that the king instructed Albemarle to go to

Chatham to take charge. Admiral Prince Rupert was sent to organise the defences at Woolwich a full three days later.

Albermarle found to his utter dismay that at Gravesend and Tilbury there were too few guns to halt a Dutch advance upon the Thames. To prevent such a disaster, he ordered all available artillery from the capital to be positioned at Gravesend. On 11 June he went to Chatham, expecting the backbone of England's naval strength to be well prepared for an attack, but found only 12 of the 800 dockyard men present. Only 10 of the 30 sloops were there because the remainder had been used to ferry to safety the cherished personal possessions of senior officers, in Commissioner Pett's case, his collection of model ships. No munitions or powder were available and the six-inch thick iron chain that blocked the Medway, installed in the Civil War to repel a possible attack of the Royalist fleet, had not been protected by batteries. Albemarle immediately ordered the transfer of the artillery from Gravesend to Chatham.

The full Dutch fleet arrived at the Isle of Sheppey on 10 June and launched an attack on the incomplete Sheerness Fort. Captain Jan van Brakel in Vrede, desperate to assuage the dishonour of his men, led and, followed by two other men-of-war, sailed as close to the fort as possible to batter it with cannon. Only the frigate *Unity*, stationed off the fort, was able to engage. It was supported by a number of ketches and fireships at Garrison Point, and by the fort itself where 16 guns had been hastily placed. The *Unity* fired one broadside, but when a Dutch fireship approached, she withdrew up the Medway, followed by the support vessels. The Dutch fired on the fort. Two men were hit and when the Scots soldiers of the garrison realised that no surgeon was on duty, they deserted. Seven remained, but their position became untenable when some 800 Dutch marines landed about a mile away. The fort and its guns were captured and blown up,

Confusion reigned on the English side, as Spragge, Monck and Admiralty officials issued conflicting orders. As his artillery would not arrive soon, Monck on the 11th ordered a squadron of cavalry and a company of soldiers to reinforce Upnor Castle. River defences were hastily improvised with blockships sunk, and the chain across the river was guarded by light batteries. Pett proposed that several big and smaller ships be sunk to block the Musselbank channel in front of the chain. HMS *Golden Phoenix*, HMS *House of Sweden*, HMS *Welcome* and HMS *Leicester* were scuttled along with the smaller vessels *Constant John*, *Unicorn*, *John* and *Sarah*. Spragge took soundings and discovered that this was not enough to block the second channel, several more were sunk, including the *Barbados Merchant*, *Dolphin*, *Edward and Eve*, *Hind* and *Fortune*. The job was done by men from the remaining warships, which were temporarily left crewless. They were placed in a too-easterly position on the line and could not be covered by fire. Monck then decided also to sink ships in Upnor Reach, presenting another barrier to the Dutch should they break through the chain at Gillingham. The defensive chain placed across the river had at its lowest point been lying practically 9ft under the waterline between its stages, leaving it possible for light ships to pass over it. The defenders tried to raise it by placing stages under it closer to the shore.

The positions of *Charles V* and *Matthais*, both captured Dutch merchantmen, just above the chain were adjusted to enable them to bring their broadsides to bear. *Monmouth* was also moored above the chain, positioned so that she could bring her guns to bear on the space between *Charles V* and *Matthias*. The frigate *Marmaduke* and the *Norway Merchant* were sunk off above the chain; the large *Sancta Maria* foundered while being moved for the same purpose. Pett also informed Monck that the *Royal Charles* had to be moved upriver. He had been ordered by the Duke of York to do this on 27 June, but as yet had not complied. Monck at first refused to make available some of his small number of sloops, as they were needed to move supplies; when he at last found the captain of the *Matthias* willing to assist, Pett answered that it was too late as he was busy sinking the blockships and there was no pilot to be found daring enough to take such a risk anyway. Meanwhile the first Dutch frigates to arrive had already begun to move the *Edward and Eve* away, clearing a channel by nightfall.

Van Ghent's squadron now advanced up the Medway on 12 June, attacking the English defences at the chain. First, *Unity* was taken by Van Brakel by assault. Then the fireship *Pro Patria* under commander Jan Daniëlsz van Rijn broke through the chain (or sailed over it according to some sources). She then destroyed the *Matthias* by fire. The fireships *Catharina* and *Schiedam* attacked the *Charles V*. The *Catharina* under commander Hendrik Hendriksz was sunk by the shore batteries but the *Schiedam* successfully set the *Charles V* alight. The crew was captured by Van Brakel.

The flagship *Royal Charles*, with only thirty cannon aboard and abandoned by her skeleton crew when they saw the *Matthias* burn, was then captured by the Irish flag captain Thomas Tobiasz. Only the *Monmouth* escaped. Seeing the disaster, Monck ordered the 16 remaining warships farther up to be sunk off to prevent them from being captured, making for a total of about 30 ships deliberately sunk by the English themselves. As Andrew Marvell observed: 'Of all our navy none should now survive, But that the ships themselves were taught to dive.' The Dutch anchored in the Medway when the tide turned.

The following day, 13 June, the whole of the Thames side as far up as London was in a panic as a rumour spread that the Dutch were transporting a French army from Dunkirk for a full-scale invasion. Many wealthy citizens fled the city, taking their most valuable possessions with them. Samuel Pepys, secretary of the Naval Board, wrote on the 13th:

No sooner up but hear the sad newes confirmed of the Royall Charles being taken by them, and now in fitting by them – which Pett should have carried up higher by our several orders, and deserves, therefore, to be hanged for not doing it – and turning several others; and that another fleete is come up into the Hope. Upon which newes the King and Duke of York have been below [London Bridge] since four o'clock in the morning, to command the sinking of ships at Barking-Creeke, and other places, to stop their coming up higher: which put me into such a fear, that I presently resolved of my father's and wife's going into the country; and, at two hours' warning, they did go by the coach this day, with about L1300 in gold in their night-bag. ... never were people so dejected as they are in the City all over at this day; and do talk most loudly, even treason; as, that we are bought and sold – that we are betrayed by the Papists, and others, about the King; cry out that the office of the Ordnance hath been so backward as no powder to have been at Chatham nor Upnor Castle till such a time, and the carriages all broken; that Legg is a Papist; that Upnor, the old good castle built by Queen Elizabeth, should be lately slighted; that the ships at Chatham should not be carried up higher. They look upon us as lost, and remove their families and rich goods in the City; and do think verily that the French, being come down with his army to Dunkirke, it is to invade us, and that we shall be invaded.

The Dutch continued their advance into the Chatham docks with the fireships *Delft*, *Rotterdam*, *Draak*, *Wapen van Londen*, *Gouden Appel* and *Princess*, under English fire from Upnor Castle and from three shore batteries. Cannon boomed and musketry rattled from Upnor. Dutch frigates suppressed the English fire, but suffered about 40 casualties in dead and wounded. The exposed structures of three of the finest and heaviest vessels in the navy, already sunk to prevent capture, now perished by fire: first the *Loyal*, set alight by the *Rotterdam*, then the *Royal James* and finally the *Royal Oak*. The latter withstood attempts by two fireships but succumbed to a third. The English crews abandoned their half-flooded ships, mostly without a fight, a notable exception being army Captain Archibald Douglas of the Scots Foot, who personally refused to abandon the *Oak* and perished in the flames. The *Monmouth* again escaped. The raid thus cost the English four of their remaining eight ships with more than 75 cannon. Three of the four largest 'big ships' of the navy were lost. The fourth, the *Royal Sovereign*, was safely but uselessly in Portsmouth. De Ruyter now joined Van Ghent's squadron in person.

Pepys wrote:

Late at night comes Mr. Hudson, the cooper, my neighbour, and tells me that he come from Chatham this evening at five o'clock, and saw this afternoon 'The Royal James,' 'Oake,' and 'London,' burnt by the enemy with their fire-ships: that two or three men-of-war come up with them, and made no more of Upnor Castle's shooting, than of a fly.

Cornelis de Witt, fearing that the English would finally get themselves organised and counter-attack, on 14 June decided against further penetration and withdrew, towing the *Royal Charles* along as a war trophy; the *Unity* was also removed with a prize crew. Dutch demolition teams rowed to any ship they could reach to burn her down as much as they could, thus ensuring their reward money. One boat even re-entered the docks to make sure nothing was left above the waterline of the *Oak*, *James* and *London;* another burnt the merchantman *Slot van Honingen*, ruining a precious salvage opportunity. The Dutch failed to completely destroy the Chatham dockyard, another missed opportunity. Such destruction could have put back the rebuilding of the English navy by decades.

The Dutch fleet, after celebrating by collectively thanking God for 'a great victory in a just war in self-defence' tried to repeat its success by attacking several other ports on the English east coast but was repelled each time.

On 27 June an attempt to enter the Thames beyond Gravesend was called off when it became known that the river was blocked by sunken ships and five fireships awaited the Dutch attack. On 2 July a Dutch force landed near Woodbridge north of Harwich, aiming to take the port, a position of immense strategic importance. But first they had to take the newly constructed Landguard Fort. What happened next did something to restore battered English military pride. Four officers and around 100 men, with 18 heavy cannon, were determined to fight. So, too, were the town militia.

Initially the Dutch fleet, due to unfavourable winds, was forced to sail north off Lowestoft before turning south to launch the attack. As they sailed northwards, the British militia, assuming another raid, marched along the coast shadowing the enemy fleet. When the Dutch turned south again, with a now favourable wind, so did the militia. De Ruyter's fleet was joined by five troop transports sent out from Holland especially for the Harwich raid, commanded by the experienced Colonel Count van Hoorn. That took the attack force to about 850 infantrymen and 400 marines. The infantry commander was Colonel Thomas Dolman, the Medway veteran who had earlier served in the British army under Cromwell.

On Sunday 30 June, 70 Dutch ships anchored behind the shelter of a large sand-bank known as the Gunfleet. The landing force embarked in a small fleet of around 20 small flat-bottomed sailing barges, known as *galiots*, At noon de Ruyter gave the signal and the *galiots* started for the shore.

Marines commander Colonel Francois Palm leaped out onto the gently sloping shingle, the first man to land, followed immediately by his men. To their right the infantry also poured ashore, led by Dolman. On the beach, the troops formed up as though on parade, while van Hoorn sent out a scouting party to ascend the low cliffs by a narrow track. Within two hours the Dutch were ashore safely, in good order, and without a shot being fired at them. The scouts brought back two civilian prisoners who told them that the fort's garrison had been heavily reinforced and that 60 guns faced the raiders. Van Hoorn refused to believe them and ordered the attack.

While the Dutch soldiers of the assault group moved under cover of a large sand dune at around 1400 hours, the footsore English militia were on the wrong side of the River Deben. The river was swift-flowing with a surging tidal current. The militia cavalry trotted eight miles upstream to cross at Woodbridge while the infantry crossed in a tiny ferry-boat capable of carrying barely a dozen men at a time. It was agonisingly slow work in the face of immense danger. De Ruyter ordered forward a few of his *galiots,* each carrying a small cannon to bombard the 250yd crossing. The part-time British militia were attempting that most difficult military manoeuvre – a river crossing under artillery fire. The crossings were halted when just a few had reached the Dutch side of the estuary. They buried themselves in marsh ditches and waited for the ebb of the tide. As the water receded, the *galiots* that had been plaguing them were forced farther and farther from the shore until out of range. The river crossing started again at about 1600 hours.

The Dutch troops of the assault group were also forced to wait. The same tidal rush frustrated the Dutch admirals sent to bombard Harwich and Landguard Fort from the south and east. Their arrival in the selected firing positions with their squadrons coincided with the fall of the tide, and they too were forced out of range – even the largest cannon on the ships could barely reach the walls of the fort. The Dutch assault force was denied the flanking fire designed to keep the defenders' heads down. The English had also removed all the marker buoys from the Harwich channels, so that the Dutch sailors had to navigate by memory and guesswork. Admiral van Nes's flagship, the *Delft*, ran aground and had to be laboriously towed off later. The Dutch ships withdrew and most of their sailors were sent to reinforce the soldiers on land.

Soon after 1600 hours – just as the falling tide allowed the militia to the north to resume their interrupted river crossing – the Dutch soldiers, marines and sailors started their attack. The soldiers were organised in 18 infantry half-companies of about 48 men each, disposed in four sections, each with four grenadiers, the rest being musketeers and pikemen. The marines were all armed with carbines – short flintlock muskets much like the old firelocks.

Surprised by the sheer volume of musket fire poured at them, the vast majority of Dutch soldiers and sailors simply refused to leave the shelter of the dunes. Their musketeers, trying to fire from behind cover, tended to fire high. Some did make several gallant assaults against the walls, using their *fascines* to fill the ditch and their ladders to scale the walls. None made it to the top. At around 1730 the Dutch began to melt away, but officers rallied sufficient of the braver men for a second major assault. That, too, failed. At 1800 the attack on Landguard Fort was called off and the Dutch retreated towards the beaches.

Part of the volume of fire which had so surprised and dispirited the Dutch troops came from a tiny *galiot* the British had sailed to the harbour mouth. This vessel used grapeshot to great effect on the retreating Dutch. Having run that gauntlet, Colonel Dolman's men made it to the beach, only to confront another threat. The English militia had come together and a mixed force of 1,500 infantry and cavalry were on high ground to the north challenging the Dutch flank guard. A separate two-hour battle now ensued as the Dutch used their musketeers to keep the British at bay, with small groups of men from both sides creeping around trying to out-manoeuvre each other. The British attempred to lure the Dutch forward from their lines by feigning a withdrawal, but instead the Dutch maintained the fire of their small portable cannon, using grapeshot against the infantry and round-shot against the cavalry. This harassing artillery fire was so effective that the British cavalry were unable to form up for a charge. Sunset ended the battle. At about 2030 hours the Dutch used the deepening darkness to disengage in a display of professional skill and they were all re-embarked by around 2200.

The casualties were never recorded properly by either side. One Dutch report listed '7 dead and 35 wounded in the whole fleet', which does not accord with a British eye-witness account of 'boat-loads of Dutch dead' being rowed out to the ships. More believable is that the Dutch casualties were seven dead and 35 wounded in the ships themselves, while the soldiers and marines ashore suffered perhaps eight dead and 30-40 wounded at the fort. British casualties were very precisely numbered at the fort as one dead and four wounded, including their commander, Captain Nathaniel Darell, who received a musket ball through his shoulder. But, like the Dutch, there was no record of casualties during the withdrawal or in the battle with the enemy flank guard. The best guesses, given the nature of the battle, are 12-15 British killed and 20 wounded, and eight Dutch dead and 20 wounded. For the British it was a small price to pay for repelling the last opposed seaborne invasion of England.

Despite that Dutch failure, panic still ruled in London amongst the ruling class. Samuel Pepys noted in his diary on 19 July 1667: 'The Dutch fleete are in great squadrons everywhere still about Harwich, and were lately at Portsmouth; and the last letters say at Plymouth, and now gone to Dartmouth to destroy our Streights' fleete lately got in thither; but God knows whether they can do it any hurt, or no, but it was pretty news come the other day so fast, of the Dutch fleets being in so many places, that Sir W. Batten at table cried, By God, says he, I think the Devil shits Dutchmen.' And on 29 July 1667: 'Thus in all things, in wisdom, courage, force, knowledge of our own streams, and success, the Dutch have the best of us, and do end the war with victory on their side'.

Wharf official John Norman estimated the damage caused by the Medway raid at about £20,000, apart from the replacement costs of the four lost capital ships; the total loss of the Royal Navy must have been close to £200,000. Pett was made a scapegoat, bailed at £5,000 and deprived of his office while those who had ignored his earlier warnings quietly escaped any blame. The *Royal James*, *Oak* and *Loyal London* were in the end salvaged and rebuilt, but at great cost and when the City of London refused to share in it, Charles had the name of the latter ship changed to simply *London*. For a few years the English fleet was handicapped by its losses during the raid, but by around 1670 a new building programme had restored the English navy to its former power.

Total losses for the Dutch were eight spent fireships and about 50 casualties. In the Republic, the populace was jubilant after the victory; many festivities were held, repeated when the fleet returned in October, the various admirals being hailed as heroes. They were rewarded by a flood of eulogies and given honorary golden chains and pensions by the States-General and the lesser States of the Provinces; de Ruyter, Cornelis de Witt and Van Ghent were honoured by precious enamelled golden chalices depicting the events. Cornelis de Witt had a large 'Sea Triumph' painted, with himself as the main subject. This triumphalism by de Witt's States faction caused resentment with the rival Orangist faction; when the States regime lost power in 1672, Cornelis's head was to be ceremoniously carved out from the painting, after Charles had for some years insisted the picture would be removed.

The Dutch success in the Medway had a major psychological impact throughout England, with London feeling especially vulnerable just a year after the Great Fire. This, together with the cost of the war, of the Great Plague and the extravagant spending of Charles's court, produced a rebellious atmosphere in London. Clarendon ordered the English envoys at Breda to sign a peace quickly, as Charles feared an open revolt.

On 31 July 1667, the Treaty of Breda sealed peace between the two nations. The treaty allowed the English to keep 27 possession of New Netherlands, which they renamed New York, while the Dutch kept control of the valuable sugar plantations of Surinam they had conquered in 1667.

The Raid on the Medway was a serious blow to the reputation of the English crown. Charles felt personally offended by the fact the Dutch had attacked while he had laid up his fleet and peace negotiations were in progress, conveniently forgetting he himself had not negotiated in good faith. His resentment was one of the causes of the Third Anglo-Dutch war, as it made him enter into the secret Treaty of Dover with Louis XIV of France. In the nineteenth century, jingoistic British writers expanded on this theme by suggesting it had been the Dutch who had sued for peace after their defeats in 1666 – although in fact these had made them, if anything, more belligerent – and that only by treacherously attacking the English had they been able to gain a victory.

The Republic was jubilant about the Dutch victory and the peace was generally seen as a personal triumph for de Witt. He consolidated his political power at home and reduced the powers of difficult provinces. But de Witt's success would sow the seeds of his eventual downfall and nearly that of the Republic with him. Charles and Louis, both humiliated in turn, intensified their secret cooperation and would, joined by the bishop of Münster, attack the Dutch in 1672. De Witt was unable to counter this attack, as he could not create a strong Dutch army for lack of money and fear that it would strengthen the position of the young William III. That same year de Witt was assassinated and William became stadtholder.

The *Royal Charles*, her draught too deep to be of use in the shallow Dutch waters, was permanently drydocked near Hellevoetsluis as a tourist attraction, with day trips being organised for large parties, often of foreign state guests. After vehement protests by Charles that this insulted his honour, the official visits were ended and *Royal Charles* was eventually scrapped in 1672.

In 1676 de Ruyter took command of a combined Dutch-Spanish fleet to help the Spanish suppress the Messina revolt and twice fought a French fleet. At the Battle of Agosta a cannonball mangled his left leg. He died on 29 April 1676. He was given a full state funeral and buried in Amsterdam.

The Medway debacle, a humiliation for Britain's military might, led to a major overhaul of coastal defences. Over 15 years, enormous sums were spent in both the Medway and the Thames, and in Portsmouth, Plymouth, Hull and Tynemouth. Many fortifications were designed by the country's famed chief engineer, Sir Bernard de Gomme. Squat forts bristling with ordnance covered the main estuaries and waterways. In military circles, the lessons were learnt and never forgotten.

During the Second World War, on 14 December 1941, the Dutch minelayer *Jan van Brakel* hit the anchor buoy of one of the vessels protecting the entrance to the Medway. The commander reported this incident to the port authorities, signalling: 'Van Brakel damaged boom defence Medway'. The instant reply was: 'What, again?'

10 THE 'GLORIOUS' INVASION

'… actuated by a higher principle'
– John Churchill, 1688

William and Mary from the Guild book of the Barber
Surgeons of York.

Propaganda is often the instant re-writing of history. That is particularly true of the events of 1688. The overthrow of James II was hailed by John Hamden the following year, and ever since, as the 'Glorious Revolution'. Edmund Burke proclaimed that: 'The Revolution was made to preserve our ancient indisputable laws and liberties, and that ancient constitution of government which is our only security for law and liberty.' That view has dominated both historical analysis and public sentiment ever since. But the alternative view is that it was the last successful military invasion of Britain, and a successful coup organised by our old trade rivals and on-off enemies, the Dutch.

Cut through the tangle of shifting allegiances, secret treaties, regal domestic disputes and complex power-play, and you have a full-scale military incursion by a foreign army, which to my mind defines an invasion, whatever spin is put on it afterwards. And the forcible combination of two trading nations was an often overlooked factor in the building of a 'British' Empire.

The momentous event, one of the most important in British history, was also known as the 'Bloodless' Revolution. Tell that to the Scots and Irish, who shed copious amounts of blood before William of Orange established himself on the throne.

❦ ❦

During his short reign, King James II was constantly trapped between the great political and religious divides, between Catholicism and Protestantism, between the divine right of kings and the power of Parliament. The low-church Whigs had failed in their attempt to pass legislation to exclude James from the throne between 1679 and 1681, and James's supporters were largely the high-church Anglican Tories.

When James inherited the English throne in 1685, he had much support in the 'Loyal Parliament', which was composed mostly of Tories. His Catholicism was a concern to many, but the fact that he had no son and his daughters were Protestants was a 'saving grace'. James's attempt to relax the penal laws – those laws enacted to uphold the Church of England by imposing forfeitures and civil disabilities on dissenters – alienated his natural supporters, because the Tories viewed this as tantamount to disestablishment of the Church. Abandoning the Tories, James looked to form a 'King's party' as a counterweight and in 1687 he supported religious toleration and issued the Declaration of Indulgence. By allying himself with the Catholics, dissenters and nonconformists, James hoped to build a coalition that would advance Catholic emancipation. He was playing a very dangerous game.

In May 1686 James, who like Charles I before him believed in the divine right of kings, decided to obtain from the English courts of the common law a ruling which affirmed his power to dispense with Acts of Parliament. He dismissed judges who disagreed with him on the matter, as well as the Solicitor General Heneage Finch. In April 1687, James ordered the fellows of Magdalen College, Oxford, to elect a Catholic as their president. They refused and he appointed the Bishop of Oxford, replacing the fellows with Catholics. James packed Parliament with his supporters, convinced that he had the support of dissenters. He purged Tories and Anglican office-holders and over 1,000 members of the city livery companies were ejected. In October James insisted on loyalty oaths for the lords lieutenants, in the form of a questionnaire. Hundreds who did not give satisfactory answers in the first three months of 1688 were sacked. Corporations were purged by agents given wide discretionary powers. The purges struck deep at every level of established order and privilege and on 24 August James prorogued Parliament without consent.

James also created a large standing army staffed by Catholic officers in key posts. His army was encamped at Hounslow, a short march from London, in a clear message to the city: comply with royal diktat, or else. English troops in in Ireland were also purged of Protestants. James had more than 34,000 men under arms in his three kingdoms.

In April 1688, James re-issued the Declaration of Indulgence and ordered all clergymen to read it in their churches. When the Archbishop of Canterbury, William

Sancroft, and six other bishops wrote to James asking him to reconsider his policies, they were arrested on charges of seditious libel, but at trial they were acquitted, to the cheers of the London crowd.

Matters came to a head in June 1688, when the king fathered a son, James. Until then, the throne would have passed to his daughter, Mary, a Protestant, and the wife of William of Orange. Following the birth, a rumour immediately spread that a call for a warming pan had been the pretext for a substitution, implying that James and Mary's baby was stillborn. Enemies whispered that the infant of a miller had been smuggled into the Queen's bedchamber. Within six months of his birth, Mary of Modena took baby James to France, worried about his safety. Despite Protestant propaganda over legitimacy, the prospect of a Catholic dynasty ruling over England, Scotland and Ireland now looked inevitable.

Mary and her husband, also her cousin, were the Protestant grandchildren of the beheaded Charles I. Before the birth of James's son on 10 June, William had been third in the line of succession. William was also stadtholder of the main provinces of the Dutch Republic, then preparing to join the War of the Grand Alliance against France. William and Mary had already secretly approached prominent English politicians opposed to James because they assumed that James' policies of broad religious tolerance was a first step towards the full return of Catholicism in England. James, he concluded, could not achieve that without French aid. Both the English and French navies had been expanded and re-organised, and William knew his own could not resist an Anglo-French attack. Furthermore, he believed that English neutrality in the approaching conflict would not be enough – he needed the Royal Navy to defeat the French. William saw himself as the main champion in Europe of the Protestant cause against Catholicism and French absolutism. He watched closely the crisis over the Channel and saw a golden opportunity to prevent an Anglo-French alliance by direct military action against his father-in-law. In November 1687 William wrote an open letter to the English people deploring James's religious policies. It was an indirect, but obvious, bid to become king himself.

William's envoy Everhard van Weede Dijkvelt visited England, ostensibly on a diplomatic mission to the court of King James. His real task was to let it be known to those plotting to oust their monarch that William would uphold the Church of England. He also aimed to reassure moderate Catholics that they would not be discriminated against. After having been assured by James that all rumours about a French alliance were malevolent fabrications, Dijkvelt returned to the Republic with letters from leading English statesmen. James tried again to gain William's support but William responded by advising James to keep to the law and not to try to extend his prerogative powers. Another supposed diplomat was sent a few months later to test the mood in the English Parliament.

Invisible ink and other devices were used in letters between William and the English plotters distributed by post and then, as the conspiracy gained momentum, via merchant vessels trading between Gravesend and Rotterdam. Eventually, fast yachts were used as a special courier service, most dodging English Customs. The failure of England's spy network to realise the scale of the conspiracy would have had Walsingham turning in his grave.

William knew he could not invade without English connivance and active support. In April he asked for a formal invitation to be issued by a group of leading English statesmen. A conversation between William and Admiral Edward Russell was noted down:

> So Russell put the Prince to explain himself what he intended to do. The Prince answered, that, if he was invited by some men of the best interest, and the most valued in the nation, who should both in their own name, and in the name of others who trusted them, invite him to come and rescue the nation and the religion, he believed he could be ready by the end of September to come over.

In May, Russell told William that the English opposition to James would not wait any longer for aid and was on the brink of rising in revolt. After the Prince of Wales had been born in June, the 'Immortal Seven', comprising Lord Shrewsbury. Lord Devonshire, Lord Danby, Lord Lumley, Henry Compton, Edward Russell and Henry Sidney, wrote to William inviting him to become their king. The letter was carried by Rear-Admiral Herbert, who was disguised as a common seaman. It declared:

> We have great reason to believe, we shall be every day in a worse condition than we are, and less able to defend ourselves, and therefore we do earnestly wish we might be so happy as to find a remedy before it be too late for us to contribute to our own deliverance … the people are so generally dissatisfied with the present conduct of the government, in relation to their religion, liberties and properties (all which have been greatly invaded), and they are in such expecta-tion of their prospects being daily worse, that your Highness may be assured, there are nineteen parts of twenty of the people throughout the kingdom, who are desirous of a change; and who, we believe, would willingly contribute to it, if they had such a protection to countenance their rising, as would secure them from being destroyed.

The Seven went on to claim that 'much the greatest part of the nobility and gentry' were dissatisfied and would rally to William, and that James's army

> … would be very much divided among themselves; many of the officers being so discontented that they continue in their service only for a subsistence … and very many of the common soldiers do daily shew such an aversion to the Popish religion, that there is the greatest probability imaginable of great num-bers of deserters … and amongst the seamen, it is almost certain, there is not one in ten who would do them any service in such a war.

The Seven also promised to rally to William upon his landing in England and 'do all that lies in our power to prepare others to be in as much readiness as such an action is capable of'.

William's spin doctor Hans Willem Bentinck presented William as a true Stuart but one blessedly free from the usual Stuart vices of crypto-Catholicism, absolutism, and debauchery. Much of the later 'spontaneous' support for William had been carefully organised by him and his agents. William also enjoyed surprisingly strong support within the English army, and James only had himself to blame for that. In January he had forbidden any of his subjects to serve the Dutch – a lucrative second career for soldiers – and had demanded that the Republic dissolve its mercenary Scottish and English regiments. That was rejected, but William agreed to release Britons from their martial oath if they wanted to return to England. William was acting out of self-interest, effectively purging his army of Jacobite supporters. In total, 104 officers and 44 soldiers returned. The officers were enlisted within the British armies and were so favoured that members of the established officer corps began to fear for their positions.

William then focused on building a powerful invasion force, and to do that he had to get funding from Amsterdam, then the world's main financial centre. Those financiers, previously pro-French for trade reasons, had been outraged by Louis's import curbs on Dutch herring, The burgomasters agreed, prompted by Bentinck's propaganda, to pay for the hiring of 260 transport ships. They were concerned, however, that the invasion expedition would leave them defenceless. Bentinck responded by recruiting 13,616 German mercenaries to man Dutch border fortresses to free an equal number of Dutch elite mercenary troops for use against England.

Further financial support was obtained from the most disparate sources. The Jewish banker Francisco Lopes Suasso lent two million guilders. When asked what security he desired, Suasso answered: 'If you are victorious, you will surely repay me; if not, the loss is mine.' Even Pope Innocent XI, an inveterate enemy of Louis XIV of France, provided a loan. Total costs were seven million guilders, four million of which would ultimately be paid for by a state loan. The Dutch navy was expanded to 9,000 sailors on the pretext of fighting the Dunkirkiers. The standard summer equipment of 20 warships was secretly doubled.

William continued to struggle to persuade the Dutch regents, powerful provincial rulers, that the expensive operation would be worth it. He also feared a surprise French invasion of his own lands. He dithered as the September target date approached. He almost cancelled it, but the French played into his hand. They warned the States-General against an English invasion and interference in French ambitions in Germany. The States-General were then convinced that there was indeed a secret Anglo-French pact, and that the French were aiming to move into Germany rather than threaten the borders of the Netherlands.

In late September, Louis XIV seized around 100 Dutch ships in French ports. The powerful city council of Amsterdam decided to support the English invasion officially. On 27 September Louis crossed the Rhine into Germany to attack Philipsburg and William began to move the Dutch field army from the eastern borders to the coast. Two days later, the States of Holland, the government of the most important Dutch province, gathered in secret session and approved the operation. They accepted William's argument that a preventive strike was necessary to avoid a repeat of the events of 1672, when England and France had jointly attacked the Republic. William denied any intention 'to remove the King from the throne or become master of England'.

The States ordered a Dutch fleet of 53 warships to escort the troop transports. The fleet was commanded by Lieutenant-Admiral Cornelis Evertsen on the *Cortgene* and Vice-Admiral Philips van Almonde on the *Provincie Utrecht*. But aware of the sensitivities of the English, it was in October nominally placed under the English defector, Rear-Admiral Arthur Herbert, who sailed on the *Leyden*. Although William was officially Admiral-General of the Republic, he abstained from operational command, sailing conspicuously on the new frigate *Den Briel*. The core regiments of the Dutch field army were under command of Marshal Schomberg.

The Dutch preparations, though carried out with great speed, could not remain secret. The English envoy Ignatius White, the Marquess d'Albeville, warned his country: 'An absolute conquest is intended under the specious and ordinary pretences of religion, liberty, property and a free Parliament.' Louis XIV threatened the Dutch with an immediate declaration of war, should they carry out their plans.

Embarkation started on 22 September and was completed on 8 October. William issued the Declaration of The Hague in which he swore that his only aim was to maintain the Protestant religion, install a free parliament and investigate the legitimacy of the Prince of Wales. He would respect the position of James, he lied. William declared:

> It is both certain and evident to all men, that the public peace and happiness of any state or kingdom cannot be preserved, where the Laws, Liberties, and Customs, established by the lawful authority in it, are openly transgressed and annulled; more especially where the alteration of Religion is endeavoured, and that a religion, which is contrary to law, is endeavoured to be introduced; upon which those who are most immediately concerned in it are indispensably bound to endeavour to preserve and maintain the established Laws, Liberties and customs, and, above all, the Religion and Worship of God, that is established among them; and to take such an effectual care, that the inhabitants of the said state or kingdom may neither be deprived of their Religion, nor of their Civil Rights.

William went on to condemn James's attempt to pack Parliament as a way of removing 'the last and great remedy for all those evils'. 'Therefore,' William continued, 'we have thought fit to go over to England, and to carry over with us a force sufficient, by the blessing of God, to defend us from the violence of those evil Counsellors … this our Expedition is intended for no other design, but to have a free and lawful Parliament assembled as soon as is possible.' The Declaration was translated into English and 60,000 copies were distributed after the landings.

For three weeks the invasion fleet was prevented by adverse south-westerly gales from departing from the naval port of Helievoetsluis. Catholics gave thanks in prayer. But eventually the 'popish wind' became the famous 'Protestant Wind' by turning to the east.

James, despite months of invasion threats, negotiations and ultimatums, only deployed around 30 ships-of-the-line, all of them third- or fourth-raters, while heavier vessels remained laid up. James regarded himself as a naval maestro and refused to believe that William would risk ferrying an army across the storm-tossed North Sea so late in the year. The Catholic Sir Roger Strickland was replaced as Admiral of the Fleet in September by the Protestant Lord Dartmouth. This was a royal sop to Protestant commanders, but it back-fired and effectively handed the navy to the enemy. Dartmouth, realising that most of his officers were reluctant to fight William, placed the fleet in a hopeless and ineffective position at the Gunfleet sandbank off the Thames estuary. James, fearing a Dutch attack on London, had already insisted that the fleet withdraw from the Downs, the most effective place to strike the Dutch supply lines in the North Sea and the Channel. It was an open invitation to William to use the Channel as his route to the southern counties. Many have long argued whether Dartmouth's actions were motivated by defeatism, incompetence or treachery. As it proved, the English fleet would be locked up in the Thames estuary by the same easterly wind that would allow the Dutch to cross.

On 16 October William boarded his ship, the *Den Briel* and his standard was hoisted, displaying the arms of Nassau quartered with those of England. The words *Pro Religione et Libertate* ('For Liberty and [the Protestant] Religion') were shown next to the House of Orange's motto, *Je maintiendrai* ('I will maintain'). William's fleet was roughly twice the size of the Spanish Armada. He had 463 ships, among which 49 warships of more than twenty cannon, 28 *galiots*, nine fireships, 76 *fluyts* to carry the soldiers, 120 small transports to carry 5,000 horses, about 70 supply vessels and 60 fishing vessels serving as landing craft.

William's fleet departed from Hellevoetsluis and got approximately halfway between the Republic and England when the wind changed to the north-west and a gale scattered it fleet, with the *Briel* returning to Hellevoetsluis. Despite suffering from sea-sickness William refused to go ashore and the fleet reassembled, having lost only one ship that grounded, although about 1,000 injured horses had been thrown into the sea. Reports were ciculated that exaggerated the damage and which claimed the expedition would be postponed until the spring.

The wind again turned to the east and, resupplied and carrying new horses, the invasion fleet departed again on 1 November and sailed north towards Harwich, where Bentinck had a landing site prepared. That may have been a feint, but in any case another wind changed the course to the south. During these movements the Dutch twice saw the English fleet, which was unable to intercept them because of unfavourable wind and tide. The invasion fleet entered the Channel in a huge square formation, 25 ships deep. The Dutch sides saluted Dover and Calais with gunfire and the troops on board discharged their muskets. Their military bands played lustily and all colours flew. It was a demonstration of strength and arrogance. William's armada passed the Isle of Wight on 4 November in a stately convoy 20 miles long, the bands still playing as it was his 38th birthday. Spectators lined the cliff-tops and beaches.

William intended to land at Torbay near Brixham, but due to fog the fleet sailed past it by mistake. The wind made a return impossible and Plymouth was unsuitable as it had a garrison. Finally the wind changed and the fog lifted, enabling the fleet to sail at last into Torbay. William came ashore on 5 November, the anniversary of an infamous Popish plot. The local populace welcomed him and a service of thanksgiving was held on the beach. That night William slept in a fisherman's hut, secure in the knowledge that an English squadron under Lord Dartmouth had been forced by the same change in wind to shelter in Portsmouth harbour. During the next two days the army disembarked in calm weather on a gently shelving shingle beach.

William brought over 11,212 horse and foot. His cavalry and dragoons amounted to 3,660. His artillery train contained 21 24-pounder cannon. Including those manning the supply train, his force consisted of about 21,000 men. He also brought 20,000 stands of arms to equip his English supporters. The Dutch army was composed mostly of foreign mercenaries; there were Dutch, English, Scots, German, Swiss, and Swedish regiments, even Laplanders, as well as '200 Blacks brought from the Plantations of the Netherlands in America', the colony of Surinam. William had his personal protection, the Dutch Blue Guards, close to him. James had total forces of around 40,000, having raised five new regiments of foot and five of horse, as well as bringing in Scottish and Irish soldiers. But they were well spread out, uncoordinated, and morale was not high.

William believed his army of experienced veterans more than enough to knock James's force off the board, but he was playing a different game. He intended to avoid battle in the hope that his father-in-law would lose the will to fight. William was well supplied for a three-month campaign, his troops were paid in advance, and he was prepared to wait. His men were under strict orders not to forage, never mind plunder, to avoid alienating potential allies in the local population. Everything they took they paid for, and two men who stole a chicken were hanged as an example to others. He moved his force slowly, steadily and methodically, first taking Exeter after the city magistrates had fled the city. With an eye to spectacle, he entered on a white palfrey, with his 200 black men forming a guard of honour, dressed in white, with turbans and feathers.

In the southern counties support from the local gentry was less than impressive, and not even the Seven joined him, each reluctant to be the first to show his hand, although in the North many nobles declared for William. In the first weeks most people carefully avoided taking sides, passively awaited the outcome of events.

James refused a French offer to send an expeditionary force, fearing that it would cost him domestic support. His forward forces had gathered at Salisbury, and James went to join them on 19 November with his main army, giving him a combined strength of about 19,000. There was anti-Catholic rioting in London, and it rapidly became clear that the troops were not eager to fight. The loyalty of many of his commanders became doubtful. James continued to dither and failed to arrest officers whom he knew were conspiring against him.

First blood was shed in a skirmish at Wincanton, Somerset, where Royalist troops retreated after defeating a small party of scouts. Both sides lost about 15 men. In Salisbury, after hearing that some officers had deserted, a worried James was overcome by a serious nose-bleed that he interpreted as an evil omen indicating that he should order his army to retreat, which the supreme army commander, the Earl of Feversham, also advised on 23 November. The next day, Lord Churchill, one of James' chief commanders and the future Duke of Marlborough, deserted to William.

Churchill, though a Protestant, had loyally served James for many years and his victory over the Monmouth rebels at the battle of Sedgemoor had help secure his crown. True to his conscience, and unlike many other courtiers, he had told James throughout that: 'I have been bred a Protestant, and intend to live and die in that communion.' He was courageous, diplomatic, and intensely ambitious. Ultimately, self-interest ruled his judgements, he believed the monarch's policy would either wreck his own career or generate a wider insurrection. He was determined to be on the winning side. When the Seven men met to draft William's invitation to rule, Churchill, although not then of sufficient political rank to be a signatory, declared his intentions through William's principal English contact in The Hague. Like many others, he was looking for an opportune moment to desert James. When William landed, Churchill was at the king's side, but privately he wrote of 'the greatest transports of joy imaginable' at the desertion of Protestant lords to the Williamist cause. He openly encouraged defection to the Orangemen. There were calls for his arrest, but James hesitated until it was too late to act. After the meeting of the council of war on 24 November, Churchill, accompanied by some 400 officers and men, slipped from the royal camp and rode towards William in Axminster, leaving behind him a letter of apology and self-justification:

> I hope the great advantage I enjoy was under Your Majesty, which I own I would never expect in any other change of government, may reasonably convince Your Majesty and the world that I am actuated by a higher principle.

James was thrown into despair by Churchill's defection. That despair was compounded a few days later when his own daughter, Princess Anne, who doubted the paternity of her new brother, and who was greatly influenced by Churchill's wife Sarah, also defected. She wrote to William to wish him 'good success in this so just an undertaking.' The family split, although long coming, had started in earnest when James banned Anne from visiting her sister Mary. Defying their father, they wrote to each other and Anne was thus aware of William's plans to invade. After her declaration for William, her father ordered she be placed under house arrest. She and Sarah Churchill fled from Whitehall by a back staircase, arriving at Nottingham on 1 December. James returned to London that same day. 'Even my children have forsaken me,' he wailed. There was treachery all around him, in his family and within his military forces. He slipped into mental decline, his confidence shattered.

Meanwhile, Plymouth surrendered to William and he began to advance. By failing to engage the invaders in the West Country, James lost all military advantage. William could not believe his luck. From now on the invasion would be won by politics rather than on the battlefield. And William was a political master, knowing exactly who to flatter and who to cajole, who to bribe and who to threaten with force. He advanced on Salisbury as the king retreated towards London. By 24 November William's forces were at Sherbourne and on 1 December at Hindon. On 4 December he was at Amesbury, and was received by the mayor of Salisbury. Three days later they had reached Hungerford, where the following day they met with the king's commissioners to negotiate. James offered free elections and a general amnesty for the rebels.

James was simply playing for time. His despair engendered at the last a simple desire for self-preservation and by now he had decided to flee the country. He feared that his English enemies would insist on his execution. Convinced that his army was unreliable, he sent orders for it to be disbanded.

After retreating from Salisbury, James's main force was stationed on Hounslow Heath. James posted an advance guard of 600 in Reading to stop the march of the Dutch towards London. These troops were composed of Irish Catholics under Patrick Sarsfield, who, wild rumour asserted, were planning to massacre the townsfolk.

While the Prince of Orange was in Hungerford, English supporters came into the town from all directions, including a body of several hundred cavalry headed by northern lords. On Saturday 8 December James sent Lord Halifax, Lord Nottingham and Lord Godolphin to Hungerford to confer with William. They were invited into William's bedroom to meet William and his advisers. James proposed to permit Parliament to debate all outstanding issues and in the meantime he asked that William's army should stay at least 30 miles outside London. William's advisers met in the Bear Inn under the chairmanship of Lord Oxford. After a long debate they rejected James's proposals, sending word to William of their decision. William in turn rejected their advice and decided to negotiate with James. In doing so, he kept up the pretence that he did not have his own designs on the English crown.

James sent part of his army to Reading to stop the march of the invasion force. The townspeople had already sent a messenger to William to ask for help. On Sunday 9 December a relief force of about 250 Dutch troops was sent to the town. Warned in advance of the Royalist positions, they attacked from an unexpected direction, and got into the centre of Reading. Forcing the Irish troops back, the Dutch attack was supported by Reading men shooting from their windows along Broad Street. The Dutch soon forced the Irish troops to retreat in confusion, leaving a number of their side slain, from 20 to 50 depending on the source. There were few deaths on the Dutch side, one being a Catholic officer. Many of the dead were buried in the churchyard of St Giles' Church.

James was already convinced that only Irish troops could be relied on to defend him, but this defeat by an inferior force and the willingness of the people of Reading to support a Dutch invasion, further underlined the desperate nature of his position. He fled London in abortive attempt to escape. William did not pursue, but instead dined lavishly at the University of Oxford. On 11 December, William set off for Abingdon, but on hearing of James's flight, he turned and headed down the Thames valley through Wallingford and Henley, accepting the submission of the Royalist troops he met on the way.

Anti-Catholic riots spread from London to Bristol, Bury St Edmunds, Hereford, York, Cambridge, and Shropshire. James knew his time was up. On the night of December 9/10, the Queen and the Prince of Wales fled for France. The next day James tried to escape, dropping The Great Seal in the Thames along the way, believing that no lawful parliament could be summoned without it. His personal talisman, the gold cross of Edward the Confessor, was snatched from him. He collapsed in the boat, crying and muttering to himself. He was captured that morning by fishermen in Faversham. The same day, 27 lords and bishops asked William to restore order but also suggested James should be returned to London to reach an honourable agreement.

On the night of the 11th there were more riots. The houses of Catholics and several foreign embassies of Catholic countries in London were looted. The following night a mass panic gripped London during what was later termed the Irish Night. False rumours of an impending Irish army attack on London circulated in the capital, and a mob of over 100,000 assembled ready to defend the city.

James was returned to London on 16 December and was welcomed by cheering crowds. He took heart from this and attempted to recommence government, even presiding over a meeting of the Privy Council. He sent the Earl of Faversham to William to arrange for a personal meeting to continue negotiations. Now for the first time it became evident to all that William had no desire, despite previous protestations, to keep James in power in England. He was well aware, however, that to imprison James would breach his own Declaration and strain relations with his wife Anne, the king's daughter. Instead, he played on James's own cowardice, saying his safety could no longer be guaranteed.

William ordered all English troops to leave the capital and his forces entered on 17 December. By then the English navy had openly declared for William. On 18 December William entered London, cheered by crowds dressed in orange ribbons or waving oranges that had been distributed in their thousands. The same day, Dutch officers loosely guarding the king were told that 'if he [James] wanted to leave, they should not prevent him, but allow him to gently slip through.' James duly left for France on 23 December after having received a face-saving plea from his wife to join her, even though his followers urged him to stay. The Archbishop of Rheims observed that James had 'given up three kingdoms for a Mass'.

William took over the provisional government, summoned an assembly of all the surviving members of parliament of Charles II's reign and set up an English convention with 513 elected members. After much constitutional wrangling over the legitimacy of the new set-up, with the ever-present danger of civil war, a new Bill of Rights was drawn up.

It listed twelve of James's policies by which James designed to 'endeavour to subvert and extirpate the protestant religion, and the laws and liberties of this kingdom'.

The Bill of Rights also vindicated and asserted the nation's 'ancient rights and liberties' by declaring, amongst much else, that the 'pretended' power to dispense with Acts of Parliament was illegal; that the election of MPs ought to be free; that freedom of speech and debates in Parliament 'ought not to be impeached or questioned in any court or place out of Parliament'. It also banned Catholics from both Parliament and, 'for ever', from the throne.

On 13 February the clerk of the House of Lords read the Declaration of Right and Lord Halifax, in the name of all the estates of the realm, asked William and Mary to accept the throne. William replied: 'We thankfully accept what you have offered us.' They then went in procession to the great gate at Whitehall. The Garter King of Arms proclaimed them King and Queen, whereupon they adjourned to the Chapel Royal, with Compton preaching the sermon.

They were crowned on 12 April, swearing an oath to uphold the laws made by Parliament. The Coronation Oath Act 1688 had provided a new coronation oath, whereby the monarchs were to 'solemnly promise and swear to govern the people of this kingdom of England, and the dominions thereunto belonging, according to the statutes in parliament agreed on, and the laws and customs of the same'.

On 19 April (Julian calendar) the Dutch delegation signed a naval treaty with England. It stipulated that the combined Anglo-Dutch fleet would always be commanded by an Englishman, even when of lower rank; it also specified that the two parties would contribute in the ratio of five English vessels against three Dutch vessels, meaning in practice that the Dutch navy in the future would be smaller than the English. On 18 May the new Parliament allowed William to declare war on France. On 9 September 1689, William as king of England joined the League of Augsburg against France.

❦ ❦

Much blood would be shed before William's authority was accepted in Ireland and Scotland.

In Scotland there had been no serious support for the rebellion; but when James fled for France, most members of the Scottish Privy Council went to London to offer their services to William. On 7 January they asked William to take over the responsibilities of government. On 14 March a Scottish Convention convened in Edinburgh, dominated by the Presbyterians because the Episcopalians continued to support James. On 4 April it decided that the throne of Scotland was vacant. On 11 May William and Mary accepted the Crown of Scotland.

Supporters of James were prepared to resist what they saw as an illegal coup by force of arms. The first Jacobite uprising in support of James in Scotland erupted in 1689, led by John Graham, 1st Viscount of Dundee, who raised an army from Highland clans. Dundee was pursued by a 3,500-strong force led by General Hugh Mackay, a Highlander who had been in Dutch service with the Scots Brigade for many years. 'Bonnie' Dundee, moving quickly, outmanoeuvred Mackay, but failed to pin him down. Dundee was determined to intercept Mackay near Blair Atholl, astride the road through the hills that Mackay would have to pass. Around 2,400 Highlanders caught the government forces in a narrow pass and after discharging their muskets swept down the hillside in a famous, blood-curdling charge. Mackay's men in the centre were 'swept away by the furious onset of the Camerons'. So fast was the Jacobite charge that many Government troops had insufficient time to fix their bayonets, leaving them defenceless at close quarters. The battle soon ended, with the entirety of Mackay's force fleeing the field. It quickly turning into a rout that killed 2,000. However, the cost of victory was enormous. About one-third of the Highlander force was killed and Dundee was fatally wounded towards the end of the battle. The Jacobite advance continued until it was stopped by government forces at the battles of Dunkeld and Cromdale.

In Ireland there was no equivalent of the English or Scottish Convention and William had to conquer by force. The English Convention presumed to legislate for Ireland as well, and the Declaration of Right deemed William to be King of Ireland as well as of England. Richard Talbot led local Catholics in a swift campaign that captured all the fortified places in the kingdom except Derry and so held the Kingdom for James. James himself landed in Ireland with 6,000 French troops to try to regain the throne.

In the meantime, the French realised that if communications between England and Ireland could be cut, the Anglo-Dutch troops would be stranded in a hostile land. A French fleet of around 100 ships under Admiral Anne Hilarion de Tourville entered the Channel in June 1690, aiming to destroy William's fleet. On the 30th, having passed the Lizard, Tourville met the Williamite fleet under Admiral Torrington off Beachy Head. Torrington put the Dutch ships in the lead and in the ensuing eight-hour battle they were badly mauled, with 400 dead and 500 wounded. Torrington was forced to retreat to the Thames estuary, again abandoning the Downs station.

In London many panicked, certain that a full-scale invasion was imminent. But William, through his spies, knew that the French had no plans to disembark. And Torrington's fleet, although mauled, was still a fighting force capable of destroying invasion barges. The French failed to follow up their advantage and instead of sailing into the Irish Sea to cut William's communications, they diverted to raid Teignmouth in Devon.

The port was looted and burnt and in the short term this only stiffened the resolve of the local population. A petition to the Lord Lieutenant from the townsfolk reported:

> … on the 26th day of this instant July 1690 by Foure of the clocke in the morning, your poor petitioners were invaded [by the French] to the number of 1,000 or thereabouts, who in the space of three hours tyme, burnt down to the ground the dwelling houses of 240 persons of our parish and upwards, plundered and carried away all our goods, defaced our churches, burnt ten of our ships in the harbour, besides fishing boats, netts and other fishing craft.

The local justices of the peace concluded:

> ... by the late horrid invasion there were within the space of 12 houres burnt downe and consumed 116 dwelling houses ... and also 172 dwelling houses were rifled and plundered and two parish churches much ruined, plundred and defaced, besides the burning of ten saile of shipps with the furniture thereof, and the goods and merchandise therein.

William issued a church brief that authorised the collection of £11,000 for the aid of the town. Churches from as far afield as Yorkshire contributed and the collections enabled the further development of the port.

The attack served no useful purpose for the French. However, it did prove that the French could make landfall on English soil, a lesson which would have consequences much later. Louis XIV, furious at the opportunity lost, dismissed Touville. Across the Channel, Torrington was also relieved of his command, although a court-martial later found him not guilty.

The war in Ireland continued until 1691. James fled Ireland following his defeat at the Battle of the Boyne, but Jacobite resistance was not ended until after the battle of Aughrim, when over half of their army was killed or taken prisoner. The Irish Jacobites surrendered under the conditions of the Treaty of Limerick on 3 October 1691. The Williamite victory in Ireland is still commemorated by the Orange Order for preserving British and Protestant dominance in the country.

Having England as an ally meant that the military situation of the Dutch Republic was strongly improved, but this very fact induced William to be uncompromising in his position towards France. That led to a large number of very expensive campaigns which were largely paid for with Dutch funds. In 1712 the Republic was financially exhausted; it withdrew from international politics and was forced to let its fleet deteriorate, making what was by then the United Kingdom the dominant maritime power of the world. The Dutch economy, already burdened by the high national debt and concomitant high taxation, suffered from the other European states' protectionist policies, which its weakened fleet was no longer able to resist. To make matters worse, the main Dutch trading and banking houses moved much of their activity from Amsterdam to London after 1688. Between 1688 and 1720, world trade dominance shifted from the Republic to Britain.

In North America, the Glorious Revolution precipitated the 1689 Boston revolt in which a well organised 'mob' of provincial militia and citizens deposed the hated governor Sir Edmund Andros, seen by some as a precedent for the American War of Independence a century later. In New York, Leisler's Rebellion caused the colonial administrator, Francis Nicholson, to flee to England. A third event, Maryland's Protestant Revolution, was directed against the proprietary government, seen as Catholic-dominated.

Princess Anne showed no concern when her father fled to France, and instead merely played her usual game of cards. She justified herself by saying that 'she was used to play and never loved to do anything that looked like an affected constraint.' She was given her reward after the deaths of Mary and then William when she became queen herself. Maureen Waller wrote that neither Mary nor Anne ever expressed a single regret over their betrayal of their father.

> Each of them in her own way had been a remarkable queen. They had done what they believed was right for their kingdoms and the Protestant religion, in which they had been indoctrinated from their childhood. They had presided over the painful transition from the turbulence of the seventeenth to the stability of the eighteenth century, heralding a more tolerant society, an age of booming commerce where Great Britain finally took its place as a great power.

Their father, and the Catholic population, would not have agreed with that verdict.

James was allowed to live in in exile in the royal château of Saint-Germaine. Some of his supporters in England attempted to restore him to the throne by assassinating William III in 1696, but the plot failed and the backlash made James's cause less popular. Louis XIV's offer to have James elected King of Poland in the same year was rejected, for James feared in his deluded mind that acceptance of the Polish crown might prevent him ever returning as king of England. During his last years, James lived as an austere penitent. He died of a brain hemorrhage on 16 September 1701. His body was laid in a coffin at the Chapel of Saint Edmund in the Church of the English Benedictines in the Rue St Jacques, Paris. He was not buried, but put in one of the side chapels. Lights were kept burning round his coffin until the French Revolution. In 1734 there was an attempt to have him canonised, but it failed.

The events of 1688-89 progressed in three more or less discrete stages: conspiracy, invasion and consolidation. The invasion was played down by Dutch propaganda that pretended it was a largely internal English affair. The Glorious Revolution is regarded as one of the most important events in the long evolution of the respective powers of Parliament and the Crown in England. With the passage of the Bill of Rights, it stamped out once and for all any possibility of a Catholic monarchy, and ended moves towards absolute monarchy. The powers of the monarch were greatly restricted. He or she could no longer suspend laws, levy taxes, make royal appointments or maintain a standing army during peacetime without Parliament's permission. Since 1689, government under a system of constitutional monarchy has been uninterrupted, and Parliament's powers have steadily increased as those of the Crown have declined. The Revolution led to the Act of Toleration 1689, which granted toleration to Nonconformist Protestants but not to Catholics, despite William's earlier promise.

The Revolution permanently ended any chance of Catholicism being re-established in England. For British Catholics its effects were disastrous both socially and politically: Catholics were denied the right to vote and sit in the Westminster Parliament for over a century; they were also denied commission in the army. The monarch was forbidden to be a Catholic or to marry a Catholic, a prohibition that continued until 28 October 2011, when this requirement was rescinded in a meeting of the 16 countries who still retain the British Monarch as the Head of State. It has been argued that James's overthrow began modern English Parliamentary democracy: the Bill of Rights has become one of the most important documents in the political history of Britain and never since has the monarch held absolute power. However, Tony Benn, like many others on the Left, disputes both the motives behind the invasion and the honesty of William's legislators, writing: 'Are we to welcome a Bill of Rights that says that papists could not sit in either House of Parliament?'

Internationally, the Revolution ended all attempts by England in the Anglo-Dutch wars of the seventeenth century to subdue the Dutch Republic by military force. However, the resulting economic integration and military co-operation between the English and Dutch Navies shifted the dominance in world trade to a Dutch-ruled England and later, to Great Britain.

Historian Frank McLynn saw 1688 as the great turning point that saw Britain achieve global dominance.

[The events of 1688] allied British and Dutch interests and put England on a collision course with France. From 1689 to 1815 these two powers engaged in a great worldwide struggle for colonies, raw materials and markets ... The monumental battle for economic preponderance was conducted on a vast scale, in North America and the Caribbean, in India and in South America and Africa too.

But Winston Churchill pointed out that William of Orange saw the invasion of England as a tiresome but necessary duty:

He was never fond of England or interested in her domestic affairs. Her seamy side was what he knew. He required the wealth and power of England by land and sea for the European war. He used the English public men who had been his confederates for his own ends, and he rewarded them for their services, but as a race he regarded them as inferior in fibre and fidelity to his Dutchmen.

William never bothered to hide his feelings and upset many with his long silences, his greedy table manners and his surliness. Many longed for the gaiety of the Jacobite court. But, as Churchill pointed out, the greatest dissatisfaction was felt within the English army, which was

... troubled in its soul. Neither officers nor men could dwell without a sense of humiliation upon the military aspects of the Revolution. They did not like to see all the most important commands entrusted to Dutchmen. They eyed sourly the Dutch infantry who paced incessantly the sentry-beats of Whitehall and St James's … As long as the Irish war continued, or whenever a French invasion threatened, these sentiments were repressed; but at all other times they broke forth with pent-up anger.

The Jacobite cause was far from dead. Many, particularly in Ireland and Scotland, continued to see the Stuarts as the legitimate monarchs of the Three Kingdoms. And that was to lead to another invasion of England.

11 THE FRENCH ARMADA OF 1692

'... if only this was for Ireland.'
– Patrick Sarsfield, 1693, reportedly his dying words

The Battle of La Hogue, by Adriaen van Diest.

The Jacobites were now the 'enemy within', aided by William's continued discrimination against Catholics. But it was the Jacobites in exile in the court of Louis XIV who would prove the most dangerous in the short term. When the French withdrew their force from Ireland, they took many Irish soldiers with them. They were known as the 'Wild Geese'. Effete courtiers and battle-hardened veterans combined to convince the Sun King that he could rely on a powerful Jacobite fifth column in England. Louis began to gather another armada.

One of the most impressive veterans was the 31-year-old Patrick Sarsfield, the first Earl of Lucan, a popular Irish hero of the Williamite war and the head of an Anglo-Norman family long settled in Ireland. In his youth he challenged Lord Grey over a slur on the Irish people and he was run through the body in another duel. In May 1682 he helped his friend Captain Robert Clifford to abduct Ann Siderlin, a wealthy widow, and was lucky not to be prosecuted. Then he abducted Elizabeth Herbert, the widowed daughter of Lord Chandos, on his own account. Elizabeth refused to marry him, but agreed not to prosecute him in exchange for her freedom. During the last years of Charles II's reign he saw service in the English regiments that were attached to the army of Louis XIV. The accession of James saw him return home.

He took part in the suppression of the Monmouth rebellion and in 1686 helped James reorganise the army to promote Catholics and purge Protestants. He went to Ireland under commander-in-chief Richard Talbot. He commanded a small Irish brigade after William had landed and saw action in the skirmishes at Wincanton and Reading (see previous chapter). But it was back in Ireland that he found martial glory. He secured Connaught for the Jacobites. James, with some reluctance because he regarded him as brave but not that bright, made him major-general. After the defeat at the Boyne he led 500 men and blew up a convoy of English stores, delaying the siege of Limerick until the winter rains forced the English to pull back. The incident made him a hero and increased James' affection for him. When both fled to France just before Christmas 1691, Sarsfield took his men with him in what became known as the Flight of the Wild Geese. According to the contemporary historian Gilbert Burnet, Sarsfield told English officers at Limerick: 'As low as we are now, change but kings with us and we will fight it over again with you.'

In total around 14,000 Irish fighting men left Ireland with Sarsfield. They included the larger-than-life Michael 'Galloping' Hogan, a former landowner and brigand. Sarsfield had given Hogan the honour of lighting the fuse which destroyed the English siege train. Sarsfield was disillusioned with what he regarded as the indecisiveness, bordering on cowardice, of his king. But he was still his king and he drilled similar loyalty into the Wild Geese.

Louis knew that there were Catholics who would rise to support James, but doubted whether they would be enough, especially given the failures of recent expeditions. Talk of another rebellious faction in England gave him heart. A powerful anti-Dutch Protestant faction was conspiring to oust William and Mary and place James's daughter Anne, Mary's sister, on the throne. At the heart of this tangled web, it was thought, was John Churchill and his wife Sarah, a close confidante of both sisters. When William heard of the plot he stripped Churchill of all his offices. Louis saw the potential of a combination of true Jacobites, mainly Catholics, and Protestant 'Anneites'. Anne could bring the Church of England on side, Churchill the army, and Admiral Edward Russell the navy. The scheme may have been fantastical, but Sarsfield and others convinced him it was a realistic scenario. He prepared for a full-scale invasion of England.

The mood at Louis's glittering new court at Versailles was behind such a grand plan. It was known that William was preparing to raid the French coast. The minister of war, the marquis de Louvois, who strongly opposed an invasion of England, had died. Both his replacement and the navy minister were raring to go.

Louis assembled an army of 24,000 during 1692 on the Cotentin peninsula in Normandy. Most of the infantrymen were Wild Geese. They were to be embarked at La Hogue under the command of the Duke of Berwick, James II's illegitimate son. The cavalry were to set off separately from Le Havre. The transport vessels were gathered. The Toulon fleet under Admiral d'Estrees was ordered from their Mediterranean station to join the main fleet under Admiral Tourville at Brest. Tourville would first take some transport ships to Torbay, both to make symbolic landfall at the port which he had raided before and to form a bridgehead. Tourville's main fleet would then return to link up with the d'Estrees squadron. Together they would keep open a cross-Channel ferry route for the invading army. William's English and Dutch fleets, it was assumed, were still languishing in their winter ports. Everything depended on secrecy to maintain the element of surprise; some hope in those cloak and dagger days.

William's intelligence service knew of the invasion plans, including the intended landing points, by April 1692. He focused on getting his fleets out to sea as fast as possible. Coastal defences were strengthened. The planned raids on the French coast were dropped to switch manpower to defence. The militia were called out, while regular troops were placed in a string of camps between Portsmouth and Petersfield. Farmers were ordered to move their cattle 15 miles inland from any point the French were sighted, a measure designed to deny forage to the invaders. Rumours of disaster abounded. The diarist John Evelyn noted on 5 May: 'The reports of an invasion, being now so hot, alerted the city, court and people exceedingly.'

The weather, however, was again in England's favour. By the start of May d'Estrees's squadron was still battling storms and had not joined Tourville at Brest. Tourville was unlucky enough to be under a royal chain of command: he was admiral of the fleet but strategic decisions were taken by kings Louis and James and their senior advisors. They both believed that the French victory at the Battle of Beachy Head two years earlier made them supreme at sea. The minister Compte de Pontchartrain sent Tourville orders to sail at the earliest possible moment and to give battle whatever the numbers the English could muster. Louis added a personal footnote in his own hand stressing that those orders must be obeyed unquestioningly. The invasion fleet's fate was sealed by the scrawl of a royal pen. Tourville would have to sail without d'Estrees' reinforcements. The Brest squadron was severely under-manned, forcing Tourville to leave 20 ships behind when he sailed on 29 April.

He began to advance up the Channel, linking up with Admiral Villette's squadron out of Rochefort. Even then his forces were inferior to those ranged against him. He had command of 44 ships of the line, including 11 80-gunners, and almost as many fireships and auxiliary vessels. But by now the English and Dutch fleets had merged and outnumbered the French by two to one. Intelligence reached Versailles and the king countermanded his original order to fight whatever the odds, but by then it was too late as Tourville was at sea.

William's naval commander Admiral Edward Russell coolly awaited the French advance off the Isle of Wight. At first light on 20 May the two fleets sighted each other 21 miles north of Cape Barfleur. Tourville saw the numbers ranged against him and realised that the invasion was a lost cause. At a hurried on-board conference his senior officers agreed. But he knew only of Louis's initial instructions, and orders were

The redoubtable shield wall of English Housecarles at Hastings, as depicted in the Bayeux Tapestry. The unarmoured man is the only example of an English bowman in the whole tapestry. His diminutive stature is indicative of his lowly rank.

King John hunting. He was criticised by many for pursuing pleasure instead of taking care of business in France.

A soldier of King John torturing prisoners. His livery indicates he serves John's General, the supposedly 'chivalric' William the Marshal. *Corpus Christi College, Cambridge*

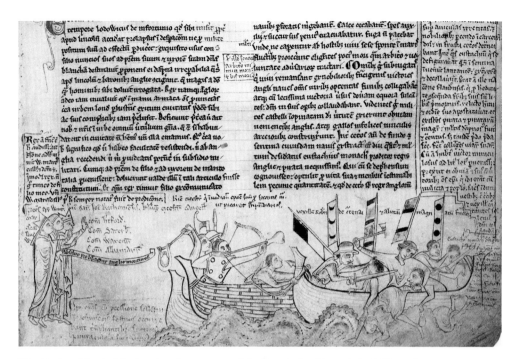

The Battle of Sandwich, showing the capture of the French flagship and the killing of Eustace the Monk, from Matthew Paris's *Chronica Majora*. *Corpus Christi College, Cambridge*

Edward III grants Aquitaine to the Black Prince; unknown artist, dated 1390. *British Library*

The Battle of Crecy, miniature from Froissart's Chronicles.

Late sixteenth-century copy of a portrait of Henry VII by unknown artist.
National Portrait Gallery

The *Mary Rose* as depicted in the Anthony Roll.

Carracks similar to the *Mary Rose* in battle in the Messina Straits, *c.*1561, by Frans Huys after Pieter Bruegel the Elder.

Elizabeth I and the Spanish Armada, the stylised panorama attributed to the celebrated miniaturist Nicholas Hilliard (1547-1619) who took part in the action.

Dutch ships bomb Tripoli in a punitive expedition against the Barbary pirates, *c.*1670, by Lieve Pietersz Verschuier.

French bombardment of Algiers by Admiral Duppere, 13 June 1830, by Antoine Leon Morel-Fatio.

Cornelius de Witt by Jan de Baen and workshop.

Prince William of
Orange landing at
Torbay, engraving by
William Miller after
J.M.W. Turner, published
in *The Art Journal*, 1852.

Bonnie Prince Charlie
after Robert Strange
(1725-1792).

Battle of Quiberon Bay – The Day After, by Richard Wright, 1760.

Engraving of the painting of 'Action Between the *Serapis* and the *Bonhomme Richard*' by Richard Paton, published 1780, engraver Balthasar Leizett. He personalised the action by calling it '*Combat mémorable entre Le Pearson et Paul Jones*'.

Famous depiction of John Paul Jones by J.M. Moreau le Jeune, engraved in Paris, 1780.

A commemorative medal created by Napoleon's engraver Romain-Vincent Jeuffroy, 'The Treaty of Amiens Broken by England, May 1803'. The Treaty provided a year-long cessation of hostilities between Britain and France during the Napoleonic Wars. The terms of the treaty were broken by both sides. *From* Napoleon's Medals: Victory to the Arts *by Richard A. Todd*

On 11 April 1814 Napoleon abdicated and the threat of invasion seemed to be over. The satirical British medal has Napoleon riding backwards on a donkey led by the Devil: 'Inseparable friends – to Elba'. *From* Napoleon's Medals: Victory to the Arts *by Richard A. Todd*

Two men who contributed so much to the abandonment of Operation *Sea Lion*, Hitler's planned invasion of Britain: R.J. Mitchell and Sir Henry Royce, pictured at RAF Colshot in 1931.

England's wooden walls eventually became steel. Seafires on the flight deck of a Royal Navy fleet carrier in 1943.

Some advice from the authorities on the island of Guernsey before the invasion. In late June and early July 1940, 17,000 of the population of 42,000 on the island were evacuated.

orders. His only hope was that English captains and crews would desert, as forecast by Sarsfield and other Jacobites. He sailed his fleet straight at the 80 English men-of-war. Russell and other allied commanders watched in awe as Tourville breached the generally prudent rules of naval engagement. The fleets slowly closed, Russell from the north-east, and Tourville from the south, on a starboard tack to bring his line of battle into contact with Russell's. Both fleets were in three squadrons, each split into three divisions and commanded by a flag officer. Favourable winds took the French in close but due to calm seas it was five hours after initial sighting before the two sides clashed. The result was an inferno in which the French sustained heavy casualties but did not lose a single ship.

Tourville had reinforced his centre, the White squadron under his own command, in order to engage Russell's Red squadron with close to equal numbers. Elsewhere, he sought to minimise damage by extending those ships in the van, to avoid them being turned and overwhelmed, while the rear was held back. Russell countered by holding fire as long as possible, to allow the French to come close. For the next few hours, both fleets bombarded each other, causing considerable damage. The English *Centurion* was engaged by *Ambitieux* and severely damaged; *Chester* was outgunned by *Glorieux* and had to withdraw. *Eagle* was forced to pull out of the line, with 70 dead, to repair damage, but was able to re-join after emergency repairs. *Grafton* suffered 80 casualties, but was also able to continue.

Tourville's flagship *Soleil Royal* was engaged by three English ships, Russell's flagship *Britannia*, supported by *London* and *St Andrew*. She was severely damaged and forced at one point out of the line. *Perle* was shot through and through, and suffered one-third of her crew as casualties. *Henri* and *Fort* were both severely damaged trying to hold the line between two squadrons, to prevent a gap opening; *Henri* was battered until she could no longer fight and only escaped capture when boats were sent to tow her to safety; *Fort* had to be pulled out of the line.

At about 1300 the light breeze strengthened and shifted to the east. This gave the weather to the allies, who immediately took advantage of it. Rear Admiral of the Red Sir Cloudesley Shovell saw a gap in the French line ahead of him, and steered towards it; his *Royal William* broke through to engage the French from both sides. He was followed by the rest of his division, while *Kent* and *St Albans* pulled round to follow the William through the breach. This allowed the Dutch to start enveloping the French van. The wind enabled the Dutch commander Philips van Almonde to extend and cross the head of the French line. Shovell's action brought Tourville's ships under fire from both sides. By 1500 *Prince* was hotly engaged on both sides, with a third across her stern. In the centre, Coetlogon and Tourville were engaged on either side by Shovell and Russell. An hour later the wind had died, the sea becoming flat calm, and visibility was hampered by battle smoke. The continuous firing also tended to push the embattled ships apart, offering some respite, as both sides were exhausted.

By 1700 the centres were re-engaged as Russell had used his boats to tow his ships back into action. The fog had lifted. As the wind strengthened, Tourville headed north-west towards Carter, in order to fight his way out of the encirclement.

Russell pursued, until the wind once again died away and the mist closed in once more. At 1800 Tourville was able to use the tide to gain a respite and at 2000 Shovell used the same tide for a fireship attack. That was dealt with by accurate French gunnery and at least one fireship exploded well out of harm's way.

By 2200 the battle was almost over. The evening was foggy and the tide turned. Again, Tourville took advantage of that, cutting his cables to be carried down-channel on the ebb, away from the scene of battle. Russell also cut when he realised what had happened, to give chase into the night. By now it was clear to all that the invasion was a lost cause despite Tourville's heroic action and superb seamanship. It was now that he would suffer his greatest losses as the English ruthlessly pursued crippled French ships. The winds and weather were against them and the French withdrawal was also hampered a lack of adequate anchors capable of withstanding the strong tidal races of the region, owing to cutbacks by the French Naval Ministry. For the same reason, there was also the lack of a fortified haven at Cherbourg.

First light saw the French fleet scattered into groups across a wide area. To the north four ships skirted the English coast and headed out into the Atlantic. They reached safety at Brest. To the south, six ships headed south-east towards the Normandy coast. Two of these would be beached at St Vaast la Hougue, while another two would later put into Le Havre, where *L'Entendu* was wrecked at the harbour entrance. The remaining two ships, *Monarque* and *Aimable*, passed through the Straits of Dover, went north around Britain and finally arrived safely at Brest.

Heading west was the main body in three groups: Villette leading with 15, followed by d'Amfreville with 12, and Tourville bringing up the rear with seven. During the day the French were able to close up, but Tourville was hampered by his efforts to save his flagship, *Soleil Royal*, which was in a pitiable condition. Later that day Tourville recognised this and transferred his flag to *L'Ambitieux*. In pursuit was Almonde and the Dutch fleet, with the various English divisions scattered behind. Many of these, particularly those of the English Red, were hampered by damage and lagged behind, leaving Almonde and Admiral of the Blue Sir John Ashby close to the French by the end of the day. Russell was forced to detach three ships to return to port for repairs.

The main French fleet anchored against the tide off Cap de la Hague. Thirteen ships with Tourville went to the east where the currents proved too powerful and several French ships dragged their anchors. Three of the most badly damaged were forced to beach at Cherbourg; the remaining 10 ships reached St Vaast la Hogue where they too were beached. Russell and the ships with him, together with some of Ashby's Blue squadron, also cut to pursue him, while Ashby and Almonde continued to shadow Pannetier's group. Admiral Pannetier made the hazardous passage through the treacherous, 15-mile Alderney Race, a task only achieved because he found among his crew an Alderney man, Hervel Riel, to act as pilot when his navigators baulked at the ordeal. Almonde and Ashby did not try to follow him and were criticised later by Russell for not doing so, although the only flag officer who knew the waters, Carter, had died of his wounds. Instead, Almonde attempted pursuit by taking his squadron west of Alderney, but the delay allowed Pannetier to pull too far ahead, and Almonde abandoned the chase. Pannetier later reached Saint Malo in safety, while Almonde and Ashby turned east to rejoin Russell at la Hogue.

Meanwhile, Russell chased Tourville eastward along the Cotentin coast. Without anchors Tourville was unable to do more than beach his ships, leaving three at Cherbourg and taking the remaining 12 to St Vaast la Hougue. The *Soleil Royal*, *Admirable*, and *Triomphant* were in such bad shape they had to be beached at Cherbourg. There they were destroyed by Vice-Admiral Delaval, attacking from long boats and with fireships.

Russell turned on the remaining ships which had sought refuge at La Hogue under the protection of the assembled land forces and a battery. The Dutch and English attacked with long boats. By now the French crews were exhausted and disheartened. The allies successfully deployed shore parties and fire ships, which burnt all 12 French ships. Just like the Spanish Armada, the journey home proved the deadliest part. Overall, including those that did limp home but were not repairable, Tourville lost 16 ships of the line and many smaller vessels, none of them in the set-piece battle.

Throughout England church bells tolled joyfully, preachers gave thanks, bonfires were lit, honours and rewards doled out and a Fleet Review aimed to show that England truly ruled the waves.

❦⸱❧

The battle of Barfleur-La Hogue was England's greatest naval victory to date, bigger even than the destruction of the Spanish Armada. It underlined to continental rivals the difficulties of mounting an invasion of England and no repeat was attempted for 50 years. Not until the Seven Years War would the navy win a greater victory.

The dispersal of the French fleet put an end to the invasion plans and the French abandoned the idea of seeking naval superiority for its own sake, adopting instead a continental strategy on land and pursuing a war against trade at sea.

However, the battle quickly faded from the consciousness of the British public. One reason was that the victorious Admiral Russell was not afforded the plaudits of others due to his tactlessness and lack of servility at court. Later, he was unable to disguise his contempt for Queen Anne's armchair generalship and ignored her orders to divide his force to guard against a later, but bogus, invasion threat. Another is that the propaganda value was mixed and there was no mileage in stressing a British victory against a heroically weaker foe. In France it is celebrated as a tale of unbelievable heroism against the odds. This disparity in English and French memories is another reason why the battle, celebrated in its day, is not celebrated in Britain in the same way as many lesser victories.

The English saw it as a single action over six days; the French as three separate battles Barfleur, Cherbourg and La Hogue. Both sides regarded the outcome differently. The English claim an outright victory, the French, while acknowledging La Hogue and Cherbourg as defeats, claimed Barfleur as a victory. Both sides, however, acknowledged the ferocious fighting ability of the French at Barfleur.

Many historians agree that the 1692 invasion bid was a close-run thing. If Tourville had been allowed to wait for d'Estrees he could have landed his French-Irish force, secured a quick victory and put James II back on the throne. History is full of such 'ifs.'

For Sarsfield and the Jacobites it was a disaster. For James it was a psychological blow from which he never recovered. He regarded it as divine judgement and morosely retreated into the seclusion of the monastery of La Trappe. Louis XIV gave up notions of invasion, largely because he was militarily at full stretch fighting the War of Spanish Succession (1701–13). The French navy, however, continued to attack and capture English and Dutch merchantmen at every opportunity.

Admiral Tourville was feted for his courage and, rarely for the times, not blamed for his losses, as was fair given his initial orders. In June 1693, he defeated a convoy of 59 English ships commanded by George Rooke at Cape St Vincent. He retired after the Peace of Ryswick and died in Paris on 23 May 1701, aged 59, a national hero.

Louis made Sarsfield a merechal-de-camp and the Anglo-Irishmen fought bravely in Flanders. He was mortally wounded at the battle of Landen on 19 August 1693 and died two or three days later. His dying words reportedly included: 'Oh, if only this were for Ireland.' In the twentieth century his descendant, Lord Lucan, notoriously disappeared after the murder of the family's nanny.

Galloping Hogan became a general in the French Army but in 1706 he was forced to leave France after killing a fellow officer in a duel in Flanders. He fled to Portugal and in 1712 led the Portuguese Army against the Spanish at the Battle of Campus Maior. He died in his adopted country.

Others of the Wild Geese fought in Cuba and South America, far from home. Many of their descendants remain there.

12 THE JACOBITE INVASION OF ENGLAND

'In person … not ill-suited to his lofty pretensions'
– Mr Home, Edinburgh, 1745

The March of the Guard to Finchley by William Hogarth, 1749-50, Thomas Coram Foundation.

A victorious army marched steadily down England's spine, throwing London into panic. At its head was a charismatic prince prone to temper tantrums. By the time they reached Derby he was in such a sulk that he would not speak to his brilliant army commander.

This was the closest the Jacobites came to achieving their grand aim. Once again brave men would be let down by aristocratic flaneurs.

James II died a broken man in 1701, convinced his God had deserted him. His successor was his only legitimate son, James Francis Edward Stuart, whose birth in 1688 had been the pretext for the Glorious Revolution which had deposed his father. His supporters proclaimed him James III of England and Ireland and James VIII of Scotland. Louis XIV and Pope Clement XI formally recognised the Catholic monarch. The Pope offered James the Palazzo Muti in Rome as his residence and a life annuity of 8,000 Roman scudi. Such aid enabled him to organise a Roman Jacobite court.

The outbreak of the War of the Spanish Succession in 1701 renewed French support for the Jacobites. In 1708 James Stuart, the Old Pretender, sailed from Dunkirk with 6,000 French troops in nearly 30 ships of the French navy. His intended landing in the Firth of Forth was thwarted by the Royal Navy under Admiral Byng. The British pursued the French fleet, forcing them to retreat round the north of Scotland, losing ships and most of their men in shipwrecks on the way back to Dunkirk.

Following the arrival from Hanover of King George I in 1714, Tory Jacobites in England conspired to organise armed rebellions against the new Hanoverian government. They were indecisive and frightened by government arrests of their leaders.

The Treaty of Utrecht ended hostilities between France and Britain. From France, as part of widespread Jacobite plotting, James Stuart had been corresponding with the Earl of Mar. In the summer of 1715 James called on Mar to raise the Clans. Mar, nicknamed Bobbin' John, rushed from London to Braemar. He summoned clan leaders to 'a grand hunting-match' on 27 August 1715. Early the following month he proclaimed James as 'their lawful sovereign' and raised the old Scottish standard. Mar's proclamation brought in an alliance of clans and northern Lowlanders, who quickly overran many parts of the Highlands.

Mar's Jacobites captured Perth on 14 September without opposition and his army grew to around 8,000 men. A force of fewer than 2,000 under the Duke of Argyll held the Stirling plain for the government and Mar indecisively kept his forces in Perth, waiting for the Earl of Seaforth to arrive with a body of northern clans. Seaforth was delayed by attacks from other clans loyal to the government. Planned risings in Wales, Devon and Cornwall were nipped in the bud with the arrest of local ringleaders.

A rising in the north of England early in October was more successful and grew to about 300 horsemen under the Northumberland squire Thomas Forster. They joined forces with a rising in the south of Scotland under Viscount Kenmure. Mar sent a Jacobite force under Brigadier William Mackintosh to join them. They left Perth on 10 October and were ferried across the Firth of Forth from Burntisland to East Lothian. They attacked Edinburgh, which was undefended, but having seized Leith citadel they were pushed back by the arrival of Argyll's forces. Mackintosh's force of about 2,000 then made their way south and met their allies at Kelso in the Scottish borders on 22 October. They wasted precious days arguing over strategy. The Scots wanted to fight government forces in the vicinity or attack Dumfries and Glasgow, but the English were determined to march towards Liverpool, claiming that there were 20,000 Jacobite recruits in Lancashire eager to fight.

The Highlanders resisted marching into England and there were some mutinies and defections, but the combined army pressed on with the second option. Instead of the expected welcome the Jacobites were met by hostile militia armed with pitchforks, and very few recruits. They were unopposed in Lancaster and found about 1,500 recruits as they reached Preston on 9 November, bringing their force to around 4,000. General Charles Wills was ordered to halt their advance and left Manchester on 11 November with six regiments, arriving on the 12th. The Jacobite leader Thomas Forster had intended to move on that day, but learning of Wills' approach decided to stay and foolishly withdrew troops from a strong defensive position at Ribble bridge, half a mile outside Preston.

The Jacobites barricaded the principal streets and Wills ordered an immediate attack, which met with fire from the barricades and houses. The government attack was repulsed with heavy losses. Wills ordered the torching of houses in the hope that the fires would spread along to the Jacobite positions. The Jacobites retaliated with similar tactics, creating a minor inferno as night fell. Snipers on both sides took advantage of the light cast by the flames. In the battle, 17 Jacobites were killed and 25 wounded. Government casualties, killed and wounded, approached 300. But the Jacobites were in an impossible position and by the morning of Sunday the 12th many Jacobites had quietly left their positions.

More government forces arrived and Wills belatedly stationed troops to prevent the remaining Jacobites from escaping. Although the Highlanders wanted to fight on, Forster agreed to open negotiations with Wills for capitulation on favourable terms. He did not tell the Highlanders and when they learnt of it they were enraged and paraded the streets threatening any Jacobites who might even allude to surrender, killing or wounding several who disagreed. Another night cooled heads, however, and they grudgingly lined up with Forster's men to lay down their arms in unconditional surrender. In all, 1,468 Jacobites were taken prisoner, 463 of them English. The Earl of Seton, the Viscount of Kenmure, the Earl of Nithsdale and the Earl of Derwentwater were among those captured and sentenced to death. Many of their clansmen were transported to America. The battle of Preston is often claimed to have been the last fought on English soil, but in fact there were further skirmishes over the next two centuries.

Meanwhile, in Scotland, at the Battle of Sheriffmuir on 13 November, Mar's forces were unable to defeat a smaller force led by the Duke of Argyll. Mar retreated to Perth while the government army built up. Belatedly, on 22 December 1715 a ship from France brought the Old Pretender to Peterhead, but he was too consumed by melancholy and fits of fever to inspire his followers. He briefly set up court at Scone, visited his troops in Perth and ordered the burning of villages to hinder the advance of the Duke of Argyll through deep snow. The Highlanders were cheered by the prospect of battle, but James's counsellors decided to abandon the endeavour and ordered a retreat to the coast, giving the excuse of seeking a stronger position. James boarded a ship at Montrose and fled back to France on 4 February 1716, leaving a message telling his Highland supporters to shift for themselves. What had briefly turned into an embryonic civil war across the north of Britain ended in ignominy and regal betrayal.

In the aftermath of the 'Fifteen', the Disarming Act and the Clan Act aimed to
subdue the Highlands. Government garrisons were built or extended in the Great
Glen at Fort William, Kiliwhimin and Fort George, Inverness, as well as barracks at
Ruthven, Bernera and Inversnaid, linked to the south by roads constructed for Major-
General George Wade. The government also attempted to 'win hearts and minds' by
allowing the bulk of the defeated rebels to slip away back to their homes and com-
mitting the first £20,000 of revenue from forfeited estates to the establishment of
Presbyterian-run, Scots-speaking schools in the Highlands. That was not generosity,
rather part of a process aimed at eradicating the Gaelic language.

With France at peace with Britain, the Jacobites found a new ally in Spain's
Minister to the King, Cardinal Guilio Alberoni. His plan was first to land 300 Spanish
marines to join up with rebellious clansmen under George Keith, the Earl Marischal
and divert English forces while the main fleet of 27 ships and 7,000 men under James
Butler, the exiled Duke of Ormonde, would disembark in south-west England or
Wales, where Jacobites were believed to be abundant. The resulting alliance would
march east to besiege London, depose George I and enthrone James Stuart.

Three weeks after leaving Cadiz, Ormonde's fleet ran into a storm near Cape
Finistere that dispersed and damaged most of the ships. Ormonde was forced to withdraw to several Spanish havens. By then, Keith had already left the Spanish port of
Pasala and occupied the Isle of Lewis, including Stornoway where he set camp. On
13 April 1719, Keith's Spaniards disembarked near Lochalsh, although the Highlanders
did not join the 'Little Rising' in the expected numbers, mistrusting the whole enterprise and with bitter memories of Preston still fresh. Keith established his headquarters
in the castle of Eilean Donan. They were joined by a few hundred Highlanders. Some
days later, the main body of the troop went south to stir up the Highlanders, leaving a
small garrison of less than 50 men at the castle. The Jacobite forces were to be led by
the Earl of Seaforth. Their plan of action was to capture Inverness.

The government deployed sea power. At the beginning of May, the Royal Navy
sent five ships to the area for reconnaissance: two patrolling off Skye and three around
Lochalsh, adjacent to Loch Duich. Early in the morning on Sunday 10 May, the latter
three, HMS *Worcester*, HMS *Llamborough* and HMS *Enterprise*, anchored off Eilean
Donan. A boat went ashore under a flag of truce to negotiate, but when the Spanish
soldiers in the castle fired at it, all three warships bombarded the castle for an hour.
Only a fresh gale prevented utter destruction. The next morning, acting on intelligence from a Spanish deserter, Captain Boyle of the *Worcester* sent the *Enterprise* up the
river to capture a house being used to store gunpowder but the rebels on the shore set
it on fire as the ship approached. The other two ships resumed the bombardment while
a landing party was prepared. In the evening, under the cover of an intense cannonade,
the ships' boats went ashore and captured the castle against little resistance. Inside they
found 'an Irishman, a captain, a Spanish lieutenant, a sergeant, one Scots rebel and 39
Spanish soldiers, 343 barrels of powder and 52 barrels of musket shot'. The government troops burnt corn stored in several barns, demolished the castle with 27 barrels of
gunpowder over the next two days and sent the Spanish prisoners to Edinburgh.

After a month of aimless wandering the main body of Spaniards realised that Ormonde would never come. Despite that, they attracted some more clansmen and prepared for one last battle with a force of barely 1,000 men. On 5 June, government forces composed of both English and Scottish soldiers under General Joseph Wightman came from Inverness to block their march. They consisted of 850 infantry, 120 dragoons and 4 mortar batteries. They confronted the Jacobites and Spaniards at Glen Shiel, just a few miles from Loch Duich, on 10 June. The Galician regiment occupied the top and the front of a hill, while the Jacobite Scots manned barricades on the sides. The great natural strength of the Jacobite position was increased by hasty barricades across the road and on the north side of the hill.

The Battle of Glen Shiel began before 0600. The left wing of the government army advanced against Lord George Murray's position on the south side of the river after the Jacobite line was softened up by mortar fire. Resistance was initially stubborn, but Murray's men were unsupported and forced to retreat. Wightman ordered his right wing to attack the Jacobite left commanded by Lord Seaforth, which was sheltered by rocky outcrops. It proved a hot fight and Seaforth was reinforced. But before a second body under Robert Roy MacGregor could reach him, a government surge took the position. Wightman concentrated his troops on the flanks, while the mortars battered the Spanish positions. The Spanish regulars stood firm until their Scottish allies deserted them. They retreated uphill and finally surrendered that evening, three hours after the first shots. The Jacobites who escaped were low on provisions and most of their ammunition was spent. Spirits fell, the rising was abandoned and the lucky ones got home.

Three of the Jacobite commanders, Lord George Murray, William Mackenzie, the Earl of Seaforth, and Robert Roy MacGregor, were badly wounded. John Cameron of Lochiel, however, after hiding for a time in the Highlands, made his way back into exile in France. George Keith, chief of Clan Keith and the last Earl Marischal, fled into exile in Prussia. In spite of a later pardon, Keith never returned to Britain and became the Prussian ambassador to France and later, to Spain. The 274 Spanish prisoners were reunited with their comrades in Edinburgh and by October, negotiations allowed their return to Spain.

In 1725 General Wade raised the independent companies of the Black Watch as a militia to keep peace in the unruly Highlands, but in 1743 they were moved to fight the French in Flanders. Their commander at the Battle of Fontein in May 1745 was the Duke of Cumberland, soon to earn the epithet 'Butcher'.

The War of the Austrian Succession drew Britain and France into unofficial hostilities. Leading English Jacobites made a formal request to France for armed intervention and the French king's Master of Horse secretly toured southern England meeting Tories and discussing their proposals. In November 1743 Louis XV authorised a large-scale invasion of southern England scheduled for February 1744. It was to be a surprise attack: troops were to march from their winter quarters to hidden invasion barges which were to take them and Charles Stewart to Maldon in Essex, where they were to be joined by local Tories in an immediate march on London. The Young

Pretender was in exile in Rome with his father and rushed to France. As late as mid-February, the British were still unaware of the invasion plans. But on 24 February one of the worst storms of the century scattered the French fleet, sinking one ship and putting five out of action and wrecking many barges as they embarked 10,000 troops. Some of the latter were sunk with all hands lost. The invasion was cancelled.

＠‑＠

'Bonnie Prince Charlie' was born in the Palazzo Muti, Rome on 31 December 1720, in his father's loaned papal residence. He spent almost all his childhood in that city and in Bologna, living an opulent life of privilege. He was raised a Catholic in a loving if fractious family, which instilled in him an unshakeable belief in both his right to kingship and the divine rights of kings. His father, swinging between depression and optimism, talked of little else other than regaining the throne of England and Scotland for the Stuart dynasty.

Early in 1744, a small number of Highland clan chieftains promised that they would rise if he arrived with as few as 3,000 French troops. He tirelessly petitioned his French hosts, often to their irritation, to commit to another invasion. He also planned to use his own royal body to force their hands. In secret he wooed a consortium of Nantes privateers and together they fitted out a small frigate, the *Du Teillay*, and a ship of the line, the *Elisabeth*, funding what was ostensibly a privateering mission by borrowing from exiled Scottish bankers and by pawning his mother's jewellery. He left Nantes bound for Scotland in July 1745, leaving a personal letter to Louis asking for help in the planned rising.

The *Elisabeth*, carrying 700 Irish Brigade volunteers, met HMS *Lion* and in the ensuing battle both vessels were badly damaged. The *Elisabeth* was forced back, but the *Du Teillay* successfully landed Charles with his seven men of Moidart on the island of Eriskay in the Outer Hebrides on 2 August 1745.

The Scottish clans at first showed only muted enthusiasm for his arrival without the expected troops, supplies and munitions, but Charles went on to raise the Scottish standard in his father's name on the mainland at Glenfinnan on 19 August. Around 1,200 clansmen joined him there, mostly from the clans MacDonald, Ranald, Keppoch and Cameron. Despite nationalist myth, not all those who joined the standard were genuine volunteers. The Cameron of Lochiel's notoriously vicious brother beat clansmen and threatened their families with eviction if they did not join the cause. The Jacobite force marched south, increasing to almost 3,000 men, some of them enthused, others more reluctant.

Britain was still in the middle of the War of the Austrian Succession and most of the British army was in Flanders and Germany, leaving an inexperienced force of about 4,000 in Scotland under Sir John Cope. He marched north into the Highlands but, believing the rebel force to be stronger than it really was, avoided an engagement and withdrew northwards to Inverness. The Jacobites captured Perth and at Coatbridge routed two regiments of the government's dragoons. In Edinburgh there was panic

with a melting away of the City Guard and Volunteers, and when the city gate at the
Netherbow Port was opened at night to let a coach through, a party of Camerons
rushed the sentries and seized control of the city. The next day, King James VIII was
proclaimed at the Mercat Cross. A triumphant Charles received joyous acclaim from
Edinburgh citizens, particularly when he chose not to enter the city on horseback,
but on foot. He stopped for a few minutes at Holyrood Palace to exhibit himself to
the people. One of the spectators, a Mr Home, wrote:

> In person Charles appeared to great advantage, not ill-suited to his lofty pre-
> tensions. He was in the bloom of youth, tall and handsome, and of a fair and
> ruddy complexion. His face, which in its contour exhibited a perfect oval, was
> remarkable for the regularity of its features. His forehead was full and high,
> and characteristic of his family. His eyes, which were large, and of a light blue
> colour, were shaded by beautifully arched eye-brows, and his nose, which was
> finely formed, approached nearer to the Roman than the Grecian model. A
> pointed chin, and a mouth rather small, gave him, however, rather an effeminate
> appearance; but on the whole, his exterior was extremely prepossessing, and his
> deportment was so graceful and winning, that few persons could resist his attrac-
> tions. The dress which he wore on the present occasion was also calculated to set
> off the graces of his person to the greatest advantage in the eyes of the vulgar.

Cope's army were supplied from Inverness then sailed from Aberdeen to meet the
Jacobites near Prestonpans to the east of Edinburgh. On 21 September 1745 a surprise attack planned by Lord George Murray routed the government forces. Charles
wrote again to France pleading for a prompt invasion of England. There was alarm
south of the border, and in London a patriotic song which included a prayer for
Marshal Wade's success in crushing the rebels was performed, later to become the
National Anthem.

The Jacobites held the city of Edinburgh, but not the castle. Charles held court
at Holyrood for five weeks but despite the great admiration and enthusiasm on
show he failed to raise a regiment locally. Many of the Highlanders went home with
booty from the Prestonpans battlefield and recruiting resumed. The French now sent
some weapons and funds; and assurances that they would carry out their invasion of
England by the end of the year. Charles's council of war led by Murray was against
leaving Scotland, but he told them that he had received English Tory assurances of a
rising if he appeared in England in arms, and the council agreed by a margin of just
one vote to march south. The Jacobite army of around 6,000 men started southward
on 3 November.

The victory at Prestonpans had been almost entirely due to Lord George Murray's
boldness and tactical skills, leading the attack on the English lines himself on his
own initiative. But as Lieutenant General he was in command of an invasion he had
grave doubts about. At the age of 18 Murray had enlisted in the army in Flanders
and three years later, against his father's wishes, he had joined the 1715 rebellion.

He commanded a regiment of Atholl men and was captured at Preston. He escaped and fled to France. He was active too in the 1719 debacle and was wounded at Glen Shiel. He hid for several months in the Highlands before escaping to Rotterdam. He was rumoured to have fought with the Sardinian army and was able to return to Scotland when his father died in 1726, after receiving a pardon as a dynastic courtesy. He had been a passionate opponent of the 1707 Acts of Union, but he finally took the Oath of Allegiance in 1739. When Prince Charles landed on Scottish soil he was sceptical about re-joining the Jacobite cause. He even dined with Sir John Cope, commander of the government troops, a meeting which fuelled later claims of duplicity. But Murray declared for Charles in September at Blair Castle. He told his brother that he was acting out of conscience whilst knowing it could ruin him. Upon joining the army, he was made Lieutenant General, but Charles' secretary John Murray intrigued against him and insinuated he was a traitor. George Murray treated such claims with contempt and concentrated on building discipline and confidence in his new army. He successfully won the respect of the Highland levies, and dissuaded Charles from interfering with their civil rights.

Although Murray had disagreed with Charles' plans to invade England, when the decision was made, he persuaded the prince to march for Cumberland where the terrain suited the Highlanders, rather than mount a direct attack on the English army assembled under General Wade at Newcastle. But first the Jacobites had to traverse the Lowlands. Success at Prestonpans had not, as is often claimed, left the rebels in control of Scotland, for the great bulk of the population remained bitterly hostile to the absolutist Stuarts who had previously presided over the notorious persecutions known as Scotland's 'Killing Times'. When the rebels passed near the town of Ecclefechan in Dumfriesshire, local loyalists mounted a raid on their baggage train. The army crossed the border into Cumberland.

Murray orchestrated the siege of Carlisle, but was constantly frustrated by the prince's interference, his impatience and his hot-headed bravado. When the town surrendered on 14 November, Murray resigned his command because his authority had been undermined and obtained permission to serve as a volunteer in the Atholl levies. The army however, were unhappy with his replacement, the Duke of Perth, and an apparently chastened Charles quickly reinstated Murray.

At Manchester about 250 Episcopalians formed a regiment, but no other Englishmen joined the prince. At the end of November, French ships arrived in Scotland with 800 men from the Écossais Royeaux (Royal Scots) and Irish regiments of the French army. The Jacobite army, however, was reduced by desertions to under 5,000 men. Murray, a tactician of genius, steered it around a second government army under the Duke of Cumberland and marched on Derby. A myth has grown that London was defenceless and might easily have fallen to the rebels had they advanced in 1745. In fact, London was garrisoned by significant forces at that time and King George II had no intention of abandoning his capital.

Charles and his army arrived in Derbyshire at the beginning of December and was met by cheering crowds in Ashbbourne, where in a speech to the assembled citizens in the market place, he proclaimed his father, James III, as rightful king. On 3 December word reached Derby that a rebel army up to 10,000 strong was approaching the gates. The Duke of Devonshire, commander of the newly formed Derbyshire Blues billeted in and around the George Inn on Irongate, chose discretion rather than valour. He took his men 50 miles to Retford, leaving Derby undefended.

The entry of the Jacobites on 4 December was carefully staged to give the impression that Charles had a force vastly superior to the bedraggled reality. At 1100 his vanguard, consisting of thirty horse, entered the town and ordered quarters for 9,000 men. About 1500 of Charles's life guards and some of the principal officers arrived on horseback. These were followed during the course of the evening by the main body, which entered in detached parties to make the army appear as numerous as possible. Charles himself slipped into the town on foot at nightfall.

About 70 Highlanders were sent to secure Swarkestone Bridge, reaching it four hours ahead of government troops, who had orders to destroy it to stop the prince's army from crossing, as it was the only route south to London. The 70 held the bridge whilst the prince and his generals held a council of war at Exeter House. As ever, the prince sulked and dithered, and the courage of his troops was wasted. Swarkestone Bridge proved the farthest point south reached by Charles's troops, less than 125 miles from London.

On 5 December Murray urged the prince to retreat, citing the lack of support from France and English Jacobites. But Murray's main concern may have been the prince's constant interference and carping. Murray's aide-de-camp, James Chevalier de Johnstone, wrote: 'Had Prince Charles slept during the whole of the expedition, and allowed Lord George Murray to act for him according to his own judgment, he would have found the crown of Great Britain on his head when he awoke.' A resentful Charles, jealous of his brilliant general, was by then barely on speaking terms with Murray. Charles was advised of progress on the French invasion fleet which was then assembling at Dunkirk, but at his council of war he was forced to admit he had greatly exaggerated the number of potential Jacobite recruits in England. While Charles was determined to press on in the deluded belief that their success was certain as regular soldiers would never dare to fight against their true prince, his council and Lord George Murray pointed out their uncomfortable position in the real world. The promised English support had not materialised, both Wade and Cumberland were approaching, London was heavily defended and there was a fictitious report from a government double agent of a third army closing on them. They insisted that their army should return to join the growing force in Scotland. This time, only Charles voted to continue the advance. He assented while throwing a tantrum and vowing never to consult the council again. He said bitterly: 'In future, I shall summon no councils since I am accountable to nobody for my actions but to God, and my father, therefore I shall no longer ask or accept advice.' He never forgave Murray for forcing him to back down. At daybreak on 6 December the Jacobites sullenly began their retreat, with a petulant Charles refusing to take any part in running the campaign. Fortunately, military command was retained by Murray, whose inspired feints and careful planning were to extract the army virtually intact. The French, hearing of the retreat, cancelled their invasion, which was by then ready to go. English Tories in London who had pledged Charles support went to ground.

Initially, most of Charles's officers were unaware they were retreating. The council believed that if this had been understood by the whole army, there would have been wholesale mutiny. To keep them unaware of their destination, a quantity of powder and ball was distributed amongst the men, as if they were going into action. The Highlanders were cheerful at the prospect of closing with the enemy, but in full daylight they realised they were merely retracing their steps and their mood changed to one of rage and melancholy. It was said that the retreat of a badly defeated army, which they were not, could not have been gloomier. The prince, still in a sulk and unwilling to face his men, stayed in his quarters until late in the morning before riding directly back to Ashbourne.

The main body of the demoralised Jacobite army camped on the first night in Ashbourne before reaching Leek the following day. The town was too small to accommodate the whole army, so two regiments of foot went on to Macclesfield. The rest of the army caught up the next day, while the advance body moved forward to Stockport. On the 9th, both of the Jacobite divisions met on the road to Manchester and entered the city as one body. They left the next day and reached Preston, where they stayed until the 12th.

James Drummond, the Duke of Perth, was despatched with 100 horse to travel north and bring reinforcements from Perth. The prince and his army arrived in Lancaster on the evening of the 13th. There, Charles decided to stand and fight. Murray and Cameron of Lochiel conducted a survey of the surrounding ground. They found it a suitable place for a battle, but when Charles heard that a large body of General George Wade's dragoons had entered Preston not long after they had left, he changed his mind. The march north resumed.

The government forces under General Wade and the Duke of Cumberland did not arrive in Macclesfield until 10 December, the day the Jacobites had arrived in Wigan. At Macclesfield the Duke heard that Charles had left Manchester and decided to snap at his heels. Leaving Lancaster on the 15th, Charles' army was scarcely out of the town by one gate when they heard troops of British horse clattering right behind them. The Jacobites formed in order of battle, but it turned out to be a false alarm. The army continued its march towards Kendal. Troops of English horse were indeed threatening their rear for three miles, but refused to engage. The Jacobite army entered Kendal that night, where they were met by the Duke of Perth and his party. On his way north, the Duke had been attacked by a mob, which he soon dispersed with volley fire. Near Penrith he met with a more serious obstruction, being attacked by a considerable body of militia, both horse and foot, and vastly outnumbered, he was obliged to retreat to Kendal. The army, apparently beset by peril on all sides, marched to the village of Shap where they overnighted. On the 17th, the Jacobite army marched to the village of Clifton, Cumberland.

On the morning of the 18th the Jacobite rearguard left Shap and parties of English light horse followed some distance behind them. Murray informed Charles of the danger, but it was assumed the distant horsemen were militia. The threat was not taken seriously. The cavalry was comprised of between 200 and 300 of Cumberland's men riding two abreast. When they disappeared behind a hill they made a great clamour with kettledrums and trumpets. That halted the Clan MacDonnell of Glengarry regiment, with Murray himself at their head. The Jacobite commanders now believed that the whole of Cumberland's force was close.

Several Jacobite officers charged forward with four companies, sword in hand, to open a passage through the supposed enemy army. Murray ordered his regiment to ascend the hill by another route, as supply wagons were blocking the main road. The two units scaled the hill and met at the summit, roaring battle cries and mad for action. They were astonished to discover not an army, merely the relative handful of light horse they had previously observed. The English cavalry, equally astonished at the two-pronged attack, fled in utter disorder. One unfortunate trooper fell from his steed and was instantly cut to pieces.

Murray and the rear-guard resumed the march and at the village of Clifton he sent the artillery and heavy baggage forward to Penrith under a small escort. In the parklands surrounding Lowther Hall the Glengarry regiment pursued some enemy horsemen but captured only two of them. These prisoners informed Murray that Cumberland himself, with a body of 4,000 horse, was about a mile behind him. Clifton was clearly a defensible position and Murray decided to hold them there with around 200 men augmented by Macpherson and Stewart of Appin clansmen. Behind hedges either side of the road he posted the Glengarry men, the Stewarts and the Macphersons. Close to the village, he placed Colonel Roy Stuart's regiment. Other skilled deployments meant that they could fire at the enemy's flank when they attacked.

Cumberland formed his men and about 500 dragoons dismounted and advanced forward to the foot of the moor. Colonel Stuart returned from Penrith but the prince's order was that he should immediately retreat back there. In the situation which the Lieutenant General was now faced, it was impossible to obey this order without great danger, as the dismounted government horse were already firing upon the Jacobites. Instead, Murray went on the attack. The Macdonnells of Glengarry men were ordered to move forward and keep up a smart fire until they came to the lowest ditch. Murray knew that if they succeeded in dislodging the enemy from the hedges and ditches, they could give them a flank fire within pistol-shot; but he gave them particular orders not to fire across the highway, or to follow the enemy up the moor. After speaking with every officer of the Glengarry regiment, Murray returned to the left, and placed himself at the head of the Macphersons.

It was an hour after sunset and the night was cloudy, but at short intervals the moon broke through and the Jacobites could see the disposition of the enemy, while their own movements could not be observed. The clansmen marched forward, firing as they advanced, but the Macphersons on the left soon came into contact with the English dragoons. Murray then drew his sword and cried: 'Claymore!' Clan chief Cluny Macpherson echoed him and his men rushed down to the bottom ditch, clearing the diagonal hedges as they went. They fell upon the enemy, many of whom were killed at the lower ditch, hacked down by Highland swords. The rest retreated across the moor, under the fire of the MacDonnell of Glengarry regiment.

Twelve Jacobites were killed in the brief, brutal melee but the government forces lost up to 100 killed and wounded, including some officers. The only prisoner taken on this occasion was one of Cumberland's footmen, who was later sent back unharmed by Charles. Such gallant gestures were common in aristocratic circles. Similar concern for their own men was not.

There was a rearguard action to the north of Penrith. The Manchester Regiment was left behind to defend Carlisle and after a siege by Cumberland had to surrender, to face hanging or transportation. Many died in Carlisle Castle, where they were imprisoned in brutal conditions along with Scots prisoners.

As the eventful year drew to a close, the Young Pretender headquartered at the County Hotel during a three-day sojourn in Dumfries. Charles demanded £2,000 from the town, together with 1,000 pairs of brogues for his kilted Jacobite army camped close by. The townsfolk got lucky when a rumour circulated that Cumberland was approaching. The prince and his army got out quickly, with only £1,000 and 255 pairs of shoes having been handed over.

By Christmas, the Jacobites were in Glasgow and forced the city to re-provision their army. On 3 January they left to seize Stirling and began an ineffectual siege of its castle against Murray's counsel. Jacobite reinforcements joined them and on 17 January about 8,000 men under Murray took the offensive to the approaching General Henry Hawley at the Battle of Falkirk and routed his forces.

The Jacobite army then turned north, losing men along the way. Sickness and desertion were beginning to take their toll on his force and Murray insisted that retreat to the Highlands was a necessity. A furious Charles was forced to acquiesce, but not before accusing Murray of treachery. Tragically for his followers, Charles took charge again, insisting on fighting an orthodox defensive action, and on 16 April 1746 they were finally defeated near Inverness at the Battle of Culloden by government forces made up of English and Scottish troops and Campbell militia, under the command of Cumberland.

Charles was true to form. He again ignored Murray's advice and perversely chose to fight on flat, open, marshy ground where his forces would be exposed to superior firepower. His men were exhausted, the enemy fresh and well-armed, but the prince took no account of that. Charles commanded his army from a position behind his lines, where he could not see what was happening. Hoping Cumberland's army would attack first, he had his men stand exposed to Hanoverian artillery. Seeing the error in this, he quickly ordered an attack, but the messenger was killed before the order could be delivered. The Jacobite attack, charging into the teeth of musket fire and grapeshot, was completely uncoordinated. The Highland sword charge against cannon and muskets had previously succeeded against unprepared or disordered troops. This time, against regulars who had time to form their ranks properly, it was suicidal. The Jacobites broke through the bayonets of the redcoats in one place, but they were shot down by a second line of soldiers, and the survivors fled. Cumberland's troops committed numerous atrocities as they hunted for the defeated Jacobite soldiers, earning him the title of 'the Butcher'. The Hanoverians believed a rumour that the Highlanders had been told to show 'no quarter' if they won, and Cumberland and his officers used that to justify the murder of the wounded. The young officer James Wolfe, later the hero of Quebec, refused to kill a downed Jacobite, offering to resign his commission on the spot. The man was instead killed by a common soldier. Such orders explain why the last major battle on British soil was so unbalanced in its casualty list – the Hanoverians lost 50 dead and 259 wounded, while the most conservative estimate of Jacobite casualties is 1,500, not counting those who later died of their wounds, or were bayoneted in their sleep, or while trying to escape.

Murray managed to lead a group of Jacobites to Ruthven, intending to continue the fight. Charles, however, had promptly abandoned his army, blaming everything on the treachery of his officers, even though his stragglers and unengaged units manfully rallied at the agreed rendezvous and only dispersed when ordered to leave. Cumberland's forces crushed the uprising and ended Jacobism as a serious political force in Britain.

Charles's subsequent flight has become the stuff of legend and is commemorated in the popular folk song 'The Skye Boat Song' and also the old Irish song *Mo Ghile Mear*. In the romantic Victorian rewriting of Scottish history it appeared heroic. In fact, it was a shameful scurry to save his own skin while so many others had lost their lives for it. Hiding in the moors of Scotland, he kept just ahead of the government forces. Though many Highlanders saw Charles, and some aided him, none of them betrayed him for the £30,000 reward offered. Assisted by such loyal supporters as the pilot Donald Macleod, he escaped by boat to the Isle of Skye. On the voyage he was disguised as Flora Macdonald's Irish maid, 'Betty Burke'. It was effective, if humiliating, and he evaded capture and left the country aboard the French frigate *L'Heureux*, arriving back in France in September. Flora Macdonald was briefly imprisoned in London. She married and settled in North Carolina where, after the onset of the 1776 American rebellion, she helped raise a Highland regiment to fight for King George III.

❦

The decline of Jacobism left Charles making futile attempts to enlist assistance and another abortive plot to raise support in England.

After his defeat, Charles indicated to the remaining supporters of the Jacobite cause in England that, accepting the impossibility of his recovering the English and Scots crowns while he remained a Roman Catholic, he was willing to commit himself to reigning as a Protestant. Accordingly, he visited London incognito in 1750 and conformed to the Protestant faith by receiving Anglican Communion. Bishop Robert Gordon, a staunch Jacobite whose house in Theobald's Row was one of Charles's safe-houses for the visit, performed the communion, and a chapel in Gray's Inn was suggested as the venue as early as 1788. Surpisingly, the news of this conversion was not advertised widely and Charles had apparently returned to the Roman Catholic faith by the time of his marriage.

In 1759, at the height of the Seven Years War, Charles was summoned to a meeting in Paris with the French foreign minister, the Duc de Choiseul. Charles failed to make a good impression, being argumentative (see following chapter) and Choiseul dismissed the prospect of Jacobite assistance in any future invasion of England. Charles, in turn, would only cross the Channel if it was to lead a rebellion in England. The proposed French invasion, which was Charles's last realistic chance to recover the British throne for the Stuart dynasty, was no longer a possibility.

Many of the Highland clans who had previously taken up arms for the Jacobite cause were now fighting with British forces around the world, where they played an important part in many British victories.

James, the Old Pretender, died in Rome on New Year's Day 1766 and was buried in the crypt of St Peter's Basilica. His 64 years, 3 months and 16 days as the Jacobite pretender to the thrones of England, Scotland and Ireland lasted longer than the reigns of any other monarch of those kingdoms or their successor states. Queen Elizabeth II, the descendant of the Hanoverians, must remain on the throne until 23 May 2016 to beat his record.

His son Charles, the Young Pretender, continued to plot and scheme, but in France his life was mainly given over to debauchery and dissipation. Charles had numerous affairs; the one with his first cousin Marie resulted in a short-lived son Charles (1748-49). In 1748 Charles was expelled from France under the terms of the treaty that brought the war between Britain and France to an end.

Charles lived for several years in exile with his Scottish mistress, Clementina Walkinshaw, whom he met and may have begun a relationship with during the 1745 rebellion. In 1753, the couple had a daughter, Charlotte. Charles was unable to cope with the collapse of the cause and took to drink with tenacity, and mother and daughter left him. Charlotte went on to have three illegitimate children with an ecclesiastical man.

In 1772, Charles married Princess Louise of Stolberg-Gerden. They lived first in Rome, then, in 1774, moved to Florence where Charles began to use the title 'Count of Albany' as an alias. In 1780, Louise left Charles. She claimed that Charles had physically abused her; this claim was generally believed by contemporaries, even though Louise was already involved in an adulterous relationship with an Italian poet. In 1783, Charles signed an act of legitimation for his illegitimate daughter Charlotte and gave her the title 'Duchess of Albany' in the peerage of Scotland and the style 'Her Royal Highness', but these honours did not give Charlotte any right of succession to the throne. Charlotte lived with her father in Florence and Rome for the next five years.

Charles died in Rome on 31 January 1788. He was first buried in the Cathedral of Frascati, where his brother Henry Benedict Stuart was bishop. At Henry's death in 1807, Charles's remains were moved to the crypt of Saint Peter's Basilica in the Vatican where they were laid to rest next to those of his brother, his mother and his father.

His heart, however, was left in a small urn in Frascati Cathedral. Whether it was a great heart depends on the judgement of history and the prejudices of the reader.

One of those who certainly did not regard the bonnie prince as a hero was Lord George Murray. Having been dismissed when Charles gave up his own cause, he wrote him a blunt letter upbraiding him for his distrust and mismanagement. Murray escaped to the continent in December 1746, but when he journeyed to Paris the following year, the prince refused to meet him. Murray led a gypsy life around the continent and died in Holland in October 1760 aged 66. If 'The Forty-Five' revealed anyone as a capable commander, it was him.

13 THE CHOISEUL PLAN

'Never … so near its oft-dreamt goal, the invasion of England.'
– A. Bourguet, Paris 1907

The Battle of Quiberon Bay by Nicholas Pocock, 1812, National Maritime Museum.

In Februrary 1759 Étienne-Francois, Comte de Stainville, soon to be le Duc de Choiseul, met Bonnie Prince Charlie in Paris. Charles Edward Stuart was drunk and believed that he again had a chance to take the British crown. The Frenchman flattered his ego while disguising his own contempt. He promised that Louis intended to invade Britain 'for and with the Prince and nothing done without him'.

In fact, the Jacobite cause was lost and everyone bar the prince knew it. His only role, in French eyes, would be to consolidate the French position in Scotland after securing a foothold there. The French aim was to defeat the English and then negotiate a peace in which France regained all the possessions it had lost since 1756 and the start of the Seven Years War.

This was courtly diplomacy of the most cynical kind, and was the prelude to another armada.

❦

The 39-year-old Étienne-François was born in Nancy, the eldest son of a senior advisor to the Duke of Lorraine, who ruled an independent state with cultural and political links to France. But he switched allegiance wholly to France when the Duke gave up his title to reign in Tuscany. He campaigned in the Austro-Turkish War and entered the French army during the War of the Austrian Succession, serving with distinction in Bohemia and Italy. He was appalled by the French defeat at Dettingen, which he witnessed at close hand, and criticised the 'indifference and ignorance' of French commanders and their troops. From 1745 until 1748 he fought in the largely siege warfare of the Low Countries, reaching the rank of Lieutenant General. In 1750 he married into a considerable fortune. He won the favour of Madame de Pompadour through obtaining indelicate letters between the king and a former mistress, his own cousin. He was rewarded by the ambassadorship in Rome in 1753. His gift for both diplomacy and intrigue won plaudits in the right circles and in 1757 he was transferred to Vienna, where he was instructed to cement the new alliance between France and Austria. He was one of the principal authors of the Second Treaty of Versailles which committed both states to a combined war in Germany against Prussia. The following year he replaced Cardinal de Bernis as foreign minister and took control of military policy overseas at the height of the Seven Years War (1756-63). That has claim to be the first truly global conflict. Its main protagonists were Britain and Hanover against the Bourbons of France and Spain, driven by conflicting trade and colonial interests. But it was also stoked by antagonisms between Prussia and the Holy Roman Empire. Britain allied with Prussia and Portugal, whilst the Bourbons allied with Austria, Sweden and Saxony.

At the opening of that war, Louis XV, driven by malice and megalomania, turned his eyes to England. He understood that this was a war for the Americas and that French Canada was being throttled by the Royal Navy's control of trans-Atlantic sea lanes. By July 1756 50,000 French troops were mustered at La Hogue, St Malo, Dunkirk, Calais, Dieppe, Le Havre, Granville and St Valery, threatening the whole of the south coast and, in particular, the naval base at Portsmouth. Louis' scheme was to bring together his Brest and Rochefort fleets to take the army across the Channel and land at a beachhead secured by French commandos, while distracting the English with feints in Scotland and Ireland. In a supposedly subtle refinement to the plan, 4,000 were mustered at Toulon to strike at the British base on Minorca. The thinking behind that was the British would have to send reinforcements to the Mediterranean, thereby weakening their hold on the Channel.

At first the project went to plan. The British delayed too long, allowing the French to easily take Port Mahon in Minorca, an error which led to the foredeck execution of the unfortunate Admiral Byng. Ironically, the Royal Navy's tardiness meant that their presence in the Channel remained just as strong. The invasion was postponed.

Britain and Prussia had the upper hand during the first three years of the war, gaining territory in North America, Africa and India, and fighting their combined enemies to a stalemate in Germany. But in December 1758 Choiseul took over the French military machine and the tide changed. He realised that France could only recapture lost ground if Britain was defeated close to home.

Within two months his bold master plan was in place. Charles Stuart was then summoned to the uncomfortable meeting in Paris. Choiseul was planning a full-scale invasion of England and he may have initially hoped to add a number of Jacobites led by Charles. However, he was so little impressed with Charles, he dismissed the prospect of Jacobite assistance. Choiseul muttered his diplomatic niceties, but in reality the hopes of a Jacobite revival were now nothing but a dream. This would be a French affair. Choiseul, rid of the complications the prince would have brought to the table, had a free hand. In early 1759, with England gripped by an invasion panic, he uprated his invasion force from 15,000 to 100,000 men. He withdrew 10,000 veterans from Germany to join 48,000 troops earmarked for the Channel crossing alone. Choiseul's plan was modern, ambitious and comprehensive and was conceived in tandem with a diplomatic *blitzkrieg*. He proposed three main strike forces and a diversionary expedition.

First, a 20,000-strong force would be taken in the Brest fleet to Scotland, land at Glasgow and march across the central belt to take Edinburgh. The Brest fleet would then sail back via the North Sea, pick up another 40,000 men and land them in Essex. The privateer Francois Thurot would create a diversion by landing 800 men in five frigates in Northern Ireland. Meanwhile a fleet of 337 flat-bottomed barges was assembled at Le Havre, each one capable of carrying hundreds of troops. Twelve Swedish cargo boats known as *prames* were built and adapted as floating batteries. The whole flotilla would sail at night in a square formation, flanked by the *prames*. This force would land on the south coast of England and deal the killer blow. Scotland and Ulster would be in uproar. The main French army would rampage through the southern counties and meet up with the Essex force on the outskirts of London. England would capitulate. Game over. It was not to be.

What most hindered the Choiseul Plan was the French tendency to over-sophistication, which divided their forces and confused their objectives. Choiseul himself put forward a short-lived deviation to combat the Royal Navy in the West Indies. The French commanders raised repeated objectives as they tried to fine-tune the Plan to their own advantage. Choiseul, fatefully, made two key amendments in response. He summoned the Toulon fleet from the Mediterranean to convey the main body troops across the Channel. And those destined for Scotland would be picked up at Quiberon Bay on the Atlantic coast by the Brest fleet under Admiral Conflans. To do that, the fleet would have to sail 100 miles south east. The French had not learnt the lesson of previous failed invasions – that a good strategist should never separate an army from its transport.

Choiseul's attempts to build up a diplomatic alliance to support the invasion also foundered. He had intended to persuade two old enemies, Russia and Sweden, to join the Scottish invasion. That proved impossible, while Choiseul's attempt to bring in Spain also collapsed. Again, he discovered, it was to be a solely French enterprise.

The 12-ship Toulon fleet under Admiral La Clue passed through the Straits of Gibraltar on 4 August, but was intercepted by Admiral Edward Boscawen off Portugal. The French suffered a crushing defeat at the battle of Lagos. Boscawen, with 14 ships of the line, overtook seven of the French ships on the 18th. The 74-gun *Centaure* was captured after a hard fight in which the British flagship *Namur* was severely damaged. That night, two of the French ships, *Souverain* and *Guerrier* altered course to the west and escaped. The remaining four fled to the north and into Portuguese waters where de la Clue's flagship, *Ocean,* and *Redoutable* were driven ashore and destroyed, while *Temeraire* and *Modeste* were captured. De la Clue was seriously wounded and carried ashore. Five of his ships had taken refuge in Cadiz before the battle and were blockaded by Boscawen's second-in-command, Admiral Broderick. The young slave Olaudah Equiano, who later became a prominent abolitionist, participated in the engagement on the English side.

The French defeat, coming on the back of other British land victories, failed to kill the invasion plan. Choiseul and General Prince le Soubise continued to amass flat-bottomed barges for the Channel crossing. But the fatal flaw in the Choiseul Plan – the division of army and navy – should have become clear when Admiral Edward Hawke moved to blockade Brest.

Hawke had acquired a reputation as a 'fighting officer' and developed the concept of a Western Squadron, keeping an almost continuous blockade of the French coast throughout the war. He was born in London in 1705, the only son of a lawyer, and joined the navy in 1720 as a midshipman. In 1725 he passed his examination as a Lieutenant, but it was 1729 before he could find a position on a ship because of a shortage of active commands in peacetime. His career accelerated and he was a captain by 1734. Hawke did not see action until the Battle of Toulon in 1744. That fight was extremely confused and, while not a defeat for the British, they had failed to take an opportunity to comprehensively defeat the Franco-Spanish fleet, leading to a mass court-martial. Hawke's ship managed to capture the only prize of the battle, the Spanish ship *Poder*, although she was subsequently destroyed by the French. Because of that pyrrhic victory, Hawke was largely spared the recriminations that followed the battle. He was promoted to Rear Admiral in 1747 and became commander of the Western Squadron the same year. Hawke put a great deal of effort into improving the performance of his crews and instilling in them a sense of pride. Hawke ambushed a French squadron returning from the West Indies in the second battle of Cape Finistere, giving Britain almost total control of the English Channel in the final months of that war, helping to secure a favourable peace. The peace, however, temporarily halted Hawke's military advancement. He was elected MP for Portsmouth, retaining the seat for 30 years.

He clashed with Lord Anson, First Lord of the Admiralty, over how the next wars with France should be fought, each regarding the peace treaty as little more than a brief armistice. When it became clear that war would indeed break out, Hawke was ordered to reactivate the Western Squadron. He successfully intercepted ships bound for French harbours. More than 300 merchant ships were captured, accelerating the drift to renewed warfare. Hawke replaced the doomed Admiral Byng as commander in the Mediterranean in 1756. He blockaded Rochefort, stormed an offshore island in a botched bid to land a force on the French coast, and directed the blockade of Brest.

He again clashed with his Admiralty superiors and was taken out of active service. Luckily, he retained the respect of the Cabinet and was returned to command in time to win a great victory.

By October, Louis XV had approved an appeal by Admiral Conflans, who was frustrated by the blockade, to sail out and engage the English fleet. Once Hawke was defeated, he argued, he could sail to Quiberon to pick up his army. Fortune appeared to smile on Conflans when winds blew Hawke off station. But Conflans quickly discovered that his fleet, held in port for too long, was in poor shape, with ships in need of repair and their crews devastated by disease. He was unable to take advantage of the opportunity the winds had given him. A furious Louis ordered him to put to sea regardless.

Then the weather took against both sides. From 6 to 9 November a ferocious gale raged. The naval commanders were faced with 50ft waves and 90mph winds. Seven French ships of the line reinforced the Brest fleet from the West Indies. Suitably reinforced and with Louis's rebukes ringing in his ears, and with the winds turning in his favour, Conflans was able to set sail. Believing that the English had been blown well away, he led his fleet into the Bay of Biscay. He was just 130 miles from Quiberon, while Hawke was 200 miles behind. That was not a big enough margin. Hawke, in an astonishing display of seamanship and finally helped by the winds, overtook him. The French, meanwhile, had been blown to the west. The two fleets converged.

On the 20th, seeing that he was outgunned, Conflans decided to run for cover in Quiberon Bay. That was the sensible decision by the normal rules of engagement. He reasoned that Hawke would not dare to follow in 40mph winds and the Atlantic swell into a shoal-strewn area unknown to him. His reasoning, though faultless in theory, proved wrong in practice. Hawke gave chase. His vanguard caught up with the French rear off the gale-lashed Cardinals, razor-sharp rocks guarding the entrance to Quiberon Bay.

The seas were so high that it was suicide to open the lower gun ports, but after the first fusillade from the upper ports, the wind dramatically veered in Hawke's favour, throwing the French into fatal confusion and blowing the English smoothly into the bay. Just before 1600 the battered *Formidable* surrendered to the *Resolution*, while *Thésée* lost her duel with HMS *Torbay* and foundered, *Superbe* capsized, and the badly damaged *Héros* struck her flag to Viscount Howe before running aground on the Four Shoal some time during the night.

Meanwhile, the wind shifted to the north-west, further confusing Conflans' half-formed line. Conflans tried to sort out the chaos but without success and in the end decided to put to sea again. His flagship, *Soleil Royal*, headed for the entrance to the bay just as Hawke was coming in on *Royal George*. Hawke saw an opportunity to rake *Soleil Royal*, but *Intrépide* got in between the two and endured the fire. *Soleil Royal* fell to leeward and was forced to run back and anchor off Croisic, separated from the rest of the French fleet. By now it was about 1700 and dark, so Hawke made the signal to anchor. Two French ships of the line had been sunk and of almost 1,300 crewmen on the two vessels, many of them untrained Breton peasants, only 22 survived. There was worse to come. Both sides spent an appalling night battling the gale rather than each other. But in the morning Hawke continued the wholesale destruction. By the close, seven French ships of the line were destroyed or captured.

During the night eight French ships managed to navigate the shoals and escape to the open seas. But seven ships and the frigates in the Villaine estuary jettisoned their guns and gear to clear sandbanks, and four of them broke their backs on the mud. The badly damaged *Juste* was lost with all hands as she made for the Loire, and *Resolution* grounded on the Four Shoal during the night. *Soleil Royal* tried to escape to the safety of the batteries at Croisic. HMS *Essex* set off in pursuit and both were wrecked on the Four Shoal beside *Heros*. On the 22nd the gale eased and three Royal Navy ships were sent to destroy the beached French vessels. Conflans set fire to *Soleil Royal* while the British burnt *Heros*.

It was the greatest British sea victory to that date, and surely one of the most decisive in history. The power of the French fleet was broken, and would not recover before the war was over. Historian Alfred Mahan wrote:

> The battle of 20 November 1759 was the Trafalgar of this war, and ... the English fleets were now free to act against the colonies of France, and later of Spain, on a grander scale than ever before.

The Comte de Germiny, the French naval historian, said of the battle: 'It brought on us a bewilderment and a sense of helplessness.'

The implications were global. Despite later land victories across the Atlantic, the French were unable to reinforce their forces in New France, determining the future of Canada. At home, France suffered a credit crunch as bankers realised that Britain could now strike at will against French trade. The French government was forced to default on its debt.

Meanwhile, the privateer Francois Thurot's diversionary invasion of Northern Ireland went ahead. Weeks before Quiberon Bay he set off from Dunkirk with six vessels and a reduced force of 1,100 troops under Brigadier Flobert. The two commanders, navy and army, squabbled at every opportunity. The force found it near-impossible to dodge the royal Navy and were kicking their heels in Gothenburg in early November, waiting for the Choiseul Plan to come together. A frustrated Thurot decided to head north to take his fleet to Ireland via Scandinavian and Hebridean waters. The fleet was quickly scattered by storms, and some ships failed to rendezvous in the Faroe Islands.

Thurot overruled a council of war decision which favoured a return to France and, Quiberon Bay notwithstanding, the fleet sailed for Ireland again in early January 1760. Reports of the French naval defeat had made him determined on a grand gesture to restore French honour.

Thurot's high-handedness played into the hands of Flobert, who convinced his officers that the mission was either vainglorious or suicidal. He refused Thurot's orders to attack Londonderry and Thurot, faced with wholesale mutiny, agreed to return to France. But he chose a route through the Irish Sea and Flobert quickly realised that the apparent capitulation has been a ruse to land on that coast. Flobert agreed to a landing only to take on water and supplies at Carrickfergus. Thurot then demanded a joint attack on that port and Belfast. Flobert agreed a compromise, in which he agreed to attack Carrickfergus alone.

Flobert and 600 of his men overwhelmed the small garrison and took both the town and the castle, at a cost of 19 men killed and 30 wounded. When word of the capture reached Dublin there was panic and a small force of dragoons was despatched by the Duke of Bedford, the Lord Lieutenant, who feared, incorrectly, that it was a feint to draw British forces to the north while a main French force was to attack Cork or Dublin. Thurot held the town for five days, menacing Belfast and demanding supplies and a ransom. But Flobert, fearing with good reason a large-scale mobilisation of militia, refused to take his men onwards to Belfast. The appearance of a Royal Navy squadron off the coast finally persuaded Thurot that it was time to go. He re-embarked his force and departed the town, but was delayed leaving Belfast Lough.

By now the British had belatedly sprung into action. The port of Liverpool, which had improved its defences on the news of Thurot's seaborne rampage, called in reinforcements, and more Royal Navy ships were sent from Portsmouth and Plymouth. On 24 February the alarm reached two Royal Navy frigates, HMS *Pallas* and HMS *Brilliant*, who were at Kinsale. They passed Dublin on the morning of 26 February, but the bad weather prevented them from entering Belfast Lough that evening. Thurot was first to benefit from improved weather, and escaped. On the night of 27-28 February the Royal Navy squadron, having heard local claims that the next target of the raiders was to be Whitehaven in Cumberland, headed south-east to round the Mull of Galloway in southern Scotland. They spotted the French squadron at anchor near Luce Bay. Thurot scrambled south towards the Isle of Man. At sunrise HMS *Æolus*, the leading ship, caught up with the *Maréchal de Belle-Isle*, Thurot's flagship. After the first broadsides, Thurot tried to grapple *Æolus*, but lost his bowsprit in the attempt, while his men were swept from the deck by small-arms fire. *Æolus* fired a second broadside and fell back so that the other two Royal Navy vessels could also fire at the *Belle-Isle*. Then *Æolus* resumed the fight, while *Pallas* and *Brilliant* dealt with the remaining French vessels, one of which, *Terpsichore,* attempted to escape but was easily caught by *Pallas*.

Thurot was killed by a musket shot and his crew surrendered to a British boarding party. Around 160 men were killed on *Belle-Isle* alone, compared to four killed and 11 wounded aboard *Æolus*. Thurot's corpse was thrown overboard, with many others, and it washed ashore near the Mull of Galloway. He was buried with full honours in the churchyard of Kirkmaiden, at the expense of the local lord, Sir William Maxwell, who also served as chief mourner. In England he was a feared but widely admired foe.

A news report observed that 'he had justly acquired, and has left behind him, the two most amiable Characteristicks of a Sailor or Soldier, intrepid Courage, and extensive Humanity.' A published letter from London reported that 'most people here are sorry for his Death, as he on all Occasions behaved like a brave Officer, and a Gentleman.' In France he became a national hero, in part because his hopeless heroism contrasted with the meek incompetence of many of their commanders at Quiberon Bay.

Thurot's attempted Irish invasion was just a sideshow; but such failures did not kill French desires to invade Britain. As the stakes were so high, grand plans to do so continued, despite the Royal Navy's command of the seas. And Choiseul was not finished with his grand plan.

✌--✌

Choiseul did not see Quiberon Bay as the last throw of the dice. He devised yet another grand plan. He was aided by Spain's move to the French side in the hostilities and Choiseul planned to use Britain's colonial responsibilities to create a diversion. Spain would invade Portugal and take Lisbon, the Royal Navy's chief supply port for the Mediterranean fleet, while besieging Gibraltar. The French fleet would sail to the West Indies to threaten Britain's islands there. In that way, both the Mediterranean and Caribbean fleets would be kept occupied. Choiseul, as another part of the smokescreen, would open peace negotiations with the newly formed government of the Marquis of Bute in London. All the time, however, Choiseul would assemble a new fleet of 28 warships at Ferrol in Spain, supposedly to be sent to attack Gibraltar. At the right time, the fleet would instead be sent to the Channel. At the last moment 50,000 troops ostensibly forming a reserve force in the lower Rhine would make a forced march to the coast. The vanguard would cross immediately in transports protected by the French navy and secure a beachhead. The English would be taken by surprise and the rest of the army would be ferried across while the English were scrambling about in panic. That, at least, was the plan.

British intelligence operations, however, were both efficient and effective. The plan leaked and Hawke concentrated all his naval forces in the Channel and off Ferrol. Choiseul's 1762 project was throttled before it could get under way.

The Treaty of Paris ended the Seven Years War, but not Choiseul's thirst for revenge for all his thwarted schemes. He was helped by the appointment of Charles-Francois, the Comte de Broglie, formerly Louis XV's secret agent on foreign policy, as minister. In 1765 he submitted a new invasion plan to the king. As well as the main attack, there would be no less than six diversions: Spain would attack Jamaica, land troops in Ireland and besiege Gibraltar. France would attack British interests in India, lay siege to Minorca and land troops in Scotland. While the Royal Navy buzzed around the globe dealing with those threats, a French army of 60,000 men would land, a division each at Rye, Winchelsea, Hastings and Pevensey, the last being the landing point of William the Conqueror. The divisions would converge and march towards London.

Choiseul tinkered with the plan, both strengthening and weakening it at crucial points. The scheme was constantly refined, and its salient objectives re-designed. In particular, the main landing points were changed from the East Sussex coastline to farther west, between Littlehampton and Chichester. The French would split, with one force advancing towards London as far as Guildford and Dorking. The other would attack the Portsea Lines defending Portsmouth, while French marines would land at Gosport to aid them. After the capture of Portsmouth and the Isle of Wight those French troops not needed to garrison those places would catch up with their compatriots and advance on London. The army would secure Thames crossings at Putney, Kew, Kingston and Hampton Court and take the heights of Hampstead and Highgate. The English capital would then capitulate. London, Portsmouth and the Isle of Wight would be used as bargaining chips in peace negotiations. Those negotiations would, in Choiseul's dreams, secure the return of French colonies lost during the seven years of global conflict.

At Versailles the idea took hold that the Isle of Wight should be held permanently in French hands, just as Calais had been an English enclave hundreds of years earlier. The deliberations outlived the King and when Louis XVI succeeded to the throne in 1774, he desired peace. All the elaborate invasion plans were put aside. But only temporarily. The concept of a French Isle of Wight fitted in with an obsession at Versailles that if the English economy could be destabilised, even wrecked, all their problems would be over. British credit would be ruined by an occupation so close to Portsmouth, the country's premier military port, French honour satisfied. And when in 1775 the Americans rebelled against the mother country that fantasy won an even stronger hold on French strategy. Two years later, when France allied herself to the American revolutionaries, there was another opportunity. Now the main target was not London, but Portsmouth.

General Dumouriez, the future Revolutionary commander, argued that the Isle of Wight was defended by only a handful of militia and could be taken in hours. Spithead Channel could be blocked by the sinking of 50 stone-laden transports, and the great naval base of Portsmouth would be destroyed. By March 1779 the new plan was in place, with two aims: secure a major naval victory in the Channel and destroy Portsmouth forever as a global naval base.

On paper, the timing was good. The Royal Navy was preoccupied across the Atlantic, and the combined French and Spanish navies were theoretically a greater force in the Channel. French morale was high. The original plan involved 30 French warships backed by numerous corvettes and frigates sailing from Brest and rendez-vousing at Corunna with 20 Spanish ships of the line. They would secure the western Channel in a battle with the Royal Navy's home fleet and then the lesser ships would be used to convey 20,000 troops from Normandy to the Solent.

Frank McLynn observed succinctly:

The 1779 invasion project was the best-conceived yet. Unlike Choiseul's 1759 venture, it began from the premise that the Royal Navy had to be engaged and defeated as a necessary condition for success. And for the first time in the eighteenth century England's enemies would have clear supremacy in numbers. Indeed, this was the first time ever that England was involved in the united fleets of the two Bourbon powers when their military strength was unbroken and not dispersed in diversionary actions. Moreover, in 1779 England was in as parlous a state as France had been 20 years before. She was now without an ally anywhere, thanks to her faulty diplomacy and the jealousies engendered by her triumph in the Seven Years War.

The British were indeed most vulnerable at this stage. The 1779 Admiralty list contains just 79 ships of the line, of which only 30 were available for home defence, the rest scattered across the globe. A French historian reported: 'Never at any other time in history … was the French navy so near its oft-dreamt goal, the invasion of England.'

French ambitions increased. Instead of merely occupying the Isle of Wight and neutering Portsmouth, they aimed to ensure permanent occupation of the port itself, with 30,000 soldiers turning Portsea Island into a redoubt. Spain's involvement in the plan was cemented by promises, probably false, that Portsmouth could then be swapped with Gibraltar.

At the beginning of May the French raided the Channel Islands to test their opponents, but gales delayed the Franco-Spanish rendezvous. The French and Spanish fleets did not combine until 23 July, and after that contrary winds delayed them further. Both fleets were stricken with sickness. But by August the fleet of 66 warships and their auxiliary vessels were off The Lizard. The forces of the French admiral, d'Orvilliers, a veteran of the battle of Ushant, outnumbered the Channel fleet under the inexperienced and possibly cowardly Admiral Charles Hardy. The scene was set for a successful re-run of the Spanish Armada. Instead, history repeated itself as farce.

The timid Hardy refused to engage and a frustrated Admiralty ordered him to attack the enemy off the Scillies. The Franco-Spanish fleet was by now heading towards Plymouth and the two opposing fleets sailed past each other on parallel courses in opposite directions. Hardy retraced his course, but when the two fleets were about to engage a great bank of fog descended. Battle was impossible and it was not until 31 August that the two fleets again sighted each other. Hardy veered off, intending to draw the enemy farther up the Channel and away from their supply lines. The Franco-Spanish fleet gave chase, but Hardy's timid behaviour proved the best tactics.

D'Orvilliers had meanwhile been given new orders from Versailles to attack Cornwall rather than Portsmouth. Provisions were short and instead the invaders were ordered to restock in Brest. When they arrived, the incompetence of the Brest commissariat meant there was insufficient food. The invasion was postponed for a year.

The fleet anchored in Brest harbour, around 100 vessels, became little more than floating hospitals. During the whole catastrophic expedition, hundreds on board had died and been thrown overboard. In harbour by mid-September there were 8,000 sick. Broken by the experience, the 71-year-old d'Orvilliers resigned. The invasion was over.

An observer midway through the enterprise blamed Versailles:

> The Court, which has shilly-shallied between plans and has been unable to
> decide anything, as one would expect from the ignorance and indecision of
> our Ministers, has wanted to play on two strings and has left M. D'Orvilles to
> decide which should be touched first … Our Ministers have done what weak
> people do who can never go whole-heartedly for things at the critical moment
> and who love to give only conditional and obscure orders. They have got thor-
> oughly tangled up in Spain and don't know how to get clear. They thought
> events would get them out of the mess and they now find themselves at the foot
> of a wall.

The next serious French invasion threat would have to wait until a Revolution and
the emergence of a new European military genius.

And Choiseul? A popular hero in France, he lived a lavish retirement in Paris, enter-
taining many great and privileged guests, particularly the faction around Madame Du
Barry, in style. He died on 8 May 1785, leaving his widow to pay off huge debts.

Horace Walpole acknowledged his influence on French foreign policy, writing that

> … he would project and determine the ruin of a country, but could not medi-
> tate a little mischief or a narrow benefit. … He dissipated the nation's wealth
> and his own; but did not repair the latter by plunder of the former.

14 JOHN PAUL JONES

'I have not yet begun to fight.'
– John Paul Jones, 1779

John Paul Jones from an engraving, *c.*1779, after the
Battle of Flamborough Head.

The Cumbrian fishing hamlet of Whitehaven grew into a substantial coal-mining
town during the eighteenth century and developed its harbour into a major commercial port. In the 1720s Daniel Defoe visited and wrote that it had

> … grown up from a small place to be very considerable by the coal trade, that
> it is now the most eminent port in England for shipping off of coals, except
> Newcastle and Sunderland and even beyond the last. They have of late fallen
> into some merchandising also, occasioned by the strange great number of their
> shipping, and there are now some considerable merchants; but the town is yet
> but young in trade.

Other notables who visited or lived there included Mildred Gale, grandmother of George
Washington. During that century it became a model of planned Georgian architecture
and its street grid system is believed to have become the blueprint for New York City.

Across the Atlantic the USS *Ranger*, a sloop-of-war in the Continental Navy, was launched on 10 May 1777 by master shipbuilder James Hackett from the shipyard on Badger's Island, Maine. The following February she received an official salute to the new American flag, the 'Stars and Stripes', given by the French fleet at Quiberon Bay.

Her captain had, aged 13, started his maritime career sailing out of Whitehaven as apprentice aboard the *Friendship*. To the British he was a pirate, a turncoat and a renegade, vilified in print and it caricatures. To the citizens of the new United States of America he was a hero and mariner of genius, celebrated in stone and on stamps.

The port, warship and captain would in 1778 come together in the first, and last, American military incursion on English soil.

John Paul Jones was born as simply John Paul on 6 July 1747 on the Arbigland estate in Kirkcudbright on the south-west coast of Scotland, where his father was a gardener. He escaped the narrow confines of estate servitude by enlisting on the *Friendship*. He was influenced by his older brother William, who had married and settled in Fredericksburg, Virginia. The pull of America was strong and it was the destination of many of the youngster's early voyages. For several years John sailed on British merchant and slave ships, reaching the rank of first mate on the *Two Friends* in 1766. He visited Virginia on many of those voyages and listened avidly to American revolutionary talk of freedom from oppression. He became disgusted with the cruelty of the slave trade and in 1768 he abandoned his prestigious position on the profitable slaver while docked in Jamaica. He found passage back to Scotland, but was soon back at sea.

On the brig *John* in 1768, both the captain and a ranking mate suddenly died of yellow fever. John successfully navigated the ship back to a safe port and as a reward the vessel's grateful Scottish owners made the 21-year-old master of the ship, giving him 10 per cent of the cargo. He then led two voyages to the West Indies. During his second voyage in 1770, John Paul allegedly viciously flogged a sailor who subsequently died after several weeks of agony. John's disciplinary regime was judged by many as 'unnecessarily cruel'. Although he escaped prosecution, his reputation in Scotland was tarnished. For 18 months he commanded the London-registered *Betsy* engaged in commercial speculation in Tobago. Another death saw that end – John killed a crew member called Blackton with a sword in a row over wages. He claimed that he had acted in self-defence against a mutineer. He refused to face trial in an Admiral's Court and fled to Fredericksburg, leaving his considerable fortune gained in speculation behind. In that Virginian town he arranged the affairs of his brother, who had died there without leaving any other family, and took over his plantation. He added the name Jones to his surname, some say in honour of Willie Jones of Halifax, North Carolina, a noted planter and statesman.

By now he clearly regarded himself as American, if not by birth, then by both conviction and necessity. He said it was 'the country of (my) fond election'. The first skirmishes of the Revolutionary War had been fought in April 1775 at Lexington and Concord and John Paul Jones was well aware that his shift in national allegiance made him, in British eyes, a rebel. He had little to lose from that – his reputation in his homeland was tattered, his fortune lost. Whether he was driven by self-interest or revolutionary ardour remains a matter for conjecture. We can guess that it was a little of both. Within months he travelled to Philadelphia and volunteered for the fledgling Continental Navy of the self-declared American Republic. When he arrived, the navy and the marines were in their infancy and there was great demand for experienced naval officers and captains. Nevertheless, Jones's talents were little known there and it was only the influence of contacts in the Continental Congress which secured him a posting as 1st Lieutenant of the newly converted 24-gun frigate *Alfred* on 7 December 1775. Jones sailed from the Delaware River the following February on the Continental Navy's maiden cruise. The fleet sailed to the Bahamas and raided Nassau, stripping it of military supplies. On return, Jones was given command of the sloop *Providence*. During a six-week rampage, Jones captured 16 prizes and inflicted significant damage along the coast of Nova Scotia. Jones was next tasked with freeing several hundred American prisoners-of-war forced to labour in the Nova Scotian coal mines by their British captors. Although the November 1776 mission failed owing to atrocious weather, Jones succeeded in capturing the British merchant vessel *Mellish* carrying vital winter clothing to British troops in Canada.

Despite such successes at sea, modest but rare against British sea power, Jones's ambitious and pugnacious nature got the better of him. He became convinced that the Continental Navy's commodore, Esek Hopkins, was blocking his advancement out of jealousy or spite. Both men took verbal potshots at each other, while for several months Jones stagnated without a ship to command. He lost the feud and was given a smaller command, that of the newly built *Ranger,* on 14 June 1777, auspiciously the day the Stars and Stripes was adopted as the flag of the new nation. With France on the brink of an alliance with America against Britain, Jones sailed for France on 1 November 1777, ordered to aid the cause in any way he deemed effective. The mission took a troublesome officer well away from the Boston naval commanders; the free rein offered him limitless opportunities to act with impunity.

Jones had grand strategic visions for winning the war, both on land and at sea. Hopkins and other commanders had not listened to the Scottish upstart. The American commissioners in France, Benjamin Franklin, Arthur Lee and John Adams, however, were all ears. They promised him the command of *L'Indien*, a warship under construction in Amsterdam, but that was blocked by British business interests who diverted the sale. Once again, Jones was without a major command. During this period of inaction he became close friends with Franklin, a fellow Mason whom he greatly admired.

On 6 February 1778, France signed the Treaty of Alliance with America, formally recognizing the independence of the new American republic. Eight days later, Captain Jones's *Ranger* became the first American naval vessel to be formally saluted by the French, with a nine-gun salvo fired from captain Lamotte-Piquet's flagship. Jones wrote: 'I accepted his offer all the more, for after all it was a recognition of our independence and the nation.'

Finally, on 10 April 1778, Jones set sail from Brest in the *Ranger*, determined to wreak havoc on for the western coasts of Britain. After some early successes against British merchant shipping in the Irish Sea, he determined to raid Whitehaven. The American rules of naval discipline were rather more lax than on British vessels – they were fighting for a democratic republic, after all – and Jones had to rule by persuasion and offers of reward rather than by the lash. This rankled, particularly when it became clear that the main aim of officers and crew was booty. Jones later wrote about his senior officers:

> Their object was gain not honour. They were poor: instead of encouraging the morale of the crew, they excited them to disobedience; they persuaded them that they had the right to judge whether a measure that was proposed to them was good or bad.

Jones had to persuade them that an attack on Whitehaven, his own home port, would be worth their while. However, contrary winds forced the abandonment of the initial raid, and drove *Ranger* towards Ireland. On the way they captured several small British merchant vessels.

On 20 April 1778, Jones learned from captured sailors that the Royal Navy man o' war HMS *Drake* was anchored off Carrickfergus. The surgeon of the *Ranger* wrote in his diary that Jones's first intention was to attack the vessel in broad daylight, but his sailors were 'unwilling to undertake it'. Therefore, the attack took place just after midnight, but in the dark the possibly drunk mate responsible for dropping the anchor to halt *Ranger* right alongside *Drake* misjudged the timing, so Jones had to cut his anchor cable and run. When the wind changed Jones sailed back across the Irish Sea to have another go at Whitehaven.

The *Ranger* stood two miles off the unsuspecting port on a clear, frosty night. Jones intended to torch the 200-plus merchant fleets anchored in the port, alongside numerous coal transporters. The target vessels lay stranded in the low water and packed tight together against the piers. He also hoped to terrorise the townspeople by lighting more fires as the townsfolk slept.

Jones personally led the raid in one of two boats of 15 men each, armed with pistols and cutlasses, just after midnight on 23 April 1778. With him with his Swedish second-in-command, one of the few officers he felt he could trust, Lieutenant Meijer. The other boat was commanded by Lieutenant Wallingford of the US marines and Midshipman Ben Hill. The journey to shore was slowed by the still shifting wind and a strong ebb tide and took three hours of hard rowing. The plan was already becoming unstuck because of the delay. They first tried to make a landing on the coast near Saltom Pit, in order to run along the shore and attack the guns of the lunette battery first, but the sea was too rough and the shore too rocky. This attempt lost them another half an hour. They then rowed past the battery around the New Quay and into the harbour.

The intention now was for the marines to burn the ships in the northern half of the harbour as Jones led a raid on the fort to prudently spike the guns covering the harbour entrance and the raiding party's escape route. Jones landed first, near the battlements. The frozen guards had gone into the guardhouse for warmth and were unaware of the intruders. Jones and a few men scaled the walls by climbing on each other's shoulders, burst into the guardhouse and captured the guards before they could snatch up their weapons. Jones stood on the battlements to encourage the rest of his reluctant men to follow. Jones left Lieutenant Meijer guarding his boat to deter any men tempted to return to the ship. The fort's guns were spiked and Jones took Midshipman Joe Green to spike those at the half-moon battery of 32-pounders 250m along the shoreline.

Meanwhile, Wallingford and his men landed at the Old Quay slip ready to start firing the anchored merchant ships. They found that their lanterns were empty, their lights extinguished. The men saw Nicholas Allison's public house was on the quay-side and secured it to prevent its occupants raising the alarm and to obtain oil and matches. The pub was well stocked and temptation proved too much for the US Marines. They stayed for a drink or three. When Jones returned he was dismayed to find that no ships had yet been set on fire, apparently because his own crew as well as Wallingford's had no light. After taking a light from the pub they headed along the pier. They focused on the largest vessel close by, the *Thompson*, laden with coal destined for Dublin. The raiders woke up two boys left aboard to guard it and the neighbouring ship, the *Saltham*, gagged them with cloth and took them onto the quay dressed only in their shirts. Wads of canvas doused in sulphur were set alight and thrown into the holds of both ships. A barrel of tar was also tossed into the *Thompson*. The fire took hold in the steerage of the ship and eventually burnt out the cabin.

Amid the confusion, one of Jones's disaffected men, David Freeman, slipped away and started knocking on doors to warn the townspeople that the fires had been started and that the whole town was in peril. The townspeople acted quickly. They needed to – the ships were packed with coal and the warehouses on the harbour's edge were full of combustibles, including rum, sugar and tobacco. A conflagration looked certain. Fortuitously, the town had invested in fire engines. All classes of people manned the pumps and extinguished the flames before they reached the rigging.

Jones, despite his later claims that he faced down the crowd, saw how vulnerable he was as dawn broke. The captured boys were held at gunpoint as hostages, but the towns-folk were too busy fighting the fire to approach. Nevertheless, Jones knew it was time to leave. Jones was short of space in the boats so only took three prisoners with him, one of the boys, a guard and a ship's master who had gone to the pier for some night fishing. As soon as Jones and his men started rowing for the ship, people ran to the forts and started working on the spiked guns. They got two working at the half-moon battery and fired upon the retreating boats but missed by a country mile.

As the *Ranger* set sail, Jones must have pondered deeply on his failure. Despite surprise and his own knowledge of Whitehaven, the raid had been a fiasco, with just a few hundred pounds worth of property damaged or destroyed. His officers and men grumbled at the lost opportunity for plunder, although Wallingford later claimed that his men had been reluctant to 'destroy poor people's property'.

The raid nevertheless shocked England and re-awakened the fear of foreign invasion. Jones always insisted that his aim was to inflict damage on England's war effort, but the result was strengthened defences at English ports and a recruitment boost for the militia.

Crossing the Solway Firth from Whitehaven to Scotland, Jones hoped to hold for ransom the Earl of Selkirk, who lived on St Mary's Isle near Kirkcudbright. He believed that the Earl could be exchanged for American sailors impressed into the Royal Navy. The Earl was absent on business. Jones's crew wanted to pillage the house and estate but Jones convinced them that there was more advantage to be had going back to sea and taking ships as prizes. He did, however, permit them to take a silver plate set adorned with the Selkirk emblem. Jones himself bought it later when it was auctioned in France and returned it to the Earl once the war was over.

Jones continued to have trouble with his officers and crew. They were disgruntled over his high-handed manner and the lack of profit from the expedition. The disaffected were led by Lieutenant Thomas Simpson, who claimed that his captain was too full of pride to command effectively or profitably. Jones repeatedly told them that they were on board a ship of war, not a privateer.

Jones took *Ranger* back across the Irish Sea to have another crack at the *Drake*, which was still anchored off Carrickfergus. Late in the afternoon of 24 April 1778, the ships, roughly equal in firepower, engaged. The *Drake* was captured after an hour-long gun battle, which cost the British captain and three crew members their lives for the loss of three American dead. Lieutenant Simpson was given command of *Drake* for the return to Brest. Both ships arrived safely, but after another altercation Jones filed for a court martial of Simpson, detaining him on the ship.

John Adams, still serving as a commissioner in France, intervened on Simpson's behalf, arguing that the lieutenant had been detained simply so he could not undermine Jones's claims of glory as he was feted by European dignitaries. Simpson was exonerated, but Jones was by no means vilified – his capture of the *Drake* was one of the Continental Navy's few significant military victories during the Revolution. It demonstrated that the Royal Navy could be beaten. And it inspired Americans at sea.

In 1779 Jones took command of the 42-gun *Bonhomme Richard*, a merchant ship rebuilt and given to America by the French shipping magnate, Jacques-Donatien. She was originally an East Indiaman named *Duc de Duras* and had sailed between France and the East. Her new name was Jones's own choice, designed to honour his friend Benjamin Franklin whose Poor Richard's Almanac was published in France under the title of *Les Maximes du Bonhomme Richard*.

On 14 August, as a French and Spanish invasion fleet approached England (see following chapter) he provided a diversion by heading for Ireland at the head of a five-ship squadron including the 36-gun *Alliance*, 32-gun *Pallas*, 12-gun *Vengeance*, and *Le Cerf*, also accompanied by two privateers, *Monsieur* and *Granville*. All sailed the

American flag, although all but the *Alliance* were loaned or donated by France. The crews were made up of Americans, French volunteers, captured Britons who served to escape captivity, and a number of freebooters and adventurers only interested in plunder. Just a few days out, *Monsieur* separated when her captain had a disagreement with Jones. Several Royal Navy warships were in pursuit of Jones and he sailed his fleet around the north of Scotland into the North Sea, creating panic along Britain's east coast as far south as the Humber estuary. As usual, Jones sparked off or suffered resentment amongst his senior officers, in particular the *Alliance* captain, Pierre Landais, who was disinclined as a Frenchman in charge of an American vessel to recognise Jones's authority.

On 23 September 1779, the squadron met a large merchant convoy off the coast of Flamborough Head off Yorkshire. The convoy of around 50 ships had been trading with Baltic ports and had rendezvoused off the Norwegian coast before heading for home ports stretching from Hull to Bristol. The 50-gun British frigate HMS *Serapis* and the 22-gun *Countess of Scarborough* placed themselves between the convoy and Jones's squadron, allowing the merchant ships to escape. Shortly after 1900, the Battle of Flamborough Head began.

Jones ordered a single line of battle to make best use of their broadsides as they passed the two larger British ships. Captain Landais on the *Alliance*, the most manoeuvrable ship on the scene, peeled off to one side to threaten the fleeing convoy, and the *Countess of Scarborough* under Captain Thomas Piercy was obliged to do the same. That left *Serapis* alone against the remaining three American ships. The *Bonhomme Richard* sailed to within pistol-shot of the British warship and Captain Pearson shouted questions to confirm her identity. After some evasive answers, both ships fired broadsides. A minute later *Alliance* and the *Countess of Scarborough* were also blazing away at each other.

Bonhomme Richard's broadside was ineffective, and two of her guns burst, killing those crewmen around them. *Serapis*, one of the Royal Navy's newest ships, was fitted with 10 18-pound guns on each side, all of which worked perfectly. *Serapis* was also able to run rings around the ponderous *Bonhomme Richard*.

While Jones and Landais were fighting their separate battles, Captains Cottineau of the *Pallas* and Ricot of *Vengeance* held back, considering it prudent not to intervene in the ship-to-ship duel.

Jones, knowing that he could not win a gun duel, concentrated on trying to grapple and board his opponent. Pearson used the superior manoeuvrability of *Serapis* to keep out of reach while continuing to bombard the slower ship. When the two ships briefly collided, Captain Pearson cheekily asked: 'Has your ship struck?' Jones famously replied: 'I have not yet begun to fight!'

Meanwhile, the broadside duel between *Alliance* and the *Countess* broke up with little damage on both sides. Piercy rushed to help the *Serapis* but could not get close.

The *Bonhomme Richard* was holed below the water line but the *Serapis*'s jib-boom got caught in the rigging of the American ship. Jones saw his opportunity and ordered his men to attach the two ships strongly together. This they did with considerable efficiency so that the ships were held bow to stern, their guns touching the other's hull planks. Pearson's crew fired broadsides straight into the *Bonhomme Richard*'s hull, tearing huge holes in its side, and doing terrible damage to the gun-decks. Jones ordered three still-usable 9-pounders to be dragged around to bear on the enemy's deck. Two were loaded with grapeshot to clear the *Serapis*'s deck of men, the third with bar-shot to bring down the main-mast. Jones's men in the rigging hurled down grenades. All were fighting to board the enemy ship before their own sank.

The moon had risen and in the semi-darkness Captain Landais of the *Alliance* passed the two locked ships and fired a broadside at *Serapis*'s bow. As much lethal shot hit Jones's men as Pearson's, and metal also flew along *Bonhomme Richard*'s gun-deck, killing some of the remaining gunners and wrecking several gun-carriages. Landais continued merrily on his way.

Jones was now in a desperate position. But just after 2130 a grenade thrown either by an American on a yard-arm or by another on the deck dropped down a hatch and ignited a charge of gunpowder placed in readiness for firing. The effect was devastating, a chain reaction of other charges that decimated the gun crews on the rear half of the ship. Many men jumped overboard to extinguish burning clothes, hair and flesh. Five guns were silenced.

A mile away *Pallas* was locked in battle with the *Countess of Scarborough* and *Alliance* was fast returning to that fray. As she approached, Piercy, with seven of his guns out of action and with his rigging too damaged to escape, surrendered.

Back on the *Bonhomme Richard*, her gun decks were now so badly damaged that most of the British shots were passing straight through without touching anything. Both ships were blazing, but Jones's vessel was about to sink, her pumps were severely damaged. An exhausted Jones slumped on the chicken-coop for a brief rest. The rumour spread that he was dead or dying. Two of his wounded men, a gunner and a carpenter, tried to strike the ship's colours in surrender, but they had been shot away. Pearson shouted across the carnage asking whether that was indeed the intention. Jones, suddenly awake, shouted back: 'I have not yet thought of it, but I am determined to make you strike.' Later newspaper reports that Jones shot three officers who tried to surrender are almost certainly wrong.

Pearson sent a boarding party onto the *Bonhomme Richard*, but they were repelled. At 2215 *Alliance* returned and Landais delivered another of his helpful broadsides. Jones's men yelled at him to stop, and Jones issued lantern orders for *Alliance* to help with a boarding operation instead. Landais ignored him.

Bonhomme Richard was again holed below the water line and started settling so rapidly that the master-at-arms released 100 or so prisoners from previous captures from the lower decks. This was a gamble, as they could have turned on Jones's crew, but instead they went to work on the damaged pumps to save themselves from drowning. Pearson, also losing men from *Alliance*'s attacks and shackled to the enemy, kept firing with his remaining guns. By then, however, it was clear that the merchant convoy he was charged with protecting was safely away. As the *Alliance* kept up its pounding he decided that his job was done and there was little point in continuing the fight. Shortly after 2215 he struck his colours.

The Americans finally boarded by invitation, but several officers and men could not believe that their captain had surrendered and Midshipman John Mayrant was stuck with a pike through his leg. Boats from both ships were used to evacuate the *Bonhomme Richard*'s crew. Several were used by British crewmen to slip away to shore under the eyes of thousands of spectators on the high Yorkshire cliffs. The clear night and full moon had given them a ringside seat at the battle.

Casualty figures for the battle are contradictory. Pearson stated that he had 'many more than' 49 dead and 68 wounded aboard *Serapis*, but his figure of 300 casualties aboard *Bonhomme Richard* appears an exaggeration to disguise defeat.

Overnight, pumping continued aboard the *Bonhomme Richard* and the guns from the lower decks were reluctantly heaved overboard, as were the dead. The following afternoon it was clear that she could not be saved. During the night, after the wounded had been transferred and important documents retrieved, the flotilla moved out with Jones in command of the captured *Serapis*. The *Bonhomme Richard* disappeared beneath the waves.

Jones, his fleet and the captured *Serapis* were pursued by the Royal Navy, and the French officers insisted that they head for neutral Holland instead of his preferred destination of Dunkirk. As a result, the *Serapis* and another prize were impounded. While turning on his diplomatic charm to solve that dilemma, Jones wrote to his mentor Benjamin Franklin to complain about the insubordination of Captain Landais. Jones, however, stopped short of demanding his dismissal. Captain Cottineau was not so circumspect and called Landais a coward to his face. A duel was fought and Landais skewered Cottineau's chest, just missing his heart.

Jones, networking furiously in Amsterdam, became the toast of continental society as 'The Terror of the English'. On 8 October the British Ambassador, Sir Joseph Yorke, wrote to the rulers of the United Provinces claiming that under international law, Jones, not being accredited by a recognised state, was a rebel and a pirate; therefore, the two captured ships should be detained for handing back to their rightful owners. Yorke also asked that the wounded from the two ships should be taken ashore and treated at British Government expense. The legal wrangling continued for weeks, causing the Dutch a massive diplomatic headache, until Jones and his fleet, including the prizes, slipped away among a group of Dutch ships on 27 December and sailed to France.

In England, although Pearson and Piercy had lost the battle, they were the only Royal Navy commanders to have engaged with the raiders and they had fulfilled their main mission – that of protecting the convoy. And, although they had lost their own vessels, they had sunk Jones's flagship. When they returned home at the beginning of November, they were honoured by the towns of Kingston upon Hull and Scarborough, and were rewarded by the convoy's owners and insurers. Pearson was knighted in 1780.

The King of France honoured Jones with the title 'Chevalier'. Jones insisted that the title be used whenever he was addressed thereafter. He also received from Louis a decoration of '*l'Institution du Mérite Militaire*' and a sword. The new United States of America had a new hero, albeit a flawed one. His actions helped convince the French that a full-blown military alliance with the new Republic really could defeat the British. By contrast, in Britain he was cursed as a pirate.

In June 1782, Jones was appointed to command the 74-gun *America*, but his command fell through when Congress decided to give it to the French as replacement for the wrecked *Le Magnifique*. As a result, he was given assignment in Europe in 1783 to collect prize money due to his former hands. At length, this too expired and Jones was left without prospects for active employment, leading him in 1788 to enter into the service of the Empress Catherine II of Russia, who placed great confidence in Jones, saying: 'He will get to Constantinople.' He took the name Pavel Dzhons.

Jones avowed his intention, however, to maintain his status as an American citizen and officer. As a rear admiral aboard the 24-gun flagship *Vladimir*, he took part in the naval campaign in the Liman against the Turks. Jones successfully repulsed Ottoman forces from the area, but the jealous intrigues of Prince Potëmkin caused him to be recalled to St Petersburg for the pretended purpose of being transferred to a command in the North Sea. Here he was compelled to remain in idleness, while rival officers plotted against him and even maliciously impugned his character with accusations of sexual misconduct. In April 1789 Jones was arrested and accused of raping a 12-year-old girl named Katerina Goltzwart. But the Count de Segur, the French representative at the Russian court and Jones's last friend and ally in Russia, conducted his own personal investigation into the matter and was able to convince Potëmkin that the allegation was baseless and that Jones had been framed by jealous rivals in the Russian court. On 8 June 1788 Jones was awarded the Order of St Anne, but he left the following month, an embittered man.

In May 1790 Jones arrived in Paris, where he remained in retirement for the rest of his life, although he made a number of attempts to re-enter the Russian service. In June 1792, Jones was appointed US Consul to treat with the Dey of Algiers for the release of American captives. Before Jones was able to fulfill his appointment, however, he died of interstitial nephritis and was found lying face-down on his bed in his third-floor Paris apartment, No. 19 Rue de Tournon, on 18 July 1792. He was buried in Paris at the Saint Louis Cemetery, which belonged to the French royal family. Four years later, France's revolutionary government sold the property and the cemetery was forgotten. It was variously used as a garden, a rubbish dump and an arena for dog and cockfights.

In 1905, Jones's remains were identified by US Ambassador to France General Horace Porter, who had searched for six years to track down the body using faulty copies of Jones's burial record. The body was ceremonially brought to the United States aboard the USS *Brooklyn*, escorted by three other cruisers. On approaching the American coastline, seven US Navy battleships joined the procession escorting Jones's body back to America. It was finally re-interred in a spectacular bronze and marble sarcophagus at the Naval Academy Chapel in Annapolis.

The *Ranger*, under Lieutenant Simpson, re-crossed the Atlantic after the return from the Whitehaven raid and joined two other ships in preying on British ships in the North Atlantic. In one expedition they captured 11 prizes which, with their cargoes, raised over a million dollars when sold in Boston. *Ranger* was herself captured when Charleston fell to the British. She was taken into the Royal Navy under the name HMS *Halifax*. She was decommissioned the following year.

15 THE BATTLE OF FISHGUARD

'… luckiest escape since the Armada.'
– Theobald Wolf Tone, 1796

Charge of the 5th Dragoon Guards on the insurgents by William Sadler.

A 47-year-old Welsh woman cobbler faced a dozen French invaders. Realising they were dispirited drunk, she brandished her pitchfork and took them prisoner. When she told them that their destination was the Royal Oak inn, they did not need any further compulsion. They were officially arrested in the bar.

Her name was Jemima Nicholas, also known as Niclas, also known as Fawr. Her actions guaranteed her a place in Welsh mythology. She died aged 82 and a plaque in Fishguard was erected in her honour. But behind the mythology and farce was a tragic tale of these islands. She had played a part, albeit a minor one, in countering that last military invasion of Britain. It was an invasion in which two factors dominated – booze and bluff.

❦––❦

The background was revolution and rebellion, the first across the Channel, the second across the Irish Sea.

The French Revolution had sent shock waves throughout the old monarchies across Europe. In Britain revolutionary fervour threatened order. The young Napoleon was emerging as a military leader of genius. What became known as the War of the First Coalition (1792–97) was the first major effort of the monarchies to contain France's revolutionary ambitions and its dreams of empire. Habsburg–ruled Austria and the Kingdom of Prussia lined up, and Britain soon joined them. Their tactics were simple – to invade France from all sides, Britain by sea and her allies from the Austrian Netherlands and the Rhine.

France suffered reverses and revolts within its borders. The response of the Committee of Public Safety in April 1793 was to conscript fit men aged 18 to 25. Suitably strengthened, the new French army fought back, repelled all invaders and took the Prussian Rhineland. French arms established the Batavian Republic in May 1795, the Austrian Netherlands was ceded to France and puppet Republics were set up across Northern Italy. France was not satisfied and wanted more conquests. Napoleon decisively won campaigns in the Po Valley and the coalition collapsed, leaving Britain to fight on alone.

It was a black period for Britain. Napoleon appeared to be winning on all fronts, having ousted the British fleet from Toulon, and British troops were suffering badly in Flanders. The threat of invasion was very real – a large force of French privateers landed at Newcastle and took away local livestock – and PM William Pitt ordered a large-scale expansion of military might on land and at sea to defend the homeland. The threat was from both Bonaparte and, at home, from civil insurrection. Naval press gangs were determinedly busy, but the public would not stand for general conscription to boost army numbers. Instead, Secretary of War Henry Dundas, in March 1794, wrote to each county Lord Lieutenant urging them to beef up local militias and volunteers. Virtually every county responded to the call, with local squires and aristocrats financing arms and uniforms and volunteer enrolments. Pembrokeshire was one of the first to respond, with Lord Lieutenant Lord Richard Milford raising the Pembroke Company of Gentleman and Yeomanry Cavalry.

Meanwhile, in 1798, Theobald Wolf Tone was leading a revolution of his own in Ireland. The 36-year-old Tone was a founding member of the Society of United Irishmen, a republican group strongly influenced by both the French and American revolutions. The long-standing cause was the anti-Catholic discrimination of the ruling Protestant Ascendancy loyal to the British crown. Catholics were barred from voting, holding office or wielding influence. The peasantry starved when crops failed. And most worked for the sole benefit of absentee landlords.

When France supported the Americans in their war of independence, London set up a voluntary militia to defend Ireland against any French invasion while British troops normally stationed there were on the other side of the Atlantic. Thousands of Protestants enlisted and used their newly strengthened position to win themselves a greater degree of self-rule. The landless, of course, were excluded, along with Catholics. The prospect of reform, however, was never off the agenda and the foremost agents of change were Ulster Presbyterians who, like Catholics, were denied the vote. A small group of Belfast Protestant liberals, Tone included, formed the Society of United Irishmen. The word 'United' sent shivers through the Establishment as it suggested a movement happy to cross the religious divide. So it proved. The Society proposed electoral reform *and* Catholic emancipation. The new Irish Parliament was deaf to such calls and the guillotining of King Louis XVI and the subsequent war with France drove the society underground. This is when Wolf Tone came to the fore.

Born in Dublin, the son of a Church of Ireland coach-maker and farmer, the young Tone tutored the child siblings of Galway MP Richard Martin, a fervent supporter of Catholic emancipation. Martin certainly influenced Tone's intellectual growth, if not his morality. Tone seduced the MP's wife, leading to a non-fatal duel. While studying law at Trinity College Tone eloped with his soon-to-be wife Matilda. He dreamt up a crackpot scheme to found a military colony in Hawaii, but when that was rejected by premier William Pitt the Younger, he turned to Irish politics.

Tone's hatred of England, he said, was 'rather an instinct than a principle', and he was initially prepared to accept reform rather than revolution. But when it became clear that genuine reform would never be delivered voluntarily by those in power, his aim became whole-heartedly an independent Irish republic. That aim, he wrote, was 'to subvert the tyranny of our execrable government, to break the connection with England, the never-failing source of all our political evils and to assert the independence of my country'.

By 1794 the Society was sworn to overthrow the state and such oaths were, by their nature, illegal. Several of Tone's friends were arrested and convicted and, through social contacts within government, Tone himself was allowed to emigrate to America in return for information about the Society's activities. Before he left, however, and despite his collusion with the established order, he attended the Cavehill summit in which he and fellow United Irishmen vowed 'Never to desist in our efforts until we subvert the authority of England over our country and asserted our independence'. Tone did not settle well in Philadelphia and after just a few months wrote from Philadelphia that he found the American people just as attached to unjust authority as the British. He described George Washington as a 'high-flying aristocrat'. He despised the American 'aristocracy of money' even more than the European 'aristocracy of birth'.

By now the United Irishmen had spread across Ireland. Insurrection and a complete break with England became its aim. It linked up with secret agrarian societies who raided the fine homes of the gentry to collect arms. Tone and his colleagues in the leadership of the Society asked for help from the French revolutionary government before calling a national rising. Tone sailed to France to press that case.

Tone's youth, passion and charm worked well in the French revolutionary salons and he worked assiduously to win over ministers and civil servants. The French revolutionary leaders were impressed by Tone's energy and clear-sighted ability. In February 1796 he persuaded them to send an expedition to invade Ireland. He was made an adjutant-general in the French army, a move designed to protect him from charges of treason if captured by the English. Apart from an invasion of Ireland to encourage a general uprising, he supported a plan to land troops of *La Legion*

Noire on the mainland as a diversionary tactic. The crack French force would burn Bristol, then England's second city, and commit atrocities designed to shock the Establishment into surrender.

❦ ❧

The *Expedition d'Irlande* was placed in the hands of General Louis Lazare Hoche. The low-born 28-year-old was a product of the Revolution. Like Tone, he was a young man of action, an ardent revolutionary with a vehement hatred of England. He had enlisted at 16 in the *Gardes Francaises* and spent all his spare time educating himself. His personal commitment and demonstrated valour received swift rewards. After serving as an NCO he was commissioned in 1792 and was promoted further for his service in the defence of Thionville, on France's northern frontier, and at the battle of Wissembourg. Innocent associations with more senior officers who deserted to the Austrians resulted in his arrest. But he redeemed himself in the defence of Dunkirk. By October 1793 he was commander of the Army of the Moselle, and later the Rhineland was added to his responsibilities. His record was not perfect – he first lost a battle at Kaiserslautern – but even during the Reign of Terror when failure normally ended in execution, the Committee of Public Safety regarded his tenacity and vigour as assets which outweighed any other shortcomings. Their confidence in him was vindicated when he stormed the famous lines of Weissenburg and followed through by sweeping aside all resistance to take much of the Rhineland in just four days. Hoche was again arrested after spurious charges of treason were laid by a general whom he had overtaken in the chain of command. He escaped execution but was imprisoned until the fall of Robespierre. During a short lull in the European wars he excelled by defeating both Vendean rebels and Royalists in successive battle. He then used flying columns, intelligence, modern and good communications to end the three-year civil war which threatened the integrity of Revolutionary France. Such successful methods made him the obvious choice to lead the expedition in support of the United Irishmen.

The French Directory appointed the experienced and talented Admiral Louis Villaret Joyeuse as naval commander. But he proved uninterested in the project, if not downright hostile, believing French naval forces should concentrate on controlling major sea routes, particularly those to and from India. He saw the Irish expedition as an ill-thought-out diversion. He was duly replaced by the less experienced, less competent and comparatively timid Admiral Justin Morard de Galles.

Hoche devised a three-pronged attack. The main focus was on the landing. The main body of his 15,000-strong force would land in Ireland. Two smaller forces would land on mainland Britain. These were aimed as diversions to draw away British forces, but they could also lead to greater things if successful. One would strike at Northern England and take Newcastle. The other would land in Cornwall and spark a revolt there before moving on to take Bristol. If successful, the two mainland forces, heavily swelled by home-grown supporters, would take Chester, Liverpool and, eventually, London.

The main expedition to Ireland was a disaster. On 15 December 1796 43 ships set sail from then Camaret roads. Brest's advanced anchorage. The fleet comprised of 17 ships of the line, supporting frigates and transports. Other ships due to join them did not arrive due to a mixture of poor weather and political intrigue. On board the fleet were 14,000 troops, a hefty supply of arms and other war materials for the Irish rebels, and Wolfe Tone, registered as 'Adjutant-General Smith'.

When they arrived in Bantry Bay, it had turned into a maelstrom. A combination of the foul winter weather, poor seamanship and indecisive leadership – much to the chagrin of Tone – scattered the fleet. Some ships managed to anchor off Bere Island, but none were able to get any troops on shore. The United Irishmen were nowhere to be seen because no-one had told them when the fleet was due to arrive. The rest of the fleet was kept out at sea for two weeks, waiting in vain for the gale to die down. Instead its savagery intensified. They were not bothered by a British fleet under Vice Admiral Robert Kingsmill. Hoche, unable to land a single soldier. overruled Tone's objections and decided to return to France. A furious Tone, on board the *Indomptable*, said: 'England has had its luckiest escape since the Armada.'

Astonishingly, given the scale of the setback, the two mainland expeditions went ahead, in a refined format. The Newcastle attack's aim was now to land 5,000 men to destroy shipping and collieries. They would then join up, the French believed, with revolutionary Jacobites, and join forces in Lancashire with the third invasion force. It was a fantasy. Unseaworthy invasion barges set off from Dunkirk but turned back at Flushing in the Netherlands due to bad North Sea weather. Once back in port many of the soldiers, who appear to have been criminal conscripts, refused to re-embark and the project was abandoned.

Even now the third attack went ahead, but with the destination changed to Wales. It could no longer be called a diversionary expedition and was probably regarded in Paris as a face-saver. On 16 February 1797 four warships left Brest flying Russian colours.

❦──❦

Commander-in Chief of this expeditionary force was Irish-American Colonel William Tate from South Carolina. Approaching 70, he was a veteran of the War of Independence but after a failed coup in New Orleans he had fled to France in 1795. He was more of an adventurer than a revolutionary. His command comprised 1,400 men of the *La Legion Noire*. The Black Legion was so-called not for any reputation for savagery, but for its use of British uniforms captured at the unsuccessful landings at Quiberon and dyed very dark brown/black. Around 600 of the force were regulars, the remaining 800 a ragbag of committed Republicans, convicts, former deserters and turned Royalist prisoners. In what followed, in the words of historian Frank McLynn, 'Never was the theory that criminals and jailbirds are revolutionary material exposed so harshly.' Some of the officers were Irish. The expedition's composition suggests that the French high command had little faith in the project and were not prepared to jeopardise crack troops. To add to his difficulties, Tate could not speak French and had to rely on bilingual officers to communicate his orders. But they were well armed and suitably provisioned, and Republican ardour was evident in the upper ranks. The commander of the British forces, Lord Cawdor, later described 600 of his foe as 'Grenadiers all over six foot and as fine a body of men as I have set eyes on'. Although the French authorities now appeared to have little interest in the adventure, Tate drew up detailed plans for advance, including the mechanics of river crossings.

Naval command was given to Commodore Castagnier. His orders were to land the troops and supplies and then sail with due haste to the Dublin roads to disrupt British naval communications with Ireland. His vessels, amongst the newest and largest in the entire French fleet, were the 40-gun frigates *La Vengeance* and *La Resistance* (on its maiden voyage), the 24-gun corvette *La Constance*, and a smaller 14-gun lugger, *Le Vautour*.

Castagnier plotted a course to land near Bristol but bad weather, the Severn estuary's treacherous tides and Tate's obstinate insistence forced him to re-route to the alternative destination of Fishguard. The fleet was spotted on Wednesday 22 February passing Ilfracombe, and again off St David's Head in Pembrokeshire. The fleet was illegally flying British colours, but retired sailor Thomas Williams was not fooled – particularly as he saw the warships were packed with troops – and raised the alarm. The news of the fleet spread along the coast either side of the Estuary. The element of surprise was lost, although the British authorities assumed the target would be either Bristol or Swansea Bay. Oblivious to that, the fleet sailed on, chased a revenue cutter into shallow water and captured a local trading sloop, the *Britannia*, carrying its load towards Fishguard. Her captain, John Owen, warned that their destination port was well defended by infantry, cavalry and artillery in a well-placed fort.

La Vautour, flying the Union Jack, was the first to be sent into Fishguard harbour to test the waters. A single cannon shot was fired from the fort and the lugger turned tail. In fact the nine-pounder had been fired simply to raise the alarm. The French did not know that the fort's eight guns only had three rounds between them. The local population, not taking the invasion threat seriously, had neglected their obligation to keep the fort supplied.

The French, under cover of darkness, dropped their plans to land at Fishguard and instead disembarked their troops three miles west of the port at secluded Carragwastad Bay. It was not a good choice as, although there was a sandy bay nearby, the landing point sloped steeply up to a rock-strewn shore. Any opposition on such a site would have seen a bloodbath, and bad weather would have wrecked the landing boats. Fortunately for the invaders, there was no-one else in sight and an area normally battered in February by winter gales from the Atlantic was blessed with clement weather. Even so, during the landing one boat capsized, several men were drowned and, more worryingly for the commander, the sole four-pounder gun carried by the troops was lost.

By 1400 on Thursday 23 February 1797, the French had landed 17 boatloads of troops, 47 barrels of gunpowder, 50 tons of cartridges and grenades, and 2,000 stands of arms for locals expected to join the uprising due to their supposed Celtic heritage.

One rowing boat was lost in the surf. Tate signed a report saying the landings had been successful and Castagnier later that day sailed off towards Ireland. The lugger sailed speedily to Brest and a report was sent on to Paris attesting to the success of the operation. It was premature.

Inshore, the commanding officer of the Fishguard and Newport Volunteer Infantry, 28-year-old Lieutenant-Colonel Thomas Knox, was enjoying a social event at Tregwynt mansion when news of the invasion came via a messenger who had ridden hard from Fishguard after the initial cannon shot. Knox was inexperienced, having bought his commission, and he had never seen combat. The Volunteers, who had been raised by his father, a prominent and wealthy landowner in response to the government's 1794 call, consisted of 270 men formed into four companies. On his way to the fort from the party, Knox met 70 of his men marching towards the enemy. He led them back to the fort. Knox was slow to respond to the danger but a subordinate had already sent instructions that the Newport Division of the Regiment was to march the seven miles to Fishguard with all haste. A wounded man who had been captured and then escaped confirmed that the enemy had indeed landed.

Thirty miles away at Stackpole Court, Lord Cawdor, Captain of the Castlemartin Troop of the Pembroke Yeomanry Cavalry, speedily assembled his force. Luckily his men had previously gathered for a funeral the following day. Even luckier, the Pembroke Volunteers and the Cardiganshire Militia were also to hand, having been on routine exercises nearby. They set off for the county town of Haverfordwest. On arrival they found that Lieutenant-Colonel Colby of the Pembrokeshire Militia had summoned together a force of 250 soldiers. Captain Longcroft had brought up the press gangs and crews of two revenue vessels based in Milford Haven, totalling 150 sailors. Nine cannon were also brought ashore, of which six were placed inside Haverfordwest Castle and the other three prepared for transit to Fishguard. Local contingency planning to counter the French threat appeared to be coming together. Lord Cawdor was given overall command by the county's Lord Lieutenant, Lord Milford. The French had already begun to move inland and secure outlying farmhouses.

By now a company of French grenadiers under Lieutenant St Leger had taken possession of Trehowel Farm on the Llanwnda Peninsula about a mile from their landing site, and it was here that Colonel Tate set up his headquarters. The French troops were told to live off the land, an, invitation to plunder. Some deserted to take advantage of that opportunity before their feet were dry. However, Tate could take some consolation from his 600 regulars who remained loyal and ready to carry out orders throughout. By dawn on the 23rd his force had moved two miles inland and occupied the rocky outcrops of Garnwnda and Carngelli, strong positions with an excellent view of the surrounding countryside.

At 0900 Knox, determined to attack the invaders as soon as was practical rather than wait for Cawdor's strong force, sent out scouting parties to assess the strength of the enemy. Knox's problem was that he had just 198 men available – 100-strong reinforcements had not yet arrived – and the scouts erroneously reported that he was facing at least 10 times that number. There was no inkling that most of the invaders were a ragbag of convicts and no-hopers with little experience of battle and even less appetite for it. The countryside was in uproar. Many locals had fled both the invasion threat and the very real activities of the convict looters. But many more were flooding in armed with farm implements and crude weapons, determined to beat off the invaders alongside the Volunteers. Lead was stripped off the roof of St David's Cathedral to make musket balls. When the outraged clergy protested they were told that the balls were for the defence of both religion and nation.

Knox wrestled with his conscience and common sense. He decided that his force was not sufficient or co-ordinated enough either to attack the French or defend Fishguard. Instead, he decided to retreat towards Haverfordwest to unite with Cawdor's superior force. His orders to spike the nine cannon in the fort were ignored by their Woolwich gunners. He set off, sending out scouts continuously to reconnoitre the French. Knox and his men met the reinforcements led by Lord Cawdor at Treffgarne, eight miles south of Fishguard, at 1330. After a short dispute between the two men, Cawdor assumed command and led the British forces back towards Fishguard.

By then the invasion was losing momentum due to Tate's inability to control his ill-disciplined ranks. Discipline collapsed utterly amongst the convicts when they discovered the locals' supply of wine collected from a Portugese ship wrecked nearby some weeks earlier. Some openly mutinied, others simply vanished during the night. They ravaged the local villages and hamlets, taking whatever loot they could carry and consuming whatever drink they could find. One group broke into Llandwnda church to shelter from the cold, and set about lighting a fire inside using a Bible as kindling and the pews as firewood. That sacrilege was guaranteed to outrage the local inhabitants. Even among the loyal grenadiers, morale plummeted. In farmhouses all over the Llanwnda Peninsula, they lay drunk and sick. Rather that rise up against the English, the Welsh locals were clearly hostile to the French. Even those who had little love for the English didn't much appreciate their homes being wrecked by drunken looters. Small clashes left at least six Welshmen and French soldiers dead.

Throughout the day there was fighting of sorts in and around the hamlet of Pencaer. A Mr Whitesides from Liverpool, an engineer building the Smalls lighthouse, gathered seafaring colleagues and marched on a French outpost. Five French troops fired and missed. The sailors took careful aim and fired back, killing one and badly wounding two others. The rest fled. Tate, witnessing the brief skirmish, was dismayed. He wondered, with good reason, what his men would do against disciplined soldiers if what he assumed were untrained local levies had put them to flight.

Near Garnwnda, two local men attacked a party of French foragers. Both died, but not until they had killed one of the invaders. Elswhere, there were numerous occasions in which local people captured invaders in ones and twos. They were often drunken deserters, but they were still the enemy. It was during the chaos that the redoubtable and rough-tongued Jemima Nicholas rounded up her French dozen with her pitchfork at Llanwnda before resolutely going out again to find more. It is thought the French troops may have mistaken local women like her, in their traditional tall black hats and red cloaks, for British Grenadiers. But the defence was not all heroics –

at Brestgarn, a panicky and drunken English soldier fired at the ticking of a clock – the bullet hole remains there still.

Many of Tate's Irish and some French officers counselled surrender. By then Castagnier and the naval squadron had long gone and there was no escape. The elderly Tate, who had expected a heroic climax to his adventurous and colourful career, had many doubts of his own about the ill-disciplined rabble he supposedly commanded.

The British reinforcements arrived in Fishguard at around 1700, and Cawdor decided to attack before dusk. His 600 men, dragging their three cannons behind them, marched up the narrow Trefwrgi Lane towards the French position on Garngelli. Lieutenant St Leger and his grenadiers were lying in ambush, having made their way down from the outcrop to crouch behind the lane's high hedges. In seconds their musket balls and grenades would have poured into a tightly compressed British column at point-blank range. It would have been carnage. But, blissfully unaware of the danger, Cawdor, concerned about the failing light, ordered his men to halt and turn around 100 yards from the ambush. They returned to Fishguard. Cawdor realised that his cannon was not viable in the tangled countryside and its narrow lanes.

That evening, two French officers arrived at the Royal Oak where Cawdor had set up his headquarters on Fishguard Square. They wished to negotiate a conditional surrender. Tate's second-in-command, Baron Jacques Phillipe de Rochemure, and his English-speaking aide-de-camp, said:

> Sir, The Circumstances under which the Body of French troops under my Command were landed at this place renders it unnecessary to attempt any military operations, as they would tend only to Bloodshed and Pillage. The Officers of the whole Corps have therefore intimated to me their desire of entering into a Negotiation upon Principles of Humanity for a surrender. If you are influenced by similar Considerations you may signify the same by the bearer and, in the mean Time, Hostilities shall cease.

The only qualification was that the French troops would be repatriated at British expense. It was an offer of retreat with honour.

Cawdor, aware, as the French were not, that his force was heavily outnumbered, bluffed. He replied that with his 'superior' force he would only accept the unconditional surrender of the French forces and issued an ultimatum to Colonel Tate. He had until 1000 on Friday 24 February to surrender on Goodwick Sands, otherwise the French would be attacked. Cawdor's actual words were grand and condescending, giving no hint of the reality of the situation:

> Sir, The Superiority of the Force under my command, which is hourly increasing, must prevent my treating upon any Terms short of your surrendering your whole Force Prisoners of War. I enter fully into your Wish of preventing an unnecessary Effusion of Blood, which your speedy Surrender can alone prevent, and which will entitle you to that Consideration it is ever the Wish of

British Troops to show an Enemy whose numbers are inferior. My Major will deliver you this letter and I shall expect your Determination by Ten o'clock, by your Officer, whom I have furnished with an Escort, that will conduct him to me without Molestation.

Tate, ignorant of the degree of bluff involved, felt he had no choice but to accept, as he communicated after a restless night. He believed that he was outnumbered two to one – the opposite of the truth. The fact that none of Cawdor's small force were regulars but mainly civilian-volunteers did not occur to him. Added to that, the French did not realise that many of those approaching the turnpike were local women, motivated by both Jemima-inspired aggression and simple curiosity. In his capitulation he referred to the British advancing 'with troops of the line to the number of several thousand'.

At 0800 the following morning the British forces lined up in battle order on the Goodwick Sands at low tide. Above them on the cliffs, the inhabitants of the town came to watch and await Tate's response to the ultimatum. Tate's fears were confirmed – among the crowd were hundreds of Welsh women clad in then fashionable scarlet mantles and low-crowned, round felt hats. At a distance, to French eyes, they looked like British redcoats. Tate tried to delay it but eventually accepted the terms of the unconditional surrender and at 1400 the sounds of the French drums could be heard leading the column down. The French piled their weapons and by 1600 the French prisoners were marched through Fishguard on their way to temporary imprisonment at Haverfordwest. Meanwhile, Cawdor had ridden out with a party of his Pembroke Yeomanry Cavalry to Trehowel Farm to receive Tate's official surrender. After brief imprisonment, Tate was returned to France in a prisoner exchange in 1798, along with most of his invasion force.

On 9 March 1797, HMS *St Fiorenzo*, under Sir Harry Neale and Captain John Cooke's HMS *Nymphe* encountered La *Resistance*, which had been crippled by the adverse weather in the Irish Sea en-route to Ireland, along with *La Constance*. Cooke and Neale chased after them, engaging them for half an hour, after which both French ships surrendered. There were no casualties or damage on either of the British ships, while the two French ships lost 18 killed and 15 wounded between them. *La Resistance* was re-fitted and renamed HMS *Fishguard* and *La Constance* became HMS *Constance*. Castagnier, on board *Le Vengeance*, made it safely back to France.

The United Irishmen went ahead with their revolt but the Establishment was more than ready. It reacted to the failed French invasion and ongoing civil disorder at home in time-honoured fashion – with repression. Martial law was declared on 2 March 1797. House-burnings, the torture and murder of captives, and the closure of the pro-United Irishmen newspaper *The Northern Star* swiftly followed. The worst pain was inflicted in Ulster on both Catholics and Presbyterians. Sectarianism was employed as an official government policy, under the 'divide and rule' principle. Brigadier-General C.E. Knox wrote to Ulster military commander general Lake: 'I have arranged ... to increase the animosity between the Orangemen and the United Irishmen, or liberty men as they call themselves. Upon that animosity depends the safety of the centre counties of the North.' The Lord Chancellor of Ireland, John Fitzgibbon, told the Privy Council: 'In the North nothing will keep the rebels quiet but the conviction that where treason has broken out the rebellion is merely popish.'

Loyalists in the newly created Orange Order supplied vital local intelligence. And the government bought off the hierarchy of the Roman Catholic Church by founding Maynooth College. The French conquest of Rome that year also helped ensure that, with a few individual exceptions, the bishops were firmly on the side of the Crown throughout.

In March 1798 the United Irishmen were betrayed by informants and most of the leadership were arrested in raids across Dublin. And a small rising at Cahir, Tipperary, was swiftly crushed. The brutality – and effectiveness – of the repression convinced the remaining leaders that they needed to act before it was too late. They agreed to rise, without French aid if need be, on 23 May. By then their membership had swelled perhaps to as much as 280,000, out of a population of around 5 million, but only a fraction of these took up arms.

The initial plan was to take Dublin, after which bordering counties would rise in support. They would block British reinforcements, and the rest of the country would tie down British garrisons. The signal to rise was to be spread by the interception of the mail coaches from Dublin. However, eleventh-hour intelligence from informants revealed the rebel assembly points in Dublin and the military occupied them in force just before the rebels were to assemble. Faced with such overwhelming odds, the rebels quickly dispersed, dumping their weapons in the surrounding lanes.

Despite the failure of the rising in Dublin, the surrounding districts rose as planned. The first armed clash came just after dawn on 24 May. Fighting quickly spread throughout Leinster, with the heaviest in County Kildare. There the rebels gained control of much of the county as military forces at Kildare withdrew. Nevertheless, the rebels were defeated at Carlow and the Hill of Tara, County Meath, ending the rebellion in those counties.

In County Wicklow, news of the rising spread panic and fear among loyalists; they responded by massacring rebel suspects held in custody at Dunlavin Green and Carnew. A baronet, Sir Edward Crosbie, was found guilty of leading the rebellion in Carlow and executed. In the town of Wicklow, large numbers rose but chiefly engaged in a bloody rural guerrilla war with the military and loyalist forces. Rebel General Joseph Hall led up to 1,000 men in the Wicklow Hills and forced the British to commit substantial forces to the area until his capitulation in October.

Mostly Presbyterian rebels rose in Antrim. They briefly held most of the county, but the rising there collapsed following defeat at Antrim town. In County Down, after initial success, rebels led by Henry Munro were defeated in the longest battle of the rebellion at Ballynahinch.

The rebels had most success in County Wexford, where they seized control, but a series of bloody defeats prevented the effective spread of the rebellion beyond the county borders. Over 20,000 troops poured into Wexford and inflicted defeat at Vinegar Hill on 21 June. The dispersed rebels spread in two columns through the midlands towards Ulster. The last remnants of these forces fought on until their final defeat on 14 July at the battles of Knightstown Bog and Ballyboughal.

The rebellion took on the worst characteristics of a civil war as neighbours fought neighbours, especially in Leinster. Vengeance replaced principle due to the ruthless repression that had preceded the rising. Rumours of massacres sparked retaliatory atrocities on both sides. And every British victory was followed by the slaughter of prisoners and wounded rebels. In Enniscorthy, rebel wounded were burned to death when soldiers set fire to a building used as a casualty station. After the defeat of a rebel attack at New Ross, between 100 and 200 prisoners were killed, some by gunshot, but the majority were burned alive at Scullabogue when the barn in which they were being held captive was set alight. There were many, many other examples. No quarter was given, whether or not a captive had played an active part in the rising. They were not regarded as prisoners of war and were summarily hanged. Civilians were murdered by the military with little or no justification, legal or otherwise. Soldiers in Wexford and elsewhere raped the womenfolk of suspected rebels. Supposedly pardoned rebels were released from military custody into the hands of local Irish yeomanry, who killed them. The rebels too were guilty of savagery towards their captives. In Wexford town 70 loyalist prisoners were marched to the bridge, stripped naked and piked to death.

Napoleon had initially promised full-scale support and the 'army of England' had been mustered on the Channel coast from Dunkirk to Honfleur. This new armada comprised 60 specially constructed gunships able to carry 10,000 men, 250 fishing vessels capable of carrying 14,750 more, plus the ships of their Dutch allies and Swedish commercial mercenaries. By the end of March the minister of marine proudly declared that, by combining with the Havre flotilla, there were enough vessels available to carry 70,000 men and 6,000 horses.

Napoleon, never wholly committed to the Irish cause and by now an Emperor who thought in terms of continents rather than mere islands, lost interest in the project. Its greatest proponent, Hoche, had died, and he had little confidence in the unwieldy flotilla's ability to evade the Royal Navy. He believed that an invasion of England was possible only after a major French victory at sea, which had eluded him. The only alternative, he reasoned, was for a flotilla of small vessels to race across the Channel under cover of darkness. But that could only be done during winter months when the night lasted the eight hours reckoned necessary for crossing and the establishment of a bridgehead. By April, as the days drew out, that was no longer feasible.

Added to such considerations, the British were well aware of the military build-up and launched a pre-emptive strike on Flushing where the invasion gunboats were being fitted out. In a precursor to later commando tactics, 1,200 men were landed, tasked with destroying the vital sluices of the Bruge canal. After a quick firefight, one sluice was destroyed and several gunboats sunk. The wind changed and the British were thus prevented from re-embarking and making their getaway. They surrendered, but the raid nevertheless shocked the French authorities.

Napoleon effectively turned his back on the Irish and headed for Egypt. Pressed by Tone, the Directory would only promise small raids on the Irish coast. The first strike was by no means small in scale but came far too late. On 22 August, nearly two months after the main uprisings had been defeated, 1,099 French soldiers under General Joseph Humbert landed at Kilcummin, County Mayo.

The leadership of the expedition had been fractious from the start, never a harbinger of military success. In July General Cherin had been put in charge of the whole operation. The plan was that his main army would assemble in Brest, with two advance divisions under Humbert and General Hardy going on ahead. Those two would sail from Brest and Rochefort and join up off the Irish coast. But a row beween Cherin and the war ministry halted the main force and Cherin was ordered to follow Napoleon to Egypt instead. Humbert, an energetic and effective soldier, set off in August and Hardy, now the overall commander, was expected to follow with 3,000 battle-ready troops under the expectation that the Irish rebellion would be almost won. That illusion was swiftly shattered, but Humbert pressed on in an already lost cause.

Joined by up to 5,000 local rebels, Humbert's army inflicted a humiliating defeat on the British at the battle of Castlebar. The British lines wavered before the French reached them and eventually turned in panic, fleeing the field. Some soldiers of the militias ran to join the republicans and even joined in the fighting against their former comrades. A unit of cavalry and British regular infantry attempted to stand and stem the tide but were quickly overwhelmed. In the headlong flight, massive quantities of guns and equipment were abandoned, including General Lake's personal luggage. Although not pursued a mile or two beyond Castlebar, the British did not stop until reaching Tuam. The Irish called the battle the Castlebar races. Although achieving a spectacular victory, the losses of the French and Irish were high, losing about 150 men, mostly to the cannonade at the start of the battle. The British suffered over 350 casualties, of which about 80 were killed, the rest either wounded or captured, including perhaps 150 who joined the republicans. Following the victory, thousands of volunteers flocked to join the French, who also sent a request to France for reinforcements and formally declared the 'Republic of Connaught'.

The victory sparked some supportive risings in Longford and Westmeath, which were quickly defeated, and the main force was defeated at the battle of Ballinamuck in September 1798. British losses were 12 killed and 16 wounded or missing. Of the French soldiers, 96 officers and 748 men were taken prisoner. Around 500 Irish lay dead on the field, and 200 prisoners were taken in the mopping up operations. The prisoners were moved to Carrick-on-Shannon where most were executed. Among those hanged was Matthew Tone, brother of Wolfe. Humbert and his men were taken by canal to Dublin and repatriated in exchange for British prisoners of war. The British army then slowly spread out into the rebel-held 'Republic of Connaught' in a brutal campaign of killing and house burning, which reached its climax on 23 September when Killala was stormed and retaken with much slaughter.

A second French raid came to disaster on the coast of Donegal. Wolf Tone took part in a third under Admiral Bompard, with General Hardy belatedly arriving with his 3,000 men. This encountered an English squadron at Buncrana on Lough Swilly on 12 October 1798. Tone, on board the ship *Hoche*, refused Bompard's offer of escape in a frigate before the action, and was taken prisoner when the *Hoche* surrendered.

When the prisoners were landed a fortnight later, Sir George Hill recognised Tone in the French adjutant-general's uniform. At his trial by court-martial in Dublin on 8 November 1798, Tone made a speech avowing his determined hostility to England and his intention 'by frank and open war to procure the separation of the countries'. Recognising that the court was certain to convict him, he asked 'that the court should adjudge me to die the death of a soldier, and that I may be shot'. Reading from a prepared speech, he defended his desire for a military separation from Britain (as had occurred in the fledgling United States) and lamented the outbreak of mass violence:

> Such are my principles, such has been my conduct; if in consequence of the measures in which I have been engaged misfortunes have been brought upon this country, I heartily lament it, but let it be remembered that it is now nearly four years since I have quit Ireland and consequently I have been personally concerned in none of them; if I am rightly informed very great atrocities have been committed on both sides, but that does not at all diminish my regret; for a fair and open war I was prepared; if that has degenerated into a system of assassination, massacre, and plunder I do again most sincerely lament it, and those few who know me personally will give me I am sure credit for the assertion.

Predictably, Tone was found guilty. He asked for death by firing squad, but when this was refused, Tone cheated the hangman by slitting his own throat in prison on 12 November and died a week later.

Small fragments of the great rebel armies of the summer of 1798 survived for a number of years and waged guerrilla war in several counties. In County Wicklow, General Holt fought on until his negotiated surrender in autumn 1798. It was not until the failure of Robert Emmet's rebellion in 1803 that the last organised rebel forces under Captain Michael Dwyer capitulated. Small pockets of rebel resistance had also survived in Wexford and the last rebel group was not vanquished until February 1804.

★★★

After the *Expedition d'Irlande* debacle Hoche returned to the Rhineland where he defeated the Austrians at the battle of Neuwied in April 1797. He was minister of war for a short period but was overwhelmed by political intrigue. He resigned for technical violations of the constitution and went back to the Rhine frontier. His health deteriorated and he died at Wetzlar on 19 September 1797 of consumption. Rumours spread that he had been poisoned. His motto was *Res non verba*, 'Deeds, not words'.

Tate was one of those repatriated to France, a country that was alien to him in most ways, including language. Little more was heard of his bluster. Jemima Nicholas became a Welsh heroine. She died, aged 82, in July 1832. She has a plaque in Fishguard dedicated to her.

In 1853, amidst fears of another invasion by the French, Lord Palmerston conferred upon the Pembroke Yeomanry the battle honour 'Fishguard'. It had the unique honour of being the only regiment in the British Army, regular or territorial, that bears a battle honour for an engagement on the British mainland. It was also the first battle honour awarded to a volunteer unit.

The wreck of a rowing boat believed to belong to the invasion fleet was found in 2003 and lies off Strumble Head. A few sodden timbers mark the last foreign invasion of the British mainland.

16 THE NAPOLEON THREAT AND BRITAIN'S 'GREAT TERROR'

'Eight hours of favourable weather will decide the fate of the universe.'
– Napoleon Bonaparte, 1803

'Bonaparte, 48 Hours after Landing! John Bull and the Volunteers' by Jamers Gilray, 1803.

The battle of Fishguard may have been a farcical sideshow to global warfare, but it again focused the minds of Britain's war leaders on the threat of invasion. Any doubts they may have harboured were swept away when Napoleon Bonaparte, newly appointed commander in Boulogne, announced in October 1797: 'Our government must destroy the British monarchy, or it will have only to wait for its own destruction by the corruption and intrigue of these insular plotters. Let us concentrate all our attention on the navy and destroy England.' He added that France must 'destroy the English monarchy, or expect itself to be destroyed by these intriguing and enterprising islanders … Let us concentrate all our efforts on the navy and annihilate England. That done, Europe is at our feet.'

The French strategy was two-fold – neutralise the Royal Navy to clear the way for an invasion across the Channel and a strike against London. Napoleon's role was to create and build up an invasion army and the means to ferry it across. Napoleon ordered a fleet of invasion craft and an English spy reported, 'On the road to Lisle (Lille) every useful tree cut down, and sawyers at work, cutting plank and other scantling, and carts transporting it to the coast in great numbers.' In London, premier William Pitt said simply: 'Expect the French every dark night.'

Napoleon's army, at that stage of planning, was around 50,000, with artillery in the same calibres as British guns to ease re-supply. But by the end of 1797, Napoleon concluded that he needed more time: 'With all our efforts, we shall not for many years obtain command of the seas. An invasion of England is a most difficult and perilous undertaking … our fleet is today as little prepared for battle as it was four months ago.' He turned his attention to Italy and Egypt, leaving General Kilmaine to continue the invasion preparations in northern France.

In early 1798 the British could raise almost 250,000 men comprising regular, militia, fencible cavalry and infantry, and yeomanry. Taken together with troops on overseas service, the combined military force topped 615,000. But strategists realised how vulnerable the coastline was and that they could not rely entirely on men. The victory at Fishguard had been the outcome of a mixture of luck and bluff. Britain was now facing oblivion in a global war of conquest. More solid defences were needed and that meant more money had to be spent. There was already an early warning system of beacons, watch-houses and semaphore telegraphs. Although these preparations were vital, it was naval power which remained the top priority.

In spring 1801, a sickly Horatio Nelson returned ennobled from the Battle of Copenhagen and was given the command of the Downs Fleet of small attack vessels based between Deal and Dungeness. As part of the Channel Fleet, he was responsible for carrying the fight to the French and for rallying the 'Sea Fencibles', an auxiliary force established to reinforce coastal defence. Nelson launched a series of daring attacks in summer 1801. Little was achieved and Nelson was pilloried by the press. Pressure only eased when Britain and France, both tired of war, signed the Treaty of Amiens in March 1802. There followed an uneasy peace which lasted just 14 months. In May 1803, after breaches in the treaty, war erupted again in May 1803. Nelson left the Channel and destroyed the French Navy off the Nile.

Napoleon fled Egypt and, back in France, turned again to his invasion flotilla. He set the invasion timetable for the winter, reasoning that fog would hide the invasion barges. By then his mustering had swelled from his initial plan to a 200,000-strong multi-national army camped in and around Boulogne, to be transported in 1,500 small craft from ports between Etaples and Flushing which had been themselves defensively strengthen against Royal Navy attack. The waiting troops were put to training manoeuvres and ceremonial parades, during which Bonaparte awarded the newly created *Legion d'Honneur*. But seaborne exercises showed the invasion craft to be of poor design and scores drowned. Napoleon considered and rejected alternatives, which can be seen as either ridiculous or far ahead of their time – troop-carrying balloons, huge rafts and even a Channel tunnel. In addition, Napoleon knew to his cost that the Royal Navy retained command of the seaways. The French fleet was constantly attacked and blockaded in port. During visits to Boulogne, he realised that only a speedy and efficient crossing, plus luck and fair weather, could bring him success. He wrote: 'Eight hours of favourable weather will decide the fate of the universe.' And: 'All my thoughts are directed towards England. I want only for a favourable wind to plant the Imperial Eagle on the Tower of London.' He planned to attack around Chatham and Dover and then strike at London, believing that it would lead quickly to both military and political victory.

Across the Channel, from the end of 1803 to 1805, the invasion threat saw thousands of volunteers being placed on military alert. For satirists it was 'The Great Terror'. The King boasted that he would personally fight the invader on the beaches, and a courtier wrote in 13 November 1803: 'The King is really prepared to take the field in case of attack, his beds are ready and he can move at half an hour's warning.' Another courtier wrote:

> The king certainly has his camp equipage and accoutrements quite ready for joining the army if the enemy should land, and is quite keen on the subject and angry if any suggests that the attempt may not be made … God forbid he should have the fate of Harold.

The King wrote to Bishop Hurd from Windsor on 30 November 1803:

> We are here in daily expectation that Bonaparte will attempt his threatened invasion; the chances against his success seem so many that it is wonderful he persists in it. I own I place that thorough dependence on Divine Providence that I cannot help thinking the usurper is encouraged to make the trial that the ill-success may put an end to his wicked purposes. Should his troops effect a landing, I shall certainly put myself at the head of my troops and my other armed subjects to repel them. But as it is impossible to foresee the events of such a conflict, should the enemy approach too near to Windsor, I shall think it right the Queen and my daughters should cross the Severn, and send them to your Episcopal Palace at Worcester; by this hint I do not the least mean they shall be any inconvenience to you, and shall send a proper servant and furniture for their accommodation. Should this event arise, I certainly would rather have what I value most in life remain, during the conflict, in your diocese and under your roof than in any other place in the island.

His government's contingency plan, as he well knew, insisted that he would meet up with the Prime Minister and the Home Secretary at Dartford if the French landed. After reviewing the situation, or if London fell, His Majesty would be transported to the relative safety of Worcester Cathedral, along with his mistress and key ministers. There they would 'use the final mainstays of sovereignty – treasure and arms – to keep up the final struggle'.

Lord Cornwallis would command the reserve army. The Royal Arsenal artillery and stores would be barged up the Grand Junction canal to a new ordnance depot at Weedon, Northamptonshire. Soldiers would be paid in gold instead of paper money. The Bank of England's books would be sent to the Tower of London and its treasure would be entrusted to Commissary General Sir Brook Watson, who would transport it in 30 wagons guarded by a relay of twelve volunteer escorts across the Midlands to join the King at Worcester. The Stock Exchange would close and the Privy Council would take charge in London. The press would be forbidden from printing troop movements and official government communiqués would be distributed.

Such contingencies were not tested as Britain embarked on an extraordinarily rapid military mobilisation. Fifty of the 93 regiments of the army gained a second battalion, known as the Army of Reserve. The aim was to raise 50,000 men by ballot within one year, serving on the home front only. Those that agreed to transfer to the regulars would be paid. Most took that route. Within one month 22,500 men had enlisted, but by the end of the year the recruitment drive was still 15,000 short of the target.

Then there were the militia, used only for home defence, raised by ballot. The government had in December 1802 held such a ballot run by churchwardens and poor law overseers in each parish. A list of men aged between 18 and 45 was posted on the front of the church door. However, there were many exceptions, such as seamen and Thames watermen. And any man could get off the list by paying a fine or persuading another to take his place. It was an accommodation which benefited the better-off and penalised the poor. After four months, and a week into the war, the militia was filled to 80 per cent of the 51,000 required.

And finally, there were the volunteers. The British government had no choice but to rely on the patriotism of the people. Their specified role was to conduct guerrilla warfare against French occupying forces. A similar underground army was established in the Second World War in the event of a Nazi invasion – small groups with extensive local knowledge who would harass the enemy, slow down advances, create panic and generally wear down the invaders.

Well aware that in an era of revolution and civil insurrection, arming the people could be dangerous, Secretary at War Charles Yorke said on 18 July 1803 in introducing a Bill for amending the Defence of the Realm Act:

I say, that in these times, it is better to run the hazard even of the people making a bad use of their arms, than that they should be actually left in a state of entire ignorance of the use of them. For my own part, I can safely aver, that I cannot see any real danger which is likely to accrue to the internal peace of the Country, when I consider the present dispositions and feelings of the people.

William Pitt, now out of his 'vast, awkward house', Number 10, agreed:

I am sure there is not a heart that palpitates in a British bosom that will not rouse for the common cause, and cordially join for the defence of the country.

... That there was a time, Sir, when it would have been dangerous to entrust arms with a great portion of the people of this country, I have strong reasons to know, because it must be in the recollection of every man that incendiaries were at work amongst them; and so successful in the promulgation of revolutionary doctrines, as to have disposed them to exert any means, however desperate, which they thought could be successful, in subverting the Government and Constitution. But that time is now past; and, I trust, those who have been so grossly deluded have seen their error. At least I am convinced, that if any such there still remain, the portion is so small, that if armed and dispersed in the same ranks with their loyal fellow subjects, they would be converted by their example; and, like them, rejoice in the blessings of our happy constitution; like them glory to live under its auspices, or die in its defence.

Prominent anti-war MP Charles James Fox also supported the Bill, saying:

This is the first measure which I could ... come down to support, being a measure for the defence of the country ... the mass of the country; acting, not in single regiments, but as a great mass of armed citizens, fighting for the preservation of their country, their families, and everything that is dear to them in life ... an armed mass of the country, who are bound by every feeling and by every tie to defend that country to the last drop of their blood, before they will give way to him and his invading forces.

The call for volunteers met with a massive response – 280,000 strong – that wrong-footed the government which could not cope with such an influx. Fears of arming the 'rabble' re-surfaced. On 18 August premier Addington issued a circular discouraging new volunteers 'in any county where the effective members of those corps, including the yeomanry, shall exceed the amount of six times the militia'. That did not dissuade a population in the grip of both patriotic fervour and fear. By early September the total reached 350,000. At least half could not provide their own arms. And when the government tried to issue them with pikes, this was met with contempt and disappointment not seen again until the time of *Dad's Army*.

The second half of 1803 marked the height of the invasion scare. When the King reviewed 27,000 volunteers in London's Hyde Park on 26 and 28 October 1803, 500,000 people were estimated to have turned out on each of the two days to witness the event. The Chief Constable of Bramfield, John Carrington, said: 'I never saw such a sight all my days.' These were the best attended of reviews of volunteers which between 1797 and 1805 'were often of daily occurrence'. By the end of 1803 480,000 volunteers had signed up. Together with the regulars and the militia, nearly one in five of able-bodied British were men in uniform. The Commons Speaker said: 'The whole Nation has risen up in Arms.' Addington called the volunteer movement 'an insurrection of loyalty'. It was a response not seen again until the First World War when the threat of invasion was not so real as those facing their Georgian forebears.

The response to the call to arms to resist invasion in these years was impressive and one historian wrote: 'If some dissentient voices were heard in 1797-8 when the aftermath of the Revolution still lingered in the land, there was increased enthusiasm in the patriotism of 1801, and burning ardour coupled with absolute unanimity in that of 1803-5.'

However, there remained the problem of physical defences against Napoleon's invasion strategy. The Duke of York, the military commander, rightly believed that the low-lying sandy beaches either side of Dover were the most likely places for a landing, particularly at Hythe and Dungeness. Since 1798, the British had adopted a defensive 'scorched-earth' policy, known as 'driving the country', knowing that Napoleon's army travelled light and relied on taking food and fodder from the land, rather than carrying supplies in heavy wagon trains. The British planned to evacuate the local population and destroy foodstuffs and the means of transport across a swathe of the southern counties. In addition, there would be three more elements of defence: ongoing and aggressive naval operations in the Channel designed to sink or at least delay the invasion fleet; a line of gun towers along the coast to provide inter-locking cannon fire in support of deployed regular troops and militia; and a canal behind Romney Marsh to hinder the French advance and supply routes in the event of a successful landing.

The military commanders charged with the defence of the realm faced problems common before and after – bureaucracy, politics and penny-pinching. This was an era in which the rich were largely untaxed and found the concept alien even at times of national crisis. The debate over the cost of a ring of towers and other permanent defensive works raged in Westminster and Whitehall, in coffee houses and glittering salons. Eventually the realisation dawned on even the most bone-headed aristocrat and minister that Napoleon meant business. By the end of 1803 the Privy Council finally agreed that the army could build Martello gun towers from East Anglia to Sussex. The Duke of York said that 'the Erection of such Works must be immediate with a view to their probable utility', placing them at 'Points where a Landing threatens the most important interests of the Country'.

Their name came from a tower on 'Mortella' Point in Corsica, which in February 1794 held off an attack by two Royal Navy ships, inflicting heavy damage. In spring 1805 work began on 74 squat towers from Folkestone to Seaford. When completed, each held one officer and 24 men who manned the gun platform on the roof. As military strongholds spaced pretty evenly along the coast, they also helped tackle the lucrative smuggling trade. In July 1803 the Duke of York argued for the construction of field fortifications as soon as possible because 'the Erection of such Works must be immediate with a view to their probable utility,' placing them at 'Points where a Landing threatens the most important interests of the Country.'

General Sir William Twiss scouted suitable sites across the south east and suggested 88 of them. At a defence conference in Rochester the plan finally got the commitment and funding it required. In the event, 74 were built, but those at Eastbourne and Dymchurch were bigger than the rest, housing 11 guns and 350 soldiers each. A second line of 29 towers, from Clacton-on-Sea to Slaghden near Aldeburgh, was constructed by 1812, including a great redoubt at Harwich, to extend the defences up the east coast. Forty were built in Ireland and more in the Channel Islands (see Appendix 4).

General Twiss also recommended a fortress at Dover. Western Heights, across the town from the massive medieval castle, was started in 1804. The Drop Redoubt, a detached fort close to the steep cliffs, surrounded by ditches and intended for soldiers to go out and attack French infantry, was completed by 1808. The Citadel was a larger fort surrounded by ditches and was still unfinished when war with France ended in 1815. The Grand Shaft was a barracks containing 60 officers and 1,300 NCOs and soldiers, begun in 1806 and completed in 1809.

During the summer of 1804 it was proposed to flood Romney Marsh by opening the sluices at Dymchurch, Scots Float, East Guldeford and Pett Level, and by breaching the walls along the rivers Brede and Rother. During the summer of 1804, Lieutenant Colonel Brown was sent to examine the proposal, which he deemed unworkable. Instead he preferred 'a cut from Shorncliffe battery, passing in front of Hythe under Lympne heights to West Hythe … being everywhere within musket shot of the heights'. Brown then proposed a water barrier 'cutting off Romney Marsh from the county, opening a short and easy communication between Kent and Sussex but, above all, rendering unnecessary the doubtful and destructive measure of laying so large a portion of the country waste by inundation'. In September it was duly agreed to build the 28-mile Royal Military Canal from Hythe to Rye Harbour. It turned every 500yds to enable enfilade fire from guns placed at the bends. On the inshore side there was a parapet, military road and a drain; on the shore side, a towpath for troop barges. Key crossing points had guardhouses for soldiers.

A manual military telegraph system using flags had already been connected in January 1796 between the Admiralty, Deal and Portsmouth. Later, another ran to Great Yarmouth. The system was tried, tested and highly efficient. A message using runners and horsemen had previously taken many hours, if not days, to travel from Portsmouth to London. It now took 15 minutes. A similar message from Hythe took 11 minutes.

However, during the period of greatest danger from Napoleon – the three years from 1805 – Britain remained vulnerable. The Royal Military Canal was not fully operational until 1809 and first line of Martello towers was not completed until the year after that, as were the great redoubts at Dover and elsewhere. At the height of the threat in 1803/1804, there were merely a few crumbling forts from other eras and hastily thrown up gun batteries. An exception were the Shorncliffe defences at the end of Hythe Bay, with a dozen 24-pounders covering the beach and a redoubt above. That was largely due to Sir John Moore, later of Peninsular War fame, who in 1802 took responsibility for the defence of Kent. He determined that his troops would mount an aggressive defence and his fortifications drew condemnation from the Treasury and Whitehall pen-pushers.

The British and French continued their preparations throughout 1804 and 1805 while skirmishing in the Channel. The Royal Navy kept a constant blockade of

French harbours. Rear-Admiral Cornwallis had a fleet off Brest and Commander-in-Chief of the North Sea Admiral Keith commanded another fleet between the Downs and Selsey Bill. A further line of British ships lay close to the English coast to intercept any French ships that broke through the blockade. The French were so reluctant to venture out that in two years only nine flotilla ships had been captured or sunk. During the end of December 1803 a violent storm blew Cornwallis's fleet from Brest and it had to stay in Torbay. Aldington and the admirals realised this gave the French a perfect opportunity to invade and issued emergency orders. But it was an opportunity the French missed. Lord St Vincent, First Lord of the Admiralty, told Parliament: 'I do not say the French cannot come, I only say they cannot come by sea.'

In October 1805 Nelson confronted the combined French and Spanish fleets off Cadiz. The victory at Trafalgar, while robbing Britain of one of its best naval commander, changed everything. In addition, Napoleon had a few weeks earlier felt under threat from the Austrians and moved his Grand Army from Boulogne to southern Germany. It was at Ulm that he received the news of his fleet's defeat by Nelson at Trafalgar. With no chance of naval superiority, the invasion of Britain was put on hold.

Nevertheless, the building of British defences continued, no-one quite believing that Boney was now himself on the defensive. Naval skirmishing continued in the Channel until around 1811. The threat of invasion never went away until Napoleon was finally defeated at Waterloo in 1815.

A new First Lord of the Admiralty, Lord Melville, noted after the war that given time Napoleon would 'have sent forth such powerful fleets that our navy must eventually have been destroyed, since we could never have kept pace with him in building ships nor equipped numbers sufficient to cope with the tremendous power he could have brought against us'.

Naval superiority, and perhaps the superbly engineered defences still visible today, helped shatter the European – and global – ambitions of the nineteenth-century conqueror.

17 THREATS FROM AMERICA AND GERMANY 1815-1939

'invasion is impracticable…'
– Committee of Imperial Defence report, Germany 1907

Alfred von Tirpitz.

Following the defeat of Napoleon, Britain's interests were scattered across her empire and military clashes tended to be far away – Afghanistan, New Zealand, the Far East – rather than close to home. The threat of invasion was miniscule by the time Queen Victoria took the throne.

There were tensions, however, which raised fears of invasions of her dominions and colonies. One such was the especially fraught relationship with the United States of America that had festered since the War of Independence and the subsequent war, which began in 1812 and saw the British shelling of Washington, the burning of the White House and the mass deportation of English residents. (The second amendment on the right to bear arms, dating from this period, has arguably been misconstrued to justify the sale of automatic weapons used in a series of school massacres up to and including that at Sandy Hook elementary school in 2012.) Neither war settled securely the border with Canada and the state of Maine. The subsequent Aroostook 'War' of 1838-39 was a confrontation in which heated rhetoric led both sides to raise and arm troops, and march them to the disputed border. President Martin Van Buren sent Brigadier General Winfield Scott to work out a compromise that created a neutral area and prevented a crisis turning into conflict. The American Civil War saw Britain instinctively siding with the Confederacy, largely because of the cotton trade, and the ill-fated Fenian invasion of Canada, although again, diplomacy prevented outright warfare.

In the meantime Britain and her allies, including the French, had defeated Russia in the Crimea and any perceived threat from across the Channel was again diminished. That did not, however, stop regular scares hitting the general population and the military high command. The reasons were both over-active imaginations and the pell-mell advances of new technology. Mass production allowed European nations to build up vast armies which could be mobilised quickly using the new railways and steam boats. As early as 1847 the Duke of Wellington warned that steam power had made possible potential new war machines and techniques available to those capable of harnessing them. Rumours of a balloon invasion had been known during the Napoleonic era, as had talk of the French digging a tunnel under the Channel. But by the time that original Chunnel was seriously proposed in the 1880s, a far more realistic threat had emerged – a united Germany fully capable of building up both army and navy into iron juggernauts.

The rise of German sea power, notwithstanding the Kaiser's family and dynastic ties with Victoria, raised the distinct possibility, some would say certainty, of a lightning strike against the British Isles themselves rather than far-flung dominions.

The Germans saw the potential long before the British. In 1896 the German Chief of Staff, Admiral von Diederichs, advocated a swift, unannounced naval attack on the Thames estuary which would give them control of the North Sea. His critics in Berlin pointed out that to be successful that would entail grabbing embarkation ports in the Netherlands and Belgium. That would in turn entail overrunning both countries, losing the element of surprise and dragging France into a war on Britain's side. For three years the secret plans were hotly debated – with the sole use of German North Sea ports emerging as the favoured strategy – until the plans were shelved. The Kaiser and his commanders from then on favoured building up the Imperial navy and, in the run-up to the Great War, buying up the technologies and submarine hardware they turned into the U-boat fleet. Blockade, rather than outright invasion, would bring Britain to its knees, they assumed. That was set out clearly by Admiral Tirpitz, whose dominance of the Kaiser's navy was secure. He told junior strategists that their advocacy of a lightning strike was based on the belief that in 1805 Napoleon needed just one clear day free of Royal Navy interference to succeed in an invasion. In a scathing memo he wrote: 'That was Napoleon's error. If he had really succeeded in getting across and was later cut off, then both he and his army would have been lost – as in Egypt, where only flight and the premature conclusion of peace saved him from total defeat.' Tirpitz was also an early advocate of submarine power and pointed out that even if the Royal Navy was lured away with some ruse, a few British submarines could cause havoc by torpedoing invasion barges.

Britain was slow to understand the change of strategy while the two nations engaged in a naval arms race. A 1907 panic followed a claim to the Committee of Imperial Defence that Germany was considering an invasion without declaring war, and there were proposals to raise a 400,000-strong militia based on the Territorial Army as a home defence force. That died down the following year when the Committee insisted that maintaining the Royal Navy as the world's strongest fleet remained the best deterrent. Its report concluded:

> So long as our naval supremacy is assured against any probable combination of Powers, invasion is impracticable … our army for home defence ought to be sufficient in numbers and organisation not only to repel small raids, but to compel an enemy who contemplates invasion to come with so substantial a force as will make it impossible for him to evade our fleet.

The onset of the First World War again raised the spectre of a German invasion when, in October 1914, the German army's march through Belgium took them to the coast and the major Channel port of Ostend. That could be the embarkation point for invasion barges assembled from the river and canal systems of Europe. Realistic numbers for the initial invading army hovered around 60,000 men, although a jittery War Office raised that at one point to 160,000. But Germany navy cover was still considered a prerequisite of any invasion and the Battle of Jutland killed off any prospect of that. The German battle fleet remained holed up in port, and the war of the Western Front became bogged down in the trenches.

America belatedly joined Britain in defeating the Kaiser, although US dominance of the treaty that ended that world war helped create the conditions that led to the next one. American isolation during the 1920s, powerful pro-German and Irish Nationalist lobbies, ambitions in and around the Pacific, recognition of the threat from Japan (a British ally at the time) and the power of industrial imperialism led to Joint Army and Navy Basic War Plan Red, also known as the Atlantic Strategic War Plan. A refinement envisaged a two-front war with both Japan and the British Empire, codenamed War Plan Red-Orange.

The trigger was the 1927 Geneva Naval Conference, which convinced some American top brass that a military confrontation was inevitable. They believed that Britain would initially have the upper hand by virtue of the strength of her navy and could use its dominion in Canada as a springboard from which to initiate a retaliatory invasion of the US. The assumption was taken that at first Britain would fight a defensive battle against invading American forces, but that the US would eventually defeat Britain by blockading the UK and economically isolating it, a scheme uncannily similar to the German U-boat campaigns in both global wars.

War Plan Red first set out a description of Canada's geography, military resources, and transportation, and went on to evaluate a series of possible pre-emptive American campaigns to invade Canada in several areas and occupy key ports and railways before British troops could provide reinforcements.

A joint US army-navy attack would capture the port city of Halifax, cutting off the Canadians from their British allies. Their next objective was to seize Canadian power plants near Niagara Falls, followed by a full-scale invasion on three fronts: from Vermont to take Montreal and Quebec, from North Dakota to take over the railhead at Winnipeg, and from the Midwest to capture the strategic nickel mines of Ontario. In parallel, the US Navy was to seize the Great Lakes and blockade Canada's Atlantic and Pacific ports.

War Plan Red did not envision striking outside the western hemisphere. The plan assumed that the British Empire would have a much larger army and slightly larger navy. Because of the empire's historical strength the United States had traditionally planned for a defensive war with it, and War Plan Red continued this attitude even as American power grew to match Britain's. Its authors saw conquering Canada as the best way to attack the British Empire, and believed that doing so would cause Britain to negotiate for peace.

Based on extensive war games conducted at the Naval War College, the plan rejected attacking British shipping or attempting to destroy the British fleet. The main American fleet would instead stay in the western North Atlantic to block British-Canadian traffic. The navy would wait for a good opportunity to engage the British fleet, and if successful would then attack British trade and colonies in the western hemisphere. In 1935 War Plan Red was updated and specified which roads to use in the invasion. America planned to build three military airfields near the Canadian border and disguise them as civilian airports. The airfields were to be kept secret, but their existence was accidentally published by the Government Printing Office and reported on the front page of the *New York Times* on 1 May 1935. The same year the plans were shelved and only de-classified in 1974.

Royal Navy commanders understood that that it would be impossible to defend Canada against invasion but, in the event of war, considered attacking the US fleet from Bermuda, while other ships based in Canada and the West Indies would attack American shipping and protect Imperial trade. The navy would also bombard coastal bases and make small amphibious assaults. India and Australia would help capture Manila to prevent American attacks on British trade in Asia and perhaps a conquest of Hong Kong. They hoped that such acts would result in a stalemate, making continued war unpopular in the United States, followed by a negotiated peace.

The Canadian Lieutenant Colonel James 'Buster' Sutherland Brown had developed an earlier response to any future American invasion called Defence Scheme No. 1 in April 1921. He planned the rapid deployment of flying columns to temporarily occupy Seattle, Great Falls, Minneapolis and Albany and divert American troops, hopefully long enough for Imperial allies to arrive with reinforcements. His scheme was abandoned two years prior to the approval of War Plan Red.

War Plan Red now seems fantastical, given the Allied efforts in the Second World War, the subsequent Cold War and the supposed 'special relationship' which developed once the British Empire no longer posed any threat to the American Empire. But it is often forgotten that isolationist Americans saw the British Empire as their main opponent in their plan for global economic dominance, while Irish nationalism was a vote-winner in many American constituencies. Many saw Germany as a natural ally in that battle for markets, while during the 1920s, Japan, America's opponent in the Pacific and rim territories, was allied to Britain. The US operated an open door policy for their own exports, but slammed the door on foreign imports. That clashed with Britain's own protectionist policy for its own empire. But then Germany began to encroach on trade in Latin America and other markets, while Britain resisted the encroachment of the Japanese in the East. Alliances, based on hard-nosed commercial realities, shifted dramatically.

Frank McLynn:

> The economic conflict of the two English-speaking power blocs, seen most dramatically perhaps in the world-wide clash between Shell and Standard Oil petroleum companies, seemed (in the 1920s) an inevitable aspect of the future. What destroyed this neat pattern was the Great Depression and its political consequences.

By the mid-1930s, in Britain at least, and despite appeasement, the main threat eventually became clear and explicit – Nazi Germany.

Even then, the majority of Americans – 80 per cent according to an aggregate of 1940 polls – continued to favour the isolationist policies of crypto-Fascist trans-Atlantic aviator Charles Lindberg and the organisation America First. They were targeted by the clandestine British Security Co-Ordination, a sub-section of the UK security services (whose members included the children's author Roald Dahl). That unit concentrated on disinformation to disrupt America First by posing as supporters, cancelling meetings, printing AF pamphlets overlaid with swastikas, planting bogus stories in newspapers and on radio, and many other schoolboy-sounding but deadly serious stunts. Their activities became redundant when the Japanese bombed Pearl Harbor in December 1941.

Author William Boyd said in December 2012 that the UK-American 'special relationship' was a myth invented by Winston Churchill after the Second World War:

> Roosevelt was dead, so Churchill rewrote the nature of their relationship, which I think was far frostier and less amicable than we think. But we were manipulating the US media for 18 months for our own ends, the media of these, our putative allies, and very successfully too … . Anglophobia was really quite extreme. Britain was an empire and America was a republic. All this has been hidden by the rosy glow of the 'special relationship'.

18 OPERATION SEA LION

'a sheer act of desperation'
– Alfred Jodl, 1940

Aircraft spotter on the roof of a building in London, 1940, National Archives and Records Administration.

In late 1940 the commander-in-chief of the German Army, Walter von Brauchitsch, directed: 'The able-bodied male population between the ages of 17 and 45 will, unless the local situation calls for an exceptional ruling, be interned and dispatched to the Continent.' That was around a quarter of the population forecast to have survived the invasion. The country would then be plundered for anything of financial, military, industrial or cultural value, and the remaining population terrorised. Civilian hostages would be taken, and the death penalty immediately imposed for even the most trivial acts of resistance. The deported male population would be used as industrial slave labour in areas of the Reich such as the factories and mines of the Ruhr and Upper Silesia. Heinrich Himmler wanted to go further and expressed an intention to kill about 80 per cent of the populations of France and England by special forces of the SS after the inevitable German victory. Adolf Hitler, who had initially hoped to forge an alliance by which he would have Europe while the nation in question would be left its empire, was furious at ongoing opposition to his diktat. He described the nation's working class as 'racially inferior'.

The nation in question was, of course, Great Britain. And the plans for its conquest was code-named *Unternehmen Seelowe*, Operation Sea Lion.

Great forests have been chopped down for the mountains of books on the Second World War, its causes, and Hitler's rise to power, so a brief summary of events is all I propose here. However, there has been a fashion to underplay Hitler's practical preparations for invasion, while deriding in *Dad's Army* terms the measures taken to counter the threat. Both issues will be addressed.

On 1 September 1939, Hitler's Germany invaded Poland and two days later Britain and France declared war in support of their ally. Within three weeks Poland was overrun by Germany from the West and by the Soviet Union from the east. A British Expeditionary Force was sent to the Franco-Belgian border, but there was no direct action in support of the Poles. There was little fighting over the months that followed, French and British soldiers trained for war and constructed and manned defences on the eastern borders of France.

On 9 April 1940, Germany invaded Denmark and Norway. Denmark surrendered immediately, and after fierce fighting, Norway also fell. The invasion of Norway was seen by the British as a dire portent. In the second week of May the British Prime Minister Neville Chamberlain, considered by most as a hapless appeaser, resigned and Winston Churchill, who for years had recognised the threat of the Nazi military build-up, succeeded him.

On 10 May 1940, Germany invaded France. The BEF consisted of 10 infantry divisions in three corps, a tank brigade and a Royal Air Force detachment of around 500 aircraft. The BEF was pinned by a German diversionary attack through Belgium and then isolated by the main attack that came through the Ardennes forest. Well equipped and highly mobile Panzer divisions of the *Wehrmacht* overran the prepared defences. After fierce fighting, most of the BEF withdrew to a small area around the French port of Dunkirk. The evacuation of British forces began on 26 May with air cover provided by the RAF at heavy cost. Over the following ten days 338,226 French and British soldiers were evacuated with the help of a flotilla of small commercial and private boats. Many of the army's vehicles, tanks, guns, ammunition and much of its heavy equipment and the RAF's ground equipment and stores were left behind. Some soldiers returned without their rifles. A further 215,000 were evacuated from ports south of the Channel during June. The defeat was turned into a propaganda victory, a miracle even, demonstrating British resilience, ingenuity and pluck. But the threat of a German invasion was now very real and immediate, as Hitler now controlled embarkation points on the Channel coast.

Before the outbreak of war Hitler and his commanders had given little thought to an invasion of Britain. The Fuhrer's main aim was unchanged since he wrote *Mein Kampf* – expansion of Germany eastwards. He believed even after Dunkirk that an honourable peace could be agreed, leaving him a free hand on mainland Europe.

His key military commanders believed that an invasion was unnecessary as Britain could be brought to its knees by a U-boat blockade. But contingency plans were nevertheless in place. As early as November 1939, the naval operations officer Kapitan Hans Jurgen Reinicke drew up a document examining 'the possibility of troop landings in England should the future progress of the war make the problem arise'. After five days' study, Reinicke spelt out five prerequisites: the elimination or sealing off of Royal Navy forces from the landing and approach areas; the destruction of the RAF; the destruction of all Royal Navy units in the coastal zone; and the blocking of British submarine action against the landing fleet. The study was well considered, and made glum reading for German military realists.

At roughly the same time the Wehrmacht issued its own study paper, *Nordwest*, and sought opinions from both the *Kriegsmarine* and Luftwaffe. The paper outlined an assault on England's eastern coast between The Wash and the River Thames by troops crossing the North Sea from Low Country ports. Seventeen divisions, including two airborne and four panzer, would strike at Yarmouth, Dunwich, Lowestoft, Hollesley Bay and Cromer. Surprise and speed would help them establish a bridgehead that would funnel reinforcements for the grand assault on London.

Reichsmarschall Hermann Goering, head of the Luftwaffe, was scathing: 'A combined operation having the objective of landing in England must be rejected. It could only be the final act of an already victorious war against Britain as otherwise the preconditions for success of a combined operation would not be met.' The *Kriegsmarine* response focused on the many difficulties to be overcome if invading England was to be a viable option. By spring 1940, the *Kriegsmarine* became even more opposed after the Norwegian 'victory' had seen most of its surface fleet either sunk or damaged, leaving the service hopelessly outnumbered by the ships of the Royal Navy.

Frank McLynn wrote that the 1939 invasion plan had 'an air of daydreaming about it' because it relied on a swift and decisive victory in France.

> But the *Blitzkreig* of May 1940, which achieved staggering results through the combined use of airpower and armoured breakthrough, and led directly to the fall of France, seemed to vindicate the most bullish advocates of air power, already buoyed up by the Luftwaffe's success in the Norwegian campaign.

McLynn added:

> In vain did the ever-circumspect German Navy point out that their heavy losses in Norway counter-balanced this. The toll on destroyers, particularly, meant that their task of protecting an invasion force bound for England would be that much more difficult. Yet the staggering ease of the French defeat led Hitler in the euphoria of the moment to underrate the difficulties of a descent on England.

In addition, new Prime Minister Churchill's ringing declaration on 18 June that Britain would never surrender convinced Hitler that his job in the west was not yet done. On 16 July, following Britain's outright rejection of his recent peace overtures, Hitler issued *Fuhrer Directive No. 16*, setting in motion preparations for a landing in Britain. He prefaced the order:

> As England, in spite of her hopeless military situation, still shows no signs of willingness to come to terms, I have decided to prepare, and if necessary to carry out, a landing operation against her. The aim of this operation is to eliminate the English Motherland as a base from which the war against Germany can be continued, and, if necessary, to occupy the country completely.

In a speech three days later Hitler spoke 'more in sorrow than anger' of the need to destroy the British Empire due to Churchill's intransigence. Hitler's directive also set preconditions: the RAF was to be 'beaten down in its morale and in fact, so that it can no longer display any appreciable aggressive force in opposition to the German crossing'; the English Channel was to be swept of British mines at the crossing points and the Strait of Dover must be blocked at both ends by German mines; the coastal zone between occupied France and England must be dominated by heavy artillery; the Royal Navy must be sufficiently engaged in the northern seas and the Mediterranean so that it could not intervene in the crossing; and British home squadrons must be damaged or destroyed by air and torpedo attacks.

This ultimately placed responsibility for Sea Lion's success squarely on the shoulders of Admiral Raeder and Göering, both openly opposed to the venture. A glaring omission from *Directive 16* was failure to provide for a combined operational headquarters under which all three service branches could work together under a single umbrella organisation to plan, coordinate and execute such a complex undertaking.

Although most of Britain's fleet was engaged in the Atlantic and Mediterranean, its Home Fleet still had a very large numerical advantage. And the vulnerability of its ships was open to question. During the Dunkirk evacuation few warships were actually sunk, despite being stationary targets. The overall disparity between the opposing naval forces made the amphibious invasion plan risky, regardless of the outcome in the air. In addition, the *Kriegsmarine* had allocated its few remaining larger and modern ships to diversionary operations in the North Sea. Even if the Royal Navy had been neutralised, the chances of a successful amphibious invasion across the Channel were remote. The Germans had no specialised landing craft and had to rely primarily on river barges to lift troops and supplies for the landing. The barges were not designed for use in open sea and even in almost perfect conditions, they would have been slow and vulnerable to attack. There were not enough barges to transport the first invasion wave, never mind those set to follow. The Germans would have to capture a port immediately, and each in the south-east sector were heavily defended. British contingency plans included the use of poison gas.

The German navy had taken some small steps to remedy the landing craft shortcomings with construction of self-propelled, shallow-draft vessels that could carry 45 infantrymen, two light vehicles or 20 tons of cargo and land on an open beach, unloading via a pair of clamshell doors at the bow. But by late September 1940, only two prototypes had been delivered. Given barely two months to assemble a large sea-going invasion fleet, the *Kriegsmarine* opted to convert inland river barges into makeshift landing craft. Approximately 2,400 barges were collected throughout Europe but of those, only about 800 were powered while the rest required towing by tugs.

The Luftwaffe had formed its own special command (*Sonderkommando*) under Major Fritz Siebel to investigate the production of landing craft for Sea Lion. Major Siebel proposed giving the unpowered Type A barges their own motive power by installing a pair of 600hp surplus BMW aircraft engines on them. The navy was highly sceptical of this venture but the army high command enthusiastically embraced it and Siebel proceeded with the conversions. By early October, 128 Type A barges had been converted to airscrew propulsion and by the end of the month this figure had risen to over 200.

Providing armour support for the initial wave of assault troops was a critical concern for Sea Lion planners, who needed to find practical ways of rapidly getting tanks onto the invasion beaches. Though the Type A barges were capable of disembarking several medium tanks onto an open beach, this could be done only at low tide when the barges were firmly grounded and would be exposed to enemy fire. A safer and faster method was needed and the Germans eventually settled on providing some tanks with floats and making others fully submersible. By the end of August, the Germans had converted 160 Panzer IIIs, 42 Panzer IVs and 52 Panzer IIs to amphibious use. This gave them a paper strength of 254 machines, about the equivalent of an armoured division. They were to carry sufficient fuel and ammunition for a combat radius of 200km. The German Army developed a portable landing bridge nicknamed *Seeschlange* (Sea Snake). This 'floating roadway' was formed from a series of joined modules that could be towed into place to act as a temporary jetty. Moored ships could then unload their cargo either directly onto the roadbed or lower it down onto waiting vehicles via their heavy-duty booms. Specialised vehicles slated for Sea Lion included the amphibious tractor *Landwasserschlepper,* which was first developed for river crossings. In an invasion they were to be used to pull ashore unpowered assault barges, and then tow vehicles across the beaches and to carry supplies directly ashore during the six hours of falling tide when the barges were grounded.

The German Army High Command originally planned an invasion on a vast scale, extending from Dorset to Kent, far in excess of what *Kriegsmarine* could supply. The final plans were more modest, calling for nine divisions to make an amphibious landing with around 67,000 men in the first echelon and an airborne division in support. The chosen invasion sites ran from Rottingdean in the west to Hythe in the east. The German Navy wanted a front as short as possible, stretching from Dover to Eastbourne. Admiral Raeder stressed that invasion shipping between Cherbourg and Dorset would be exposed to attacks from the Navy based in Portsmouth and Plymouth. General Halder rejected this, saying, 'From the army's point of view I regard it as complete suicide, I might just as well put the troops that have landed straight through the sausage machine.'

The final battle plan, issued on 17 July, called for six crack German divisions under Field-Marshal von Rundstedt to be launched from Boulogne to Eastbourne, Calais to Folkestone, and Dunkirk and Ostend to Ramsgate. Paratroopers would land near Brighton and Dover. Four more divisions would leave Le Havre to take the coast between Brighton and the Isle of Wight. Three more divisions would cross from Cherbourg to Lyme Bay. The General Staff envisaged 90,000 men put ashore on the first day, rising to 260,000 by the third day. Close behind would follow six panzer and three motorised divisions. In all, the invasion was expected to eventually involve 39 divisions. Once a long coastal bridgehead was secured, the invaders would move inland to the first objective, a line from Gravesend to Southampton, while the Dorset force would take Bristol. They would push north, taking Gloucester and encircling London and bombarding the capital into submission. German forces would secure England up to Northampton and a line from East Anglia to the Severn, whereupon, the planners believed, the rest of England would surrender. Key Midlands industrial centres would be taken by fast-moving armoured and motorised divisions. Further occupation of the north of England and Scotland was deemed unnecessary – it could be left as a puppet neighbour, as with Vichy France. The whole operation was planned to take four weeks. That was the plan and success seemed attainable.

With Germany's occupation of the Pas-de-Calais region the possibility of closing the Strait of Dover to Royal Navy warships and merchant convoys by use of land-based heavy artillery became apparent, both to the German High Command and to Hitler. Even the *Kriegsmarine*'s Naval Operations Office deemed this a plausible and desirable goal, especially given the short 21-mile distance between the two coasts. Orders were therefore issued to assemble and begin emplacing every army and navy heavy artillery piece available along the French coast. This work was assigned to *Organisation Todt* and its slave labour and commenced on 22 July 1940.

To strengthen German control of the Channel narrows, the Army planned to quickly establish mobile artillery batteries along the English shoreline once a beachhead had been firmly established. The *Artillerie Kommand 106* was slated to land with the second wave to provide fire protection for the transport fleet as early as possible. This unit consisted of 24 15cm (5.9in) guns and 72 10cm (3.9in) guns. The presence of these batteries was expected to greatly reduce the threat posed by British destroyers and smaller craft along the eastern approaches, as the guns would be sited to cover the main transport routes from Dover to Calais and from Hastings to Boulogne. They could not entirely protect the western approaches, but a large area of those invasion zones would still be within effective range.

The British military was well aware of the dangers posed by German artillery dominating the Dover Strait and on 4 September 1940 the Chief of Naval Staff issued a memo stating that if the Germans 'could get possession of the Dover defile and capture its gun defences from us, then, holding these points on both sides of the Straits, they would be in a position largely to deny those waters to our naval forces.' Should the Dover defile be lost, he concluded, the Royal Navy could do little to interrupt the flow of German supplies and reinforcements across the Channel, at least by day, and he further warned that 'there might really be a chance that they might be able to bring a serious weight of attack to bear on this country.'

Following the invasion, Britain and Ireland were to be divided into six military–economic commands, with headquarters in London, Birmingham, Liverpool, Newcastle, Glasgow and Dublin. Hitler decreed that Blenheim Palace, the ancestral home of Churchill, was to serve as the overall HQ of the German occupation military government. The Nazi Leadership compiled lists of those they thought could be trusted to form a new government along the lines of that in occupied Norway. The list was headed by the Blackshirt leader Oswald Mosley. For a time at least, Hitler intended to restore the abdicated Edward VIII to the throne in the event of a German occupation. The Duke of Windsor was initially highly sympathetic to the Nazi government, a feeling that was reinforced by his and his bride Wallis Simpson's 1937 visit to Germany. The former king was spirited away to a new post as governor of the Bahamas, where he could do little harm.

Had Operation Sea Lion succeeded, *Einsatzgruppen* under Dr Franz Six were to follow the invasion force to Great Britain to establish the New Order. Six's headquarters were to be in London, with regional task forces in Birmingham, Liverpool, Manchester and Edinburgh. They were provided with a 'Black Book' listing people to be arrested immediately. The *Einsatzgruppen* were also tasked with liquidating whatever remained of Britain's Jewish population, over 300,000 people. Mass deportations amongst the general male population for forced labour in Nazi-occupied Europe would be given high priority. Six was also told to secure 'aero-technological research result and important equipment' as well as 'Germanic works of art'. He toyed with the idea of moving Nelson's Column to Berlin.

But the clock was ticking towards winter and the German navy was clearly not ready for decisive action in the crucial summer months. The navy was meant to complete its task by mid-September before the weather made it more difficult. But that could only be achieved if the Luftwaffe could deliver air supremacy and Goering was under orders to do just that – destroy the RAF and lower British morale by aerial bombardment.

❈--❈

In June 1940 the British had 22 infantry divisions and one armoured division. The infantry divisions were, on average, at half strength, had only one-sixth of their normal artillery and were almost totally lacking in transport. There was a critical shortage of artillery shells and none could be spared for practice. Tanks were also in short supply after the fall of France. Estimates of numbers vary from just 50 infantry tanks and 200 light tanks armed only with machine guns to 102 cruiser tanks, 132 infantry tanks and 252 light tanks, the equivalent of just three to four Panzer Divisions. But Britain did possess over 290 million rounds of .303 ammunition in June, rising to over 400 million in August.

In a reorganisation in July, the divisions with some degree of mobility were placed behind the 'coastal crust' of defended beach areas from the Wash to Newhaven, Sussex. The General Headquarters Reserve was expanded to two corps of the most capable units. VII Corps was based in Surrey to the south of London and comprised 1st Armoured and 1st Canadian Divisions with the 1st Army Tank Brigade. IV Corps was based to the north of London.

On 14 May 1940, Secretary of State for War Anthony Eden announced the creation of the Local Defence Volunteers (LDV) – later to become known as the Home Guard. Far more men volunteered than the government expected and by the end of June, there were nearly 1.5 million. There were initially no uniforms and equipment was in critically short supply. At first, the Home Guard was armed with guns in private ownership, a knife or bayonet on a pole, Molotov cocktails and improvised flamethrowers. By July 1940 the situation had improved, with uniforms, a modicum of training and the arrival of hundreds of thousands of rifles and millions of rounds of ammunition from the US. New weapons were developed that could be produced cheaply without consuming materials that were needed to produce armaments for the regular units. The sticky bomb was a glass flask filled with nitroglycerin and given an adhesive coating allowing it to be glued to a passing vehicle. In theory, it could be thrown, but in practice it would most likely need to be placed – thumped against the target with sufficient force to stick – requiring courage and good fortune to be used effectively. An order for one million sticky bombs was placed in June 1940, but various problems delayed their distribution in large numbers until early 1941, and it is likely that fewer than 250,000 were produced. Mobility was provided by bicycles, motorcycles, private vehicles and horses. A small number of units were equipped with armoured cars, some of which were of standard design, but many were improvised locally from commercially available vehicles by the attachment of steel plates.

An extensive programme of field fortification was launched. On 27 May 1940 a Home Defence Executive was formed under General Sir Edmund Ironside, Commander-in-Chief Home Forces, to organise the defence of Britain. At first, defence arrangements were largely static and focused on the coastline and on a series of inland anti-tank 'stop' lines which the modern traveller can still see the remnants of moving inland across the southern counties. The longest and most heavily fortified was the General Headquarters anti-tank line, GHQ Line, which ran across southern England, wrapped around London and then ran north to Yorkshire. It was intended to protect the capital and the industrial heartland of England. Another major line was the Taunton Stop Line, which defended against an advance from England's south-west peninsula. London and other major cities were ringed with inner and outer stop lines. Some 50 stop lines were constructed but not all were completed.

Military thinking shifted rapidly. Given the lack of equipment and properly trained men, Ironside had had little choice but to adopt a strategy of static warfare and was criticised for having a siege mentality. Churchill was not satisfied with Ironside's progress, especially regarding the creation of a mobile reserve. General Brooke (later Viscount Alanbrooke) duly replaced Ironside. Brooke's appointment coincided with more trained men and better equipment becoming available, and new strategies and tactics were devised. More concentration was placed on defending the coastal crust, while inland a hedgehog defence strategy of defended localities and anti-tank islands was established. Many of these anti-tank islands were established along the already constructed stop lines, where existing defences could be integrated into the new strategy and, especially, at towns and villages where there was a Home Guard to provide personnel.

Emergency Coastal Batteries were constructed to protect ports and likely landing places. They were fitted with whatever guns were available, which mainly came from naval vessels scrapped since the end of the First World War. These included 6in (152mm), 5.5in (140mm), 4.7in (120mm) and 4in (102mm) guns. These had little ammunition, sometimes as few as 10 rounds apiece. Beaches were blocked with barbed wire entanglements, usually of concertina wire fixed by metal posts, or a simple fence of straight wires supported on waist-high posts. Extensive anti-tank and anti-personnel minefields were created on and behind the beaches. Portions of the Romney Marsh were flooded. Piers, ideal for landing of troops and situated in large numbers along the south coast of England, were disassembled, blocked or had their landward section destroyed. Where a barrier to tanks was required, a fence of scaffolding tubes 9ft (2.7m) high and was placed at low water along hundreds of miles of vulnerable beaches. An even more robust barrier to tanks was provided by long lines of anti-tank cubes. These were made of reinforced concrete 5ft (1.5m) to a side. Thousands were cast in situ in rows sometimes two or three deep. The beaches themselves were overlooked by pillboxes, sometimes placed low down to get maximum advantage from enfilading fire, others placed high on cliffs making them much harder to capture (see Appendix 5). Searchlights were installed on the coast to illuminate the sea surface and the beaches for artillery fire.

The primary purpose of the stop lines and the anti-tank islands that followed was to hold up the enemy, slowing progress and restricting the route of an attack. The defences generally ran along pre-existing barriers to tanks such as rivers and canals, railway embankments and cuttings, thick woods and other natural obstacles. Thousands of miles of anti-tank ditches were dug, usually by mechanical excavators, but occasionally by hand. Elsewhere, anti-tank barriers were made of massive reinforced concrete obstacles, cubic, pyramidal or cylindrical. Pimples were pyramid-shaped concrete blocks designed to counter tanks which, when attempting to pass them, would climb up, exposing vulnerable parts of the vehicle and hopefully slip back down with the tracks between the points.

Roads of course offered the enemy fast routes and were blocked at strategic points. Bridges and other key points were prepared for demolition at short notice by preparing chambers filled with explosives. A depth charge crater was a place in a road, usually at a junction, prepared with buried explosives that could be detonated to instantly form a deep crater as an anti-tank obstacle. Crossing points in the defence network – bridges, tunnels and other weak spots – were called nodes, or points of resistance. These were fortified with removable roadblocks, wire, and land mines. These passive defences were overlooked by trench works, gun and mortar emplacements and pillboxes. In places entire villages were fortified using barriers of scaffolding, sandbags and loopholes in existing buildings. The modern traveller often sees small windows, or blocked-up openings in buildings overlooking streams or main village streets, which were first cut as loopholes. The rate of construction was frenetic: by the end of September 1940, 18,000 pillboxes and countless other preparations had been completed. Volunteers were encouraged to use anything that would delay the enemy and one recalled:

> In the villages use was made of any existing walls or buildings, loopholes for firing or passing heavy chains and cables through to form barriers strong enough to slow down or stop soft-skinned vehicles. The chains and cables could also be made into psychological barriers to tanks by attaching an imitation bomb to them, an impression which could be augmented by running a length of cable from it to a position out of sight of a tank commander. These positions could be made even more authentic by breaking up the surface immediately in front of the obstacle and burying an old soup plate, or similar object. For occasions where time did not permit the passing of cables and chains we had concrete cylinders the size of a 45-gallon oil or tar barrel ready to roll into a roadway or other gap. These generally had a large metal loop cemented into one end through which a cable could be passed to link several together. Again, suspicious looking parcels could be attached to strengthen the illusion.

Open areas were vulnerable to invasion from the air. Open areas with a straight length of 500yds or more within five miles of the coast or an airfield were blocked by trenches or other obstacles, even old cars. Airfields considered extremely vulnerable to ground attack were protected by trench works and pillboxes which faced inwards towards the runway, rather than outwards. It was difficult to defend large open areas without creating hazards to friendly aircraft. Solutions to this problem included the pop-up Picket Hamilton fort – a light pillbox that could be lowered to the ground when the airfield was in use. Other basic measures included the removal of signposts, milestones and railway station signs. Petrol pumps were taken from service stations near the coast and there were careful preparations for the destruction of those that were left. Detailed plans were made for destroying anything that might prove useful to the invader such as port facilities, key roads and rolling stock. In seaside resorts, homes near the beach were sometimes bulldozed to provide a clear field of fire for shore batteries. In some coastal areas non-essential citizens were evacuated; in Kent, 40 per cent of the population was relocated; in East Anglia it was 50 per cent. In June 1940 the ringing of church bells was banned; henceforth they would only be rung by the military or the police to warn that an invasion – generally meaning by parachutists – was in progress.

That month, the Ministry of Information published *If the Invader Comes*. It began:

The Germans threaten to invade Great Britain. If they do so they will be driven
out by our Navy, our Army and our Air Force. Yet the ordinary men and women
of the civilian population will also have their part to play. Hitler's invasions of
Poland, Holland and Belgium were greatly helped by the fact that the civilian
population was taken by surprise.

The pamphlet concluded that, unless told to evacuate, 'THE ORDER IS "STAY
PUT".' Refugees on the road would be a major problem. Warnings were given not to
believe rumours and not to spread them, to be distrustful of orders given by anyone
and even to check that an officer giving such orders really was British. The phrase
'keep calm' naturally made an appearance in the instructions. The enemy was to be
denied food, fuel, transport and maps; how this was to be achieved was unclear. All
should be ready to block roads 'by felling trees, wiring them together or blocking the
roads with cars'. 'THINK BEFORE YOU ACT. BUT THINK ALWAYS OF YOUR
COUNTRY BEFORE YOU THINK OF YOURSELF.'

The war and the invasion threat affected every aspect of life on the Home Front.
Families suffered loss through separation or bereavement, careers were interrupted
by the call-up, further education was shelved, holidays were cancelled, travel was
restricted, food and fuel was rationed. Juries were reduced from 12 to seven to save
manpower, fashion models showed off washable corduroy siren suits, among the
rich, family portraits were commissioned in case of untimely death, gardens were
turned into allotments, curfews and black-outs were rigorously enforced, factories
were switched to munitions and the hardware of war – the list is endless. Yet morale
remained astonishingly high in the summer of 1940. A *Times* leading article put forward one explanation in early June: 'We have almost ceased to look forward. The days
of looking forward used to pass slowly and heavily because they had merely to be
lived through, for the sake of others to come, but now the days are all lived through
for their own sake.' Britons or all ranks seized the day.

Churchill considered the formation of a Home Guard Reserve, given only an
armband and basic training on the use of simple weapons such as Molotov cocktails.
The reserve would only have been expected to report for duty in an invasion. He also
later recorded how he intended to use the slogan 'You can always take one with you.'

In 1938, a section funded by MI6 had been created for propaganda, headed by
Sir Campbell Stuart. It was allocated premises at Electra House and was dubbed
Department EH. On 25 September 1939 the unit was mobilised to Woburn Abbey
where it joined a subversion team from MI6, known as Section D, and by July these
teams became a part of the newly created Special Operations Executive (SOE). Their
task was to spread false rumours and conduct psychological warfare. Inspired by a
demonstration of petroleum warfare, one false rumour was that the British had a
new bomb: dropped from an aircraft it caused a thin film of volatile liquid to spread
over the surface of the water, which it then ignited. Such rumours were credible
and rapidly spread. American broadcaster William Shirer recorded large numbers of
burns victims in Berlin. Documents found after the war showed the German high

command were deceived. The rumour seemed to take on a life of its own on both sides leading to persistent stories of a thwarted German invasion, in spite of official British denials. On 15 December 1940, *The New York Times* ran a story claiming that tens of thousands of German troops had been 'consumed by fire' in two failed invasion attempts.

Auxiliary Units were a specially trained and secret organisation that, in an invasion, would provide resistance behind enemy lines. Selected for aptitude and local knowledge, men were mostly recruited from the Home Guard – which also provided a cover for their existence. Organised into patrols of four to eight men, each patrol was a self-contained cell, expected to be self-sufficient. They were provided with a concealed underground operational base, usually built in woodland and camouflaged. The units were well equipped and supplied with food for 14 days, their expected lifespan.

In mid-1940, the principal concern of the RAF was to contest the control of British airspace with the Luftwaffe. For the Germans, achieving at least local air superiority was an essential prerequisite to any invasion. If the German air force had prevailed and attempted a landing, a much-reduced RAF would have been obliged to operate from airfields well away from the south east of England. Any airfield that was in danger of being captured would have been made inoperable and there were plans to remove all portable equipment from vulnerable radar bases and completely destroy anything that could not be moved. Whatever was left of the RAF would have been committed to intercepting the invasion fleet in concert with the Royal Navy. However, the RAF would have kept several advantages, such as being able to operate largely over friendly territory, as well as having the ability to fly for longer as, until the Germans were able to operate from airfields in England, Luftwaffe pilots would still have to fly significant distances to reach their operational area. A contingency plan called Operation Banquet required all available aircraft to be committed to the defence. In the event of invasion almost anything that was not a fighter would be converted to a bomber – student pilots, some in the very earliest stages of training, would use around 350 Tiger Moths and Magister trainers to drop 20lb (9.1kg) bombs from rudimentary bomb racks.

Shortly before the outbreak of the Second World War, the Chain Home radar system began to be installed in the south of England, with three radar stations being operational by 1937. Although the German High Command suspected that the British may have been developing these systems, test flights had proved inconclusive. As a result the expanding Chain Home radar system, and aircraft-based radar first fielded in 1940, became a vital piece of Britain's defensive capabilities during the Battle of Britain.

Both Britons and Americans believed during the summer of 1940 that a German invasion was imminent. They studied the forthcoming high tides of 5-9 August, 2-7 September, 1-6 October, and 30 October-4 November as likely dates.

Beginning in August 1940, the Luftwaffe began a series of concentrated aerial attacks (designated *Unternehmen Adlerangriff* or Operation Eagle Attack) on targets throughout the UK in an attempt to destroy the RAF. That opened what later became known as the Battle of Britain. Spitfire and Hurricane fighter pilots, memorably labelled 'The Few' by Churchill, fought the Luftwaffe over the fields and towns of southern England.

Operation Eagle was delayed for 10 days by bad weather but on 13 August the Luftwaffe launched major raids on airfields and radar stations in southern England with 1500 aircraft. The battle continued daily until September 16. However, on 7 September a change in emphasis switched Luftwaffe bombing from RAF airfields to London. That, many have argued, lost the Luftwaffe any opportunity of winning air superiority before the weather window closed. The RAF was close to exhaustion through sheer attrition, even though, unlike the Germans flying far from home, many downed British pilots were back in action above their own turf within hours. Hitler's strategic decision, though uncomfortable for Londoners, arguably lost him the Battle of Britain. Along with, of course, the courage of RAF pilots, the efficiency of their ground crew, the wonder of radar and the, albeit sometimes flawed, strategies of their commanders.

There is an overall consensus among historians that the Luftwaffe simply could not crush the RAF. The RAF proved to be a robust and capable organisation, which was to use all the modern resources available to it to the maximum advantage. Richard Evans wrote:

> Irrespective of whether Hitler was really set on this course, he simply lacked the resources to establish the air superiority that was the *sine qua non* of a successful crossing of the English Channel. A third of the initial strength of the German air force, the Luftwaffe, had been lost in the western campaign in the spring. The Germans lacked the trained pilots, the effective fighter planes, and the heavy bombers that would have been needed.

The Germans launched some spectacular attacks against important British industries, but they could not destroy the British industrial potential, and made little systematic effort to do so. Hindsight does not disguise the fact that the threat to Fighter Command was very real, and for the participants it seemed as if there was a narrow margin between victory and defeat. Nevertheless, even if the German attacks on the 11 Group airfields which guarded south-east England and the approaches to London had continued, the RAF could have withdrawn to the Midlands out of German fighter range and continued the battle from there. The victory was as much psychological as physical. Dr Alfred Price wrote:

> The truth of the matter, borne out by the events of 18 August is … [that] neither by attacking the airfields, nor by attacking London, was the Luftwaffe likely to destroy Fighter Command. Given the size of the British fighter force and

the general high quality of its equipment, training and morale, the Luftwaffe could have achieved no more than a Pyrrhic victory. During the action on the 18th it had cost the Luftwaffe five trained aircrewmen killed, wounded or taken prisoner, for each British fighter pilot killed or wounded; the ratio was similar on other days in the battle. In the Battle of Britain, for the first time during the Second World War, the German war machine had set itself a major task which it failed to achieve, and so demonstrated that it was not invincible. In stiffening the resolve of those determined to resist Hitler the battle was an important turning point in the conflict.

While Britain may have been militarily secure in 1940, both sides were aware of the possibility of a political collapse, one of the prime objectives of the London Blitz. If the Germans had won the Battle of Britain, the Luftwaffe would have been able to strike anywhere in southern England and with the prospect of an invasion, the British government would have come under pressure to come to terms. However, the extensive anti-invasion preparations demonstrated to Germany and to the people of Britain that whatever happened in the air, the United Kingdom was both able and willing to defend herself.

After the evacuation of Dunkirk, people had believed that the threatened invasion could come at almost any time. German preparations would require at least a few weeks, but all defensive precautions were made with an extreme sense of urgency. The weather deteriorates significantly after September, but an October landing was not out of the question. On 3 October, General Brooke wrote in his diary: 'Still no invasion! I am beginning to think that the Germans may after all not attempt it. And yet! I have the horrid thought that he may still bring off some surprise on us.'

The Battle of Britain was deemed won by early autumn and between 11 and 14 September Hitler came close to completely abandoning Sea Lion. He changed his mind at the last moment, knowing that Germany needed a quick win in the west before realising his ambitions in the east. He subbed down Sea Lion, which had envisaged deploying 39 divisions over a month to 23 divisions over six weeks, landing on a much narrower front. Under the revised plan, four divisions would embark from Rotterdam, Antwerp, Ostend, Dunkirk and Calais and land between Bexhill and Hastings, as The Conqueror had done in 1066. Two more divisions would land between Bexhill and Eastbourne and three more between Beachy Head and Brighton. The first landings would be backed by 250 amphibian tanks and paratroopers would seize the heights above Folkestone. A 16-mile deep bridgehead would be defended until, within two weeks, a further 11 divisions would be ashore.

But it soon became clear that the Luftwaffe had failed and mid-September was the last date an invasion could be ordered – the logistics of which would demand a further 10 days to assemble – before bad weather set in. On 17 September 1940, Hitler met Goering and Field Marshal Gerd von Rundstedt and was finally convinced that the operation was not viable. Control of the skies was lacking and coordination among three branches of the armed forces was out of the question.

Later that day, Hitler ordered the postponement of the operation. On 12 October 1940 and unknown to the British, Hitler rescheduled Sea Lion for the spring of 1941. He ordered the dispersal of the invasion fleet in order to avert further damage by British air and naval attacks.

Adolf Galland, commander of Luftwaffe fighters, claimed that there was a palpable sense of relief in the *Wehrmacht* when it was finally called off. Von Rundstedt also took this view and thought that Hitler never seriously intended to invade Britain and the whole thing was a bluff, to put pressure on the British Government to come to terms. He observed that Napoleon had failed to invade and the difficulties that confounded him did not appear to have been solved by the Sea Lion planners. Grand Admiral Karl Donitz believed air superiority was not enough and admitted, 'We possessed neither control of the air or the sea; nor were we in any position to gain it.' As early as 14 August 1940, Hitler had told his generals that he would not attempt to invade Britain if the task seemed too dangerous, before adding that there were other ways of defeating the UK than invading.

Britain's defences had much improved, with many more trained and equipped men becoming available and field fortifications reaching a high state of readiness. With national confidence rising, Prime Minister Churchill, was able to say: 'We are waiting for the long promised invasion. So are the fishes.'

When Germany invaded the Soviet Union on 22 June 1941, it became unlikely that there would be any attempted landing as long as that conflict was undecided. In July 1941, construction of field fortifications was greatly reduced and concentration given to the possibility of a raid in force rather than a full-scale invasion. On 7 December 1941, a Japanese carrier fleet launched a surprise attack on the US fleet at Pearl Harbor and America entered the war on Britain's side. With America's 'Germany first' strategic policy, resources flooded into the UK, effectively ending the danger of invasion after two years.

❦

The question that remains, still argued over by historians, is: Could Sea Lion have succeeded?

General Brooke frequently confided in his private diary. When published, he included additional annotations written many years later:

> I considered the invasion a very real and probable threat and one for which the land forces at my disposal fell far short of what I felt was required to provide any degree of real confidence in our power to defend these shores. It should not be construed that I considered our position a helpless one in the case of an invasion. Far from it. We should certainly have a desperate struggle and the future might well have hung in the balance, but I certainly felt that given a fair share of the fortunes of war we should certainly succeed in finally defending these shores.

British intelligence calculated that each German division landing on British soil would require a daily average of 3,300 tons of supplies. They reckoned that Folkestone, the largest harbour falling within the planned German landing zones, could handle 150 tons per day in the first week of the invasion, even if the retreating British demolition squads and the RAF halved its capacity. Within seven days, maximum capacity was expected to rise to 600 tons per day once German shore parties made repairs to the quays and cleared the harbour of any obstacles and blockships. This meant that, at best, the nine German infantry and two airborne divisions slated for the initial landings would receive less than a fifth of the 3,300 tons of supplies they required each day through a port, and would have to rely on airdrops. The capture of Dover and its harbour facilities was expected to add another 800 tons per day; but that figure assumed little or no interference from the Royal Navy and RAF with the German supply convoys.

During the period 19 to 26 September 1940, sea and wind conditions on and over the Channel were generally good and a crossing even by converted river barges was feasible. Winds for the remainder of the month were rated as 'moderate' and would not have prevented the German invasion fleet from successfully depositing the First Wave troops ashore during the first 10 days. Beginning the night of 27 September, strong northerly winds prevailed, making passage more hazardous, but calm conditions returned on 11–12 October and again from 16 to 20 October. After then, light easterly winds prevailed, which would have actually assisted any invasion craft travelling from the Continent towards the invasion beaches. But by the end of October, force 8 south-westerly winds would have prohibited any non-seagoing craft from risking a Channel crossing.

If the notional crossing had succeeded, the question of whether the British defences would have been effective is difficult to answer. England's defences relied heavily on fixed field fortifications. The First World War showed that assaulting prepared defences with infantry could be deadly, but similar preparations in Belgium had been overrun by well-equipped German Panzer divisions in the early weeks of 1940 and with so many armaments left at Dunkirk, British forces were woefully ill-equipped to take on German armour. On the other hand, while British preparations for defence were ad hoc, so were the German invasion plans, Until the Germans captured a port, both sides would have been short of tanks and heavy guns.

The Royal Navy would have attacked the enemy landing and bridgehead zones, and while German naval forces and the Luftwaffe could have extracted a high price, they could not have hoped to prevent interference with attempts to land a second wave of troops and supplies that would have been essential to German success. In this scenario, British land forces would have faced the Germans on more equal terms than otherwise and it was only necessary to delay the German advance, preventing a collapse until the German land forces were, at least temporarily, isolated by the Royal Navy and then mounting a counter-attack.

Several German General Staff members were long convinced that, regardless of the Battle of Britain, Sea Lion could not have succeeded. Grand Admiral Karl Donitz believed air superiority was 'not enough'. Erich Raeder, commander-in-chief of the *Kriegsmarine* in 1940, stressed

> … the emphatic reminder that up until now the British had never thrown the full power of their fleet into action. However, a German invasion of England would be a matter of life and death for the British, and they would unhesitatingly commit their naval forces, to the last ship and the last man, into an all-out fight for survival. Our Air Force could not be counted on to guard our transports from the British Fleets, because their operations would depend on the weather, if for no other reason. It could not be expected that even for a brief period our Air Force could make up for our lack of naval supremacy.

When Franz Halder, the Chief of the Army General Staff, heard of the state of the Kriegsmarine and its plan for the invasion, he noted in his diary on 28 July 1940: 'If that [the plan] is true, all previous statements by the navy were so much rubbish and we can throw away the whole plan of invasion.' Chief of Operations Alfred Jodl remarked, after Raeder said the *Kriegsmarine* could not meet the operational requirements of the Army, 'then a landing in England must be regarded as a sheer act of desperation.'

Most military historians concur. Sea Lion could only have got through its first stages if the Royal Navy left the invasion fleet alone and even then, only if the invasion had been launched in July 1940. Hitler's ambivalence about the enterprise was also crucial and demonstrated his characteristic tendency to forge grand schemes on the hoof and blame others when his improvisations failed to deliver. By summer 1940 he was also obsessive about the Soviets and, although that initially added weight to his invasion plans in the west, eventually that obsession dominated his thinking. Len Deighton called the German amphibious plans a 'Dunkirk in reverse'. The massive superiority of the Royal Navy over the *Kriegsmarine* would have made Sea Lion a disaster.

War games at the Royal Military Academy Sandhurst in 1974 found that while German forces would have been able to land and gain a significant beachhead, intervention of the Royal Navy would have been decisive and even with the most optimistic assumptions, the German army would not have penetrated farther than GHQ Line before being annihilated.

19 THE BATTLE OF GRAVENEY MARSH

'I got a set of enamel Luftwaffe wings'
– Piper George Willis, 1940

London Irish Regiment training on Graveney Marsh in 1940.

On the night of 27 September 1940, Luftwaffe pilot Fritz Ruhlandt and his crew dropped their 4,000lb cargo of bombs over London and headed home. Flying over Kent, their Junkers 88 bomber was hit by anti-aircraft fire from a gun emplacement beside the Medway at Upnor Castle. One engine was destroyed.

Spitfires and Hurricanes from 66 and 92 squadrons gave chase, under instructions to destroy it if they had to or, better still, force it to land. The Junkers 88 had come into service the previous September as soon as the war had broken out and had seen action over Poland, France and southern England. In those skies it had proved capable of taking heavy flak and continuing to fly. Its maximum speed was 292mph, its ceiling was 17,290ft and it had a range of 1,696 miles. It was a valuable asset and RAF scientists and designers dearly wanted to know its secrets. A general order had been issued to all units to capture one more or less intact. The RAF pilots succeeded in their aim, harrying the damaged aircraft engine until Ruhlandt had no option but to attempt a forced landing on Kent's Graveney marshes. *Unteroffizier* Ruhlandt, despite being wounded, brought down his plane and he and his injured crew members crawled from the wreckage.

The descent and crash landing was heard by a unit of A Company, 1st Battalion, the London Irish Rifles at their billet at the Sportsman Inn in nearby Seasalter. As the threat of invasion by the Germans eased, their task changed to capturing any enemy aircrew brought down in the Kent countryside. During the Battle of Britain and throughout the late summer of 1940, the marshy flats had gained a new role as an emergency landing ground for crippled aircraft, both British and German. A Dornier Do 17 came down on the mudflats at Seasalter on 13 August 1940. Another bomber crash-landed just beside The Neptune pub at Whitstable on 16 August. The London Irish riflemen recognised what they had heard and around a dozen men rushed to the scene. They fully expected the four-strong Luftwaffe crew to give themselves up without a fight, but as they approached the plane, the Germans opened fire with a machine gun.

The British servicemen hit the deck. The soldiers returned fire but were forced to take cover under a hail of bullets. The Irish Rifles regrouped and a small group crept along a dyke towards the Germans. When they were about 50yds away one of the airmen waved a white flag but as the soldiers closed in fighting erupted again before the Germans were overpowered. One of them was shot in the foot during the brief battle. Nobody was killed.

During the exchange, the Rifles' commanding officer, Captain John Cantopher, arrived at the pub for an inspection. According to the regiment's official records, a Sergeant Allworth explained he had sent the men to the downed aircraft.

'They took arms I hope,' Cantopher said. 'No sir …' The sergeant broke off. Sounds of machine gun fire could be heard. 'It looks as if they should have done,' commented Cantopher. 'Forget the inspection, I am going over there. Bring some of your men with rifles and ammo.'

Witness Nigel Wilkinson said:

On approaching the aircraft the men were fired on by the German crew with the aircraft's two machine guns. The London Irishmen got into attack formation and having laid down heavy rifle fire on the aircraft mounted an assault of the Junkers across the marsh. By now the enemy aircrew had been wounded by the rifle fire and decided to surrender. It was at this stage that Captain Cantopher came on the scene.

The soldiers knew that enemy bombers were fitted with time bombs that enemy crew would prime on crash landing. The soldiers discovered such a device and removed it. Unknown to the prisoners, one of the soldiers could speak German and he heard the fliers talking about a second time bomb due to go off at any moment. Cantopher dashed back to the aircraft, located it under one of the wings and threw it into the ditch, saving the prized aircraft for British engineers to examine.

The soldiers took the captured Germans back to the pub. Corporal George Willis, the regiment's piper, was in the *Sportsman* when the men returned with the Germans. He recalled: 'The men were in good spirits and came into the pub with the Germans. We gave the Germans pints of beer in exchange for a few souvenirs. I got a set of enamel Luftwaffe wings.'

The Luftwaffe aircrew went to prisoner-of-war camps. The riflemen were mentioned in dispatches for their tactical ability, which had forced the surrender of the heavily armed Luftwaffe crew. Unofficially, however, it is said the riflemen had their knuckles rapped for opening fire without being ordered to do so.

The Junkers 88 was transported to Farnborough airfield where RAF technicians discovered it was only two weeks old and had been fitted with a secret and extremely accurate new bombsight. The aircraft was characterised by extended wings, improved handling and upgraded navigational aids, and represented a state-of-the-art example of the Luftwaffe's bomber stable. Which explains why the crew, doing their own patriotic duty, were so willing to fight until their aircraft was destroyed.

Cantopher was awarded the George Medal for his bravery. But otherwise the incident was kept quiet during the war as the British did not want the Germans to know that they had captured nearly intact one of their most modern bombers. Newspapers made no mention of it and memories faded over 70 years.

In September 2010, the London Irish Rifles Regimental Association marked its seventieth anniversary by unveiling a commemorative plaque at the Sportsman pub.

The 'battle' of Graveney Marsh was the last exchange of fire involving a foreign invading force to take place on mainland Britain.

20 THE OCCUPATION OF THE CHANNEL ISLANDS

'not absolutely useless to a possible enemy'
– William Ewart Gladstone

German soldiers in King's Street, St Helier, later
the site of the Croix de la Reine monument,
August 1941. *German Federal Archives*

The Channel Islands are remnants of the Duchy of Normandy and remain British Crown Dependencies. Its Bailiwicks have been administered separately since the late thirteenth century. Their proximity to the French coast made them vulnerable to invasion for centuries. During the nineteenth century the British erected massive fortifications. They were presciently described by William Ewart Gladstone as 'a monument of human folly, useless to us … but perhaps not absolutely useless to a possible enemy, with whom we may at some period have to deal and who may possibly be able to extract some profit in the way of shelter and accommodation from the ruins.' The influx of English and Irish labourers employed on the constructions, along with a large English garrison, resulted in greater Anglicisation of the population.

On 15 June 1940, the British Government decided that the Channel Islands were of no strategic importance and were indefensible against German military might. The British government gave up the oldest possession of the Crown without firing a single shot. The archipelago was declared an 'open town'.

The islands had little strategic value for the Germans either, but the previous month islander Frank Johnson had written in the *Jersey Evening Post*:

> We are told that Jersey is the last place the Germans would attack ... the exact opposite is true, and at the present juncture no part of the Empire is in greater peril. Just try to imagine the tremendous effect on his people, were Hitler able to tell them that the oldest part of the British Empire – Jersey – was in German hands. He would proudly point to it as the beginning of the end, the break-up of the Empire.

Jersey schoolteacher Harry Aubin wrote:

> We were ditched by the UK government. We felt stripped naked. After demilitarisation, we had no means of defending ourselves. There's no resentment, we realised Britain had its back to the wall and we realised that Britain had to stay in the war to get our liberty back. But the local politicians were amateur, and they were frightened.

The British Government consulted the islands' elected bodies over evacuation, but opinion was divided and, without a policy being imposed on the islands, chaos ensued and different policies were adopted by the different islands. The British Government made available as many ships as possible so that islanders had the option to leave if they wanted to. The authorities in Alderney recommended that all islanders evacuate, and nearly all did so, against the wishes of the Dame of Sark, Sybil Mary Hathaway. Guernsey evacuated all children of school age, giving the parents the option of keeping their children with them, or evacuating with their school. In Jersey, the majority of islanders chose to stay.

Guernsey teenager Dolly Joanknecht recalled:

> When I got back to my mother's house after the evacuation, it had already been vandalised. All the drawers were tipped upside down and the china smashed. They must have picked out what they wanted. That was before the Germans arrived; it wasn't touched at all in the five years of Occupation.

As the Germans did not realise that the islands had been demilitarised, they approached with some caution. On 28 June 1940, they bombed the harbours of Guernsey and Jersey. In St Peter Port, Guernsey, lorries lined up to load tomatoes for export to England were mistaken for troop carriers and strafed. Forty-four islanders were killed in the raids.

The *Wehrmacht* prepared to land two battalions, but a reconnaissance pilot landed on Guernsey and the island authorities immediately surrendered to him. The Germans landed unopposed on each island in turn. On Sark, Dame Sybil's wishes were obeyed and all 471 inhabitants stayed. Hathaway (1884-1974) was the 21st Seigneur of Sark and had seven children by her first husband. He died of Spanish flu after serving in the trenches of the First World War. In 1929 she married an American and her fluent German and imperious manner gained the respect of the occupiers.

Day-to-day running of island affairs became the responsibility of a German Controlling Committee. Occupation money (scrip) was issued to keep the economy going. German military forces used their own scrip for payment of goods and services. The Channel Island time zone was put into line with continental Europe and driving on the right was introduced.

As part of Hitler's Atlantic Wall, between 1940 and 1945 the occupying German forces and the *Organisation Todt* constructed concrete fortifications, bunkers, gun emplacements, air raid shelters, an underground hospital, roads and other facilities in the Channel Islands. Hitler had decreed that 10 per cent of the steel and concrete used in the Atlantic Wall should go to the Channel Islands. The Islands were better defended than the Normandy beaches, given the large number of tunnels and bunkers. Light railways were built in Jersey and Guernsey to supply the coastal fortifications. All that construction was done by imported forced or slave labour.

The Germans built four concentration camps in Alderney, technically subcamps of the Neuengamme concentration camp outside Hamburg. *Organisation Todt* operated each subcamp. The camps commenced operation in January 1942 and had a total inmate population of about 6,000. The Borkum and Helgoland camps were 'volunteer' labour camps and their labourers were treated harshly but marginally better than the slave labour inmates at the Sylt and Norderney camps. The latter held Jewish and mainly Eastern European prisoners, with a few Spaniards and Soviets. Over 700 of the inmates died of brutal treatment, disease and starvation before the camps were closed and the remaining inmates transferred to Germany in 1944.

The policy of the island governments, acting under instructions communicated by the British Government before the occupation, was passive co-operation. This has been criticised, particularly with regard to the treatment of Jews. Those remaining in the islands, often Church of England members with one or two Jewish grandparents, were subjected to the nine orders, including closure of their businesses and staying indoors for all but one hour per day. These measures were administered by the Bailiff and the Aliens Office.

On 7 August 1940, Ambrose Sherwill, the Attorney-General and President of Guernsey's Controlling committee, addressed a meeting of the Guernsey States watched by *Kommandant* Lanz. He set out the policy of the Islands' governing authorities:

> May this occupation be a model to the world. On the one hand, tolerance on the part of the military authority, and courtesy and correctness on the part of the occupying forces, and on the other, dignity and courtesy and exemplary

behaviour on the part of the civilian population. I do not know how long the occupation will last … when it is over I hope that the occupying force and the occupied population may each be able to say: 'of different nations, having differing outlooks, we lived together with tolerance and mutual respect.'

He went on:

> The German forces, fighting troops, flushed with success on the Continent, came to Guernsey and found the civilian population calm, dignified and well-behaved. Having us in their power, they behaved as good soldiers … we, the civilian population, were sober, law-abiding, giving no cause for offence, courteous and polite …

Some days later Sherwill horrified Britons with a cack-handed attempt to reassure them that their relatives on the islands were safe. He broadcast on German overseas radio, saying:

> I am proud of the way my fellow-islanders have behaved and grateful for the correct and kindly attitude towards them of the German soldier. On the staff is an officer speaking perfect English, a man of wide experience … . To him I express my grateful thanks for his courtesy and patience.

This is not what the British population expected during the Blitz and the Battle of Britain.

The occupying force did indeed behave better than elsewhere in occupied Europe and was under orders to treat civilians properly, to pay for goods and refrain from looting. Hitler saw it as a testing ground for a model occupation of Britain, encouraging co-operation with established civic authority before imposing a regime of slave and forced labour, and racial and religious genocide.

There was no resistance movement in the Channel Islands on anything like the scale of that in mainland France. There were obvious reasons – they were islands, there was a German soldier for every two islanders left and the absence of the Gestapo reduced the chances of atrocities recruiting resisters amongst the family and friends of the victims. Much of the population of military age had already joined the British or French armed forces. And the attitude of their civilian representatives, such as Sherwill, hardly encouraged open acts of defiance.

There was resistance, but it was generally passive, acts of minor sabotage, sheltering and aiding escaped slave workers and publishing underground newspapers containing news from the BBC. Listening to all radio stations was banned and wireless sets confiscated. They were replaced by homemade crystal sets and such disobedience continued despite the ever-present threat that the users would be exposed, sometimes by neighbours with a grudge. Artists Claude Cahun and Suzanne Malherbe produced flyers of English-to-German translations of BBC reports.

The couple attended many German military events in Jersey and put the flyers in soldiers' pockets. In 1944 Claude and Suzanne were arrested and sentenced to death, but the sentences were never carried out. Islanders also daubed Churchill's 'V' (for Victory) over German signs.

For many youngsters the Occupation provided a great excuse for vandalism and fun, tinged with danger and patriotic fervour. Eighteen-year-old Mike Le Cornu recalled:

> We put chisels in German car radiators when I was working as a mechanic in a garage. There was a little group of us called the Sab Squad. Everyone of that age wanted to do something. When I was arrested and questioned, I just acted really stupid and dopey.

Some individual acts of resistance, serious or farcical, sometimes had tragic results. A Guernsey woman, possibly pursuing a personal vendetta, reported a 'simple-minded' local boy, John Ingrouille, for allegedly possessing a gun and plotting an uprising. No gun was found but the lad was sentenced to five years for treason and espionage. He died of tuberculosis in a German gaol. Seventeen-year-old James Houillebecq was arrested for espionage and sabotage and died in Neuengamme concentration camp. Five more Jerseymen died while serving sentences for sabotage. Clarence Painter and his son Peter were arrested for listening to the BBC and the Germans found a First World War souvenir pistol. They both died in Natzweiler concentration camp in 1944. Canon Clifford Cohu of St Saviour's, Jersey, was informed on for giving hospital patients BBC reports to cheer them up. He and two others arrested with him died in various camps. Some arrestees survived. Cinema projectionist Stanley Green was also taken for radio offences and tortured by the Gestapo in Paris. He was finally transferred to Buchenwald where he spent over seven months, some of them carting bodies to the crematorium. He was the only inmate to successfully smuggle out photographs of the horror there, Those images were later used as evidence in the Nuremberg war crimes trials. He returned to Jersey but never recovered from his ordeals and his memories of the extermination camp.

There were other such heroes and heroines, but perhaps the most effective resistance was the selfless help given to foreign slave and forced labourers. It was a serious offence to aid them in their soul-crushing daily toil, never mind helping them escape. Housewives left food scraps and used clothing out for them, a sacrifice given the shortages of food and supplies which grew steadily worse. Guernsey teenager Herbert Nichols recalled:

> When they built the bunkers it was close to Christmas. I was living with my grandmother, and we were huddled around the fire … It was early evening and the weather was terrible. We suddenly heard a noise on the porch, and my grandmother went to look. It was a young Frenchman of about my age. He was absolutely frozen and completely exhausted. He was very scared. My grandmother brought him to the fire to get warm and rubbed his hands. She got him

some old clothing and gave him a drop of soup, and told him to come back the next day. He came every night for about a week, and she would keep a little bit of food, and he'd gobble it up. He never said much. On the last time he came, he gave my grandmother a present. It was wrapped in newspaper. She kissed him on the cheek. When she opened it, it was a piece of soap which wasn't much thicker than the newspaper. It was so thin, it was transparent. He promised to come back after the war. He was the kind who would have done. I think he must have died.

A number of islanders, escaped, particularly after D-Day, when conditions in the islands worsened as supply routes to the continent were cut off and the desire to join in the liberation of Europe increased.

Some island women fraternised with the occupying forces. They were known by disapproving neighbours as 'Jerry-bags'. Records released by the Public Records Office in 1996 suggest that 900 babies of German fathers were born to Jersey women during the occupation.

The British Government's reaction to the German invasion was muted, with military necessity, realistic expectations and a certain sense of shame intermingled.

On 6 July 1940, 2nd Lieutenant Hubert Nicolle, a Guernseyman serving with the British Army, was dispatched on a fact-finding mission to Guernsey. He was dropped off the south coast of Guernsey by a submarine and rowed ashore in a canoe under cover of night. This was the first of two visits which Nicolle made to the island. Following the second, he missed his rendezvous and was trapped in the island. After six weeks in hiding, he gave himself up to the German authorities and became a PoW.

In October 1942, a British Commando raid on Sark was code-named Operation Basalt. On the night of the 3rd, 10 men of the Special Operations Executive and No. 12 Commando landed on Sark for reconnaissance and to capture prisoners. Nine broke into a local while the tenth went to a covert rendezvous with an undercover agent who had been posing as a forced Polish labourer. The house's occupant, Frances Pittard, told the raiders there were about 20 Germans in the nearby Dixcart Hotel. In front of the hotel was an unguarded hut containing five sleeping German soldiers. They were easily captured but none were officers. The Commandos decided to move on to the hotel and capture more of the enemy, leaving the prisoners' hands bound with toggle ropes to minimise the necessary guard. One prisoner started shouting to alert those in the hotel and was instantly shot dead. The enemy now alerted, incoming fire from the hotel became considerable and the raiders returned to the beach with the remaining four prisoners. En route, three prisoners made a break. It was never conclusively established whether they were still bound. Two were shot and the third stabbed. The fourth was conveyed safely back to England for interrogation, along with the SOE agent. A few days later, the Germans issued a communiqué implying at least one prisoner had escaped and two were shot while resisting having their hands tied. That led to Hitler's order instructing that all captured Commandos or Commando-type personnel be executed as a matter of course.

In 1942, the German authorities, under direct orders from Hitler, announced that all residents of the Channel Islands who were not born in the islands, as well as those men who had served as officers in the First World War, were to be deported. The majority of them were transported to the south-west of Germany. Guernsey nurse Gladys Skillett, who was five months pregnant at the time of her deportation to Biberach, became the first Channel Islander to give birth while in captivity in Germany.

In 1943, Vice Admiral Lord Mountbatten proposed a plan to retake the islands, Operation Constellation, but it was never mounted.

In June 1944, the Allied forces launched the D-Day landings and decided to bypass the Channel Islands due to their heavy fortifications. German supply lines for food and other supplies through France were completely severed. The islanders' food supplies were already dwindling, and the islanders and German forces alike were on the point of starvation. Churchill's reaction to the plight of the starving German garrison was to 'let 'em rot', even though this meant that the islanders had to suffer with them. The heavily fortified islands were simply bypassed by Allied commanders who had more pressing priorities. It took months of protracted negotiations before the International Red Cross ship SS *Vega* was permitted to relieve the starving islanders in December 1944, bringing food parcels, salt and soap, as well as medical and surgical supplies. The *Vega* made five further trips to the islands before liberation.

In December 1944 four German paratroopers and a naval cadet escaped from a PoW camp in Allied-occupied France, stole an American landing craft and made their way to the Islands. They were greeted as heroes and reported that several ships were in the harbour at Granville discharging coal that was in short supply in the beleaguered Islands. The new garrison commander, Admiral Friedrich, a former captain of the battleship *Scharnhorst*, used the intelligence to plan a raid against the Allies to restore morale to his garrison and obtain needed supplies. The raid, led by *Kaptanleutnant* Carl-Friedrich Mohr, took place on the night of 8-9 March 1945 with four large minesweepers, three light barges, three fast motor launches, two smaller minesweepers and a tug. Allied resistance delayed the timetable so only one collier, the *Eskwood* with 112 tons of coal, could be taken back to the Islands due to the low tide. A German minesweeper, the M-412 *De Schelde*, ran aground, eventually being blown up by the Germans.

The Germans mined and badly damaged the British freighters *Kyle Castle*, *Nephrite*, *Parkwood* and the Norwegian merchantman *Helen* but they remained aground at this low tide. The Captain of the *Kyle Castle* refused to cooperate and was killed. German forces also damaged the locks and harbour and started fires. Several American prisoners were taken and two marines killed, while 14 US seamen, a Royal Navy officer and five of his men also died during this attack. Mohr was awarded the Knight's Cross. But the raid had failed in its bid to bring supplies. The Islands continued to starve.

On 8 May 1945 at 10 a.m., the islanders were told by the German authorities that the war was over. Churchill made a radio broadcast at 1500 during which he announced: 'Hostilities will end officially at one minute after midnight tonight, but in the interests of saving lives the "Cease fire" began yesterday to be sounded all along the front, and our dear Channel Islands are also to be freed today.'

The following morning HMS *Bulldog* arrived in St Peter Port, Guernsey, and the German forces surrendered unconditionally aboard the vessel at dawn. British forces landed shortly afterwards, greeted by crowds of joyous but malnourished islanders. HMS *Beagle* performed a similar role in liberating Jersey. Two naval officers, one of whom was Surgeon Lt Ronald McDonald, were met by the Harbour Master who escorted them to the Harbour Master's Office where they together hoisted the Union Jack, before also raising it on the flagstaff of the Pomme D'Or Hotel.

The first place actually liberated in Jersey was the General Post Office's Jersey repeater station. Mr Warder, a GPO lineman stranded in the island during the occupation, was not prepared to wait. He told the German officer in charge that he was taking over the building on behalf of the GPO.

Sark was not liberated until 10 May 1945 and for the following week Dame Sybil was left in command of the German garrison on her island. The German troops in Alderney did not surrender until 16 May 1945. The German prisoners of war were not removed from Alderney until 20 May 1945 and its population could not start to return until December 1945, after clearing up had been carried out by German troops under British military supervision.

Following the liberation of 1945, allegations of collaboration with the occupying authorities were investigated. By November 1946, the UK Home Secretary told the House of Commons that most of the allegations lacked substance and only 12 cases of collaboration were considered for prosecution, but the Director of Public Prosecutions had ruled out prosecutions on insufficient grounds. In particular, it was decided that there were no legal grounds for proceeding against those alleged to have informed to the occupying authorities against their fellow-citizens.

In Jersey and Guernsey, laws were passed to confiscate retrospectively the financial gains made by war profiteers and black marketeers, although these measures also affected those who had made legitimate profits during the years of military occupation. In the hours following the liberation, members of the British liberating forces were obliged to intervene to prevent revenge attacks on 'Jerry-bags', women who had fraternised with German soldiers.

For two years after the liberation, Alderney was operated as a communal farm. Craftsmen were paid by their employers, whilst others were paid by the local government out of the profit from the sales of farm produce. Remaining profits were put aside to repay the British Government for repairing and rebuilding the island. The Occupation, particularly in Guernsey, which evacuated the majority of school-age children, weakened the indigenous culture of the island. Many felt that the children 'left as Guernsey and returned as English'. The abandoned German equipment and fortifications posed a serious safety risk and there were many accidents after the occupation, resulting in several deaths.

After the war, a court-martial case was prepared against ex-SS *Hauptsturmführer* Max List, the former commandant of the Norderney and Sylt concentration camps, citing atrocities in Alderney. He did not stand trial and is believed to have lived near Hamburg until his death in the 1980s.

In 2002 St Helier was twinned with Bad Wurzach, where numbers of deported Channel Islanders were interned.

On 9 March 2010 the award of British Hero of the Holocaust was made posthumously to four Jersey people in recognition of their helping Jews. They were Albert Bedane, Louisa Gould, Ivy Forster and Harold Le Druillenec. It was the first time that the British Government recognised the heroism of Islanders during the German Occupation.

Many of the bunkers, batteries and tunnels can still be seen today. Some have been restored, but after the Occupation, most were stripped out for scrap and by souvenir hunters and left abandoned. One bunker was transformed into a fish hatchery and a large tunnel complex was made into a mushroom farm.

⊗⃝⃠ ⃝

Some people have tried to portray the Occupation of the Channel Islands as a snapshot of what would have happened if Hitler had succeeded in his British invasion plan.

Madeleine Bunting put the unanswered questions well:

> Who would have plotted resistance? Who would have made a handsome profit selling guns and cloth to the Germans and trading in black market whiskey? How would the majority of the British people have muddled their way through? The Channel Islands were as close as Hitler got; they were the one bit of British soil he conquered. That is why those blurred black-and-white photos … are so riveting: German soldiers marching past Lloyds Bank or flirting with island girls outside Boots the Chemists, or getting directions from a smiling British bobby. This is what life could have been in Britain, with Germans on British streets and in British shops.

That is a fair point, and Britain then, as now, had its fair share of unscrupulous industrialists and bankers, aristocratic chancers, jobsworth officials, black marketeers and home-grown natural fascists who may well have embraced the invaders. But any direct extrapolation from the experience of the Channel Islands is fallacious. The Islands were isolated communities, small territories with little or no hiding place for organised resistance. There was precious little the islanders could do but survive.

That said, however, they were also small communities infected with petty jealousies and with an inbred predilection for obeying one's masters, whoever they were. The heroism of the few, and the resilience of the majority, is balanced by the collaboration of petty officials and privileged, if frightened, civilian rulers.

After the war, Dame Sybil Hathaway and Ambrose and Mary Sherwill were the honoured guests in his Bavarian castle of Baron Max von Aufsess, the Head of Civic Affairs during the latter part of the Occupation.

CONCLUSION

The successful invasions of Britain have been dynastic struggles involving an element of civil war in which an invader could count on a good measure of domestic support, as was seen in 1216 and in 1688. Those which expected such domestic support – the Jacobite efforts with French and Spanish backing, the revolutionary incursions involving the Irish, Americans and French – and didn't get it, were doomed to failure.

The other main elements in Britain's invincibility are, obviously, Britain's island geography compounded by the unpredictability of the weather, and over time the increasing dominance of the Royal Navy.

The first may be obvious, but it is a complicated issue. During medieval and later times seas and rivers were by far the easiest and quickest ways to transport an invading force. The Channel should have been a pathway to invasion, rather than a barrier. What scuppered so many attempts was the refusal of the British weather to fit in with foreign notions of the seasons. William the Conqueror was forced to wait all summer for favourable winds and calm seas to ferry across his invasion fleets. If King Harold had not been engaged in beating off the Scandinavian threat in the North, the outcome would have been different, allowing the Saxons to bottle up the Norman bridgehead and slaughter them at their leisure.

The so-called 'Protestant wind' also played its sometimes overrated part in seeing off the Spanish armada and several other attempts. The same wind, blowing in the other direction, enabled William of Orange to invade.

Another factor often forgotten, is that any great purpose in an invasion of England before she became a great seafaring nation was often not recognised. The cross-Channel warfare of the Middle Ages was a largely dynastic matter engaged in largely by French speakers on both sides. England itself was a marginal country, poor by the standards of the great European powers, and hardly worth the effort of invasion. The discovery of America and the birth of global trade routes changed all that, particularly once England had lost her Normandy territories, by making her both richer and a serious rival in the trade wars. British monarchs and strategists were instinctively and politically aware of the transformation in geopolitics and were forced to look both at the wider world, where they were creating an empire, and to the Continent where their traditional foes had always dominated. From the Tudor age onwards, the need for a navy which both defended Britain and dominated the world was recognised and acted upon.

Technically, the development of firepower changed the nature of naval warfare. Before then, warships were merely fighting platforms used to grapple at close quarters with the enemy, ram opponents and sink or capture rudimentary invasion ferry-boats. Afterwards they became floating artillery platforms, which could both defend themselves and attack the enemy at increasingly long ranges. For a potential enemy there were now three strategies available:

- Combined operations in which warships and the invasion transports they protect sail together in close formation. That was the strategy employed by the Spanish Armada and others which followed it. To succeed it had to have overwhelming naval supremacy and close liaison between naval and army commanders. Once landed, the invaders had to ensure that supply routes were maintained and that their ground forces moved swiftly and effectively to avoid becoming bottled up. For centuries potential invaders believed that could only be achieved by a coalition with other English rivals; however, such a strategy usually led to confusion in the chains of command and conflicting priorities amongst allies of different nationalities.

- Prior action by a battle fleet acting independently. This could in theory mean searching out and destroying the English forces before launching the invasion barges. In practice, the dominance of the Royal Navy meant it was more realistic to lure the English into an engagement far away from the route of the actual invasion, allowing the barges to slip across the Channel, the tactic favoured by Napoleon.

- Surprise assault without declaration of war. The French tried that in 1743-44 and others before and after built up invasion fleets in preparations for lightning strikes. The flaw in that scenario was secrecy. To build up an invasion army and fleet involves huge logistics, the transport of men and materials, feints and counter-feints to misdirect, and the issuing of complex orders to all naval, army and ordnance ranks. In every case, such preparations were exposed by British agents who, particularly after the work of Elizabethan spymaster Walsingham, were masters of espionage.

To counter such strategies the Royal Navy used two tactics that went beyond its simple, dominating existence. First, a pre-emptive strike: Sir Francis Drake's fireship attack on the Spanish fleet was a prime example, setting back invasion plans by a year. Second, supplementary flotillas to destroy enemy transports while the main ships-of-the-line were engaged elsewhere. Such ancillary forces relied on frigates and privateers ever-ready to take the battle to the enemy before they could reach shore. In this Britain was lucky in having its string of superb naval ports from the Solent to the Thames.

The Royal Navy's ability to achieve defensive success while dominating the world's oceans and trade routes begins with the Tudors. Henry VIII created a standing navy with its own dockyards building warships, funded by the wealth of wool, and its own bureaucracy. During Elizabeth's reign that standing navy combined with privately owned vessels to plunder Spanish bullion ships and colonies in the Americas. It was a sixteenth-century public-private finance initiative which rewarded the best captains and crews, improved design to provide faster and better-armed vessels, and gave England an advantage in seamanship, gunnery and discipline.

During the early seventeenth century, England's relative naval power deteriorated to the point where it was even ineffective against Barbary corsairs. Charles I undertook a major programme of warship building but the huge costs incurred, and the taxes he imposed, contributed to the English Civil Wars which ended in his execution. The new Commonwealth under Cromwell, beleaguered on all sides, again expanded the navy. The introduction of navigation acts imposing an English shipping monopoly on all seaborne imports and exports led to war with the Dutch Republic. Superior Dutch tactics at first threatened stalemate but the English soon learnt their lessons from the First Anglo-Dutch War with a series of stunning victories that left them with the most powerful navy in the world.

After the Restoration such victories were repeated against the Dutch, and the navy for the first time ceased to be a royal possession and instead became a national institution. But lack of hard cash under Charles II forced it to lay up in ports. That in turn led to the humiliating Dutch raid on the Medway.

Following the Glorious Revolution, the War of the Grand Alliance ended the brief sea supremacy of France and gave the Royal Navy a dominance it would not lose until the twentieth century.

During the eighteenth century the Royal Navy was transformed from a semi-amateur organisation into a fully fledged professional institution, generally ahead of the rest in terms of cutting edge naval technology, including the design of vessels, firepower, navigation and map-making, which cleverly (and often surreptitiously) combined military and trade interests. Funding was placed on a regular footing and although press gangs continued to be necessary beyond Nelson's day, it gradually created a professional officer class in place of the earlier mixture of free-booters and aristocratic ex-soldiers. As Frank McLynn wrote:

> In aristocratic England the fool of the family could find a career in the army, but rarely in the navy. The meritocracy in the Royal Navy that produced men like Captain Cook contrasted with the stultifying nepotism and grandee traditions in the French Marine before the Revolution, a tradition in which blood and rank were everything.

In the American War of Independence the rebel frigates were easily destroyed but the entry of France, Spain and the Netherlands briefly robbed Britain of the naval superiority it had become used to. The Royal Navy recovered that dominance and reached a peak of efficiency during the Napoleonic Wars, achieving its finest hours under Nelson at the battles of the Nile and Trafalgar.

The eradication of scurvy by the introduction of fresh lemons in diets strengthened crews, reducing the occurrence of an often fatal illness that could cripple a fleet well out of earshot of enemy cannon. The depradations of this vitamin deficiency cannot be overestimated: in the Seven Years War alone, the Royal Navy reported that it conscripted 184,899 sailors, of whom 133,708 died of disease or were 'missing' – and scurvy was stated to be the principal disease. There were further improvements in supply, sanitation and treatment, lessons which were not learned by the army until the Crimea.

During the Napoleonic era the Royal Navy also became adept at amphibious landings, capturing French Caribbean islands and the Dutch colonies in South Africa and the East Indies.

Between 1815 and 1914 the Navy saw little large-scale action, owing to the absence of any opponent strong enough to challenge its dominance. During this period, naval warfare underwent a comprehensive transformation, brought about by steam propulsion, metal ship construction, and explosive munitions. Despite having to completely replace its war fleet, the Navy managed to maintain its overwhelming advantage over all potential rivals. Britain's leadership in the Industrial Revolution gave it unparalleled shipbuilding capacity and financial resources, which ensured that no rival could take advantage of these revolutionary changes to negate the British advantage in ship numbers. In 1889, Parliament passed the Naval Defence Act which formally adopted the 'two-power standard', which stipulated that the Royal Navy should maintain a number of battleships at least equal to the combined strength of the next two largest navies.

But although the Royal Navy was too powerful to engage in set-piece sea battles, during the Victorian era it was effectively engaged in the innumerable imperialist wars of empire, anti-piracy actions in the Mediterranean and the South China Sea, and anti-slave trade blockades. It also participated in the Crimea – both in the Black Sea and the Baltic – and heavy-handed policing actions on both the east and west coasts of Africa and the Far East.

The end of the nineteenth century saw structural changes enforced by the First Sea Lord Jackie Fisher who retired, scrapped, or placed into reserve many of the older vessels, making funds and manpower available for newer ships. He also oversaw the development of HMS *Dreadnought*, whose speed and firepower rendered all existing battleships obsolete. The industrial and economic development of Germany had by this time overtaken Britain, however, enabling it to try to outpace British construction of dreadnaughts. Britain won the subsequent arms race, but for the first time since 1805 another navy now existed with the capacity to challenge the Royal Navy in battle. The Battle of Jutland, however, saw off the Imperial German Navy and the emphasis switched to submarine warfare, the protection of convoys and, eventually, airpower in the retaking of Nazi- and Japanese-occupied territories.

Ultimately, both the threat of invasion, and Britain's ability to defend herself from invasion, derived from her position as an imperial power. Britain's colonial expansion provoked the Spanish, while the struggle for global dominance mobilised the French and Nazi Germany. Conversely, it was Britain's mastery of the sea, which would have been impossible without the wealth which poured in from the empire, which saw off invasions. Once the days of empire were over, so too was the threat of invasion.

APPENDIX 1

CHRONICLERS' ACCOUNTS OF THE 1377 RAIDS

'Many noble feats of arms …'

Thomas Walsingham (An early English translation of Walsingham's Latin text, taken from Higden's Polychronicon, Volume 8):

> After that men of France entered into the Isle of Wight, and did great hurt; which taking a thousand marks for ransom returned to the sea, keeping the coasts of England, and burning many noble places, slaying men whom they could find in the south parts, and taking many beasts with them. For more hurt was done in England in that year, as it was said, than in the forty years afore. Also men of France made an assault to the town of Winchelsea, but they could not enter into the town, nevertheless they sent diverse men which burnt the town of Hastings. Also men of France entered in the same year into the town of Rottingdean, in Sussex, where the prior of Lewes met them with a little number of people, which was taken and brought to their ships with other two knights, Sir John Falvesley and Sir Thomas Cheyne, with a squire John Brocas. But a squire born in France being in the service with the said [prior] fought manfully against men of France, in so much that his belly [was] cut, he fought sore, his bowels remaining behind him a great space, and followed his enemies. In which conflict a hundred Englishmen were slain, and many more of the Frenchmen; which took the dead men away with them, other else they burnt their faces with iron that they should not be known, and that Englishmen should not solace of their death. Where a man of France was taken, confessing afore his death that the realm of England should not have been troubled by the men of France if that the Duke of Lancaster had been made king.

Froissart. An English translation taken from P.E. Thompson's *Contemporary Chronicles of the Hundred Years' War* (London 1966, pages 176-7):

> As they sailed along the coast of England, Jean de Vienne and Jean de Rye, the French admirals, and the Spanish admiral harried the land and made every effort to force a landing for their own advantage. They came shortly before a considerable town near the sea called Lewes, where there is a very rich priory.

The people of the surrounding country had taken refuge there with the prior and two knights, Sir Thomas Cheyne and Sir John Falvesley. The Earl of Salisbury and his brother were unable to get there in time, because of the rough roads and difficult going between Lewes and the country they were in.

The French reached the port, which they entered in formation, bringing their ships as close to the land as they could; they effected their landing in spite of the English defenders, who did what they could. As they entered Lewes there was a deal of fighting, and many French were wounded by arrows; but they were so numerous that they drove back their enemies, who gathered in a convenient square in front of the monastery to await the foe approaching in close order for a hand-to-hand fight. Many noble feats of arms were performed on both sides, and the English defended themselves very well considering their numbers, for they were few in comparison with the French. For this reason they exerted themselves all the more, while the French were all the more eager to inflict losses on them. Finally the French conquered the town and dislodged the English; two hundred of them were killed and a large number of the more important men taken prisoner, rich men from the surrounding parts who had come there to win honour; the prior and the two knights were also taken. The whole town of Lewes was ransacked and burnt or destroyed, together with some small villages round about. By high tide the French were already back in their ships, and they set sail with their booty and their prisoners, from whom they learned of the death of King Edward and the coronation of King Richard.

Jean Cabaret D'Orronville. *La Chronique du bon duc Loys*, 1876, pages 71-2. An English translation from the original French text by D.A. Crowder:

And Messire Renier de Grimaldi having returned bringing the things that he had promised, to the Admiral, they embarked their army for the crossing, numbering 400 horses and 2,000 troops, both men-at-arms and support troops, and they reached the coast of England, where the English on the coast tried to prevent them from landing, but without success because the Admiral and his force landed and pursued them for a good league and more as far as Rye; and in that pursuit many English were killed. And the town was then taken, overrun and burnt that day, when many people were killed and a fair number taken to the vessels as prisoners, and an abundance of cloth and other riches of many kinds were seized. And a wealthy English prior, known as the Prior of Lewes, who had learnt of the emergency from the refugees from Rye, reaching his monastery, which was not far away, had assembled a large force to drive out the French if he could. And to this end, during the evening the prior arrived with a good 500 troops, some of the best men he had; but the Admiral, who was no fool and had a strong suspicion that someone would arrive, had laid a great ambush of 300 cavalry, hand-picked men. They saw the English coming a long way off and let them get close, then they emerged from ambush and attacked them, routed them and captured their leader, who was wearing armour covered with red velvet; and the Prior of Lewes became the Admiral's prisoner as his share of the spoils and was held captive for a year, and the Admiral was paid a ransom of 7,000 nobles. The Admiral with his fleet withdrew from Rye honourably and without loss and went to Paris to join the King.

LATER HISTORY OF CASTLES AND FORTIFICATIONS FEATURED

'a sett of drunken wretches'

Rochester

Rochester was besieged for the third time in 1264 during the Second Barons' War (1264-7). The castle's royal constable, Roger de Leybourne, held Rochester in support of Henry III against the rebel armies of Simon de Montfort and Gilbert de Clare. On 17 April they laid siege. Having marched from Tonbridge de Clare's force attacked from the Rochester side of the river. While the army advanced towards the city the Royalist garrison set alight the suburbs. An army under Simon de Montfort marched from London with the intention of attacking the city from another direction. The first two attempts to cross the Medway were fought back, but the rebels were partially successful on Good Friday, 18 April. A fire-ship was used to provide smoke cover for the rebels as they crossed the bridge across the Medway. In a co-ordinated attack both rebel armies fell on the city. That night the cathedral was raided. The following day the rebels captured the castle's outer enclosure and the royal garrison retreated to the keep. Because the next day was Easter Sunday there was no fighting, though hostilities resumed on the Monday. Siege engines were set up and targeted the keep. As in 1215, the keep proved resistant to missiles, and after a week had not succumbed. According to one contemporary source, the besiegers were about to dig a mine beneath the tower, but the siege was abandoned on 26 April when the earls received news of a relief force led by Henry III and his son, Prince Edward. Although the garrison did not surrender, the castle suffered extensive damage that was not repaired until the following century.

It was noted in 1275 that the castle's constables had not only failed to make any effort to repair the structure but had caused further damage: they stole stone from the castle for reuse elsewhere.

Between May 1367 and September 1370 repairs costing £2,262 were carried out. Records show that sections of the curtain wall were repaired and two mural towers built, one of them replacing a tower on the same site. The towers were positioned north-east of the keep and still stand.

Rochester Castle saw fighting for the final time during the Peasants' Revolt of 1381. It was besieged and captured by a group of rebels who plundered the castle and released a prisoner.

The decline of the castle's military significance is marked by the leasing of the surrounding ditch, beginning in 1564 at the latest. Between 1599 and 1601 stone from Rochester Castle was reused to build nearby Upnor Castle.

Samuel Pepys commented on the condition of Rochester Castle, and as early as the seventeenth century the castle may have acted as a tourist attraction.

The castle fell out of use, its materials were reused elsewhere and custodianship relinquished by the Crown. The castle and its grounds were opened to the public in the 1870s as a park. At various points during the nineteenth and twentieth centuries repairs were carried out.

Dover Castle

By the Tudor age, the castle defences had been made redundant by the new supremacy of gunpowder. They were improved by Henry VIII, who made a personal visit and added the Moat Bulwark.

During the English Civil War it was held for the king but then taken in 1642 by a Parliamentarian force without a shot being fired, thereby avoiding destruction.

Massive rebuilding took place at the end of the eighteenth century. William Twiss, Commanding Engineer of the Southern District, completed the remodelling of the outer defences by adding the huge Horseshoe, Hudson's, East Arrow and East Demi-Bastions to provide extra gun positions on the eastern side, and constructing the Constable's Bastion for additional protection on the west. Twiss further strengthened the Spur at the northern end of the castle, adding a raised gun platform.

Dover became primarily a garrison town and Twiss and the Royal Engineers built a complex of barracks tunnels about 15m below the cliff top. The first troops were accommodated in 1803 and at the war's height housed more than 2,000 men.

At the end of the Napoleonic Wars, the tunnels were partly converted and used by the Coast Blockade Service to combat smuggling. The tunnels then remained abandoned for more than a century.

The outbreak of the Second World War in 1939 saw the tunnels converted first into an air-raid shelter and later into a military command centre and underground hospital. In May 1940, Admiral Sir Bertram Ramsey directed the evacuation of French and British soldiers from Dunkirk from his headquarters in the cliff tunnels. The castle's batteries and communications centre played a major role in the Battle of Britain and subsequent operations in the Straits of Dover and beyond.

During the Cold War the tunnels were to be used as a shelter for the regional seats of government in the event of a nuclear attack. This plan was abandoned when it was realised that the chalk cliffs would not provide significant protection from radiation.

Lincoln

After the siege of Lincoln, a new barbican was built onto the west and east gates of the castle. Later the castle was used as a secure site in which to establish a prison. At Lincoln, the prison gaol was built in 1787 and extended in 1847. Imprisoned debtors were allowed some social contact but the regime for criminals was designed to be one of isolation. By 1878 the system was discredited and the inmates were transferred to the new gaol on the eastern outskirts of Lincoln. The prison in the castle was left without a function until the Lincolnshire archives were housed in its cells.

Lincoln Castle remains one of the most impressive Norman castles in the UK, with immense twelfth-century walls and ramparts. Within its walls is displayed one of the four surviving originals of Magna Carta.

Castles of the Downs

Henry VIII's Castles of the Downs – Deal, Sandown and Walmer –were not tested in battle during Tudor times. That came with the English Civil War. In 1648 all three came under siege.

They were first held for Parliament but their commanders and garrisons switched to the Royalist cause after the naval vessels in the Downs declared for the King. A 2,000-strong Parliamentary force under the Puritan Colonel Nathaniel Rich, 2nd Earl of Warwick, marched into Kent and, after raising the Royalist siege of Dover Castle, turned its attention to the three Downs castles. The Royalists attempted to relieve them by sea and at Deal and Sandown they succeeded. But at Walmer they were beaten back after an indecisive engagement, and after three weeks that castle surrendered.

Rich besieged Deal and Sandown in earnest. A sally from Deal Castle was described by a contemporary:

> [they] intended to surprise our forlorn guard, which was between three and four hundreds yards of the Castle; but they were soon discovered, and by a Reserve guard they were gallantly repulsed, and driven back to the very gates of the Castle, and this with the loss of three of our men and some few wounded. As for the losses on the Enemies' part, it is not certain, yet some of our Soldiers observed about eight or nine of them to be carried off on pick-pack.

The Royalists tried again to land a strong relief force, but were again beaten off with heavy losses. According to Rich, out of a relief force of 800 men the Royalists lost 80 killed, 100 taken prisoner including their commanders, and 300 stands of arms captured. The Parliamentarians lost seven men. Both remaining castles surrendered, their last hope of relief gone.

Walmer

In 1708 Walmer Castle became the residence of the Lord Warden of the Cinque Ports, an eleventh-century confederation in which the five ports of Hastings, Romney, Hythe, Dover and Sandwich joined forces to provide ships and men for the defence of the coast and protection of cross-Channel trade. In return for these services they received substantial local privileges including immunity from all external courts of justice and from national taxation.

Over the years successive Wardens converted the fort and its grounds into a comfortable country house and gardens. Resident Wardens included William Pitt the Younger, who used local militia to create impressive gardens, the Duke of Wellington who died there, Sir Winston Churchill and Queen Elizabeth, The Queen Mother.

Deal

The castle was fortified during the Napoleonic Wars, with numerous alterations keeping pace with advances in military firepower during the eighteenth and eighteenth centuries. From May 1940 until September 1944, the castle was used as the Battery Observation Post and accommodation for the nearby coastal battery of six-inch naval guns. The Governor's lodgings were destroyed in 1941 by German bombs. Since 1951 it has been owned by English Heritage.

Sandown

Sandown Castle was in a ruinous state by the end of the seventeenth century and the sea had breached the moat walls by 1785. The castle was repaired and garrisoned in 1808 to counter Napoleon's threat, but in 1863 it was sold by the War Office. By 1882 it had been largely demolished for building materials. Further damage has been caused by coastal erosion. Only fragments of the landward side remain, battered by storm-tossed shingle rather than enemy cannonades.

Southsea

In the early part of the seventeenth century the castle was unarmed and in March 1625 a fire started that caused significant damage to the fortification. The damage was repaired in fits and starts over 10 years but much of that work was undone by a fire in March 1640.

During the Civil War the castle was initially held by Royalist forces under the command of Captain Challoner. He pointed its cannon inland leaving the seaward side undefended. Inevitably, the castle was captured during the siege of Portsmouth in

September 1642. By then only a dozen men defended it, no match for a Parliamentary forces of 400 infantry backed by cavalry. Equipped with ladders, the Parliamentarians approached the fort by night and although spotted and fired on by the guns of Portsmouth were able to make to the seaward side of the castle. At the same time a small party approached the main gate called on the castle to surrender. Captain Challoner was drunk and asked them to come back in the morning. Under renewed cannon fire from the port, the Parliamentarians scaled the walls and captured the castle without further opposition. A Parliamentarian garrison was then installed.

After the civil war the castle became a prison, before being rebuilt in the 1680s to the design of the military architect of genius, Bernard de Gomme. It was damaged in an accidental gunpowder explosion in August 1759 that killed 17 people. Another rebuild began in 1814 with the castle being extended north by 20-30ft. In 1828 an Admiralty lighthouse was constructed on the western gun platform. In 1844 the castle reverted to a gaol before its strategic position was again appreciated in 1850. Seven modern gun emplacements were built, followed 10 years later by flanking batteries. It turned from a stand-alone fortification to the hub of a sophisticated system of port defences.

During the First World War the castle was at first manned by Royal Garrison artillery and No. 4 company of Hampshire RGA territorials. Later these units were transferred to France and were replaced by the Hampshire RGA Volunteers. Postwar, the castle became a magnet for tourists eager to see practice firings out to sea. The castle was hit by several incendiary bombs during the Second World War, although they did little damage.

On 23 June 1940 the castle became involved in an armed standoff with the French ships that had escaped the fall of France. The garrison was ordered to prepare to fire on the French craft while the destroyer *Leopard* aimed her guns at the castle. The test of nerves ended on 3 July when British forces boarded the French ships in Operation Catapult. In 1960 Portsmouth city council took control of the castle and in 1967 it was opened as a museum.

Hurst

In 1561 Thomas Carew captained the castle situated on a curved spit reaching towards the Isle of Wight. Under him were 12 gunners, eight soldiers and two porters. He died at his post and was succeeded by Sir Thomas Gorges who in 1593 petitioned for the repair of the platforms, which were so decayed as to be incapable of supporting the guns. His son, Sir Edward, succeeded him as captain in 1610. The castle's defences were neglected and in 1628 had insufficient shot and powder to halt a suspicious ship. Of 27 cannon, only four of five were operable and only then only for 'a shot or two'.

In 1642, in the absence of the captain, the castle was occupied by Captain Richard Swanley for Parliament. It was the last prison of King Charles I before being moved to Windsor prior to his trial and execution.

Following the Restoration, in January 1661 Charles II ordered the garrison to be disbanded and the castle demolished. The latter plan was dropped due to the expense of demolition. In 1671 the castle commander, Sir Robert Holmes, reported that there was scarcely a gun mounted and no stores or provisions. Nothing was done to rectify the matter for three years until repairs were done and a proper garrison re-installed. A Captain Roach murdered a fellow-officer and, borrowing a black cloak, sailed by boat to Hurst where he was arrested.

The fort's tower was rebuilt around 1805 and in the 1850s a dock and the west battery were added. Recommendations by the 1859 Royal commission report led to the castle being refortified, and two large wing batteries were built to house 30 heavy guns. In 1873 a new east wing was built and a new entrance to the castle was driven through the north-east bastion. Around 1889 the magazine roof was reinforced with more concrete; the staircases and rooms within the tower were rebuilt; and the tower roof was adapted for modern gun mountings. A coastal battery was built in 1893

By December 1902 the battery was armed with three 12-pounder and three 6-pounder quick-firing guns and ten 12.5-inch and fifteen 10-inch rifle muzzle-loading (RML) weapons. In 1905 the RML and 6-pounder guns were removed from the armament. The battery was closed in 1928.

The fort was recommissioned again during the Second World War. By 1941 it was armed with two 12-pounder and two 6-pounder quick-firing guns.

Other Key Fortifications Commissioned by Henry VIII

Isle of Wight: East Cowes Castle, Sandown Castle, Sharpenode Bulwark, St Helen's Bulwark, West Cowes Castle, Worsleys Castle, Yarmouth Castle.

Hampshire: Calshot Castle, Netley Castle, St Andrews Castle.

Dorset: Sandsfoot Castle, Portland Castle.

Sussex: Camber Castle.

Kent: Sandgate Castle, Gravesend Blockhouse, Higham Blockhouse, Milton Blockhouse.

Essex: East Tilbury Blockhouse, West Tilbury Blockhouse.

Cornwall: Pendennis Castle, Little Dennis Blockhouse, St Mawes Castle, St Catherine's Castle.

Devon: Devil's Point artillery tower.

St Mawes

The castle, and Pendennis across the river, was built on the shore of the Fal Estuary near Falmouth to protect the Carrick roads, one of the world's biggest natural harbours.

It was occupied by the Royalists in the Civil War but, indefensible from land attack, surrendered to Parliamentary forces in 1646. Later a lead-covered dome was added to the stair turret as a navigational aid.

At the end of the eighteenth century, a lower gun battery beneath St Mawes castle was built during the Napoleonic wars, armed with twelve guns and built with three flanks. In about 1870, the battery was armed by four 64-pounder guns, but the battery was remodelled in 1898 to house two 6-pounder quick-firing guns and a heavy machine gun. These were served by a new underground magazine situated beneath the battery. The lower battery was superseded by a more powerful battery built on higher ground by 1903. During the Second World War, the battery was part of an extensive system of defences set up on the headland.

Pendennis

Pendennis Castle was the last Royalist position in the West of England, withstanding a five-month siege by Parliamentarians until August 1646. It survived an attack from both land and sea, but the garrison under 70-year-old Sir john Arundel with 1,500 men, women and children, were starved out.

A battery was built on Crab Quay, the most suitable landing place, and a battery was built, first recorded on a map of 1715. By 1815 five 18-pounder guns were mounted, firing through embrasures in a thick retaining wall. In 1855 the battery was upgraded to five 32-pounders on dwarf traversing carriages, but by 1880 these had in turn been replaced by two 64-pounder rifled muzzle-loaders. In 1898 the battery was reconstructed to provide two concrete emplacements for a pair of 6-pounder quick-firing guns, which, together with a sister battery at St Mawes, would prevent fast torpedo boats evading the heavier guns on the headland and entering the Carrick Roads. They were removed in 1904. The battery was briefly rearmed around 1942 with two 3-pounder QF guns while the twin 6-pounder battery at Middle Point was being constructed, but these were dismantled by 1943.

Upnor

In 1668, as part of the upgrading of Chatham's defences, new batteries were built at Cockham Wood. The chain was no longer used, and as new fortifications extended towards the Medway and Thames estuaries, the redundant castle became a storehouse for gunpowder shipped from Tower of London Wharf. Records show that in 1691, after floors were strengthened to take the weight, there were 5,206 barrels of powder.

In 1718 barracks were built. Life followed a regular uneventful pattern for the two officers and 64 soldiers. The master gunner patrolled every night to see that the gunners were safely in bed. Boredom set in, however, and in 1746 the garrison was described as a 'sett of drunken wretches'. The magazine closed in 1827 and by 1840 it became an ordnance laboratory. In 1891 the Castle was transferred from the War Office to the Admiralty. It continued in service until 1945 when it became a museum.

Post-Tudor

Western Heights, Dover

The fortifications built to protect the key port of Dover during the Napoleonic era remain impressive. The initial earthworks expanded into a series of forts, strongpoints, ditches, batteries and barracks, with tunnels cut into the chalk cliffs.

To assist with the movement of troops between Dover Castle and the town defences Twiss made his case for building the Grand Shaft in the cliff:

> ... the new barracks ... are little more than 300yds horizontally from the beach ... and about 180ft (55m) above high-water mark, but in order to communicate with them from the centre of town, on horseback the distance is nearly a mile and a half and to walk it about three-quarters of a mile, and all the roads unavoidably pass over ground more than 100ft (30m) above the barracks, besides the footpaths are so steep and chalky that a number of accidents will unavoidably happen during the wet weather and more especially after floods. I am therefore induced to recommend the construction of a shaft, with a triple staircase ... the chief objective of which is the convenience and safety of troops ...

The shaft was built for an estimated £4000 and was completed by 1807.

The Drop Redoubt is one of the two forts on Western Heights, and is linked to the other, the Citadel, by a series of dry moats. The artillery at the Redoubt faced mostly inland; it was intended to attack an invading force attempting to capture Dover from the rear. It was built in two phases: from 1804 to 1808 during the Napoleonic Wars, and from 1859 to 1864 following the recommendations of the 1859 Royal Commission.

During the Second World War, the Redoubt housed a squad of commandos who would have been responsible for destroying Dover Harbour in the event of an invasion. Their presence was secret and the lines around the Redoubt were mined.

The barracks have been demolished and the Citadel, after a period as a young offenders' institution, became the area's removal centre for illegal immigrants.

Royal Military Canal

The defensive ditch linking Hythe in Kent and Iden Lock over the border in East Sussex was built between the end of October 1894 and April 1809 at a total cost of £234,000. Gun positions along the canal were generally located every 500yds. Any troops stationed or moving along the Military Road was protected by the earthen bank of the parapet.

Although the canal never saw military action, it was used to try to control smuggling from Romney Marsh. Guard houses were constructed at each bridge along its length. This met with limited success because of corrupt guards. Although a barge service was established from Hythe to Rye, the canal was abandoned in 1877 and leased to the Lords of the Level of Romney Marsh. During the early stages of the Second World War it was fortified with concrete pillboxes.

The canal is now an important environmental site.

SAMUEL PEPYS'S DIARY EXTRACTS

'… to be hanged for not doing it'

Samuel Pepys (1633–1703), who had no experience at sea, rose through patronage and a genius for administration to become Chief Secretary of the Admiralty. But he is best known for the detailed, often raunchy, private diary he kept between 1660 and 1669. It has become an invaluable primary source for historians of the Restoration because of its immediacy and his access to the power-brokers of the era. The diary is most often quoted on the Great Plague and the Great Fire of London, both in 1666. But his entries the following year on the Second Anglo-Dutch War vividly reveal first the complacency, then the sense of panic at Charles II's court, and within Whitehall and the City, at the threat of invasion.

23 March:

> At the office all the morning, where Sir W. Pen come, being returned from Chatham, from considering the means of fortifying the river Medway, by a chain at the stakes, and ships laid there with guns to keep the enemy from coming up to burn our ships; all our care now being to fortify ourselves against their invading us.

24 March:

> … all their care they now take is to fortify themselves, and are not ashamed of it: for when by and by my Lord Arlington come in with letters, and seeing the King and Duke of York give us and the officers of the Ordnance directions in this matter, he did move that we might do it as privately as we could, that it might not come into the Dutch Gazette presently, as the King's and Duke of York's going down the other day to Sheerenesse was, the week after, in the Harlem Gazette. The King and Duke of York both laughed at it, and made no matter, but said, 'Let us be safe, and let them talk, for there is nothing will trouble them more, nor will prevent their coming more, than to hear that we are fortifying ourselves'.

18 April 1667:

> … then to the office, where the news is strong that not only the Dutch cannot set out a fleete this year, but that the French will not, and that he [Louis XIV]

hath given the answer to the Dutch Embassador, saying that he is for the King of England's, having an honourable peace, which, if true, is the best news we have had a good while.

3 June:

… the Dutch are known to be abroad with eighty sail of ships of war, and twenty fire-ships; and the French come into the Channell with twenty sail of men-of-war, and five fireships, while we have not a ship at sea to do them any hurt with; but are calling in all we can, while our Embassadors are treating at Bredah; and the Dutch look upon them as come to beg peace, and use them accordingly; and all this through the negligence of our Prince, who hath power, if he would, to master all these with the money and men that he hath had the command of, and may now have, if he would mind his business. But, for aught we see, the Kingdom is likely to be lost, as well as the reputation of it is, for ever; notwithstanding so much reputation got and preserved by a rebel that went before him. This discourse of ours ended with sorrowful reflections upon our condition, and so broke up.

8 June:

Up, and to the office, where all the news this morning is, that the Dutch are come with a fleete of eighty sail to Harwich, and that guns were heard plain by Sir W. Rider's people at Bednallgreene, all yesterday even. So to the office, we all sat all the morning, and then home to dinner, where our dinner a ham of French bacon, boiled with pigeons, an excellent dish. The news is confirmed that the Dutch are off of Harwich, but had done nothing last night. The King hath sent down my Lord of Oxford to raise the countries there; and all the Westerne barges are taken up to make a bridge over the River, about the Hope, for horse to cross the River, if there be occasion.

9 June:

Being come home I find an order come for the getting some fire-ships presently to annoy the Dutch, who are in the King's Channel, and expected up higher.

10 June:

… news brought us that, the Dutch are come up as high as the Nore; and more pressing orders for fireships.

11 June:

Up, and more letters still from Sir W. Coventry about more fire-ships, and so
Sir W. Batten and I to the office, where Bruncker come to us, who is just now
going to Chatham upon a desire of Commissioner Pett's, who is in a very fearful stink for fear of the Dutch, and desires help for God and the King and
kingdom's sake. So Bruncker goes down, and Sir J. Minnes also, from Gravesend.
This morning Pett writes us word that Sheernesse is lost last night, after two or
three hours' dispute. The enemy hath possessed himself of that place; which is
very sad, and puts us into great fears of Chatham.

12 June:

… met Sir W. Coventry's boy; and there in his letter find that the Dutch had
made no motion since their taking Sheernesse; and the Duke of Albemarle
writes that all is safe as to the great ships against any assault, the boom and
chaine being so fortified; which put my heart into great joy.

Later entry:

… his clerk, Powell, do tell me that ill newes is come to Court of the Dutch
breaking the Chaine at Chatham; which struck me to the heart. And to White
Hall to hear the truth of it; and there, going up the back-stairs, I did hear some
lacquies speaking of sad newes come to Court, saying, that hardly anybody in
the Court but do look as if he cried … all our hearts do now ake; for the newes
is true, that the Dutch have broke the chaine and burned our ships, and particularly 'The Royal Charles', other particulars I know not, but most sad to be sure.
And, the truth is, I do fear so much that the whole kingdom is undone, that I
do this night resolve to study with my father and wife what to do with the little
that I have in money by me …

13 June:

No sooner up but hear the sad newes confirmed of the *Royal Charles* being
taken by them, and now in fitting by them – which Pett should have carried
up higher by our several orders, and deserves, therefore, to be hanged for not
doing it – and turning several others; and that another fleete is come up into
the Hope. Upon which newes the King and Duke of York have been below –
[London Bridge] – since four o'clock in the morning, to command the sinking
of ships at Barking-Creeke, and other places, to stop their coming up higher:
which put me into such a fear, that I presently resolved of my father's and wife's
going into the country; and, at two hours' warning, they did go by the coach
this day, with about 1300l. in gold in their night-bag. Pray God give them good

passage, and good care to hide it when they come home! but my heart is full of fear: They having gone, I continued in fright and fear what to do with the rest. W. Hewer hath been at the banker's, and hath got 500l. out of Backewell's hands of his own money; but they are so called upon that they will be all broke, hundreds coming to them for money: and their answer is, 'It is payable at twenty days – when the days are out, we will pay you;' and those that are not so, they make tell over their money, and make their bags false, on purpose to give cause to retell it, and so spend time. I cannot have my 200 pieces of gold again for silver, all being bought up last night that were to be had, and sold for 24 and 25s a-piece. So I must keep the silver by me, which sometimes I think to fling into the house of office, and then again know not how I shall come by it, if we be made to leave the office. Every minute some one or other calls for this or that order; and so I forced to be at the office, most of the day, about the fire-ships which are to be suddenly fitted out: and it's a most strange thing that we hear nothing from any of my brethren at Chatham; so that we are wholly in the dark, various being the reports of what is done there; insomuch that I sent Mr Clapham express thither to see how matters go: I did, about noon, resolve to send Mr. Gibson away after my wife with another 1000 pieces, under colour of an express to Sir Jeremy Smith; who is, as I hear, with some ships at Newcastle; which I did really send to him, and may, possibly, prove of good use to the King; for it is possible, in the hurry of business, they may not think of it at Court, and the charge of an express is not considerable to the King. So though I intend Gibson no further than to Huntingdon I direct him to send the packet forward.

My business the most of the afternoon is listening to every body that comes to the office, what news? which is variously related, some better, some worse, but nothing certain. The King and Duke of York up and down all the day here and there: some time on Tower Hill, where the City militia was; where the King did make a speech to them, that they should venture themselves no further than he would himself. I also sent, my mind being in pain, Saunders after my wife and father, to overtake them at their night's lodgings, to see how matters go with them. In the evening, I sent for my cousin Sarah [Gyles] and her husband, who come; and I did deliver them my chest of writings about Brampton, and my brother Tom's papers, and my journalls, which I value much; and did send my two silver flaggons to Kate Joyce: that so, being scattered what I have, something might be saved. I have also made a girdle, by which, with some trouble, I do carry about me 300l. in gold about my body, that I may not be without something in case I should be surprised: for I think, in any nation but our's, people that appear (for we are not indeed so) so faulty as we, would have their throats cut.

In the evening comes Mr. Pelling, and several others, to the office, and tell me that never were people so dejected as they are in the City all over at this day; and do talk most loudly, even treason; as, that we are bought and sold – that we are betrayed by the Papists, and others, about the King; cry out that the office of the Ordnance hath been so backward as no powder to have been at Chatham nor Upnor Castle till such a time, and the carriages all broken; that Legg is a Papist; that Upnor, the old good castle built by Queen Elizabeth, should be lately slighted; that the ships at Chatham should not be carried up higher. They look upon us as lost, and remove their families and rich goods in the City; and do think verily that the French, being come down with his army to Dunkirke, it is to invade us, and that we shall be invaded.

Mr. Clerke, the solicitor, comes to me about business, and tells me that he hears that the King hath chosen Mr Pierpont and Vaughan of the West, Privy-councillors; that my Lord Chancellor was affronted in the Hall this day, by people telling him of his Dunkirke house; and that there are regiments ordered to be got together, whereof to be commanders my Lord Fairfax, Ingoldsby, Bethell, Norton. And Birch and other Presbyterians; and that Dr. Bates will have liberty to preach. Now, whether this be true or not, I know not; but do think that nothing but this will unite us together.

Late at night comes Mr. Hudson, the cooper, my neighbour, and tells me that he come from Chatham this evening at five o'clock, and saw this afternoon 'The Royal James,' 'Oake,' and 'London' burnt by the enemy with their fire-ships: that two or three men-of-war come up with them, and made no more of Upnor Castle's shooting, than of a fly; that those ships lay below Upnor Castle, but therein, I conceive, he is in an error; that the Dutch are fitting out 'The Royall Charles;' that we shot so far as from the Yard thither, so that the shot did no good, for the bullets grazed on the water; that Upnor played hard with their guns at first, but slowly afterwards, either from the men being beat off, or their powder spent. But we hear that the fleete in the Hope is not come up any higher the last flood; and Sir W. Batten tells me that ships are provided to sink in the River, about Woolwich, that will prevent their coming up higher if they should attempt it. I made my will also this day, and did give all I had equally between my father and wife, and left copies of it in each of Mr. Hater and W. Hewer's hands, who both witnessed the will, and so to supper and then to bed, and slept pretty well, but yet often waking.

14 June:

Up, and to the office; where Mr. Fryer comes and tells me that there are several Frenchmen and Flemish ships in the River, with passes from the Duke of York for carrying of prisoners, that ought to be parted from the rest of the ships, and their powder taken, lest they do fire themselves when the enemy comes, and so spoil us; which is good advice, and I think I will give notice of it; and did so. But it is pretty odd to see how every body, even at this high time of danger, puts business off of their own hands! He says that he told this to the Lieutenant of the Tower, to whom I, for the same reason, was directing him to go; and the Lieutenant of the Tower bade him come to us, for he had nothing to do with it; and yesterday comes Captain Crow, of one of the fireships, and told me that the officers of the Ordnance would deliver his gunner's materials, but not compound them, but that we must do it; whereupon I was forced to write to them about it; and one that like a great many come to me this morning by and by comes Mr Wilson, and by direction of his, a man of Mr. Gawden's; who come from Chatham last night, and saw the three ships burnt, they lying all dry, and boats going from the men-of-war and fire them.

But that he tells me of worst consequence is, that he himself, I think he said, did hear many Englishmen on board the Dutch ships speaking to one another in English; and that they did cry and say, 'We did heretofore fight for tickets; now we fight for dollars!' and did ask how such and such a one did, and would commend themselves to them: which is a sad consideration. And Mr. Lewes, who was present at this fellow's discourse to me, did tell me, that he is told that when they took 'The Royall Charles,' they said that they had their tickets signed, and showed some, and that now they come to have them paid, and would have them paid before they parted. And several seamen come this morning to me, to tell me that, if I would get their tickets paid, they would go and do all they could against the Dutch; but otherwise they would not venture being killed, and lose all they have already fought for: so that I was forced to try what I could do to get them paid.

This man tells me that the ships burnt last night did lie above Upnor Castle, over against the Docke; and the boats come from the ships of war and burnt them all which is very sad. And masters of ships, that we are now taking up, do keep from their ships all their stores, or as much as they can, so that we can despatch them, having not time to appraise them nor secure their payment; only some little money we have, which we are fain to pay the men we have with, every night, or they will not work. And indeed the hearts as well as affections of the seamen are turned away; and in the open streets in Wapping, and up and down, the wives have cried publickly, 'This comes of your not paying our husbands; and now your work is undone, or done by hands that understand it not.' And Sir W. Batten told me that he was himself affronted with a woman, in language of this kind, on Tower Hill publickly yesterday; and we are fain to bear it, and to keep one at the office door to let no idle people in, for fear of firing of the office and doing us mischief. The City is troubled at their being put upon duty: summoned one hour, and discharged two hours after; and then again summoned two hours after that; to their great charge as well as trouble. And Pelling, the Potticary, tells me the world says all over, that less charge than what the kingdom is put to, of one kind or other, by this business, would have set out all our great ships. It is said they did in open streets yesterday, at Westminster, cry, 'A Parliament! a Parliament!' and I do believe it will cost blood to answer for these miscarriages.

We do not hear that the Dutch are come to Gravesend; which is a wonder. But a wonderful thing it is that to this day we have not one word yet from

Bruncker, or Peter Pett, or J. Minnes, of any thing at Chatham. The people that come hither to hear how things go, make me ashamed to be found unable to answer them: for I am left alone here at the office; and the truth is, I am glad my station is to be here, near my own home and out of danger, yet in a place of doing the King good service.

The dismay that is upon us all, in the business of the kingdom and Navy at this day, is not to be expressed otherwise than by the condition the citizens were in when the City was on fire, nobody knowing which way to turn themselves, while every thing concurred to greaten the fire; as here the easterly gale and spring-tides for coming up both rivers, and enabling them to break the chaine. D. Gawden did tell me yesterday, that the day before at the council they were ready to fall together by the ears at the council-table, arraigning one another of being guilty of the counsel that brought us into this misery, by laying up all the great ships.

Mr. Hater tells me at noon that some rude people have been, as he hears, at my Lord Chancellor's, where they have cut down the trees before his house and broke his windows; and a gibbet either set up before or painted upon his gate, and these three words writ: 'Three sights to be seen; Dunkirke, Tangier, and a barren Queene.' It gives great matter of talk that it is said there is at this hour, in the Exchequer, as much money as is ready to break down the floor. This arises, I believe, from Sir G. Downing's late talk of the greatness of the sum lying there of people's money, that they would not fetch away, which he shewed me and a great many others. Most people that I speak with are in doubt how we shall do to secure our seamen from running over to the Dutch; which is a sad but very true consideration at this day.

Dined, and Mr. Hater and W. Hewer with me; where they do speak very sorrowfully of the posture of the times, and how people do cry out in the streets of their being bought and sold; and both they, and every body that come to me, do tell me that people make nothing of talking treason in the streets openly: as, that we are bought and sold, and governed by Papists, and that we are betrayed by people about the King, and shall be delivered up to the French, and I know not what ...

At night come home Sir W. Batten and W. Pen, who only can tell me that they have placed guns at Woolwich and Depford, and sunk some ships below Woolwich and Blackewall, and are in hopes that they will stop the enemy's coming up. But strange our confusion! that among them that are sunk they have gone and sunk without consideration 'Franakin,' one of the King's ships, with stores to a very considerable value, that hath been long loaden for supply of the ships; and the new ship at Bristoll, and much wanted there; and nobody will own that they directed it, but do lay it on Sir W. Rider. They speak also of another ship, loaden to the value of 80,000l, sunk with the goods in her, or at least was mightily contended for by him, and a foreign ship, that had the faith of the nation for her security: this Sir R. Ford tells us: And it is too plain a truth, that both here and at Chatham the ships that we have sunk have many, and the first of them, been ships completely fitted for fire-ships at great charge.

But most strange the backwardness and disorder of all people, especially the King's people in pay, to do any work, Sir W. Pen tells me, all crying out for money; and it was so at Chatham, that this night comes an order from Sir W. Coventry to stop the pay of the wages of that Yard; the Duke of Albemarle having related, that not above three of 1100 in pay there did attend to do any work there.

… and they say the Duke of Albemarle did tell my Lord Bruncker to his face that his discharging of the great ships there was the cause of all this; and I am told that it is become common talk against my Lord Bruncker. But in that he is to be justified, for he did it by verbal order from Sir W. Coventry, and with good intent; and it was to good purpose, whatever the success be, for the men would have but spent the King so much the more in wages, and yet not attended on board to have done the King any service…

So to supper, and then to bed. No news to-day of any motion of the enemy either upwards towards Chatham or this way.

15 June:

No newes more than last night; only Purser Tyler comes and tells me that he being at all the passages in this business at Chatham, he says there have been horrible miscarriages, such as we shall shortly hear of: that the want of boats hath undone us; and it is commonly said, and Sir J. Minnes under his hand tells us, that they were employed by the men of the Yard to carry away their goods; and I hear that Commissioner Pett will be found the first man that began to remove; he is much spoken against, and Bruncke is complained of and reproached for discharging the men of the great ships heretofore. At noon Mr. Hater dined with me; and tells me he believes that it will hardly be the want of money alone that will excuse to the Parliament the neglect of not setting out a fleete, it having never been done in our greatest straits, but however unlikely it appeared, yet when it was gone about, the State or King did compass it; and there is something in it.

17 June:

At the office all the afternoon, where every moment business of one kind or other about the fire-ships and other businesses, most of them vexatious for want of money, the commanders all complaining that, if they miss to pay their men a night, they run away; seamen demanding money of them by way of advance, and some of Sir Fretchville Hollis's men, that he so bragged of, demanding their tickets to be paid, or they would not work: this Hollis, Sir W. Batten and W. Pen say, proves a very … , as Sir W. B. terms him, and the other called him a conceited, idle, prating, lying fellow …

... the King and Court are all troubled, and the gates of the Court were shut up upon the first coming of the Dutch to us, but they do mind the business no more than ever...

... every body cries out of the office of the Ordnance, for their neglects, both at Gravesend and Upnor, and everywhere else.

18 June:

This day comes news from Harwich that the Dutch fleete are all in sight, near 100 sail great and small, they think, coming towards them; where, they think, they shall be able to oppose them; but do cry out of the falling back of the seamen, few standing by them, and those with much faintness.

28 July (Lord's Day):

Up and to my chamber, where all the morning close, to draw up a letter to Sir W. Coventry upon the tidings of peace, taking occasion, before I am forced to it, to resign up to his Royal Highness my place of the Victualling, and to recommend myself to him by promise of doing my utmost to improve this peace in the best manner we may, to save the kingdom from ruin. By noon I had done this to my good content, and then with my wife all alone to dinner, and so to my chamber all the afternoon to write my letter fair, and sent it away, and then to talk with my wife, and read, and so by daylight (the only time I think I have done it this year) to supper, and then to my chamber to read and so to bed, my mind very much eased after what I have done to-day.

3 July:

Here I find all the newes is the enemy's landing 3,000 men near Harwich and attacking Landguard, and being beat off thence with our great guns, killing some of their men, and they leaving their ladders behind them; but we had no Horse in the way on Suffolk side, otherwise we might have galled their Foot.

APPENDIX 4

MARTELLO TOWERS

'never tested in battle'

The British were never shy about adapting foreign military designs. The Martello towers were a copy of the round fortress at Mortella (Myrtle) Point in Corsica, designed by Giovan Giacomo Paleari Fratino and completed in 1565.

The Corsicans had previously built similar towers at strategic points to protect themselves from pirates. They were two storeys high and measured 12-15m (36-45ft) in diameter, with a single doorway 5m off the ground accessible only by a removable ladder. Watchmen, employed by local villagers, would signal the approach of suspected threats by lighting a rooftop beacon which would alert the local defence forces to the threat.

On 7 February 1794, the British warships HMS *Fortitude* and HMS *Juno* unsuccessfully attacked the Mortello tower and were repelled. Only heavy fighting by land troops took the town below the tower. Vice-Admiral Lord Hood reported:

> …The *Fortitude* and *Juno* were ordered against it, without making the least impression by a continued cannonade of two hours and a half; and the former ship being very much damaged by red-hot shot, both hauled off. The walls of the Tower were of a prodigious thickness, and the parapet, where there were two eighteen-pounders, was lined with bass junk, 5ft from the walls, and filled up with sand; and although it was cannonaded from the Height for two days, within 150yds, and appeared in a very shattered state, the enemy still held out; but a few hot shot setting fire to the bass, made them call for quarter. The number of men in the Tower were 33; only two were wounded, and those mortally.

The British were hugely impressed by the tower's effectiveness and copied the design, misspelling the name. When the British withdrew from Corsica in 1803, with great difficulty they blew up the tower.

The classic British Martello tower, built to repel a Napoleonic invasion, consisted of three storeys above a basement. The ground floor held the magazine and storerooms, the first floor housed 24 men and one officer, and had fireplaces built into the walls for cooking and heating. The flat roof was surmounted with one or two cannon on a central pivot that enabled the guns to rotate 360 degrees. A well or cistern within the fort supplied the garrison with water. An internal drainage system linked to the roof enabled rainwater to refill the cistern.

Around 140 were initially built, mostly along England's south coast. Great Britain and Ireland, united as a single political entity in 1801 to 1922, used Martellos as a defensive screen covering both main islands. Chains of Martello towers were built.

Between 1804 and 1812 the British authorities built 103 in England, at regular intervals from Seaford in Sussex to Aldeburgh in Suffolk. Most were constructed under the direction of General William Twiss (1745-1827) and a Captain Ford. There were also three much larger circular forts or redoubts that were constructed at Harwich, Dymchurch and Eastbourne which acted as supply depots for the smaller towers as well as being powerful fortifications in their own right. None were tested in combat against Napoleon's forces, but they were effective in combating smuggling.

After the threat had passed, of the Martello towers in England, 15 were demolished for raw materials, 30 were washed away by the sea, and four were reduced to rubble as part of an exercise to test the power of new artillery. During the Second World War many were used as observation posts and as anti-aircraft gun platforms. Of the remaining 47, some have become museums and galleries, others distinctive private homes, while a few are derelict.

Three Martello towers were built in Scotland, two at Hackness and Crockness the Orkney Islands, between 1813 and 1815 to guard against the threat of French and American raiders attacking convoys assembling offshore. A third Scottish tower was built on offshore rocks facing the Firth of Forth in 1807-09 to defend Leith Harbour.

A small number of Martello towers were also built in Wales but few survived. The most notable exceptions are in Pembrokeshire Dock.

Around 50 martellos were built around the Irish coastline, from Drogheda, to Bray on the easy coast, around Dublin Bay and around Cork Harbour. The most famous, but for non-martial reasons, is that along the coast from Dublin at Sandycove. James Joyce lived there for a few days with the surgeon, politician and writer Oliver St John Gogarty. In *Ulysses*, Joyce's fictional character Stephen Dedalus lives in the tower with a medical student, Malachi 'Buck' Mulligan. During the 1980s, the rock star Bono owned the Martello in Bray, County Wicklow.

Martellos were built across the Channel Islands. Three, built in 1804, are in Guernsey: Forts Grey, Hommet and Saumarez. The oval Brehon Tower, built in 1856, represents the final evolution of the Martello tower.

Eight were built in Jersey, three between 1808 and 1810 and five between 1834 and 1837, one of which, L'Etacq, the German occupation forces destroyed during the Second World War. The three original towers are the Tower, Portelet, and la Tour de Vinde. The four surviving, later towers are Lewis's and Kempt, both in St Ouen, Victoria and La Collette. In addition, there are the Jersey Round Towers and the Guernsey loop-hole towers, often called Martellos, built in the late eighteenth century as precursors.

Martellos were copied across the globe until the 1870s, although by then it had long been clear that they could not withstand the new generation of rifled artillery.

The French themselves built similar towers along their own coastline as platforms for optical telegraphs. The United States and the Dutch also built a number. But the greatest number remained British-built, protecting her swiftly expanding empire.

During the British occupation (1798-1802) of Minorca, Governor Sir Charles Stuart ordered Engineer Captain Robert D'Arcy to build 12 Martello towers along the coast. These, when added to the three Spanish towers already in place, gave Minorca 15 towers. One tower, the Princess Tower, or the Erskine Tower, was incorporated into the Fortress of Isabelli, built between 1850 and 1875. The tower was converted to a powder magazine, but when lightning struck, the subsequent explosion destroyed it.

In Minorca the British erected Stuart's Tower in 1798 on Hangman's Hill at San Estaban or Saint Stephen's Bay. In 1756 and again in 1781, batteries on the hill had supported successful attacks on the Fortress. The tower was built both to secure the hill and protect the entrance to the bay. To protect the harbour of Fornells, a tower was built on the rocky headland overlooking the harbour's mouth, and a small tower on the island of Sargantana. Finally, Another was built at Santandria to protect the old capital of Ciudadela.

During the British 'Protectorate' of Sicily after the escape of the Bourbons from Naples, Sicily began to build towers to resist an invasion by Napoleon's armies. The new higher rate of fire of ships' guns led to the choice of the Martello tower as the model. The Sicilian Martello towers were built around 1810. One was the Magnisi tower at Syracuse, later used by the Italian Navy as an observation post during the Second World War.

On Bermuda, Martellos were built behind Ferry Island fort and at Ferry Reach. The latter was built of Bermuda limestone from 1822-1823, with walls up to 11ft thick and surrounded by a dry moat. Its role was to impede any attack on St George's Island from the main island of Bermuda. Two more Martello towers were planned, but never built, to protect the dockyard.

On Jamaica the Spanish slave agent had in 1709 built a fort in Harbour View, to guard his home against attack. The later English Governor, George Nugent, later strengthened the fort to guard the eastern entrance of the city of Kingston Harbour. Fort Nugent was built between 1808 and 1811 at a cost of some £12,000.

Fourteen Martellos were built in Canada, nine of which remain. The Canadian Martellos were fitted with removable cone-shaped roofs to protect against snow. Halifax, Nova Scotia, had five. The oldest, the Prince of Wales tower in Point Pleasant Park, is also the oldest of that style in North America. Built in 1796, it was used as a redoubt and a powder magazine. Quebec originally had four Martellos. Tower No. 1 is on the Plains of Abraham, overlooking the St Lawrence River, scene of Wolfe's earlier victory. Four more were built at Kingston, Ontario, to defend its harbour and naval shipyards. Fort Frederick was constructed with elaborate defences, including earthen ramparts and a limestone curtain wall. The Shoal tower is the only one completely surrounded by water.

In April 2006 that the Canadian military named a Forward Operating Base in Afghanistan FOB Martello.

The British built five Martello towers in Mauritius between 1832 and 1835 at Grand River North West, Black River and Port Louis, of which three survive.

A Martello was built at Freetown, Sierra Leone, in 1805 to defend the port from attacks by the warlike Temne tribe, one of the two dominant ethnic groups there. It was significantly modified in 1870 when it was truncated to allow the installation of a water tank to supply Government House (Fort Thornton) with water. The tower is now part of the Parliament Buildings.

The British built three Martello towers in South Africa, one at Simon's Town naval base, one at Cape Town, and one at Fort Beauford. The Cape Town tower was demolished over a century ago, but that at Simon's Town, built in 1795, lays claim to being the oldest Martello in the world. That is arguable, because it is not a 'classic' Martello.

A Martello tower on St Helena, Napoleon's last home in exile, was incorporated into High Knoll fort.

One Martello was built in Sri Lanka, at Hambantota on the south coast. There is purely circumstantial evidence that it repelled a French attack. British engineers commenced work on three towers to protect Trincomalee but never completed them.

The last Martello tower built in the British Empire is part of the larger Fort Denison, built on small Pinchgut Island in Sydney Harbour, New South Wales. Fortification of the island began in 1841 following a night-time incursion into the harbour by two American warships, but were not completed. Construction resumed in 1855 to provide Sydney with protection against the threat of a naval attack by the Russian navy during the Crimean War. It was not completed until 1857, well after the war had ended.

The tidal wave which followed the volcanic explosion of Krakatoa in 1883 damaged the Martello tower of Menara that the Dutch East India Company had built in 1850 on Bidadari Island (Pulau Bidadari), a former leper colony, as part of a set of fortifications that protected the approaches to Batavia.

The US government built several Martello towers along the eastern seaboard, two at Key West, and others protecting the harbours of Portsmouth, New Hampshire; Charleston, South Carolina; and New York. Two more sprang up at Tybee Island, Georgia, and Bayou Dupre, Louisiana.

The Americans copied the design from the Canadian Martellos, but there were significant differences. Those on Key West were square instead of round and had thin walls with long gun loops. They were encircled by a curtain wall of heavy guns, making them, effectively, keeps instead of stand-alone towers. The Tybee Island tower built around 1815 was made mainly of wood rather than stone, with gun loops cut into the garrison deck.

Like most Martellos across the world, they were never directly tested in battle.

APPENDIX 5

PILLBOXES

Pillboxes are concrete firing positions or guard posts, equipped with loopholes for firing. The originally jocular name arose from their perceived similarity to the cylindrical and hexagonal boxes in which medical pills were once sold. Thick walls offer protection from small-arms fire and grenades while the positions, though camouflaged, are generally raised to improve the field of fire.

They were probably first used by the Germans on the Hindenburg Line during the First World War, but the Second World War survivors remain scattered across the British countryside.

In May 1940, the Directorate of Fortifications and Works (FW3) was set up at the War Office under Major-General G.B.O. Taylor. Its purpose was to provide a number of basic pillbox designs which could be constructed by soldiers and local labour at appropriate defensive locations. In the following June and July, FW3 issued six basic designs for rifle and light machine gun pillboxes, designated Type 22 to Type 27. In addition, there were designs for gun emplacements suitable for either the Ordnance QF 2-pounder or the Hotchkiss 6-pounder and a design for a hardened medium machine gun emplacement.

There were also designs for pillbox-like structures for various purposes including light anti-aircraft positions, observation posts and searchlight positions to illuminate the shoreline. In addition, the Air Ministry provided designs of fortifications intended to protect airfields from troops landing or parachuting. These would not be expected to face heavy weapons so that the degree of protection was less and there was more emphasis on all-round visibility and sweeping fields of fire. Many of these were later reinforced.

A small number of pillboxes had been constructed in the First World War and where possible these were integrated into the defence plans. Some pillboxes may predate the publication of the FW3 designs, but in any case some local commanders introduced modifications to the standard FW3 designs or introduced designs of their own. These non-standard design pillboxes may have been produced in some numbers or as completely ad hoc designs suited to local conditions. Other designs were produced as commercial ventures.

About 28,000 pillboxes and other hardened field fortifications were constructed in the United Kingdom of which about 6,500 still survive.

Embrasures were available precast and factory produced to standard designs, but as these were in short supply some embrasures were improvised from brick or concrete paving. Embrasures were frequently fitted with a steel or concrete-asbestos shutter. From March 1941, some pillbox embrasures were fitted with a Turnbull mount, a metal frame that supported a medium machine gun.

The degree of protection offered by a pillbox varied considerably: the thickness of the walls and roof generally varied from just 12in to 3ft 6in (0.3 to 1.1m) or more, although the commercially produced designs were often much thinner. In March 1940, General Brooke carried out penetration trials and recorded that a 25mm anti-tank gun could easily penetrate up to 2ft (60cm) of reinforced concrete. Despite such results the thick-walled pillboxes were designated as shell-proof, whereas the thinner-walled pillboxes were designated as bulletproof.

Internally, pillboxes are generally cramped and spartan. Some internal concrete shelves and tables were provided to support weapons and some were whitewashed inside. Only the Type 28s provided a little space – sufficient for a few home comforts.

The basic designs were adapted to local circumstances and available building materials such that, outwardly, two pillboxes of the same basic design could look quite different. The height of a pillbox could vary significantly according to local needs: some were half buried so that the embrasures might be as low as ground level, others were raised up to give a better view; those built into hillsides might lack embrasures on some walls; the entrance could be moved and its size varied as might be convenient and there may be additional walls to protect the entrance, a freestanding blast wall or a steel door.

Appearance also varied according to to the building materials used, although all the FW3 designs are formed from reinforced concrete. Where brick was used as a shuttering, the bricks essentially formed a mould into which concrete was poured, the bricks being left in place. Otherwise, the pillbox was formed using shuttering of wood (usually planks, but sometimes plywood) and/or corrugated iron. Wood shuttering was removed, whereas corrugated iron was sometimes left in place. Construction often took advantage of whatever materials were available locally (for example, at the coast, beach sand and pebbles would be used) and this expedient use of local materials had the added advantage of aiding camouflage. The reinforced concrete used in construction was generally conventional, making use of thin steel rebars (reinforcing bars) with floor, walls and roof all mutually bonded. However, several instances are known where scrap metal had been used such as parts of an old bed or park railings. All pillboxes were carefully camouflaged and some were constructed to look like innocent buildings such as cottages, railway signal boxes and bus shelters. Near Axminster, one was disguised as a Romany caravan, complete with a scarecrow and a horse of straw.

Pillbox Varieties

Type 22: A regular hexagon in plan with an embrasure in five of the sides and an entrance in the other. The embrasures were suitable for rifles or light machine guns. Each wall was about 6ft (1.8m) long and it was generally built to the bulletproof standard of 12in (30cm) thick, although 'tank-gun proof' versions with walls around 40in (1.0m) thick were also built. Internally there was a Y- or T-shaped anti-ricochet wall. It is the second most common type, with 1,209 surviving.

Type 23: Rectangular in plan with two squares, one of which was roofed and the other open, with embrasures in each of the available sides of the covered section suitable for rifles or light machine guns. The open section was for a light anti-aircraft defence with a Bren or Lewis gun on a mounting. The walls were 8ft (2.4m) wide by 16ft (4.9m) long and usually built to a bulletproof standard of 12in (30cm) thick. Only 156 are believed to survive.

Type 24: An irregular hexagon in plan. The rear wall was the longest at about 14ft (4.3m), with the entrance with an embrasure on either side. The other walls vary from 7-8ft (2.2-2.5m) each with a single embrasure. Internally there was a Y-shaped anti-ricochet wall. It was always built to at least bullet-proof standard of 12in (30cm) thick, but often was thicker. A thick walled variant was introduced to a shellproof standard; it was larger externally and had walls 36-50in (91-127cm), thick. The type 24 is the most common type, with more than 1,787 surviving.

Type 25: The only circular FW3 design, with a diameter of 8ft (2.4m). The walls were just 12in (30cm) thick with no internal walls. There were three embrasures and a small entrance like a low window. This design was made from reinforced concrete shuttered by corrugated iron. Just 46 are believed to have survived.

Type 26: A simple square in plan, each wall being 10ft (3m) long. There was a door in one side and embrasures in each of the remaining three walls with, possibly, an additional embrasure next to the door. There were no internal walls. Occasionally, there were two embrasures in one of the walls. Walls were normally constructed to bulletproof standard at about 18in (46cm) thick. The type 26 also had an important prefabricated variant – shuttering inside and out – was provided by precast concrete slabs slotted into reinforced concrete posts. The shuttering was filled with concrete in situ. It is uncommon, with 199 recorded survivors.

Type 27: The most varied of the FW3 designs, it was either octagonal or hexagonal in plan with walls between 9ft 9in and 11ft 6in (3.0-3.5m). The outer walls had embrasures on each facet. Its defining characteristic was a central well open to the sky that could be used as a light anti-aircraft position. Only 127 survivors are recorded.

Type 28: The largest of the FW3 designs and the only one with a specific anti-tank capability. It was almost square in plan with the forward facing corners chamfered. The walls were about 20 by 19ft (6.1 x 5.8m) long constructed to shell-proof specification at about 42in (107cm) thick. The gun shield of the enclosed anti-tank gun or Hotchkiss 6-pounder would largely fill the forward embrasure. There were usually embrasures in each of the two side walls. The traverse of the gun was limited to about 60°. Generally, these pillboxes were positioned to fire along fixed lines, such as enfilading fire across an anti-tank ditch or at a bridge and in such positions the limited traverse of the gun creates no real disadvantage; whereas, the small size of the embrasure provides greater protection for the gun and its crew. Around 350 of these survive.

Vickers MMG Emplacement: Square in plan with the forward facing corners chamfered. The walls were 14ft (4.3m) long and there was usually generally a free-standing blast wall covering the entrance. The walls were constructed to shellproof standard of 36in (91cm). There were no internal walls. There was a large embrasure and inside a concrete table, on which to mount the weapon's tripod. The other walls would each have an embrasure. They are frequently sited in pairs and were often dug-in with overhead earth cover. Just over 75 are recorded as surviving, but there were also many local variants of the design.

BIBLIOGRAPHY AND SOURCES

Chapter 1: After Hastings

Berkhofer, R.F. (ed.) *The Experience of Power in Medieval Europe* (Western Michigan University, 1974)

Crouch, D., *The Birth of Nobility – Constructing Aristocracy in England and France 900-1300* (Longman, New York, 2005)

Douglas, D.C., *William the Conqueror: The Norman Impact Upon England* (University of California Press, 1964)

Fleming, R., *Kings and Lords in Conquest England* (Cambridge University Press, 1991)

Golding, B., *Conquest and Colonisation – The Normans in Britain 1066-1100* (Macvmillan, London, 1994)

Huscroft, R., *The Norman Conquest – A New Introduction* (Longmans, New York, 2009)

Hutchinson, G., *The Battle of Hastings – A Brief History* (M. & W. Morgan, Hastings, 1996)

Stenton, F.M., *The First Century of English Feudalism 1066-1166* (Oxford University Press, 1961)

Strong, R., *The Story of Britain* (Oman Productions, London, 1996)

Vincent, N., *The Birth of a Nation – A Brief History of Britain 1066-1485* (Constable and Robinson, London, 2011)

Williams, A., *The English and the Norman Conquest* (Beydell and Brewer, Woodbridge, 1995)

Chapter 2: King Louis of England?

Barlow, F., *The Feudal Kingdom of England 1042-1216* (Pearson Education, Harlow, 1999)

Bradbury, J., *Philip Augustus, King of France 1180-1223* (Longman, London, 1998)

Brown, R.A., *Rochester Castle, Kent* (English Heritage, London, 1989)

Brown, C., *Real Britannia – Our Ten Proudest Years – The Glory and the Spin* (Oneworld Publications, London, 2012)

Carpenter Burgess, G.S., *Two Medieval Outlaws: Eustace the Monk and Fouke Fitz Waryn* (D.S. Brewer, Woodbridge, 1997)

Cannon, H.L., *The Battle of Sandwich and Eustace the Monk* (English Historical Review 27, October, 1912)

Church, Stephen D., *The Household Knights of King John* (Cambridge University Press, 1999)

Churchill, Winston S., *A History of the English-Speaking Peoples, Volume 1* (Cassell, London, 1958)

Carpenter, D., *The Struggle for Mastery, The Penguin History of Britain 1066-1284* (Penguin Books, London, 2004)

Harding, A., *England in the Thirteenth Century* (Cambridge University Press, 1993)

Huscroft, R., *Ruling England, 1042-1217* (Pearson, Harlow, 2005)

McGlynn, S., *Blood Cries Afar – The Forgotten Invasion of England 1216* (The History Press, Stroud, 2011)

Paris, M., *Chronica Maiora II* (Rolls Series, London, 1874)

Poole, S., *From Domesday Book to Magna Carta 1087-1216* (Oxford University Press, 2005)

Ramsay, J.H., *The Angevin Empire* (Sonneschein, London, 1903)

Turner, R.V., *King John: England's Evil King?* (History Press, Stroud, 2009)

Vincent, N., *A Brief History of Britain: The Birth of a Nation 1066-1485* (Constable and Robinson, London, 2011)

Warren, W. Lewis, *King John* (Methuen, London, 1991)

Chapter 3: The Hundred Years' War

Bartlett, R., *England Under the Norman and Angevin Kings 1075-1225* (Oxford University Press, London, 2000)

Favier, J., *La Guerre de Cent Ans* (Fayard, Paris, 1980)

Gormley, L., *The Hundred Years War – Overview* (Ohio State University, 2007)

Green, H., *Guide to the Battlefields of Britain and Ireland* (Constable, London, 1973)

Grummitt, D., *The Calais Garrison: War and Military Service in England, 1436-1558* (The Boydell Press, Woodbridge, 2008)

James, R., 'The Skirmish at Rottingdean' (www.rgi.net/Rottingdean)

Le Patourel, J., *Feudal Empires: Norman and Plantagenet* (Continuum, London, 1984)

Pratt, W., *Winchelsea – The Tale of a Medieval Town* (Pratt, East Sussex, 2005)

Prestwich, M., *English Monarchs* (University of California, 1988)

Prestwich, M., *Plantagenet England* (Oxford University Press, 2005)

Previte-Orton, C.W., *The Shorter Cambridge Medieval History 2* (Cambridge University Press, 1978)

Rogers, C.J. (ed.) *The Oxford Encyclopaedia of Medieval Warfare and Military Technology, Vol. 1* (Oxford University Press, 2010)

Seaward, D., *The Hundred Years War* (Constable and Robinson, London, 1978)

Sumption, J., *The Hundred Years War I: Trial by Battle* (University of Pennsylvania Press, 1991)

Thompson, P.E., *Contemporary Chronicles of the Hundred Years' War* (Folio Society, London, 1966)

Chapter 4: The Pretenders

Ashley, M., *British Kings & Queens* (Carroll & Graf, New York, 2002)

Beeston, D., *A Strange Accident of State: Henry VII and the Lambert Simnel Conspiracy* (self-published, 1987)

Bennett, M.J., *Lambert Simnel and the Battle of Stoke* (Sutton, Stroud, 1987)

Dunlop, D., 'The Masked Comedian – Perkin Warbeck's Adventures in Scotland and England from 1495 to 1497' (Scottish Historical Review, October 1991)

Ford, J. & Ure, P., *The Chronicle history of Perkin Warbeck: A Strange Truth* (Methuen, London, 1968)

Gairdiner, J., *History of the Life and Reign of Richard the Third, to which is added the story of Perkin Warbeck* (Kraus Reprint Co., New York, 1968)

Mackie, J.D., *The Earlier Tudors: 1485-1558, Oxford history of England 7* (Oxford University Press, 1994)

Roberts, D.E., *The Battle of Stoke Field 1487* (Newark and Sherwood D.C., 1987)

Vincent, N., *A Brief History of Britain – The Birth of a Nation 1066-1485* (Constable & Robinson, London, 2011)

Wroe, A., *Perkin: A Story of Deception* (Vintage, London, 2004)

Chapter 5: Henry's Castles and the Invasion of the Isle of Wight

Coad, J.G., *Walmer Castle* (English Heritage, London, 1992)

Colvin, H.M. et al., *The History of the King's Works, Volume 4: 1485-1660* (HMSO, 1982)

Donnelly, J.A., 'A study of the Coastal Forts built by Henry VIII', *Fort* 10: 105-126 (1982)

Elton, G.R., *England Under the Tudors* (Routledge, London, 1991)

Glete, J., *Warfare at Sea, 1500-1650: Maritime Conflicts and the Transformation of Europe* (Routledge, London, 2000)

Harrington, P., *The Castles of Henry VIII* (Osprey, Oxford, 2010)

King, D.J.C., *The Castle in England and Wales: An Interpretative History* (Croom Helm, London, 1988)

Loades, D., *The Tudor Navy: An Administrative, Political and Military History* (Scolar Press, Aldershot, 1992)

Marsden, P., 'Sealed by Time: The Loss and Recovery of the Mary Rose' in *The Archaeology of the Mary Rose, Volume 1* (The Mary Rose Trust, Portsmouth, 2003)

Morley, B.M., *Henry VIII and the Development of Coastal Defence* (HMSO, London, 1976)

O'Neill, B.H. St J., *Deal Castle* (HMSO, 1983)

Rodger, N.A.M., *The Safeguard of the Sea: A Naval History of Britain 660-1649* (W.W. Norton & Company, New York, 1997)

Rule, M., *The Mary Rose* (Conway Maritime Press, London, 1982)

Scarisbrick, J.J., *Henry VIII* (The Folio Society, London, 2004)

Starkey, D. (ed.) *The Inventory of Henry VII* (Harvey Miller, Turnhout, 1998)

Chapter 6: The Spanish Armada

Alcalá-Zamora, J.N., La empresa de Inglaterra: (la 'Armada invencible': fabulación y realidad) Taravilla: Real Academia de la Historia (2004)

Alford, S., *The Watchers – A Secret History of the Reign of Elizabeth I* (Allen Lane, London, 2012)

Corbett, J.S. *Drake and the Tudor Navy: With a History of the Rise of England as a Maritime Power* (1898, facsimile edition, Adamant Media, 2004)

Cruikshank, D., *Invasion: Defending Britain from Attack* (Boxtree Ltd, London, 2002)

Fernández-Armesto, F., *The Spanish Armada: The Experience of War in 1588* (Oxford University Press, 1988)

Froude, J.A., *The Spanish Story of the Armada, and Other Essays* (1899, facsimile edition HardPress, 2013)

Knerr, D., 'Through the 'Golden Mist': A Brief Overview of Armada Historiography' *American Neptune* 1989 49(1): 5-13

Konstam, A., *The Spanish Armada: The Great Enterprise against England 1588* (Osprey, Oxford, 2009)

Lewis, M., *The Spanish Armada* (T.Y. Crowell Co., New York, 1968)

McDermott, J., *England and the Spanish Armada: The Necessary Quarrel* (Yale University Press, New Haven and London, 2005)

Martin, C. & Parker, G., *The Spanish Armada* (2nd ed. 2002)

Mattingly, G., *The Defeat of the Spanish Armada* (Jonathan Cape, London, 1959)

Parker, G., 'Why the Armada Failed' (History Today, May 1988)

Pierson, P., *Commander of the Armada: The Seventh Duke of Medina Sidonia* (Yale, New Haven, 1989)

Rodger, N.A.M., *The Safeguard of the Sea: A Naval History of Britain 660-1649 Vol. 1* (Penguin, London, 1999)

Rodriguez-Salgado, M.J. & Adams, S. (eds) *England, Spain, and the Gran Armada, 1585-1604* (John Donald, Edinburgh, 1991)

Strong, R., *The Story of Britain* (Hutchinson, London, 1996)

Chapter 7: Mousehole

Carew, R., *Survey of Cornwall* (1602, facsimile edition Tor Mark Press, 2000)
Halliday, F.E., *Richard Carew of Antony* (Melrose, London, 1953)
Pool, P., *History of the Town and Borough of Penzance* (Penzance Corporation, 1974)
Rowse, A.L., *Tudor Cornwall – Portrait of a Society* (Jonathen Cape, London, 1941)
San Juan, V., La batalla naval de las Dunas: la Holanda comercial contra la España del Siglo De Oro (Silex
　　Ediciones, 20070)

Chapter 8: The Barbary Pirates

Colley, L., *Captives – Britain, Empire and the World* (Pimlico, London, 2003)
Davis, R.C., *Christian Slaves, Muslim Masters: White Slavery in the Mediterranean, The Barbary Coast, and Italy,
　　1500-1800* (Palgrave Macmillan, New York, 2003)
Earle, P., *The Pirate Wars* (Thomas Dunne, New York, 2003)
Forester, C.S., *The Barbary Pirates* (Random House, London, 1953)
Lambert, F., *The Barbary Wars* (Hill and Wang, New York, 2005)
Leiner, F.C., *The End of Barbary Terror: America's 1815 War Against the Pirates of North Africa* (Oxford University
　　Press, 2006)
Milton, G., *White Gold: The Extraordinary Story of Thomas Pellow and North Africa's One Million European Slaves*
　　(Sceptre, London, 2005)
Severn, D., 'The Bombardment of Algiers, 1816' (*History Today* 28, 1978)
Silverstein, P.A., *The New Barbarians: Piracy and Terrorism on the North African Frontier* (The New Centennial
　　Review 5, 2005)
Tinniswood, A., *Pirates of Barbary: Corsairs, Conquests and Captivity in the Seventeenth-Century Mediterranean*
　　(Riverhead Books, New York, 2010)
Vikus, D.J., *Piracy, Slavery and Redemption: Barbary Captivity Narratives from Early Modern England* (Columbia
　　University Press, 2001)

Chapter 9: The Battle of the Medway

Boxer, C.R., *The Anglo-Dutch Wars of the 17th Century* (HMSO, London 1974)
Cox, A., 'The Dutch Invasion of England 1667' (*Military Affairs* 13, 1949)
Fox, F.L., *A Distant Storm – The Four Days' Battle of 1666, The Greatest Sea Fight of the Age of Sail* (Sail
　　Publications, Rotherfield, 1996)
Jones, H.M. (Battlefield Review, www.battlefieldreview.com)
Jones, J.R., *The Anglo-Dutch Wars of the Seventeenth Century* (Longman House, London/New York, 1996)
Macfarlane, C., *The Dutch on the Medway* (James Clarke & Co., Cambridge, 1897)
Meurer, A., *Seekriegsgeschichte in Umrissen* (Hase & Koehler, Leipzig, 1942)
Saunders, A.D., *Upnor Castle* (HMSO, London, 1967)
Rodger, N.A.M., *The Command of the Ocean: A Naval History of Britain 1649-1815* (Penguin, New York, 2004)
Rogers, P.G., *The Dutch on the Medway* (Oxford University Press, 1970)

Chapter 10: The 'Glorious' Invasion

Ashley, M., The Glorious Revolution of 1688 (Hodder & Stoughton, London, 1966)
Baxter, S.B., *William III* (Longmans, London, 1966)
Beddard, R., *A Kingdom Without a King: The Journal of the Provisional Government in the Revolution of 1688*
　　(Phaidon, London, 1988)
Childs, J., *The Army, James II, and the Glorious Revolution* (Manchester University Press, 1980)
Churchill, W.S., *A History of the English-Speaking Peoples, Volume III, The Age of Revolution* (Cassell and Company,
　　London, 1957)
Cruickshanks, E., *The Glorious Revolution* (Palgrave Macmillan, London 2000)
Dalrymple, J., *Memoirs of Great Britain and Ireland; From the Dissolution of the Last Parliament of Charles II Till the
　　Capture of the French and Spanish Fleets at Vigo* (London, 1790)
DeKrey, Gary S., *Restoration and Revolution in Britain: A Political History of the Era of Charles II and the Glorious
　　Revolution* (Palgrave Macmillan, London, 2007)
Horwitz, H., *Parliament, Policy and Politics in the Reign of William III* (Manchester University Press, 1977)
Israel, J.I., *The Dutch role in the Glorious Revolution* (Cambridge University Press, 1991)

Israel, J.I., *The Anglo-Dutch Moment: Essays on the Glorious Revolution and its World Impact* (Cambridge University Press, 2003)

Israel, J.I. & Parker, G., *Of Providence and Protestant Winds: the Spanish Armada of 1588 and the Dutch Armada of 1688* (Cambridge University Press, 1991)

Jardine, L., *Going Dutch: How England Plundered Holland's Glory* (Harper, London, 2008)

Jones, C., *The Protestant Wind of 1688: Myth and Reality* (European Studies Review III, 1973)

Jones, J.R., *The Revolution of 1688 in England* (Weidenfeld & Nicolson, London, 1988)

McLynn, F., *Invasion – From the Armada to Hitler 1588-1945* (Routledge & Kegan Paul, London and New York, 1987)

Pincus, S., *1688: The First Modern Revolution* (Yale University Press, New Haven, 2009)

Pincus, S., *England's Glorious Revolution 1688-89: A Brief History with Documents* (Bedford/St Martin's, London 2005)

Prall, S., *The Bloodless Revolution: England, 1688* (Anchor Books, London, 1972)

Rodger, N.A.M., *The Command of the Ocean: A Naval History of Britain 1649-1815* (Penguin, London, 2004)

Peck, W.A., *Reluctant Revolutionaries. Englishmen and the Revolution of 1688* (Oxford University Press, 1989)

Prall, S., *The Bloodless Revolution: England, 1688* (Anchor Books, London, 1972)

Schwoerer, L.G., *The Revolution of 1688-89: Changing Perspectives* (Cambridge University Press, 2004)

Waller, M., *Ungrateful Daughters – The Stuart Princesses Who Stole their Father's Crown* (Hodder and Stoughton, London, 2002)

Western, J.R., *Monarchy and Revolution: The English State in the 1680s* (Blandford Press, London, 1972)

Chapter 11: The French Armada of 1692

Aubrey, P., *The Defeat of James Stuart's Armada, 1692* (Leicester University Press, Leicester 1977)

Clowes, W.L., *The Royal Navy: A History* (1897, Chatham, 2003)

Ehrman, J., *The Navy in the Wars of William III* (Harvard, Cambridge, Mass. 1953)

Rodger, N.A.M., *The Command of the Ocean* (Allen Lane, London, 2004)

Mahan, A.T., *The Influence of Sea-Power upon History 1660-1805* (1890)

Marcus, G.J., *A Naval History of England* (Longmans, Green and Co., London, 1971)

Pemsel, H., *Atlas of Naval Warfare* (Arms and Armour Press, London, 1979)

Chapter 12: The Jacobite Invasion of England

Colley, L., *Britons – Forging the Nation 1707-1837* (Yale University Press, New Haven, 1994)

Lavery, B., *Maritime Scotland* (B.T. Batsford Ltd, London, 2001)

Maclean, F., *Bonnie Prince Charlie* (Canongate Books, Edinburgh, 1989)

Maclean, F., *A Concise History of Scotland* (Thames and Hudson, London, 1981)

Moore, E., Register article (*The Times*, 22 Dec. 2012)

Pittock, M.G.H., *The Myth of the Jacobite Clans* (Edinburgh University Press, 1995)

Prebble, J., *The Lion in the North* (Penguin, London, 1973)

Speck, W.A., *The Butcher – The Duke of Cumberland and the Suppression of the 45* (Blackwell, Oxford, 1981)

Smith, H., *Georgian Monarchy: Politics and Culture 1714-1760* (Cambridge University Press, 2006)

Smith, P.J.C., *The Invasion of 1745: The Drama in Lancashire and Cheshire* (Neil Richardson, Manchester, 1993)

Szechi, D., *The Jacobites* (Manchester University Press, 1994)

Chapter 13: The Choiseul Plan

Anderson, F., *Crucible of War: The Seven Years' War and the Fate of Empire in British North America, 1754-1766* (Faber and Faber, London, 2000)

Brown, P.D., *William Pitt, Earl of Chatham: The Great Commoner* (George Allen & Unwin, London, 1978)

Browning, R., *The War of the Austrian Succession* (Sutton, Stroud, 1994)

Clowes, W.L. (ed.) *The Royal Navy; A History, From the Earliest Times to the Present, Volume III* (London, 1898, Chatham, 2003)

Corbett, J.S., *England in the Seven Years War: A Study in Combined Operations, Volume II* (London, 1907)

Dull, J.R., *The French Navy and the Seven Years' War* (University of Nebraska, 2005)

Jenkins, E.H., *A History of the French Navy* (Macdonald, London, 1973)

Lambert, A., *Admirals: The Naval Commanders Who Made Britain Great* (Faber and Faber, London, 2009)

Marcus, G., *Quiberon Bay: The Campaign in Home Waters, 1759* (Barre, London, 1960)

McLynn, F., *1759: The Year Britain Became Master of the World* (Vintage, London, 2005)

Rodger N.A.M., *Command of the Ocean: A Naval History of Britain, 1649-1815* (Penguin Books, London, 2006)

Smith, D., *Armies of the Seven Years War* (Spellmount, Stroud, 2012)

Chapter 14: John Paul Jones

Boudriot, J., *John Paul Jones and the Bonhomme Richard* (Collection Archeologie Navale Française, Paris, 1987)

Frost, J., *The Pictorial Book of the Commodores, Comprising Lives Of Distinguished Commanders in The Navy of the United States* (Nafis & Cornish, New York, 1845)

Jones, J.P., *Report to Benjamin Franklin October 3 1779* (John Paul Jones Cottage Museum)

Jones, J.P., *Extracts from the Journals of My Campaigns 1785* (John Paul Jones Cottage Museum)

Koven, R., *The Life and Letters of John Paul Jones* (Werner Laurie, London, 1913)

Maclay, E.S., Smith, Roy Campbell, *A History of the United States Navy from 1775 to 1893* (D. Appleton, New York, 1894)

Morrison, S.E., *John Paul Jones: A Sailor's Biography* (Naval Institute Press, Annapolis, 1999)

Pearson, R., 'Report on the capture of his ship Serapis, October 6, 1779' (yorkshirehistory.com)

Purcell, L., *Edward Who Was Who in the American Revolution* (Facts on File, New York, 1993)

Walker, F., *John Paul Jones, Maverick Hero* (Spellmount, Stroud, 2004)

Chapter 15: The Battle of Fishguard

Kinross, J., *Fishguard Fiasco* (H.G. Walters, London, 1974)

Latimer, J., 'The Last Invasion of Britain' (URL, 12 July 2003)

Latimer, J., *Deception in War* (Overlook Press, London, 2001)

McLynn, F., *Invasion – From the Armada to Hitler* (Routledge, London, 1987)

Thomas, J.E., *Britain's Last Invasion – Fishguard 1797* (The History Press, Stroud, 2007)

Chapter 16: The Napoleon Threat and Britain's 'Great Terror'

Fedorak, C.J., *Henry Addington, Prime Minister, 1801-1804: Peace, War and Parliamentary Politics* (The University of Akron Press, Ohio, 2002)

Forrest, A., *Napoleon's Men – The Soldiers of the Revolution and Empire* (Continuum, New York, 2002)

Glover, M., *Warfare in the age of Bonaparte* (BCA in UK, Barnsley 1980)

Haythornthwaite, P.J., *Napoleon's Military Machine* (Spellmount, Stroud, 2007)

Kimber, A., www.wildrye.info

Longmate, N., *Island Fortress: The Defence of Great Britain 1603-1945* (Pimlico, London, 2001)

Lloyd, P.A., *The French Are Coming! The Invasion Scare 1803-05* (Spellmount, Stroud, 1992)

McLynn, F., *Invasion: From the Armada to Hitler: 1588-1945* (Routledge, London, 1987)

Muir, R., *Tactics and the Experience of Battle in the Age of Napoleon* (Yale University Press, New Haven, 2000)

Pocock, T., *The Terror Before Trafalgar* (John Murray, London 2002)

Sutcliffe, S., *Martello Towers* (Tower Books, Newton Abbott, 1972)

Richmond, H.W., *The Invasion of Britain: An Account of Plans, Attempts & Counter-Measures from 1586 to 1918* (Methuen, London, 1941)

Terraine, J., *Trafalgar* (Wordsworth, London, 1998)

Vine, P., *The Royal Military Canal* (David and Charles, Newton Abbott, 1972)

Wheeler, H.F.B. & Broadley, A.M., *Napoleon and the Invasion of England: The Story of the Great Terror* (Nonsuch, Stroud, 2007)

The Times, 19 July 1803

Chapter 17: Threats from America and Germany 1815-1939

Bell, C.M., 'Thinking the Unthinkable: British and American Naval Strategies for an Anglo–American War, 1918-31' (*International History Review*, Vol. XIX, No. 4, November 1997)

Carroll, F.M., 'The Passionate Canadians: The Historical Debate About the Eastern Canadian-American Boundary' (*New England Quarterly*, Vol. 70, No. 1, March 1997)

Garraty, J.A., *The American Nation* (Longman, London, 1997)

Joint Army-Navy Board, 'Joint Estimate of the Situation – Red and Tentative Plan – Red' (declassified correspondence, 1910-42, Joint Board 325, serial 274)

Jones, H., 'Anglophobia and the Aroostook War' (*New England Quarterly*, Vol. 48, No. 4, Dec. 1975)

Jones, H., *To the Webster-Ashburton Treaty: A Study in Anglo-American Relations, 1783-1843* (University of North Carolina Press, Chapel Hill, 1977)

Jones, W.D., 'The Influence of Slavery on the Webster-Ashburton Negotiations' (*Journal of Southern History*, Vol. 22, No. 1, Feb. 1956)

LeDuc, T., 'The Maine Frontier and the Northeastern Boundary Controversy' (The American Historical
    Review Vol. 53, No. 1, Oct. 1947)
LeDuc, T., 'The Webster-Ashburton Treaty and the Minnesota Iron Ranges' (Journal of American History, Vol.
    51, No. 3, Dec 1964)
McLynn, F., Invasion – From the Armada to Hitler 1588-1945 (Routledge & Kegan Paul, London and New York, 1987)
Preston, R.A., The Defence of the Undefended Border: Planning for War in North America 1867-1939 (McGill-Queen's
    University Press, Montreal and London, 1977)
Rudmin, F.W., Bordering on Aggression: Evidence of U.S. Military Preparations Against Canada (Voyageur Publishing,
    London, 1993)
Wagner, E., Interview with William Boyd (The Times, 22 Dec. 2012)

Chapter 18: Operation Sea Lion

Ansel, W., Hitler Confronts England (Duke University Press, Durham, NC, 1960)
Banks, D., Flame Over Britain (Samson Low, London, 1946)
Burdick, C. & Jacobsen, H.-A., The Halder War Diary 1939-1942 (Navatop Press, California, 1988)
Churchill, W.S., Their Finest Hour, The Second World War, Volume II (Penguin, London, 2005)
Corum, J., The Luftwaffe: Creating the Operational Air War, 1918-1940 (Kansas University Press, Lawrence, 1997)
Cox, R., Operation Sea Lion (Presidio Press, New York, 1977)
Cruickshank, D., Invasion – Defending Britain from Attack (Boxtree, London, 2001)
Evans, M.M., Invasion! Operation Sealion 1940 (Pearson Education Ltd, London, 2004)
Fleming, P., Operation Sea Lion (Simon & Schuster, New York, 1957)
Haining, P., Where the Eagle Landed: The Mystery of the German Invasion of Britain, 1940 (Robson, London, 2004)
Hooton, E.R., The Luftwaffe: A Study in Air Power, 1933-1945 (Classic Publications, London, 2010)
Kieser, E., Cassell Military Classics: Operation Sea Lion: The German Plan to Invade Britain, 1940 (Cassell, London,
    1987)
Lampe, D., The Last Ditch: Britain's Resistance Plans Against the Nazis (Greenhill Books, Barnsley, 2007)
Longman, N., If Britain Had Fallen (Greenhill Books, Barnsley, 1972)
Lowry, B., British Home Defences 1940-45 (Osprey Publishing, Oxford, 2004)
Macksey, K., Invasion: The German Invasion of England, July 1940 (Macmillan, London, 1980)
McLynn, F., Invasion – From the Armada to Hitler 1588-1945 (Routledge and Kegan Paul, London, 1987)
Raeder, E., Grand Admiral: The Personal Memoir of the Commander in Chief of the German Navy From 1935 Until
    His Final Break With Hitler in 1943 (Da Capo Press, New York, 2001)
Ruddy, A., British Anti-Invasion Defences 1940-1945 (Historic Military Press, Billingshurst, 2003)
Schenk, P., Invasion of England 1940: The Planning of Operation Sealion (Conway Maritime Press Ltd, London,
    1990)
Taylor, T., The Breaking Wave: The Second World War in the Summer of 1940 (Simon and Schuster, New York, 1967)
The Times, 3 July 1940
Ward, A., Resisting the Nazi Invader (Constable and Co., London, 1997)

Chapter 19: The Battle of Graveney Marsh

Green, R. & Harrison, R., 'Forgotten Frontline' (Kent Online, 30 Sept. 2009)
Daily Mail, 20 Aug 2010
Daily Telegraph, 20 Aug 2010
London Gazette Supplement No. 35050 (21 Jan. 1941)
Recommendations for Honours and Awards (Army) (National Archives) Spitfire Site, Stories of the Battle of
    Britain 1940, Graveney Marsh (spitfiresite.com)

Chapter 20: The Occupation of the Channel Islands

Bunting, M., The Model Occupation: The Channel Islands Under German Rule, 1940-1945 (Harper Collins, London,
    1995)
Cohen, F., The Jews in the Channel Islands During the German Occupation 1940-1945 (Jersey Jewish Congregation)
    jerseyheritagetrust.org
Cruickshank, C.G., The German Occupation of the Channel Islands (The Guernsey Press, 1975)
Hamlin, J.F., "'No 'Safe Haven': Military Aviation in the Channel Islands 1939-1945' (Air Enthusiast No. 83,
    September/October 1999)
Jersey Evening Post, 21 May 1940

Maughan, R.C.F., *Jersey under the Jackboot* (New English Library, London, 1980)

Mawson, G., *Guernsey Evacuees* (The History Press, Stroud, 2012)

Read, B.A., *No Cause for Panic – Channel Islands Refugees 1940-45* (Seaflower Books, St Helier, 1995)

Sanders, P., *The British Channel Islands Under German Occupation, 1940-1945* (Jersey Heritage Trust, 2005)

Toms, C., *Fortress Islands* (New English Library, London, 1967)

Woods, A. & Woods, M., *Islands in Danger: The Story of the German Occupation of the Channel Islands 1940-45* (Evans Brothers, London, 1955)

Appendix 2: Later History of Castles and Fortifications Featured

Brooks, S., *Southsea Castle* (Pitkin Guides, Andover, 1996)

Coad, J.G., *Walmer Castle* (English Heritage, 1992)

Coad, J.G., *Hurst Castle* (English Heritage, 1990)

Colvin, H.M., *The History of the King's Works, Volume 4: 1485-1660* (HMSO, 1982)

Elton, G.R., *England Under the Tudors* (Routledge, London, 1991)

Foot, W., *Beaches, Fields, Streets and Hills: The Anti-Invasion Landscape of England 1940* (Council for British Archaeology, York, 2006)

Harrington, P., *The Castles of Henry VIII* (Osprey, Oxford, 2007)

James, J., *Hurst Castle – An Illustrated History* (Dovecote Press, Stanbridge, 1986)

Jenkins, S.C., *St Mawes Castle* (Fortress Study Group Vol. 35, 2007)

Jenkins, S.C., *Pendennis Castle* (Fortress Study Group Vol. 25, 1997)

King, D.J.C., *The Castle in England and Wales: An Interpretative History* (Croom Helm, London, 1988)

Linzey, R., *The Castles of Pendennis and St Mawes* (English Heritage, 1999)

Harrington, P., *The Castles of Henry VIII* (Osprey, Oxford, 2007)

Morley, B.M., *Henry VIII and the Development of Coastal Defences* (HMSO, London, 1976)

Appendix 4: Martello Towers

Brock, B.B. & Brock, B.G., *Historical Simon's Town* (Taylor and Francis, Abingdon, 1976)

Ciucevich, R.A., *Tybee Island: The Long Branch of the South* (Arcadia Publishing, London, 2005)

Clements, W.H., *Towers of Strength: Story of Martello Towers* (Pen & Sword, Barnsley, 1998)

Davy, G., 'English Smugglers, the Channel, and the Napoleonic Wars, 1800-1814' (Journal of British Studies, 2007)

Grundy, M., 'The Martello Towers of Minorca' (Fortress Study Group, Oxford, 1991)

Harris, E., 'The Martello Tower at Ferry Point, St George's Island, Bermuda' (*Mariner's Mirror*, Bermuda, 1988)

McCall, M., 'The Martello Tower in Hambantota, Sri Lanka' (Fortress Study Group, Oxford, 1999)

Mead, H.P., 'The Martello Towers of England' (*Mariner's Mirror*, Bermuda, 1948)

Millward, J. 'The East Coast Martello Towers' (Fortress Study Group, 2007)

Saunders, I.J., 'A History of the Martello Towers in the Defence of British North America, 1796-1871' (Occasional Papers in Archaeology and History No. 15) (National Historic Parks and Sites Branch, Thorn Press Limited, 1976)

Sutcliffe, S., *Martello Towers* (Associated Universities Press, Cranbury, 1973)

Ward, S.G.P., 'Defence Works of Britain, 1803-1805' (*Journal of the Society for Army Historical Research*, 1949)

Appendix 5: Pillboxes

Foot, W., *Beaches, Fields, Streets, and Hills: The Anti-Invasion Landscapes of England, 1940* (Council for British Archaeology, 2006)

Lowry, B., *British Home Defences 1940-45* (Osprey Publishing, Oxford, 2004)

Osborne, M., *Defending Britain: Twentieth-Century Military Structures in the Landscape* (Tempus, Stroud, 2004)

Osborne, M., *Pillboxes of Britain and Ireland* (Tempus, Stroud, 2008)

Ross, S., *World War II Britain: History from Buildings* (Franklin Watts, London, 2006)

Wills, H., *Pillboxes: A Study of UK Defences* (Leo Cooper, Barnsley, 1985)

INDEX